Prayer and Power

Prayer and Power

George Herbert and Renaissance Courtship

Michael C. Schoenfeldt

The University of Chicago Press

Chicago and London

Michael C. Schoenfeldt is associate professor of English at the
University of Michigan at Ann Arbor.

The University of Chicago Press, Chicago 60637
The University of Chicago Press, Ltd., London
© 1991 by The University of Chicago
All rights reserved. Published 1991
Printed in the United States of America

00 99 98 97 96 95 94 93 92 91   5 4 3 2 1

Library of Congress Cataloging-in-Publication Data

Schoenfeldt, Michael Carl.
    Prayer and power : George Herbert and Renaissance
  courtship / Michael C. Schoenfeldt.
        p.   cm.
    Includes bibliographical references (p.   ) and index.
    ISBN 0-226-74001-3 (cloth).—ISBN 0-226-74002-1 (paper)
    1. Herbert, George, 1593–1633—Political and social
  views.   2. Politics and literature—England—History—17th
  century.   3. Devotional literature, English—History and
  criticism.   4. Power (Social sciences) in literature.   5. Social
  problems in literature.   6. Courtship in literature.   I. Title.
  PR3508.S36 1991
  821'.3—dc20   90-25408
                                                       CIP

To my father and to the memory of my mother

Contents

Illustrations

Acknowledgments

This book is in large part a product of the forms of benefaction and indebtedness it surveys. I gratefully acknowledge the Graduate Division at the University of California at Berkeley, which funded two formative trips to the Huntington and Clark libraries. The Bancroft Library provided me with a graduate fellowship which allowed me to use its fine collection of Renaissance documents without the distractions of teaching. At the University of Michigan, a Rackham Summer Fellowship and a Rackham Travel Grant enabled me to continue research on the project, as did an NEH Travel to Collections Grant. The final stages of book production were accomplished in the intense *otium* of the Michigan Institute for the Humanities. I am grateful to the Fred Wilpon Foundation, which created the A. Bartlett Giamatti Fellowship I held.

Less tangible but no less important aid was provided by a variety of individuals. Steven Zwicker first introduced me to the promise and the perils of doing literature and history. The accomplishment and the encouragement of Stephen Booth and Stephen Greenblatt were profoundly enabling. Donald Friedman directed the dissertation on which this book is based, and has continued to serve as friend and unofficial adviser, providing me with a model of intellectual magnanimity and rigorous scholarship. Readers who generously responded to portions of the manuscript include Richard Burt, Stanley Fish, Stanton B. Garner, Jr., Dayton Haskin, John R. Knott, Jr., Ted-Larry Pebworth, Debora Shuger, Thomas Sloane, Claude J. Summers, and James Grantham Turner. Kerry Larson and Ilona Bell read the entire manuscript, and improved it vastly with their suggestions. Kenneth Alan Hovey shared with me his translations of Herbert's Latin works. Like all Herbert scholars, I am grateful to John R. Roberts for his bibliography, as well as for his assistance on a few hard-to-locate items. The two readers for the University of Chicago Press—Richard Strier and Frank Whigham—bestowed on the manuscript a blend of generosity and tough-mindedness which greatly improved it.

Two nonacademic debts must be recorded. My wife Mary provided the emotional support and intellectual companionship that made it all possible and enjoyable. The dedication to my parents records my oldest and most outstanding debt.

For permission to reprint, I owe thanks to the University of Missouri Press, which published a shorter version of chapter 5 in *"Bright Shootes of Everlastingnesse": The Seventeenth-Century Religious Lyric*, eds. Claude J. Summers and Ted-Larry Pebworth. Reprinted by permission of the University of Missouri Press. Copyright 1987 by the Curators of the University of Missouri. Earlier versions of chapters 1 and 6 were published in *The Historical Renaissance: New Essays on Tudor and Stuart Literature and Culture*, ed. Heather Dubrow and Richard Strier (© 1988 by The University of Chicago), and *Soliciting Interpretation: Literary Theory and Seventeenth-Century Poetry*, ed. Elizabeth D. Harvey and Katharine Eisaman Maus (© 1990 by The University of Chicago), both by the University of Chicago Press.

All references to the Bible are to the 1611 Authorized Version, unless otherwise indicated. All references to Shakespeare's plays are to *The Riverside Shakespeare*, ed. G. Blakemore Evans et al. (Boston: Houghton Mifflin, 1974). All references to Herbert's English works are to *The Works of George Herbert*, ed. F. E. Hutchinson (Oxford: Clarendon Press, 1941), hereafter cited as *Works*.

Introduction

The opinion that art should have nothing to do with
politics is itself a political attitude.
                                        —George Orwell

Are not Religion & Politics the Same Thing?
                                        —William Blake

"When he is to read divine services," observes George Herbert in *The Country Parson*, his conduct manual for rural clergy, the parson "composeth himself to all possible reverence; lifting up his heart and hands, and eyes and using all other gestures which may express a hearty and unfeyned devotion."[1] The parson has two motives for attending so fastidiously to the details of his behavior: "first, as being truly touched and amazed with the Majesty of God . . . Secondly . . . that being first affected himself, hee may affect also his people, knowing that no Sermon moves them so much to a reverence . . . as a devout behaviour in the very act of praying" (p. 231). The parson's act of self-composure, like the poet's act of composition, is a creative and coercive gesture. Profoundly aware at once of the effect of his divine auditor upon him and of the effect his conduct has upon his congregation, the parson, like the devotional poet, addresses two very different audiences involving opposite political situations. Moved by the one and moving the other, parson and devotional poet must submit and control, amaze and be amazed, simultaneously. "If the direction of speech toward God is charged by devotion," proposes William Shullenberger, "the direction of the speech toward its human auditors carries the burden of persuasion. Paradoxically, 'Holiness,' in this remarkable prose mixture of the sublime and the practical, takes its place as a *strategy* in the context of effective persuasion."[2]

Yet once holiness and reverence are revealed as persuasive strategies, they begin to lose connection with the interior spiritual reality they ostensibly represent. Keeping these two audiences and motives separate, moreover, proves difficult, if not impossible. Manipulative tactics directed towards the mortal "thou" addressed in "The Church-porch" do not desert language simply because such language is turned to God. Rather, they continue to invade the allegedly submissive utterances directed to the divine "thou" that supplies the ultimate audience of *The Temple*. The parson, Herbert remarks, "procures attention by all possible art, both by earnestnesse of speech . . . and by a diligent, and busy cast of his eye on his auditors" (pp. 232–33). The situations of parson and devotional poet demand a nearly impossible blend of earnestness and art, of sincerity and self-composure, of submission and manipulation; with one eye on heaven and the other on earth, both parson and poet are engaged in inherently duplicitous and deeply rhetorical performances. "The exercise of power," asserts Michel Foucault, is "a mode of action upon the actions of others." In their efforts to influence the conduct of mortal and divine readers, the poems of *The Temple*, like the words of the parson, are exercises of power.[3]

Throughout *The Temple*, the institutions and practices by which political power exhibited itself in Herbert's culture—monarchy, patriarchy, masculinity, and punishment—invest Herbert's deity. The "intimate friend" of Sir Robert Filmer, whose posthumously published *Patriarcha* supplied the period's most extensive defense of patriarchal politics, Herbert replicates in his portrait of God the fusion of divine and sacred authority underpinning Stuart absolutism.[4] The ideological dimension of such portraiture is obvious; as Raymond Williams argues in his account of seventeenth-century pastoral mystification, "it matters very much . . . that the name of the god and the name of the master are significantly single—our Lord."[5] But Herbert's poems do not rest complacently in the conservative political vision that maintains an absolute continuity between earthly and heavenly authority. Rather, they allow the terms of each realm to critique the other, probing the way that the earthly hierarchy of wealth and prestige continues to rasp against the Christian hierarchy of poverty and humility. To imagine the king as a kind of god was an essential ingredient of Stuart absolutism; but the representation of God as a king could be deployed, as it was by many English revolutionaries, to reveal all earthly kingship as a usurpation of divine prerogative. In their nervous conflation of heavenly and earthly authority, Herbert's poems contain such opposite political intentions.

Moreover, instead of collapsing all devotional motives into the desire for submission, Herbert investigates the ruses by which inferiors manage to preserve some residue of integrity and independence in the face of a hierarchy which would deny both. Lacking by definition the strength to challenge his omnipotent deity, Herbert instead makes use of "the weapons of the weak"—the forms of minimal compliance and nonconfrontational resistance by which the socially impotent at once protect themselves and register their insubordination.[6] The medium of Herbert's resistance is, remarkably, courtesy, the very code of behavior originating from and licensed by the centers of power at court. Unlike Spenser, for whom courtesy's relation to the court may only be a false etymology ("Of Court it seemes, men Courtesie doe call"), Herbert still believes that "Courtesie grows in court" ("Church-porch," line 292).[7] Yet this belief does not preclude Herbert from using the discourse of courtesy as a weapon against the very authorities its practices are meant to legitimate. Courtesy, declares Stefano Guazzo, is "that common mean and instrument, whereby mens hearts are wonne."[8] Herbert's poems continually aim this instrument at God. In *1 Henry IV*, King Henry tells his prodigal son Hal how he "stole all courtesy from heaven" in order to "pluck allegiance from men's hearts."[9] In *The Temple*, Herbert reverses the process, reclaiming the strategies of courtly supplication in order to command the allegiance of his heavenly superior.

Prior to Frank Whigham's *Ambition and Privilege: The Social Tropes of Elizabethan Courtesy Theory*, accounts of courtesy literature had been marred by a tendency to idealize or moralize the variegated project this literature undertakes.[10] Even Daniel Javitch's incisive investigations of the manifold relations between poetic and courtly conduct are inclined to aestheticize courtly politics rather than to politicize the question of courtly aesthetics.[11] Whigham, by contrast, emphasizes the bitter historical irony by which the literature of courtesy, "a repertoire of actions invoked by, and meant to order, the surge of social mobility that occurred at the boundaries between ruling and subject classes in sixteenth-century England," actually enabled the socially mobile to mime the conduct of their courtly superiors.[12] The materials constituting the fences of the elite thus were reassembled as the ladders of the ambitious.

Herbert's poems, I want to argue, provide in part a minute and nuanced version of the strategic phenomena that Whigham views in terms of class; they show how courtesy is not simply a rehearsal of the social hierarchy but also a repertoire of techniques for bending the hierarchy to one's will. Yet courtesy is not the exclusive province of the privileged and the ambitious. Whigham's emphasis upon the relationship between courtesy literature and "the dominant ideology of the Elizabethan ruling elite" does not allow room for Herbert's profound investigation of courtesy as a vocabulary of affection as well as power. Moreover, in Herbert's remarkably self-conscious recourse to the tropes of courtly conversation, the language of the dominant courtly culture becomes a tool for resisting many of the claims of that culture. His emphatic redirection of courtly submission involves motives unaccounted for by Whigham's emphasis upon courtesy as a collection of tropes for elite self-justification and social-climbing ambition. Herbert takes a discourse of social control and finds in it a lexicon for investigating his own subjectivity and for expressing his bond with God. By purposefully relocating courtly discourse in two realms often opposed to the arena of political power—the temple of God and the rural world of the country parson—Herbert makes it a vehicle for critiquing the Renaissance court.

Herbert does not, however, allow his critique of the court to quell the manipulative energies of his courtly language. "As princes have arts to govern kingdoms," remarks George Herbert's brother Edward in his celebrated history of Henry VIII, "courtiers have those by which they govern their princes."[13] The lyrics of *The Temple* attempt to perform what Norbert Elias terms "the prime requirement" of courtly interaction: "To lead one's higher-ranking interlocutor almost imperceptibly where one wishes."[14] Because of the impertinence implicit in their project of attempting to lead not a mortal monarch but a divine sovereign—an impertinence nevertheless licensed by the Judeo-Christian injunction to pray—Herbert's poems reveal the glimmers of aggression and manipulation couched in the most apparently humble and benign social maneuvers. The fact that God is the audience of Herbert's utterances amplifies rather than silences the echoes of persuasion and resistance that linger amidst their genuine desire for submission. When directed to God, panegyrical hyperbole becomes understatement, while rhetorical persuasion involves an audacity that verges on defiance. The divinity of Herbert's audience illumines the darker corners of the Renaissance language of courtesy, and throws into relief its subtler maneuverings.

What this book proposes, then, is a mode of reading devotional poetry that is attentive to its social undertones and political valences. Although I make frequent reference to works of Renaissance courtesy literature, I am not arguing that these works exercise a direct literary influence on Herbert, but rather that courtesy literature textualizes the social conduct that Herbert's poems bend to God. "It is the symbolic life of our ancestors which will be the most difficult to handle," remarks Peter Laslett in his pioneering work on social history, "and especially their symbols of status."[15] Courtesy literature provides a handle on the diurnal conduct of this symbolic life. Herbert's writings, moreover, continually betray a fascination with the issue of proper conduct which might have led him, as it did his elder brother Edward, to consult the major works of Renaissance courtesy literature.[16] In 1618, George writes to his younger brother Henry, about to leave for France, "to impart unto you some of those observations which I have framed to myself in conversation" (*Works*, pp. 365–66). It has been argued that "The Church-porch," the versified courtesy book prefacing "The Church," originated in this letter to Henry.[17] At the end of his life, George Herbert again frames certain behavioral precepts, this time to himself, "that I may have a Mark to aim at"; the result is *The Country Parson*, in which Herbert turns the strategies for ingratiating behavior to the goal of winning immortal souls, not secular place (*Works*, p. 224). *The Country Parson*, asserts M. M. Mahood, "has the form and tone and, to a certain extent, the temper of Caroline courtesy-books."[18] Cristina Malcolmson has recently identified in *The Country Parson* "that rhetorical self-consciousness so important in both *The Courtier* and *The Prince*."[19] Despite the enormous differences between the glamorous courtly world negotiated in "The Church-porch" and the provincial world inhabited by *The Country Parson*, both texts are preoccupied by the rhetorical aspects of proper behavior. A little book, able (as did so many works of courtesy literature) to fit comfortably up a sleeve, *The Temple* is itself a kind of spiritualized courtesy book, proffering a rich variety of responses to divine authority which may "turn to the advantage of any dejected poor Soul."[20] Like "The Church-porch" and *The Country Parson*, Herbert's two conspicuous manuals of conduct, the poems of *The Temple* record the immense changes and notable continuities limned by Herbert's life and career.

Herbert's intention to implicate his discourse with God in the strategies by which a social inferior petitions and gratifies his superior is broadcast in the first poem a reader of *The Temple* encounters: "The Dedication." Herbert deliberately constructs this short poem from the conventions secular authors use to address their literary performances to superiors in hopes of protection and reward: "Lord, my first fruits present themselves to thee; / Yet not mine neither: for from thee they came, / And must return." By committing his poems

to God in a language steeped in both the Thames and the Jordan—
"first fruits" invokes at once Old Testament sacrifice and stock de-
dicatory practice—Herbert locates his devotional activity on the axis
spanning political obligation and religious affiliation.[21] The follow-
ing poem—"The Church-porch"—sustains this alignment, suggest-
ing by its location as well as its recommendations that shrewd advice
on social comportment is contiguous with rather than divorced from
the sacred lyrics it introduces.[22] In admonishing the reader to "Doe
all things like a man, not sneakingly," for example, Herbert declares,
"Think the king sees thee still; for his King does" (lines 121–22). Sim-
ilarly, Herbert encourages prompt arrival at church because

> God then deals blessings: If a king did so,
> Who would not haste, nay give, to see the show?
> (lines 389–90)

Behavior before God is coterminous with behavior towards earthly
authority. Power, whether secular or sacred, monitors and rewards hu-
man conduct.

Herbert's poems, then, parade rather than occlude their blend of
secular and sacred, of divine and human. At the same time, they di-
rect attention to the unstable compound of submission and aggres-
sion, of sanctity and anger, that results. In "The Church-porch," Her-
bert recommends a mode of oxymoronic conduct towards superiors:
"Towards great persons use respective boldnesse" (line 253). "Pitch
thy behaviour low, thy projects high," he continues; "So shalt thou
humble and magnanimous be" (lines 331–32). The prescription for
successful demeanor, asserts Herbert, is "a grain of glorie mixt with
humblenesse" (line 335). Dazzlingly and dizzyingly, the lines mix
ambition and submission, humility and magnanimity. Surprisingly
like Jonson's Mosca, the ultimate social parasite who dextrously "can
rise, / And stoope (almost together) like an arrow," Herbert endorses
a mode of conduct towards superiors in which the ingratiating power
of humility offers the surest way to rise.[23] Throughout *The Temple*,
Herbert translates such lessons of civil behavior into the terms of his
sacred conversation with God.

The confluence of sacred and secular modes of reverence in Her-
bert's poems is not a unique phenomenon, but part of a much larger
cultural movement. Erasmus' immensely popular *De Civilitate Mor-
um Puerilium* (translated into English in 1532 as *A Lytell Booke of
Good Manners for Children*) has consecutive chapters entitled "Of
apparayle," "Of Manners in the Temple," and "Of manners at table,"
locating religious behavior somewhere between issues of proper dress

and commensal etiquette.[24] One of the earliest English texts on conduct, *The Babees Book*, at once aligns and segregates sacred and secular behavior in its suggestion that children should kneel on only one knee to their lord, reserving the privilege of both knees to God.[25] The English Renaissance witnessed an explosion of works devoted to these two forms of submission. The burgeoning popularity of manuals of courtesy and of devotional literature testifies to the pressing need for imitable patterns of behavior in a time of baffling change.[26] Both literatures involve modes of discourse intended to discipline an unruly self for presentation to a superior being—just what was needed by a culture made anxious by the great social and theological upheavals it experienced but could not fully comprehend.[27] Gertrude Noyes argues that in the seventeenth century, "gradually the courtesy book merges into the manual of devotion."[28] The merger is so smooth because the projects are so alike.

Indeed, in *The Diamond of Devotion* (1608) Abraham Fleming exploits the parallels between civil and devotional discipline to trumpet the virtues of his work: as courtesy literature teaches one how "to grow in favour with Princes, Potentates, and Governors," Fleming promises "the true Christian Reader" that this work shows how "to please [God], & to direct our lives after his good pleasure."[29] Not only does Fleming allow devotional literature to absorb the energies and motives of courtesy literature; he also suggests the ultimate superiority of devotional efforts, since "God is omnipotent, all princes are impotent: he immortall, they mortal: he above, they below: he Creator, they creature: finally, he a cleare fountaine of all goodnes, they filthy puddles of wickednes."[30] Throughout *The Temple*, Herbert engages in a process similar to that outlined by Fleming, at once assimilating and supplanting the courtly tradition. Addressing heavenly authority in a language at times strikingly similar to that used before political authority, the lyrics of *The Temple* rest precariously on the cusp of these two projects.

Herbert's reputation as an Anglican saint has, I feel, hindered our understanding of his poetry by diverting attention from the amount of time and energy he invested in the world. Draping Herbert in robes of righteousness obscures rather than reveals the greatness of the man and the utterances. In the pages that follow, I try to give Herbert credit for being the kind of human being he claims to be in "The Pearl"— not a plaster saint but one who knows quite well the ways of learning, of honor, and of pleasure, and who feels this knowledge genuinely enriches his gestures of devotion. Even Izaak Walton, whose biography of a man he never met has exerted an undue influence over responses to Herbert in the past three hundred years, credits Herbert with the ambitious desire for courtly promotion (although he does so for his own ideological reasons—to encourage other similarly gifted young men to follow suit and join the church).[31] If I attend to the less hallowed aspects of Herbert, it is intended as a corrective to the hagiographic tendency, inherited from Walton, that continues to mar Herbert criticism. "Pardon all but thy selfe" observes one of the *Outlandish Proverbs* Herbert collected (*Works*, p. 344, no. 677). Herbert's lyrics demonstrate his rigorous refusal to pardon even his own best tendencies—a refusal we readers should honor. *The Temple* is not a portrait of perfect piety but a ledger of what T. S. Eliot terms "the cost at which [Herbert] acquired godliness."[32] Appreciation for Herbert's poetic and religious achievement is enhanced, not diminished, when this achievement is located among the sometimes grimy materials of Herbert's culture.

In my attempt to link Herbert's secular and sacred experience, I do not mean to diminish the immense adjustments in attitude and experience involved in the transition from ambitious youth to humble parson. But I do not want to let an emphasis upon the conspicuous changes preclude attention to the considerable continuities. Herbert's profound insight in *The Temple* and *The Country Parson* into courtliness does not always insulate him from implication in its practices. The irony and humor Herbert directs at his more manipulative and aggressive speakers often result in self-inflicted wounds; as Herbert attests in "The Church-porch," "Wit's an unruly engine, wildly striking / Sometimes a friend, sometimes the engineer" (lines 241–42). The poems are not simple autobiography, but neither are they disingenuous spiritual drama. As Herbert's prophetic poem "The Church Militant" depicts sin dogging the heels of the church, so do his devotional lyrics demonstrate the way that aggression follows upon submission as inexorably as systolic pulses succeed diastolic ones. Edward Herbert remembers two details about his younger brother George's character: that his "life was most holy and exemplary, in so much that about Salisbury where he lived beneficed for many years, he was litle less than Sainted," and that George "was not exempt from passion and Choler."[33] Throughout Herbert's *Temple*, elements of sanctity are nervously interwoven with the insubordinate emotions of passion and anger. "No sooner is a Temple built to God," observes another of Herbert's *Outlandish Proverbs*, "but the Devill builds a Chappell hard by" (no. 674, p. 343). The devil builds beside, and sometimes within, Herbert's finest edifices.

I am not the first reader to suggest the propriety of social terminology to the interpretation of Herbert's poems. Yet it is a curious irony of Herbert criticism that those critics for whom the social is most crucial continue to recoil from the force of their own argument, leaving the strongest statements of the importance of social forms to those critics for whom the social was of only incidental importance. Louis Martz, for example, emphasizes how Herbert's meditative practices are geared to cultivate the "presence of a friend."[34] Although working outside the theological traditions explored by Martz, Helen Vendler articulates at greater length the conspicuous affability of Herbert's poems:

> Social exchange . . . is as congenial to him as life itself, and the tactical advances and retreats of poems like "Heaven," "Love Unknown," "Dialogue," "Conscience," "Assurance," "Hope," "Love (III)," and so many others are based on the infinite variety that social dialectic and response can take . . . Herbert has a genius for social inflection . . . Herbert's dialogues with himself and with God run such a gamut of moods as almost to exhaust one form of social life. The problem for Herbert as a religious poet was to find the mode that would allow him social discourse in religious forms.[35]

As both Martz and Vendler indicate, Herbert's poems are deeply enmeshed in the language of human relationships.

Yet those critics who have dealt in some detail with the social and political components of Herbert's poetry do so as if brief exposure to politics would inoculate Herbert against infection by political concerns. M. M. Ross, for example, correctly asserts that "too little attention has been given to any concern Herbert may have shown in his poetry for the world about him."[36] But ironically, he sets out to correct this oversight by showing how little, except in a negative way, Herbert's poetry has to do with the world. Herbert, he declares, "is not concerned with *Realpolitik* and the exercise of power," striking instead an "antihistorical note of withdrawal" in his poetry.[37] Although conceding that Herbert imagines his God as a monarch, Ross argues that "God retains his kingship in a completely otherworldly realm," thus vitiating the impact of his inquiry.[38] In *Childhood and Cultural Despair*, Leah Marcus likewise recoils from the implications of some cogent insights. She perceptively remarks that "the God of *The Temple* is a master as well as a father, the Lord of a rich manor ('Redemption'), a great territorial magnate whose household, the church, keeps for all comers the standing feast of the eucharist."[39] But to Marcus, Herbert's use of social metaphors for God is the product of a nostalgia for a "near-extinct social institution," the late-feudal household, into which Herbert "retreat[s] from society," rather than a measure of his engagement with the social world.[40]

The tendency of Ross and Marcus to segregate Herbert's sacred utterances from a social world traditionally viewed as corrupt is developed at length in a recent book, Marion White Singleton's *God's Courtier: Configuring a Different Grace in George Herbert's "Temple."*[41] Rather than attending to the fascinating and troubling interplay between courtly supplication and devotional petition in Herbert's religious lyrics, Singleton quarries them only for evidence of their unremarkable anticourtly sentiments. Singleton subjects both Renaissance history and courtesy literature to a fallacious historical paradigm of increasing moral decay from which Herbert necessarily withdraws. Politics are invoked solely as a force which taints and constrains, never as an environment which sustains and enables.

In contrast, some of the richest recent criticism of Herbert has been executed by critics whose concerns are largely nonpolitical—Stanley Fish, Barbara Harman, Chana Bloch, and Richard Strier. Yet in each of these critics I find an urge towards stability and assimilation that ultimately belies the unsettling, restless insurgence of Herbert's poetry. To Stanley Fish, Herbert's God is an omnipotent other who denies by definition a relationship of reciprocity or equality with humanity. Fish apprehends the insidious pride that suffuses Herbert's ostensibly humble poetry, asserting that "every withdrawal from a prideful claim only reconstitutes it on the other side of a gesture."[42] But where Fish argues that Herbert's self is finally "absorbed into the deity whose omnipresence he has acknowledged," I attend to the vestiges of aggression lurking within the terms of the surrender the poet extends to God.[43]

Like Fish, Barbara Harman views Herbert's poems as complex acts of self-representation, attempts to dismantle a self by embodying it in narrative. Her discussion of Herbert's relationship with the authorizing text of the Bible is particularly provocative in the context of my concern with Herbert's attitude to social authority. "The Bible," she observes,

> may sanction literary productivity, but what it also sponsors . . . is a writer whose agency is immediately subverted by the discovery that he is not only the writer but the written-upon . . . the Bible provides a model for activity only to subvert activity . . . it transforms subjects into objects, embodiers into embodiments.[44]

10

Harman finds Herbert's self and poems to be contained, even erased, by the religious narratives to which they continually refer. Chana Bloch, by contrast, claims that Herbert finds in the Bible not an authority that precludes activity but a repertoire of images and models that enable the comprehension and expression of mortal devotional experience.[45] Yet her sense of the easy fit between biblical injunction and religious motivation fails to account for the aggression that Herbert frequently expresses towards his divine superior and the text he has written. The authority of the Bible neither fully encompasses nor totally obliterates the recalcitrant self. The hints of rebellion surfacing among even Herbert's most devout gestures offer the site of the subject's self-affirmation.

Unlike Bloch, whose Herbert cooperates fully with the divine authority he worships, Richard Strier argues that Reformation theology bestows upon Herbert a vocabulary of profound psychological insight into "the subtle, seemingly innocent, and even laudable forms that egotism, ungratefulness, and self-assertion can take."[46] By exploring the importance to Herbert of the Lutheran doctrine of justification by faith, Strier supplies a theological model that anticipates my own concern with the politics of Herbert's relationship with God. As Strier shows, the God for whom justification is a matter of faith rather than works has nothing to gain from the efforts of his creature, nor does his creature have any actual or rhetorical leverage against him. Yet such knowledge does not stop Herbert from seeking that leverage. The experience of the poems sometimes chafes against the theology that underpins them; in such moments, Strier opts for the theology. Moreover, Strier's emphasis upon the irresistible love that Herbert's deity feels for his creatures leads him to undervalue both Herbert's attention to the more unsettling aspects of this deity and his stress upon the mortal capacity for resistance. Where Strier tends to stabilize the poems by reference to the Lutheran doctrines of justification by faith and of the irresistibility of grace, I attend to the lingering instability and moments of political resistance in Herbert's devotional performances.

Strier's claim that "we can grasp the human content of Herbert's poetry only through, not apart from the theology" functions as a kind of challenge to works such as the present study, which would locate Herbert in a context that is not overtly theological.[47] As a site of intense ideological contest in the period, theology is ultimately inseparable from political concerns. Moreover, the experience of seeking rewards from superiors, so central to seventeenth-century social life, is a crucial element in Reformation debates about mortal conduct towards God. If theology is understood as the effort to fix Herbert's doctrinal allegiances, then this study is largely nontheological; my emphasis upon the slighted social constituent of Herbert's poetry necessarily precludes my giving the complex subject the detailed attention it deserves. Many such works do exist, and offer a baffling array of conclusions; as Ilona Bell has recently remarked, "Scholars have placed Herbert at every point along the spectrum of English Protestantism, from ceremonial Anglo-Catholicism to radical Puritanism."[48] If, however, theology entails attending to the gamut of relations between humans and the divine, and to the various materials used to represent them, then this study is deeply theological. I would endorse but reverse Strier's linkage of theological and human content. When he emphatically asserts that "the more deeply we understand the theology of the poetry the more deeply we understand its human content," I would argue that attending to the historically embedded language of Herbert's poetry allows us to arrive at the human ground on which theology rests.[49]

"Implicit in persuasion," argues Kenneth Burke, "there is *theology*, since theology is the ultimate reach of communication between *different classes* of beings . . . The 'theology' that Marx detected in 'ideological mystification' is the *last reach of the persuasive principle itself*."[50] Herbert's conscientious exposure of the suasive aspects of devotional behavior achieves its apogee at the nexus of theological and rhetorical practice. By bending towards God the strategies of courtly supplication, Herbert pushes language to "the ultimate reach of communication between *different classes* of beings." Yet this practice is itself licensed by Herbert's biblical models; even Old Testament forms of prayer are, as Moshe Greenberg argues, modelled upon petitionary address to a monarch or some other powerful person.[51] Furthermore, as G. B. Caird observes in his study of the sources of biblical imagery, "Man's sense of obligation to God, though by no means identical with his human loyalties and relationships, is inseparably bound up with them . . . Thus the language of human relationships furnishes not only the natural vocabulary for talking about obligation to God, but the indispensable vehicle for experiencing it."[52] To focus on the neglected social component of Herbert's poetry, then, is not to slight the vexed but compelling questions of Herbert's theology; it is rather to foreground the social and political presuppositions of theological doctrine.

By interrogating the oppositions we have traditionally used to organize our analyses of Herbert, and of seventeenth-century literature in general (private/public, secular/sacred, court/country, plain/ornate),

I hope to reconstruct a Herbert at once worldly and saintly, sophisticated and seraphic, whose sincere devotional motives are entangled in and enriched by the manipulative tactics of supplication that he practiced in the social world. Because his subject is by definition otherworldly but his idiom so strikingly worldly, Herbert's devotional performances supply a consummate example of the intertwining of literary, theological, and political concerns. Throughout the book, my sense of the inevitable interpenetration of devotional and social experience is deeply indebted to the recent explosion of work in the Renaissance attending to the relations between literature and history often called "the new historicism," or perhaps more felicitously, "cultural poetics."[53] New historicist critics have taught us to appreciate the immense and varied forces that cultures exert upon the formation of individual identity. But we must try to remember that individuals shape the culture that shapes them. If identity is culturally constructed, so is culture constructed from an aggregate of individual identities. Individuals are not absolutely contained within the closed circuit of their culture. Rather, they participate actively in the production of the culture that binds them.

I have also discovered among the practitioners of new historicism a refreshing readiness to juxtapose literary texts with less "literary" materials. Nevertheless, I try to remember that many of the materials I use have been made available by the painstaking archival work of an older historicism against which the new historicism self-consciously reacts. Moreover, I locate the full political impact of Herbert's devotional performances by means of the close textual analysis pioneered by new criticism even as I dispute the notion of ahistorical textual autonomy on which this mode of criticism was originally based. In my attempt to come to terms with the issues of gender and sexuality in Herbert, I have drawn on the work of feminist critics and social historians in order to find a functional yet fully historical notion of gender.[54] Throughout the book, I have worked to synthesize the compelling claims of these at times contradictory approaches. I would not want to practice a criticism intended to establish connections among different discourses from the past while refusing to do so with the range of critical discourses available in my own historical moment.[55] Doctrinal consistency seems to me a far less attractive goal than critical cogency.

In *The Country Parson*, Herbert contends that the parson must struggle with "ambition, or untimely desire of promotion to an higher state, or place, under colour of accommodation, or necessary provision," as well as with "originall concupisence," which "is such an active thing, by reason of continually inward, or outward temptations, that it is ever attempting or doing one mischief or other" (*Works*, p. 238). The first five of my chapters are concerned with Herbert's confrontation with the former temptations of power, pride, and place. My final chapter analyzes Herbert's attempts to harness the restless and insurgent energies of sexual passion. Although Herbert's battles with "the sicknesse that destroyeth at noone day, [Ghostly pride and self-conceite]" are somewhat more conspicuous than his encounters with "the pestilence that walketh in darkenesse, [carnall impurity,]" both are aspects of the same basic project—disciplining the self (p. 238; the brackets are Herbert's). These two "proper and peculiar temptations" continue to surface in various and manifold forms throughout *The Temple*. I conclude this study with the issue of sexuality because for Herbert, the spiritual longing for union with God as well as the obstacles to this union the self produces receive their most subtle and cogent statement in implicitly libidinal terms.

This study is divided into three parts of two chapters each. Part One, "The Distance of the Meek," explores Herbert's explicit engagement with and criticism of the court. In my first chapter, " 'Subject to Ev'ry Mounters Bended Knee': Herbert and Authority," I excavate the profound if recondite relationships between Herbert's utterances to figures of secular power and his lyric addresses to divine power. As University Orator at Cambridge, Herbert honed the remarkable laudatory and supplicatory abilities that the divine lyrics bend to God. In his performances before secular power, moreover, Herbert developed a discourse capable of venting the anxieties and strains incumbent upon a subordinate status in a framework that remained pleasing to authority. Herbert's panegyrics of divine power reverberate with the tactical praise he directed to secular authority. The power of his otherworldly poetry derives, remarkably, from his familiarity with the world of social power.

The next chapter, " 'My God, My King': Socializing God," analyzes a range of poems by Herbert that employ conspicuous metaphors of social superiority to represent God. Where chapter 1 explores the alignment of social and sacred as a criticism of misguided religious aspirations, this chapter attends to the implicit critique of mortal political behavior that emphasis upon God's kingship can produce. Many of the poems register Herbert's disquiet about the necessity and impossibility of serving an omnipotent being who by definition has no need of servants; others record Herbert's linguistic anxiety about imagining and addressing a God whose ultimate power resides in his inscrutability. This chapter investigates Herbert's abiding need for the divine authority he often resists in the process of constructing a manageable self.

Part Two, "I Live to Shew His Power," foregrounds the political components of affliction and petition throughout *The Temple*. God's art of imposing pain, and the mortal art of supplication, are seen as corollary activities geared to reveal divine power. My third chapter, "'Storms are the Triumph of His Art': The Politics of Affliction," analyzes the chilling image, which recurs with unsettling frequency throughout *The Temple*, of God as a torturer, imposing upon his creatures immense if ultimately salutary suffering. God's actions share a remarkable consonance with the cruelties practiced by the governments of Renaissance England. As something imposed by God and experienced by humanity, pain offers the ultimate evidence of divine power. The difficult task of the mortal sufferer is to interpret the acute agony he feels as evidence of solicitous divine love.

Yet as something to which God willingly subjected himself in the incarnation and passion, suffering can register not only mortal alienation from God but also divine accessibility. In the next chapter, "'Engine Against th' Almighty': The Poetics of Prayer," I explore the corollary violence that mortal supplication directs at God. Herbert shows in detail how the tacit aggression of courtly petition, when leveled at God, replays the scenario of the Passion, where God willingly condescends to be wounded by his creatures. This chapter highlights Herbert's profound investigation of the powers and limitations of human art. The poems it considers struggle to find a way of showing God's power without appropriating that power, and of praising God without occasioning self-display.

Part Three, "Love Bade Me Welcome," considers the final lyric of *The Temple*—"Love (III)"—as the culmination of two kinds of behavior which the courteous injunctions of Herbert's culture subjected to increasing regulation: table manners and sexual conduct. The penultimate chapter, "Standing on Ceremony: The Comedy of Manners in 'Love (III),'" locates this remarkable poem amidst the vast Renaissance literature on hospitality and behavior at meals. In this poem, Herbert makes a perfectly common social interaction—the exchange of greetings between a guest and host—adumbrate a transcendent experience which at once summarizes and revises the rest of *The Temple*. Throughout *The Temple*, Herbert attempts to approach God through what he terms "the distance of the meek," discovering in the deference of an earthly supplicant a model for his own conduct. But in

"Love (III)," he is compelled to "sit and eat" while his Lord serves him, a scenario which discloses his true status as the unilateral and undeserving recipient of God's benefits. With remarkable brevity and grace, the poem exploits the political ramifications of dining at the table of the great to display the extreme difficulty and immense rewards of the Christian devotional life.

In my final chapter, " 'That Ancient Heat': Sexuality and Spirituality in *The Temple*," I discuss the tacit eroticism imbuing Herbert's presentation of the human encounter with God. Where my third chapter foregrounds the body as the object of pain, this chapter features the body as the subject of pleasure. I demonstrate how Herbert's lyrics record the profound ambivalence suffusing Christian attitudes to sexuality and gender since Augustine. Christian discipline and courtly conduct intersect in the need to subjugate instinct. Where the previous chapter explored the fastidious regulation of social conduct at meals, this chapter analyzes the insistent socialization of the corollary appetites for food and sex. Again, the extraordinary lyric that concludes *The Temple*—"Love (III)"—gets the lion's share of attention, supplying the most conspicuous example of the surprisingly carnal motives infusing Herbert's spiritual aspirations. Throughout *The Temple*, Herbert's courtship of God plays on a complex set of homologies between social and sexual courtship. Both an urge competitive with devotional desire and the highest expression of the devotional self, erotic longing affords Herbert a resonant vocabulary for expressing religious passion.

Throughout the work I make liberal use of all of Herbert's writings, not just the often-discussed *Temple* and *Country Parson*, discovering in his Latin and English letters, his orations, his Latin poems, his collection of proverbs, and his translations concerns which illuminate, and are illuminated by, the more commonly discussed works. Although I sometimes refer to certain Renaissance paintings as striking visual responses to the devotional issues confronting Herbert, I am not arguing that Herbert was influenced by any of these paintings (indeed, it is almost certain that he never saw any of them). But I do think that the graphic acts of worship produced by Dürer, Gentile da Fabriano, Tintoretto, Simone Martini, Botticelli, and Leonardo da Vinci can illustrate elements of Herbert's verbal artistry. The paintings helped me comprehend, with the impact only a visual medium allows, certain aspects of Herbert's project; they are reproduced and discussed here in the hope that they will do the same for my reader.

In his introduction to the first edition of *The Temple*, Nicholas

Ferrar, Herbert's good friend, declares that he feels compelled to give some details of Herbert's life for the reader's benefit:

> onely for the clearing of some passages, we have thought it not unfit to make the common Reader privie to some few particularities of the condition and disposition of the Person. (*Works*, p. 3)

The chapters that follow proceed from a related set of assumptions: that literature is neither created nor interpreted in a vacuum, but is inextricably bound up with political, social, and biographical circumstances; that religious and political discourse are intertwined like the aristocratic "silk twist" let down from heaven to Herbert in "The Pearl"; that Herbert lived not only in those "sacred volumes of Divinity" for which he seeks money in his letters but also in the acts of supplication represented by these letters, and in the complex, hierarchical culture that continually demanded such conduct. Ferrar also notes that Herbert, "to testifie his independencie upon all others . . . used in his ordinarie speech, when he made mention of the blessed name of our Lord and Saviour Jesus Christ, to adde, *My Master*" (p. 4). The assertion of dependence upon one authority sanctions the expression of independence from another. Yet the term representing divine authority—master—is borrowed from the forms of political dependence that it purportedly escapes. Even as secular and sacred subordination are segregated, they are admixed.

In turning to God, then, Herbert does not just turn away from the social and political world but also turns the language of this world into the medium for his lyric worship of God. Only by attending to the political nuances of Herbert's devotional discourse can we fully apprehend the extraordinary blend of mastery and modesty, order and urgency, that marks his poetry. The penetrating and unforgiving gaze to which Herbert subjects his own gestures of devotion throughout *The Temple* was made possible by his habitation of a social world demanding daily declarations of submission and dependence. Herbert never allows himself the illusion of having attained in his poetry what Kenneth Burke terms an act of "pure persuasion," that is, "the saying of something, not for an extra-verbal advantage to be got by the saying, but because of a satisfaction intrinsic to the saying."[56] By exposing rather than repressing the impure, insurgent, advantage-seeking tendencies of the language of submission made available to him by his society, Herbert achieves in his poems a spiritual rigor and lyric intensity which continue to impress readers who may not share his religious beliefs and who inhabit a public world quite different from the social hierarchy of early seventeenth-century England. At once devious and devout, these poems translate the particular idiom of Herbert's social, political, and theological experience into the familiar vocabulary of negotiation between an intractably beneficent being and an impertinently recalcitrant self. The capacity of the poems of *The Temple* to transcend their culture is largely a function of the degree to which they are embedded in that culture. By construing them as a product of rather than an escape from their historical moment, we assist in the mysterious consubstantiation of local and indigenous matter into legible and accessible phenomena. We experience the immanent presence of a distant past.

I
"The Distance of the Meek"

1

"Subject to Ev'ry Mounters Bended Knee": Herbert and Authority

An artist true-born . . . is both tribune and troublemaker.
—Andrei Voznesensky

In 1631, two years before his death, Herbert addressed a letter to Anne Clifford, the countess of Pembroke and Montgomery. This letter, written to a great lady at court from Herbert's country parsonage at Bemerton, measures in reverse the geographical, social, and linguistic distance covered by Herbert's career. "A Priests blessing," remarks Herbert, "though it be none of the Court-stile, yet doubtless Madam, can do you no hurt" (*Works*, p. 377). This opposition between the blessings of a priest and "the salutations, and complements, and formes of worldly language"—so appropriate for one who has just left one realm for the other—is developed by Herbert in *The Country Parson*, his manual of conduct for rural clergy. There Herbert asserts that

> if a Minister talke with a great man in the ordinary course of complementing language, he shall be esteemed as ordinary complementers; but if he often interpose a Blessing, when the other gives him just opportunity, by speaking any good, this un-usuall form begets a reverence, and makes him esteemed accord-ing to his Profession. (*Works*, pp. 285–86)

Herbert suggests that religious and social discourse are different, and that the parson, by replacing the compliments through which one renders respect to "a great man" with the novelty of religious blessing, accents this difference; at the same time, he signals his separation from ordinary men, and so attains the reverence of that superior from whom ordinary compliments would elicit only common esteem.

These discourses, however, and the experiences they represent, are not as discrete as Herbert or his critics would like to make them. Even religious language remains, in the words of Joseph Summers, an "incorrigibly social medium,"[1] inevitably implicating the otherworld in the terms of this one. While Herbert opposes the "unusual form" of blessing to the deferential compliments of ordinary discourse with superiors, he nevertheless reveals the motives of both—winning the respect of superiors—to be astonishingly alike. Benediction, finally, is recommended because it fulfills this social and rhetorical function more effectively than ordinary compliments. A priest's blessing, it turns out, has more to do with "the Court-stile" than Herbert's letter to Anne Clifford would reveal.

As Herbert's dialogue with authority in *The Country Parson* begins to blur the distinction between social and religious demeanor that it attempts to draw, so throughout *The Temple* Herbert's intimate experience of political authority infiltrates and enriches his discourse with divinity. In an important but overlooked essay on Herbert, Kenneth Burke asks:

> where matters of "reverence" are concerned, should we not consider such possibilities of fusing social eminence with divine eminence as would be indicated by the similarity between "My Lord" and "milord"? . . . why should we not consider also such relationships between the language of worldly hierarchy and the language of the supernatural hierarchy, each with its great stress upon the exercising of one's desire freely to praise?[2]

As Burke's questions indicate, the two discourses that Herbert wishes to separate—the courtly and the religious—share similar motives and a common rhetoric. In both, praise of and reverence for hierarchical authority are expressed in a nearly identical vocabulary of submission. Bemerton may be far removed from the court, but both Bemerton and the court require the continual subordination of the self to superior power.

In "The Priesthood," for example, the poem in which Herbert most forthrightly ponders changing a secular for a sacred vocation, the terms he uses to denote these different careers nevertheless stress their continuity. This lyric is remarkable not only for its demonstration of how fully Herbert's purported turn from the world is involved in the discourse of this world, but also for its perception of the potentially insidious consequences of aligning behavior towards heavenly authority with actual courtly practice. Herbert depicts the contemplated career change as an "exchang[e]" of his "lay-sword / For that of th' holy Word." The sword, an emblem of social and martial power, is traded in for a "sword of the spirit," but the visual and auditory rhyme between "word" and "sword" emphasizes their likeness.[3] Besides, "sword" encloses the "Word" to which it is opposed, the "Word" that should contain it. The conclusion of the poem, moreover, reinstates the courtly values ostensibly surrendered with the gentleman's "lay-sword." Both attracted and repelled by the awesome power and responsibility of the priesthood, Herbert can only prostrate himself before his heavenly superior: "I throw me at his feet." Yet in this posture of complete submission, he discovers a method for ingratiating divine authority that is strikingly similar to secular and courtly strategies of social climbing.

> There will I lie, untill my Maker seek
> For some mean stuffe whereon to show his skill:
> Then is my time. The distance of the meek
> Doth flatter power. Lest good come short of ill
> In praising might, the poore do by submission
> What pride by opposition.

Deference functions as a device for celebrating sacred as well as secular power. The calculated observation of occasion ("Then is my time") and hierarchical distance, so much a part of behavior in the world of the "lay-sword" allegedly abandoned, is fused with the ideal of Christian patience.[4] At the precise moment of turning from the court to the church, when one would anticipate a heightening of the distinctions between earthly and heavenly service, Herbert foregrounds their dissolution. Likewise, he allows the differences between praise and flattery, good and ill, submission and opposition, to blur in a world of political and spiritual opportunism. Frank Whigham argues that the common courtly mechanism of paradiastolic ambiguity—the redescription of "an utterance or action in such a way as to reverse the polarity of its meaning"—produced at the Renaissance court a rhetorical "matrix in which praise and blame, flattery and slander, interpenetrate absolutely."[5] In "The Priesthood," Herbert brilliantly uses this matrix to convey the profound complexity of his own devotional motives, at once euphemistically putting the best face on the opposition of the proud and investing the submission of the meek with insurgent energies.

The conclusion of "The Priesthood" indicates, then, that opposition only furthers the interests of the power it intends to resist. It implies, furthermore, that power encloses and in some sense even produces the site of resistance. In doing so, the poem seems to endorse a notion underpinning much new historicist work on Renaissance literature, that of the inescapability of power. As Walter Cohen has recently argued, new historicist analyses, although attending to ambivalence or subversion, "almost always demonstrate the triumph of containment."[6] This victory seems particularly appropriate when dealing not just with the subject of most new historicist work—the implicitly contestatory forum of theatre—but with the unmistakably submissive mode of devotional discourse addressed to an omnipotent God. In *Paradise Lost*, John Milton similarly proposes that rebellion against God inevitably supplies the occasion for admiring, not threatening, this being's might:

> Who seeks
> To lessen thee, against his purpose serves
> To manifest the more thy might: his evil
> Thou usest, and from thence creat'st more good.[7]

Like Herbert, Milton is fascinated by the irresistible and omnipresent lines of force by which divine power encloses the efforts of its creatures. But what is remarkable in Herbert's lines, and strikingly absent from Milton's, is their use of the opposition of the ill to set the standard by which the submission of the good is measured: "Lest good come short of ill / In praising might." Milton is interested in only one side of the equation—the way that God turns rebellion into evidence of his "might." Herbert, by contrast, is fascinated both by the capacity of divine power to absorb gestures of opposition and by the ability of mortal submission to exude opposition. Herbert, that is, allows the osmosis between submission and opposition to flow in both directions. One indication of the ideological complexity of the seventeenth century is the fact that on this point, the actively revolutionary Milton takes a less radical position than the purportedly conservative Herbert. Herbert shows not only how social concerns constantly interpenetrate the sacred world to which they are contrasted but also how devotional postures of submission are continually infiltrated by the subtle forms of opposition or ambition they both enable and disguise. Surprisingly, the submission of the poor and the opposition of the proud produce the same result, however different they may be in appearance and intention: the flattery of power. By equating the virtuously submissive activity of praise with the duplicitously ambitious practices of flattery, Herbert underscores the rhetorical intentions of his own devout utterances. His profound attention to submission as a site of opposition requires a mode of analysis which resists the impulse to fold all acts of resistance into the unconstrained victory of divine power.

Such scrupulous attention to the affinity between obedience and opposition, between placating authority and challenging it, could only come from one who had practiced the manipulative powers of submission in his own career. The shape of Herbert's biography and the vitality of his poetry are, I want to argue, intimately related. Deeply aware of the striking continuities between his own secular and sacred careers, John Donne proposes that one's worldly experience inevitably invades the terms one selects to address the divine: "the Prophets, and the other Secretaries of the holy Ghost in penning the books of Scriptures, do for the most part retain, and express in their writings some impressions, and some air of their former professions . . . ever inserting into their writings some phrases, some metaphors, some allusions, taken from the profession which they had exercised before."[8] Although such continuities necessarily took very different form for the Dean of St. Paul's than they did for the rector of Bemerton, both Donne and Herbert cultivated the cross-fertilization of their earthly and heavenly experience.[9]

Indeed, Herbert's political career begins with his expression of the hope that secular office might be integrated with sacred duty. The "dignity" of University Orator, Herbert reassures his stepfather Sir John Danvers, "hath no such earthiness in it, but it may very well be joined with Heaven" (p. 370). Yet in this secular occupation Herbert learned that submission is indeed an act of opposition, that deference and praise are tactics for manipulating authority, and self-deprecation a way to scale both the social and the religious hierarchy. Thus, when Herbert asserts in "The H. Scriptures (I)" that the Bible, the ultimate authority, the word of the King of Kings, is "subject to ev'ry mounters bended knee," he acknowledges not only the striking availability of Scripture to the humble but also the coercive power that gestures of humility can exert over figures of authority. As "the distance of the meek / Doth flatter power," so is the bended knee the mark of the social and spiritual mounter, he who would attempt to acquire power over those powerful personages to whom he submits. By examining closely Herbert's verbal performances before secular authority, we can more fully comprehend the accomplishment of poems such as "The Thanksgiving" and "The Reprisall," in which Herbert exposes the political presumption and social aggression inherent in the lexicon of gratitude, submission, and dependence. The lyrics of *The Temple* do not occupy a realm of discourse completely separate from the court; rather, they concatenate, and consummate, Herbert's social and political experience.

Indeed, Herbert's social status and political situation forced him to practice daily the modes of submission to authority that the divine poetry exploits. The Herbert family was, in the words of T. S. Eliot, "conspicuous for warlike deeds, administrative gifts and attendance at court."[10] As the child of such a family, George Herbert would have nourished great expectations for his political future. Two of his brothers, in fact, became influential court figures—Edward was ambassador to France, and Henry was Master of the Revels—by successfully translating verbal talent into political place. Yet as a younger son, Herbert possessed few means to fulfill these expectations save his ability to ingratiate his superiors.[11] Cristina Malcolmson describes well the "paradoxical situation" of the younger son of an aristocratic family: "one has to work desperately to become what one already is, since status is ascribed by birth, and yet must be achieved through labor."[12] Herbert did receive an annuity of thirty pounds, but this was apparently insufficient (considering Herbert's many pleas for money in his letters) and often tardy.[13] In a social structure composed of a chain of dependence leading up to the monarch, the only theoretically self-sufficient figure, Herbert had to rely upon his ability to please potential patrons for his very sustenance.

Equipped with great verbal dexterity and a talent for witty praise that pleased both the intellect and the vanity of many Renaissance superiors, Herbert attempted to win the good graces of those in authority. In what may have been his first public performance, Herbert, as Reader in Rhetoric at Cambridge, was appointed to give the "Barnaby" lectures, in which he was expected to "expound in English, for the special benefit of first-year students, such authors as Cicero or Quintilian."[14] Herbert, however, chose as the appropriate text for analysis not the classical orators but instead the words of his monarch, King James I. The oration, unfortunately, has not survived, but an account by one of Herbert's classmates—John Hacket—has. In writing about James's address to the Parliament of 1624, Hacket recalls a day six years earlier when Herbert had praised James's eloquence:

Mr. *George Herbert* being praelector in the Rhetorique School in *Cambridg anno* 1618. Pass'd by those fluent Orators, that Domineered in the Pulpits of *Athens* and *Rome*, and insisted to Read upon an Oration of King *James*, which he Analyzed, shew'd the concinnity of the Parts, the propriety of the Phrase, the height and Power of it to move Affections, the Style utterly unknown to the Ancients, who could not conceive what Kingly Eloquence was, in respect of which those noted Demagogi were but Hire-lings, and Triobulary Rhetoricians.[15]

We do not know whether James was in attendance, or even if word of this speech got back to him. But two years later Herbert had been elected to the position of University Orator, an office requiring just the kind of artful flattery apparently displayed by his explication of James's eloquence.

The oratorship, observes A. G. Hyde,

> was instituted as a practical means of securing the good-will of influential persons in the outer world by paying them compliments (in elegant Latin) when they visited the University. The writing of letters, in the same tongue, to obtain privileges for the academic body, or to defend or maintain its existing privileges, was an especially important part of the office, together with conveying thanks for services rendered by Secretaries of State and others, and for gifts of all kinds.[16]

Performance of such tasks, concludes Hyde, demanded "the courtier's gifts as well as the graces of scholarship." As such, the position provided an appropriate transition between the academic hierarchy of the university and the political hierarchy of the court. Indeed, the two previous holders of the office—Sir Francis Nethersole and Sir Robert Naunton—had ascended from the oratorship into positions as secretaries of state, and Herbert had no reason to think that he would interrupt that pattern.

In the letters to Danvers in which Herbert discusses his hopes for the position, we can glimpse the developing political acumen of an aspiring and gifted twenty-six-year-old excited at the prospect of the civic world opening up to him. "The Orator's place," Herbert tells Danvers,

> is the finest place in the University, though not the gainfullest . . . but the commodiousness is beyond the Revenue; for the Orator writes all the University Letters, makes all the Orations, be it to King, Prince, or whatever comes to the University; to requite these pains, he takes place next the Doctors, is at all their Assemblies and Meetings, and sits above the Proctors, is Regent or Non-regent at his pleasure, and such like Gaynesses, which will please a young man well. (*Works*, pp. 369–70)

To Herbert, the primary value of the Oratorship is not in its monetary reward (equal to his annuity) but in the political importance of those whom it gives him the privilege to address ("King, Prince, or whatever") and in the physical and social place it grants him ("next the Doctors . . . above the Proctors"). Even as he attempts to distance himself by means of humor from the ambitious young man who would be pleased with such "gaynesses," Herbert acknowledges that the "commodiousness" of the post is not so much the revenue it bestows as the honor it confers.

The letter shows Herbert deeply engaged in the network of patronage and dependence by which place was won at the Jacobean court; yet it also shows Herbert's uneasiness with this network in his surprising eagerness to display his relative independence of his stepfather's connections. About Sir Francis Nethersole, the current orator, Herbert remarks that "he and I are of ancient acquaintance, and I have a strong opinion of him, that if he can do me a courtesie, he will *of himself*; yet your appearing in it, affects me strangely" (p. 369; my italics). The final locution cautiously reflects Herbert's ambivalence about Danvers's intervention. This ambivalence becomes more explicit in the course of the letter. Herbert encloses a letter from "our Master" (i.e., John Richardson, Master of Trinity) which he hopes Danvers will send on to Nethersole; "yet if you cannot send it with much convenience, it is no matter, for the Gentleman needs no incitation to love me." Herbert finally declares to Danvers that "I hope I shall get this place without all your *London* helps, of which I am very proud, not but that I joy in your favours, but that you may see, that if all fail, yet I am able to stand on mine own legs" (p. 370). According to Perez Zagorin, "Persons desiring success in a suit of advancement attached themselves to men of rank in order to obtain their recommendation."[17] The convoluted syntax of Herbert's final phrases to Danvers suggests the vast qualifications that must couch any declaration of independence in such a world. Independence from one authority requires dependence upon another. To stand on one's own legs is only to switch crutches. The crisscrossing letters trace the complicated network of influence that Herbert was quickly learning to negotiate.

In the conclusion of this letter, Herbert asks Danvers to send on to him as soon as possible a letter he anticipates from Nethersole "that I may work the heads to my purpose." The phrase cunningly recognizes the kinds of political manipulation required to ascend the hierarchies of university and court. And Herbert continued to "work the heads" on behalf of the university, and himself, once he had been officially elected to the position. In the first letter that Herbert wrote as University Orator, he thanks King James for donating a copy of his

Opera Latina to the university library. He apostrophizes James as "incomparable wisdom," apparently aware of James's desire to be considered the English Solomon, and declares in an epigram that Cambridge now has the equal of the Vatican and the Bodleian libraries, because James's volume is a library unto itself. Herbert also praises James for a creative, life-giving power that approaches divinity: "your right hand alone . . . quickens the globe with life and action." He suggests that by becoming an author, James displays a Christlike condescension towards his creatures: "laying aside thy majesty, thou dost offer thyself to be gazed upon on paper, that thou mayst be more intimately conversant amongst us. O astonishing benignity!" Herbert concludes with a prayer "that to your crown, civil and literary, [God] may at a far-off hour add a third, celestial (crown)."[18]

This fulsome commingling of sacred and secular power is on one level simply a presentation of James as he most wanted to be imagined: a kind of god on earth. In a speech to Parliament on March 21, 1610, for example, James explicated at length the parallels between his own power and that of God:

> Kings are justly called gods for that they exercise a manner or resemblance of divine power upon earth . . . God hath power to create or destroy, make or unmake, at his pleasure; to give life or send death, to judge all and to be judged not accountable to none; to raise low things and to make high things low at his pleasure; and to God are both soul and body due. And the like power have kings: they make and unmake their subjects; they have power of raising, and casting down; of life, and of death, judges over all their subjects, and in all causes, and yet accountable to none but God only. They have power to exalt low things, and abase high things, and make of their subjects like men at the chess . . . And to the king is due both the affection of the soul and the service of the body of his subjects.[19]

By echoing the terminology in which James advertised his own power, Herbert not only placates the monarch but also asserts continuity between spiritual and political pursuits. The prayer with which Herbert concludes his oration on the departure of James from Cambridge—that James "may connect heaven and earth by a lesser space than that we now discern"—effectively voices Herbert's own desire to conjoin the ambitions of secular office with the aspirations of spiritual service.[20] The conjunction of the political and divine hierarchies, then, provides Herbert with a convenient language for integrating secular ambition and spiritual aspiration. By praising figures of secular power in divine terms, Herbert fulfills his civil office of Orator while maintaining his devotion to "Divinity, at which . . . I aim" (p. 370).[21]

A variation of this tack may be glimpsed in the *Musae Responsoriae*, Herbert's only work of explicit theological controversy. Commencing with flattering dedications to King James, Prince Charles, and Bishop Andrewes and concluding with equally laudatory epigrams to James and to God, the volume attempts to span the range of political, ecclesiastical, and heavenly authorities upon whose commendation preferment would depend. Even Amy Charles, whose Herbert is unabashedly seraphic from birth, concedes that this "triple dedication . . . could be construed as an attempt to gain royal or ecclesiastical favor."[22] The text itself—a witty if immature defense of Conformist liturgy against the Puritan Andrew Melville's censure—bestrides the boundary dividing political from spiritual pursuits. Moreover, as Arthur F. Marotti argues in his provocative study of Donne, "the very act of composing sacred verse in the reign of a monarch [such as James] who had himself written religious poetry and especially favored pious and polemical writing was a political gesture."[23] In this context, Herbert's vindication of Conformist worship in Latin verse can be seen to reflect royal generic taste as well as Herbert's own liturgical preferences. The entry into religious disputation is also a gesture paying court to secular authority.

Although vigorously defending one authority, the church, the *Musae* is at the same time an aggressive attack on another form of authority—that represented by Melville's age. The second epigram, "Ad Melvinum," emphatically highlights the differences between their ages:

> Nor to attack, vet'ran, my age befits,
> Nor conquer thee; but yet the theme permits.
> Let my good cause my want of years supply;
> So thou a youth art found, an old man I.[24]

Herbert consciously inverts the situation of youth and age in order to license the social rupture involved in his quarrel with an elder. "In early modern England," Keith Thomas asserts, "the prevailing ideal was gerontocratic: the young were to serve and the old were to rule."[25] Herbert's attack on Melville does not so much assail this ideal as appropriate it. By claiming that the authority of his "good cause" renders him the older of the two, Herbert avoids making a frontal assault on the seniority underpinning primogeniture. Like the biblical

Jacob, he usurps the prerogative of his elder rather than rebelling—
like Shakespeare's Edmund—against the system itself.

In these early performances, then, we can see Herbert endeavoring
to display his endorsement of the system of hierarchical privilege
that would exclude younger brothers such as himself. By rehearsing
the values of the hierarchy and profusely praising those at the top,
Herbert hopes to make a place for himself within it. Yet the ever-
present need to please must have resulted in intense performative
pressure on all acts of speech. Although his forum was the university
rather than the court, "the universities," as Whigham maintains, "in
particular were rhetorical arenas with a courtly audience"; in both
realms, "public life was governed by a rhetorical imperative of perfor-
mance."[26] The stilted and farfetched quality of Herbert's encomia
adumbrates the severe strain of serving at once the courts of earth and
heaven. King James was not God, "quicken[ing] the globe with life,"
and the more he liked to hear such things, the clearer the differences
became. Accompanying the continual performance of effusive praise
and official apology runs a quiet but powerful undercurrent of ap-
prehension, resentment, and aggression.

In a letter containing "passages of newes which this time affords,"
written to Sir Robert Harley, Herbert reveals himself an acute ob-
server, and nervous recorder, of the vagaries of the courtly favor he
seeks. Appropriately, the letter itself is the product of a request by
a superior—"I am enioined to write to you by Sr John Danvers,"
Herbert tells Harley, his first cousin by marriage. In addition to com-
menting at some length on the marital difficulties of "Sr Charles
Howard & his Lady," Herbert also engages in some innuendo about a
swiftly ascending courtly favorite: "My Lord of Buckingham was ob-
served on Christmas day to bee so devout as to come to the Chappell
an howre before prayers began, of wch is doubted whether it have
some further meaning" (p. 368). The insinuation of "further mean-
ing" in Buckingham's "devout" activities parodies the fusion of
courtly and spiritual aspiration that Herbert attempted. "Buck-
ingham," notes Hutchinson, "was rising rapidly; a month later he
was appointed lord high admiral" (p. 579). Herbert was just beginning
to glimpse the capricious nature of courtly favor.

Such favor, moreover, was not always exercised in a positive direc-
tion. This gossip-laden epistle relates in noteworthy detail an inci-
dent which demonstrates Herbert's awareness of the difficulties and
dangers of attempting to translate linguistic talent into political re-
ward at the Stuart court. "There is a Frenchman," Herbert reports,

who writt a poem heere in England & presented it to the King,
who because of his importunities gaue him a reward, but not so
great as he expected & therfore he grumblingly said that if he
had giuen it to the pope he should haue had a greater reward.
upon this he was forbid Court & kingdome, yet was seene lately
neere the king, wch some observing who heard the interdiction
denounced to him, told the King & so he is committed to prison.
(*Works*, pp. 368–69)

Herbert's surprising fascination with this anonymous foreigner be-
trays a preoccupation with the acute political anxieties that resulted
from the continual pressure to please superiors within the Renais-
sance patronage network. Unable to escape the pull of the very court
that disappoints and then banishes him, this unfortunate figure allows
his disgruntlement to surface in an infelicitous witticism. James, how-
ever, apparently did not appreciate the comparison between his own
remunerative powers and those of the Pope. As a result, the poetic
labors of this Frenchman are requited not with promotion but with
prison. Like so many Englishmen who attempted unsuccessfully to
attain appropriate recompense for the exercise of their verbal abilities,
this Frenchman testifies to the centripetal attractions and pressing
dangers of the court. In recording at once the ascent of Buckingham and
the descent of the Frenchman, Herbert may be hinting not only at his
growing disenchantment with the pressures of praise but also at his
disgruntlement over his meager rewards.

Despite such discontent, Herbert persevered in his bid for the favor
of those in authority over him. This political climate, however, neces-
sitated the development of a mode of discourse through which one
could articulate this discontent in a language of submission and in-
gratiation. Hutchinson cites a contemporary account of the circum-
stances in which Herbert presented an oration to King James that il-
luminates the inherent theatricality of the Orator's role while elu-
cidating the ways such a discourse might be attained. After having
observed the performance of a Latin play entitled *Loiola*, and express-
ing "no remarkable mirth thereat," the king was brought "to the door,
entring into ye Court, where his Coach did wait for him: but his Maj-
esty was pleased to stay there, while the Orator Mr. Herbert did make
a short Farewell Speech unto him. Then he called for a copy of the
Vice-Chancellor's Speech, & likewise for an Epigram the Orator
made."[27] Following directly a dramatic performance, the oration is in
fact another performance, an entertainment intended to please the
king. The epigram that James apparently relished, "*Dum petit In-*

fantem," wittily compares Prince Charles's visit to Spain in search of a spouse with King James's visit to Cambridge. "The question is," asserts Herbert, "whose love the greater showes," James's or Charles's; Herbert then answers the question by opting for James, whose "wit's more / Remote from ours, then Spaine from Britains shoare."[28] The ironies on which the conventionally overblown wit rests are conspicuous in Joseph Mede's admiring paraphrase: "The king descended more miles to visit us at Cambridge than the Prince is gone to see the Infanta. Ergo the King's love is the greater."[29] Both Charles and James are adroitly praised for a beneficence towards their creatures the Orator intends to encourage.

Herbert's ingenious and successful encomium of James, however, leaves open the possibility that the recognition of distance between James's wit and that of the members of the university denigrates rather than celebrates the royal intelligence. The ambivalence that the brilliant young orator might have experienced, surrounded by the university community, and assigned the task of praising the intellect of a figure he probably knew to be his intellectual inferior, seems to permeate the terms of his praise. Even panegyrical hyperbole cannot fully license the epigram's assertion that James was more distant from the university intellectually than Spain was from England geographically. Whether intentionally or not, the epigram equivocates on the question of James's wit, allowing Herbert to flatter and belittle the king in a single utterance. Concurrently eulogizing and satirizing the mental capacity of his political superior, Herbert uses "the distance of the meek" to praise and oppose power. Hostility to authority is expressed in a discourse that is nevertheless acceptable and pleasing to authority.[30]

Indeed, in the next and final extant oration given by Herbert, praise of and opposition to power are so completely enmeshed that many scholars have suggested it as the major reason for Herbert's apparent loss of favor at court.[31] The occasion of this oration was the return of Prince Charles and the duke of Buckingham from Spain, angry at their failure to complete negotiations for a Spanish marriage, and intent upon war. As University Orator, Herbert was placed in a politically sensitive and rhetorically difficult situation: by advocating war, he would alienate the peace-loving King James, but by counseling peace, he would antagonize the already indignant Prince Charles. Herbert responded by praising the prince fulsomely, but for an attribute more appropriate to the king: the desire for peace. As S. R. Gardiner explains, "Herbert disliked war, and he could not refrain from the maladroit compliment of commending Charles for going to

Madrid in search of peace."[32] In this oration, Herbert attempts to command authority by commending it for qualities it lacks in the hope that it will then try to live up to the terms of the praise. Such a tactic supplies one of the few means by which a dependent might sway a superior without losing favor. Francis Bacon, for example, recommends that courtiers deal with authority through the tactic of *"laudando praecipere,* when by telling men what they are, they represent to them what they should be."[33] Herbert's coercive praise, however, was unsuccessful. Perhaps the aging King James appreciated Herbert's extensive praise of peace, but "from Charles, rushing headlong into war, the lover of peace had no favour to expect."[34]

Yet the oration is curious not only for its impolitic praise of peace but also for its disingenuous declaration of plainness amidst such covertly manipulative tactics:

> I do not speak to rustics or to barbarians, whom it were easy to circumvent by the grandeur of a statement, and to astonish their inexperienced minds by the force of (mere) words . . . I do not play the orator, O collegians . . . that wild folly and empty noise of words I have long ago laid aside; bubbles and rattles are for boys . . . I truly am conscious both who I am myself (a beard, alas, so grave!) and amongst whom I am speaking—men of polished and nice ear, whose gravity and position [purple robes] I will not trifle with.[35]

Although conventional, Herbert's protestation of candor and simplicity far exceeds the needs of the convention or the occasion. This overwrought refusal to "play the orator" adumbrates a deep discomfort with the project of praising superiors who may not necessarily merit it. Where in his writings against Melville Herbert had usurped the authority of age, here he mocks the peculiar aggregation of his youth—"a beard, alas, so grave"—and the authority his position grants. Likewise, his description of the "polished and nice ear" of his audience is a clear example of praise charged with negative innuendo. Furthermore, even as he covertly attempts to counsel royalty by extolling Charles for seeking "peace at the risk of his own life," Herbert declares that the counsels of ordinary mortals "lie open," but "hidden are the counsels of gods and kings."[36] Such irony inexorably percolates through the prior and subsequent praise of Charles for qualities which contravene those the prince exhibits. Herbert's own complex motives are revealed even as they are veiled by his declarations that they are untainted by the orator's art.

In addition, the oration contains many passages which glance critically at the court and rest uncomfortably beside the oration's labored praise. "How I am ashamed of effeminate Caesars," declares Herbert, "who, plunged in lusts, . . . feed themselves daily as if their bodies would not pass at some time into the elements, but into cakes and sweetmeats." "Why should I mention to you the gluttony of Neroes or Heliogabali?" the orator asks, "Why the belchings of drunkenness in possession of a throne? . . . the incredible luxury of Roman emperors from Tiberius Caesar to Constantine the Great, whose empire was not equal to their appetite?" Why indeed? Such utterances sound far more like Puritan denunciations of the sensual excesses of the Jacobean court than celebrations of a glorious prince's return. The criticism is only partially recuperated as praise by its displacement onto a Roman past, and its subsequent contrast with the conduct of Charles: "But our prince, despising pleasures, casting aside allurements (honeyed stranglings), encounters a journey and labours." The unstated implication, however, is that Charles's voyage to Spain was a temporary respite from the courtly excesses Herbert has just castigated. Herbert issues a reminder, indecorous to the aging king and inappropriate to the youthful prince, that "in that last dissolution there is no distinction of people or prince; there are no sceptres in the elements . . . The vapours from slaves exhaled into the clouds will produce equally loud thunder with the vapours from kings."[37] On the heels of such unsavory imagery, Herbert admonishes his royal audience to beware of "flattery and flatterers, who are always tickling the ears of princes 'as if they were tickled in their ears with feathers.'"[38] Although the situation is structurally similar, Herbert's performance is miles away from his epigram praising James's condescension in visiting the University while Charles goes to Spain in search of a spouse. Where in the epigram criticism and compliment had been held in artful suspension by means of syntactical ambiguity, here criticism shatters the panegyrical framework that should license and contain it.

Ultimately, such boldness towards monarchical power leads Herbert daringly to claim for his own status an authority equal to that of the royal audience he essays to manipulate. In describing how Charles represented the king in Spain just as the Orator speaks on behalf of Cambridge, Herbert discovers a parallel between their respective missions: "kings have ambassadors, stationary and resident, which position our sweetest prince occupied; he himself acted the orator, that I may glory a little in this title."[39] As he endeavors to manipulate authority through strategies of indirection and praise, Herbert discovers a model for his own authority. By means of complex rhetorical gestures expressing "the distance of the meek," Herbert attempts simultaneously to applaud and to appropriate power.

The "respective boldnesse" Herbert displays towards "great persons" in his oration upon Charles's return from Spain is precisely the demeanor towards authority that Herbert advises in "The Churchporch" (line 253). "That temper," Herbert counsels, "gives them theirs, and yet doth take / Nothing from thine" (lines 254–55). But as Herbert discovered, that *via media* of behavior was enormously difficult to sustain. Although his oration delicately interlaced respect and boldness, adulation and admonition, it must have only infuriated the already irate prince. Authority, Herbert learned, was subject to him only as long as he exuded praise and reverence unadulterated by resentment or assertion; as long, in other words, as his bended knee did not stiffen or ache.

Herbert's subsequent political life leaves few other records. He does represent Montgomery in Parliament in 1624, resulting in an enthusiastic endorsement of the educational value of parliamentary experience: "there is no School to a Parliament."[40] Herbert probably was ordained deacon sometime in 1624, as Amy Charles has shown; but this did not necessarily signal the abandonment of worldly aspiration that Charles argues. "Many men," notes A. L. Maycock, "in the ordinary course, entered the diaconate without any intention of becoming priests."[41] Herbert retained the position of Orator until 1628, but apparently fulfilled few if any of its duties.[42] When King James died in 1625, Herbert Thorndike, not George Herbert, delivered the official funeral sermon at Cambridge. The promising youth who had attracted the notice of the king then becomes nearly invisible to the public and to history until his ordination as priest in 1630, when presented with the living of Fugglestone-with-Bemerton six days after his cousin Philip Herbert became the fourth earl of Pembroke.[43]

The first editor of Herbert's *Country Parson* and *Outlandish Proverbs* (1652), Barnabus Oley, remembers hearing "sober men censure [Herbert] as a man that did not manage his brave parts to his best advantage and preferment, but lost himself *in a humble way*."[44] Bemerton is certainly humble; the benches in the small church could accommodate at most thirty-six parishioners.[45] Aubrey describes it as "a pittifull little chappell."[46] There in the country emerges the legend of saintly Parson George, a figure whose shadow has nearly effaced the experiences of the first thirty-seven years, but whose poetry and prose reflect, and reflect upon, those experiences. Unlike Donne, whose appointment as dean of Saint Paul's was not so much an alternative to as a fulfillment of his secular goals, providing him with the courtly audience he had sought so fervently throughout his career, Herbert concluded his career and his life at a great social and geographical distance from the court, among country people, whom he characterized as "thick, and heavy" (*Country Parson*, p. 233). Rather than rubbing elbows with the rich and powerful of the realm, Herbert as country parson had to learn to disdain not "to enter into the poorest Cottage, though he even creep into it, and though it smell never so lothsomly."[47] Yet humble as it is, Bemerton is also located midway between the ecclesiastical splendors of Salisbury Cathedral, where Herbert was ordained, and the aristocratic magnificence of Wilton House, inhabited by Herbert's powerful kinsman, Philip Herbert, the fourth earl of Pembroke; it is, furthermore, walking distance to both. Although in the letter to Anne Clifford with which this chapter began Herbert describes his parish as "Your poor Colony of Servants," implying that living at Bemerton was akin to settling a strange new country, Bemerton was geographically on the diagonal connecting political and religious power in the period (p. 376). Moreover, attaining even such a humble benefice was not easy; the descriptively titled *The Art of Thriving. Or, The plaine path-way to Preferment* describes in detail the necessary jockeying for ecclesiastical position, insisting that "I can advise you of no better course, than to learne the way to the backe stayres."[48] "It is far more likely," proposes Amy Charles, "that most of Herbert's English poems were probably written before he went to Bemerton than that the major part of his composition of poetry was postponed until the busiest period of his life."[49] I would agree; but where Charles sees this as a sign that Herbert's intentions were from the beginning uninterruptedly divine, I view it as a manifestation of the deep intermingling of sacred and secular concerns throughout Herbert's work. The sacred writings Herbert produced before and during the last three years there, moreover, exert great verbal and spiritual labor in the effort to ingratiate a monarch who bears at times an unsettling resemblance to the inscrutable, praise-loving, godlike king whose favor Herbert had originally sought.[50] Perhaps from the divine perspective, such effort was as unnecessary as the adulation of James proved unsuccessful. But from a human perspective, much of the aesthetic power of this work derives from Herbert's deliberate blend of sacred and secular political power.

"The Poet," *observes Ben* Jonson in the *Discoveries*, "is the neerest Borderer upon the Orator, and expresseth all his vertues."[51] This is certainly true in Herbert's case, although the very real differences in

style, tone, and content between Herbert's Latin performances as Orator and his English poems to God have prevented readers from exploring this rich border territory. Much of the energy and meaning of the sacred lyrics, though, is drawn from the well of Herbert's secular experience. "The Thanksgiving," for example, is a poem whose situation and motives correspond closely to those Herbert confronted in the social world. A figure of superior power, here a "king of grief," has performed an act of beneficence that requires in return a proffer of gratitude. In this poem Herbert attempts a conventional tender of thanks; yet he also exploits his experience of gratitude in the political world to reveal the implicitly aggressive aspects of giving thanks. "The Altar," the first poem in "The Church," concludes by imploring God to "let thy blessed SACRIFICE be mine." The divine speaker of the subsequent poem—"The Sacrifice"—challenges the very capacity of mortals to respond in kind to his sacrifice: "Onely let others say, when I am dead, / Never was grief like mine."[52] The task of "The Thanksgiving," the poem immediately following these two, is to take up this challenge, to attempt to appropriate a prior, superior, and unique act of suffering.

Gifts of course bear immense social and cultural weight. Both Louis Adrian Montrose and Patricia Fumerton have used the anthropological work of Marcel Mauss to explore the cultural significance of gift exchange in Elizabethan England.[53] Mauss is fascinated by the social phenomenon of "prestation," forms of gift-giving "which are in theory voluntary, disinterested and spontaneous, but are in fact obligatory and interested." "Total prestation," declares Mauss, "not only carries with it the obligation to repay gifts received, but it implies two others equally important: the obligation to give presents and the obligation to receive them." Such obligation is enhanced rather than diminished when directed not to other humans but to the gods; "with them," argues Mauss, "it was particularly necessary to exchange and particularly dangerous not to." "A whole aspect of the theory of sacrifice," proposes Mauss, can be explained by "the connection of exchange contracts among men with those between men and gods."[54] It is just this connection that Herbert explores in "The Thanksgiving," using his experience of gifts and gratitude in the social world to investigate the impossibly beneficent economy of divine-human exchange both demanded and denied by the sacrifice of Christ.

The speaker of "The Thanksgiving" addresses his God in explicitly political terms; yet these terms also express the vast differences between his divine monarch and earthly sovereigns:

> Oh King of grief! (a title strange, yet true,
>   To thee of all kings onely due)
> O King of wounds! how shall I grieve for thee,
>   Who in all grief preventest me?

The dilemma of responding to a monarch whose overwhelming beneficence disables response was one Herbert confronted in his political career as well. In the letter thanking James for donating a copy of his *Opera Latina* to the University library, Herbert pauses from his task of praise to complain: "But now thou thyself, by writing, hast broken in upon our methods of requital, and hast carried them away [*scribendo irrupisti in compensationes nostras, et abstulisti*]. Art thou such a robber of all glory [*adeon' es praedo omnis gloriae*], that thou wilt not even leave us the praise of gratitude?"[55] By writing, James has in some sense usurped the only medium left to his beneficiaries for the offering of gratitude. His gift has taken something from the recipients of his largesse. The surprising violence with which Herbert characterizes James's beneficent conduct—breaking in and robbing—quietly betrays the aggression that can imbue generosity and gratitude.

"The Thanksgiving" similarly explores the impoverishing potential of an act of munificence. Like the orator, the speaker questions his capacity to respond properly to the document his monarch has penned: "But how then shall I imitate thee, and / Copie thy fair, though bloudie hand?" He views emulation as a possible answer to his superior's largesse, and portrays the giving of thanks as a reciprocating literary performance. Remarkably, Herbert begins his first letter to Danvers in like manner, with the same question of his own ability to express appropriately witty gratitude—"though I had the best wit in the World, yet it would easily tyre me, to find out variety of thanks for the diversity of your favours" (*Works*, p. 363). He concludes, furthermore, by promising Danvers that "I will strive to imitate the compleatness of your love, with being in some proportion, and after my manner, Your most obedient Servant" (p. 364).

The predicament of answering the favors of a superior—whether divine or mortal—is voiced in strikingly similar terms. In the letters to James and Danvers, however, Herbert wants to conceal the manipulative and combative impulses inherent in expressions of gratitude; in "The Thanksgiving," by contrast, he chooses to expose them. "If it is not to constitute an insult," argues Pierre Bourdieu, "the counter-gift must be *deferred* and *different*, because the immediate return of an exactly identical object clearly amounts to a refusal (i.e., the return of the same object)."⁵⁶ In its intention to erase such difference and deferral, imitation is a kind of refusal parading as gratitude. The immediate response of the speaker of "The Thanksgiving" to his rhetorical question ("How then shall I imitate thee?") allows the politically competitive potential of the desire to *give* thanks by imitating the benefactor to surface: "Surely I will revenge me on thy love, / And trie who shall victorious prove." The speaker proposes to engage in a contest with his monarch, to pit his own abilities against those of his king in what "The Pearl" calls "vies of favours." He will *revenge* himself on his monarch (a verb with intentionally violent as well as imitative connotations) through the accomplishment of a series of purportedly pious resolves:

> If thou dost give me wealth, I will restore
> All back unto thee by the poore.
> If thou dost give me honour, men shall see,
> The honour doth belong to thee.

Yet in these lines exuding an admirable civic virtue, the speaker also endeavors to appeal to the self-interest of his monarch by suggesting what profits future acts of beneficence would reap. Rather than acknowledging what the syntax implies, that his own good deeds depend upon a prior act of beneficence by his superior ("*If* thou . . . *then* I will . . . "), the speaker presumptuously promises to return to his superior whatever gifts that superior bestows upon him.

"Herbert," asserts Richard Strier, "is presenting the desire to imitate Christ as the essence of misguided good intentions."⁵⁷ Both Strier and Ilona Bell stress how in "The Thanksgiving" Herbert undermines the mimetic aspirations of Catholic spirituality in order to reveal "the separation of our past grief and our present commemoration of it."⁵⁸ I would agree, but would argue further that Herbert is not just rejecting an outmoded form of devotion but also demonstrating the difficulty of purging the implicitly aggressive tendencies this devotion represents. "Giving," contends Bourdieu, "is also a way of possessing . . . in the absence of any juridical guarantee, or any coercive force, one of the few ways of 'holding' someone is to *keep up* a lasting asymmetrical relationship such as indebtedness."⁵⁹ Throughout the poem the speaker attempts to make his offering of thanks coercive and to shun the acknowledgment of his own inability to reciprocate. He does this because such an acknowledgment would also require the recognition of his own complete subordination. Donne sees clearly that the beneficent sacrifice to which "The Thanksgiving" responds subjugates as well as enriches its human benefactors: "by Christs taking my sins, I am made a *servant of my God*, a *Beads-man* of my God, a *vassall*, a *Tributary* debtor to my God."[60] By aspiring to equal his lord's suffering, the speaker of "The Thanksgiving" hopes to avoid such political and economic subjugation. Furthermore, as Lorenzo Ducci, author of the *Ars aulica*, argues, humanity naturally resists a status of indebtedness:

> that facultie wherein thankfulness and gratitude reside, doth not desire by nature (which makes us ever strive to be more than other men) only to give equall recompense with the benefit, but much more then what hath beene received . . . so that in love he answereth not alone in just proportion to his dutie, but by the foresaid reason endevours to outstrip the same.[61]

The competitive gratitude manifested by the speaker of "The Thanksgiving" derives from a desire not just to equal but in fact to surpass his monarch. What appears to be a humble offering of thanks and a pledge of pious performance is in effect a covert bid for political superiority, as the speaker chafes against the weight of indebtedness placed upon him by his superior's beneficence.

Even gifts, Herbert demonstrates in "The Thanksgiving," can oppress. The dynamics of potlatch exchanges demand that the recipient of a benefit is both materially enriched and politically impoverished by it. As Mauss declares, "To give is to show one's superiority, to show that one is something more and higher, that one is *magister*. To accept without returning or repaying more is to face subordination, to become a client and subservient, to become *minister*."[62] In the letters of thanksgiving to Danvers, glimmers of the onerous nature of the favors that Danvers graciously bestows upon his stepson emerge from the language of Herbert's proffered gratitude. When the young Herbert wittily remarks that Danvers's gift of a horse "come[s] a Horseback," the image of a burden can be discerned. This image is developed in a later letter, where Herbert asserts that "this Week hath loaded me with your Favours" (*Works*, p. 369). Moreover, as the monarch of "The Thanksgiving" "preventest" (meaning both "to go before" and "to hinder") the speaker's attempts to respond in kind, so does Danvers's beneficence disable Herbert's effort to express appropriate gratitude: "I can never answer what I have already received; for your favours are so ancient, that they *prevent* my memory" (p. 367; my italics). The inexpressibility topos, employed often by Herbert as

41

University Orator, functions rhetorically to flatter authority and politically to remind authority that one is accepting, by declaring one's inability to respond properly, a status of inferiority.[63]

Yet rather than rest in a confession of his inability to utter sufficient gratitude, as Herbert does with Danvers and with the benefactors whom he addressed as Orator, the speaker of "The Thanksgiving" refuses to accept the political liability and social subordination such a confession would incur. His desire to equal and surpass his monarch interlards the ridiculous and the sublime:

> For thy predestination I'le contrive,
> That three yeares hence, if I survive,
> I'le build a spittle, or mend common wayes,
> But mend mine own without delayes.
> . . . .
> My musick shall finde thee, and ev'ry string
> Shall have his attribute to sing;
> . . . .
> Nay, I will read thy book, and never move
> Till I have found therein thy love,
> Thy art of love, which I'le turn back on thee:
> O my deare Saviour, Victorie!

Yet this exclamation of triumph proves to be premature: "Then for thy passion—I will do for that— / Alas, my God, I know not what." That quality of his monarch with which the poem begins—his suffering—proves inimitable and unrequitable.[64]

In attempting to mime the actions of his heavenly monarch, the speaker of "The Thanksgiving" at once inaugurates an inevitably imperfect *imitatio christi* and engrosses the primary model for literary composition in Renaissance educational theory. " 'Imitate' and 'Copie,' " maintains Bell, "were technical terms for the writing of poetry as well as devotional terms for the imitation of Christ."[65] By asking "how then shall I imitate thee, and / Copie thy fair, though bloudie hand?" the speaker interrogates the relationship between his own poetic creations and the text written by Christ's "fair hand." Would the literary imitation proposed by the speaker of "The Thanksgiving" constitute a complete effacement of the authorial self in the effort to ventriloquize the exemplary text of the Bible? Or would it entail the generation of a discourse which could rival and supplant that exemplary text? Such questions are implicit in what G. W. Pigman III terms the "persistent ambivalence" in Renaissance concepts of imitation. As Pigman shows, "imitation" designated both an act of submissive copying as well as one of aggressive emulation.[66] "Imitation aims at similarity," argues Erasmus, "emulation, at victory."[67] But what Herbert demonstrates in "The Thanksgiving" is just how difficult these two goals are to keep apart.

The same difficulty surfaces in another realm in which the imitation of exemplary models was prescribed—that of courtly behavior. According to Lorenzo Ducci, the courtier who desires the favor of his monarch "is to adapt and fit himselfe by all the meanes he may unto his will, and make himselfe, if it bee possible, the very portract [sic] of his properties and fashions."[68] By imitating one's monarch, one subordinates one's desires and inclinations to those of the monarch. Such subordination wins the favor of superiors, explains Ducci, "because selfe *love* which is the roote of all other loves, chiefly extends it selfe unto his like, and more towards those who conforme themselves in maners and natural inclination thereunto."[69] Just as Herbert's orations and letters praising James manage to present back to James the godlike, sapient image the king most desired to project, so does the successful courtier, finally, fashion himself into a flattering mirror of his superior.

Yet there is in the imitation of political and spiritual authority a hazard corollary to the ambivalence surrounding Renaissance attitudes to literary imitation: the ease with which reproduction of authority precipitates rivalry with it. A gesture by which the self is shaped and subordinated to the whims of authority can nevertheless threaten that authority with supplantation or appropriation. In the *Discoveries*, Jonson recommends that the poet "make choise of one excellent man above the rest, and so to follow him, till he grow very *Hee*: or, so like him, as the Copie may be mistaken for the Principall."[70] But if one indeed imitates one's superior so well that "the Copie may be mistaken for the Principall," one subverts the hierarchical subordination one's imitation was intended to express. Towards an earthly lord, such imitation could obviously be impudent and imprudent; towards the heavenly Lord, such imitation contains an arrogance verging on blasphemy.

Indeed, it is just this sort of arrogance which Martin Luther finds so repulsive in the Catholic devotional project of imitating Christ. As Strier, who has demonstrated the profound relevance of Lutheran theology for the comprehension of Herbert's poetry, remarks, Luther "inveighed against those who 'set Christ out unto us as an example to be followed.'"[71] In a passage Strier does not cite, but which is particularly pertinent to "The Thanksgiving," Luther asserts that "all hypo-

43

Figure 1.   Albrecht Dürer, *Self-Portrait* (1500). Munich, Alte Pinakothek.

crites and idolators essay to do those works which properly pertain to divinity and belong to Christ solely and alone. They do not indeed say with their mouth: I am God, I am Christ, yet in fact they arrogate to themselves the divinity and office of Christ. And so, in fact, they say: I am Christ, I am saviour, not only of myself, but also of others."[72] To Luther, the *imitatio Christi* contained within it the seeds of a presumption which effaced the unique superiority of divinity.

Poised on the verge of the Reformation, the historical and theological movement that aimed to repudiate this presumption, Albrecht Dürer's *Self-Portrait* of 1500 offers a striking visual parallel to the spiritual peril of imitating God that is exposed in "The Thanksgiving." As Erwin Panofsky remarks, "It is indeed unquestionable that Dürer deliberately styled himself into the likeness of the Saviour. He not only adopted the compositional scheme of His image, but idealized his own features so as to make them conform to those traditionally attributed to Christ."[73] Yet the possible motives behind such a portrait span the extremes of self-aggrandizement and self-effacement. "How could so pious and humble an artist as Dürer resort to a procedure which many religious men would have considered blasphemous?" asks Panovsky. Panovsky's learned recourse to the traditions of *imitatio christi* and to an analogy between the creative powers of God and the craft of the artist fails to assuage fully the uneasiness one experiences in meeting the painting's gaze. The figure seems to shout, in Luther's terms, "I am Christ, I am saviour." Has Dürer made himself into Christ, or Christ into himself? Has the artist been absorbed into the deity he worships, or has his act of worship supplied the occasion for the self-aggrandizing absorption of divinity? The painting fosters but refuses to resolve such questions. Although probably arising like "The Thanksgiving" from genuinely pious intentions, the painting oscillates eternally between the tenaciously intertwined extremes of self-approbation and self-immolation.

The hazards of spiritual imitation exposed in Dürer's *Self-Portrait* have a political counterpart in the challenge to secular authority that an act of successful imitation entails. The good courtier, announces Baldassare Castiglione, "must evermore set all his diligence to be like his maister, and (if it were possible) chaung him selfe into him."[74] But the threat to authority implicit in such imitability must somehow be dodged. Although one should study to imitate an earthly prince in matters "wherein the Prince would seeme an example of vertue, and would not mislike to be egalled by others," one should also remember, as George Puttenham warns, that princes "must be suffred to have the victorie and be relented unto," and that "in gaming with a Prince it is decent to let him sometimes win of purpose, to keepe him pleasant."[75] Similarly, Denys de Refuges cautions in his *Treatise of the Court* that "as soone as [our prince] knowes that wee surpasse and excell him" in any enterprise, "he will begin to looke on us with frowning eye."[76] If courtly *sprezzatura* (translated by Hoby as "a certaine disgracing to cover arte withall"[77]) is the capacity to accomplish difficult actions with apparent ease, then what is required, finally, of the expert courtier is a kind of inverted *sprezzatura*, by which one deliberately tries and fails to imitate the monarch, thus declaring simultaneously the monarch's exemplary and inimitable nature. As de Refuges advises,

> it sufficeth not to stoope and yeelde to [the prince] in words: but wee must likewise in effects and deedes make it appeare, that in all things wee are inferiour to him: yea, and in plaine earnest, doe something grossely and sleightly, so it may please him.[78]

Or, as Berowne observes in *Love's Labor's Lost*, " 'tis some policy / To have one show worse than the King's and his company."[79]

Such policy would have been particularly pertinent for behavior at the Jacobean court, presided over by a king who prided himself on his innate superiority to other men. "Two sorts of men King James never had kindness for," remarked one contemporary, "those whose hawks and dogs flew and run as well as his own, and those who were able to speak as much reason as himself."[80] To perform before this figure without upstaging him, to show one's wit to him without showing him up, would have required heroic self-control. For an educated, intelligent, and ambitious youth such as Herbert, the necessity of expressing artful yet submissive gratitude and praise to so vain a monarch must have exerted tremendous intellectual and psychological pressure.

This pressure is assessed and recorded in "The Thanksgiving." By attempting to offer gratitude befitting the sacrifice of his king through a mixture of ludicrous and pious proposals, Herbert demonstrates the impassable gulf separating him from his sovereign. Yet in the discovery of his inability to imitate his superior's behavior, the speaker of "The Thanksgiving" is forced into a sputtering acknowledgment of his sovereign's absolute superiority. Finally, then, "The Thanksgiving" fulfills the speaker's purported intention of praising his "king of griefs," but only in the painful discovery of his inability to imitate his monarch or to offer appropriate thanks.

In "The Church-porch," Herbert advises, "Envie not greatnesse: for thou mak'st thereby / Thy self the worse, and so the distance greater" (lines 259–60). This is exactly what happens to the speaker of "The Thanksgiving." In his envy and emulation of divinity, he exposes the vast distance separating him from divinity. The poem is, finally, an act of gratitude and praise despite, not because of, the speaker's behavior. The failure rather than the success of his mimetic gratitude plumbs the distance of the meek. The submission of the poor and the opposition of the proud are revealed not only to have the same outcome—the glorification of superior power—but in fact to be one and the same gesture. "He that followes the Lord," declares one of the *Outlandish Proverbs* Herbert collected, "hopes to goe before" (no. 994, p. 354). In "The Thanksgiving," Herbert shows how genuflection is not only a gesture of submission but also a posture of social climbing. He exposes the self-serving aspects of serving another.

"The Reprisall," the poem immediately following "The Thanksgiving" and originally entitled "The Second Thanks-giving," appears to resolve many of the dilemmas plaguing its predecessor. Yet as C. A. Patrides notes, " 'reprisal' is used in the (military) sense of retaliation as well as in the (musical) sense of returning to the original subject."[81] Although more successful than "The Thanksgiving" at disguising its aggression, "The Reprisall" is nevertheless a reprise, in a more compliant key, of its contentious energies, as well as a retaliation for their repudiation. It is the portrait of a speaker who cannot win for losing. "Wee so insist in imitating others," declares Ben Jonson in the *Discoveries*, "as wee cannot (when it is necessary) return to our selves."[82] In "The Reprisall," Herbert demonstrates the difficulty of this project, exposing the process by which a return to the self through confession entails behavior as belligerent as that implicit in the imitation proposed in "The Thanksgiving."

"The Reprisall" begins with an acknowledgment of the failure of "The Thanksgiving" to offer gratitude suitable to the Lord's beneficent suffering.

> I have consider'd it, and finde
> There is no dealing with thy mighty passion:
> For though I die for thee, I am behinde;
> My sinnes deserve the condemnation.

By admitting defeat, the speaker endeavors to recoil from the coercive and competitive discourse practiced in "The Thanksgiving." Yet this sincere confession of inability is at the same time a blend of two rhetorical figures: "Paramologia, or the figure of Admittance," described by Puttenham as "when the matter is so plaine that it cannot be denied or traversed, it is good that it be justified by confessall," and "metanoia," when "we speake and be sorry for it, as if we had not wel spoken, so that we seeme to call in our word againe, and to put in another fitter for the purpose: for which respects the Greekes called this manner of speech the figure of repentance: then for that upon repentance commonly followes amendment, the Latins called it the figure of correction, in that the speaker seemeth to reforme that which was said amisse."[83] Even the effort to escape a coercive discourse is enclosed by the lexicon of an inherently manipulative rhetoric. Both Ira Clark and Barbara Harman have effectively applied Puttenham's definition of metanoia to Herbert.[84] But their emphasis upon the moral goal of repentance needs to be tempered by attention to the rhetorical function of apology. As Whigham contends, "metanoia would also allow the poet to smuggle criticism into comment and then deny it . . . the negative element does get voiced; only then is it disavowed."[85] In just this way, "The Reprisall" censures but does not erase the aggression of "The Thanksgiving." Moreover, the language of quantification ("I am behinde") and requital ("My sinnes deserve the condemnation") reiterates rather than rejects the terminology of rivalry in "The Thanksgiving." Although earnestly attempting to renounce the manipulative motives of "The Thanksgiving," "The Reprisall" replays them under the colors of submission and confession.

As if acknowledging the calculated nature of his surrender, the speaker sues to be cleansed of such motives: "O make me innocent, that I / May give a disentangled state and free." But the request replicates the situation of "The Thanksgiving." The speaker of "The Reprisall" wants to be made innocent so that he will be able to *give* to God from a "state," or status, that is "free," not "entangled" in debt. Like the speaker of "The Thanksgiving," he hopes through an act of benefaction to avoid acknowledging his own subordination. But even as he voices this wish, the speaker of "The Reprisall" realizes the impossibility of its fulfillment: "And yet thy wounds still my attempts defie, / For by thy death I die for thee." The two meanings of "attempt" active here—"endeavor" and "assault upon a person's life"—underscore the aggression lingering in his poses of submission. The speaker's realization of his own utterly subordinate status forces a bitter sigh from him:

> Ah! was it not enough that thou
> By thy eternal glorie didst outgo me?
> Couldst thou not griefs sad conquests me allow,
> But in all vic'tries overthrow me?

While conceding his lord's supremacy in "eternal glorie," the speaker wonders why his lord must also flaunt his preeminence in grief. The speaker self-centeredly suggests that Christ suffered only to "outgo" and "overthrow" him. Moreover, he displaces onto Christ his own

competitive motives, implying that the reprisal of the title may in-
clude not only human retaliation against God but also God's retalia-
tion against humanity. "The Reprisall" could thus be seen to fulfill
the ambiguous revenge threatened by the suffering Christ in the final
stanza of "The Sacrifice": "Onely let others say, when I am dead, /
Never was grief like mine."[86]

The final stanza of "The Reprisall" appears to elude the quandary
of gratitude exposed in "The Thanksgiving":

> Yet by confession will I come
> Into thy conquest: though I can do nought
> Against thee, in thee I will overcome
> The man, who once against thee fought.

Rather than competing with his maker, the speaker pledges to con-
fess, to cultivate a discourse of his own inferiority. Although his com-
bative tendencies are not completely purged, the speaker does prom-
ise to direct them towards himself, "The man who once against thee
fought," rather than towards his superior. Yet the language by which
the speaker distinguishes his submissive and aggressive selves dem-
onstrates the difficulty of keeping them apart. The proximity in
sound and location of "Against thee, in thee," for example, blurs the
distinction between submission and aggression that the speaker is at-
tempting to draw. Likewise, the consonance of "conquest" and "con-
fession" belies the contrast between the conquering and confessing
selves on which our sense of the resolution of the poem depends. The
emphasis upon the "will" of the speaker, moreover, sounds sus-
piciously like the catalog of actions the speaker of "The Thanksgiv-
ing" promises to perform. The tangled syntax and intricate acoustics
suggest some of the difficulty of the project that the speaker of "The
Reprisall" has set out for himself: disentangling from his gestures of
submission the agonistic and manipulative motives voiced in "The
Thanksgiving."

This difficulty is reproduced in the wide range of critical reactions
engendered by the poem's close. For Louis Martz, "The Reprisall"
"solves the dilemma of gratitude for the Passion with which the first
Thanksgiving, with a witty inconclusion, ends." This view has re-
cently been affirmed by two critics approaching the poem from quite
disparate directions: Barbara Leah Harman asserts that "the speaker
does find an authentic and acceptable labor . . . the task of overcom-
ing the self who produces poems like this," while Richard Strier ar-
gues that "The Reprisall" achieves "a true rather than an 'incomplete'
resolution." Yet Stanley Fish suspects the speaker of rationalizing "if

you can't beat him, join him." Michael McCanles is even more skeptical of the speaker's sincerity: "by 'confessing' Christ's transcendent redemption he may conquer the 'man, who once against thee fought'; but he may also become Christ's secret enemy in still hoping to make his own part something to be valued, to 'come / Into thy conquest' in a way that would 'conquer' God by the very act of flourishing his humility before Him."[87] Such diversity among some of Herbert's best interpreters provides the best gauge of the indeterminacy of the speaker's aspirations. Both versions of the speaker's motives, I would argue, are correct but partial. Although voicing a wish to utter submission untainted by resentment or the desire for power, the poem nevertheless implicates its gestures of compliance in the covertly manipulative discourse with authority that it ostensibly rejects.

As University Orator, Herbert had responded to the situation of complimenting a superior for an accomplishment or award by identifying with the superior's success. In a letter to Buckingham congratulating him on his marquisate, for example, Herbert declares, "Marquis, thy glory we account our own, and in thy honours we congratulate our own advantage."[88] Likewise a letter to Thomas Coventry, newly appointed Attorney General, begins: "Permit that we also should come to a share of the spoil with thee."[89] The speaker of "The Reprisall" attempts in like manner to assimilate the success of his superior. He desires, in the words of the speaker of "The Thanksgiving," to "side with thy triumphant glorie." His surrender is simultaneously tactical and sincere, an act of legitimate resignation like that sought by the speaker of "Easter-wings" ("With thee / Let me combine / And feel this day thy victorie") and a Pyrrhic defeat exercising the pragmatic wisdom of one of Herbert's *Outlandish Proverbs*: "Sometimes the best gaine is to lose" (no. 224, p. 328). Like so many of Herbert's poems, including the poem it purports to resolve, "The Reprisall" contains both submissive and aggressive impulses. It sublimates, but does not fully subordinate, its insurgent energies.

Moreover, the mode of speech proposed by "The Reprisall"—confession—contains the same problematic blend of pious intentions and brazen insurgence possessed by imitation, the activity it aspires to replace. Herbert does praise the "antient and pious ordinance" of confession in *The Country Parson*, asserting that "there is no help for fault done, but confession" (*Works*, pp. 249, 240). Yet he also suggests that one must exercise a constant suspicion towards this ordinance, always "doubt[ing] . . . whether his repentance were true, or at least in that degree it ought to be" (p. 279). "Doubtlesse the best faith in us is defective," remarks Herbert in his *Briefe Notes on*

*Valdesso's "Considerations," "*and arrives not to the point it should"
(p. 319). Moreover, in "The Holdfast" Herbert displays his suspicions
of the potentially proud, even truculent behavior that can parade as
confession:

> We must confesse that nothing is our own.
> Then I confesse that he my succour is:
> But to have nought is ours, not to confesse
> That we have nought.

Like the devout "threat" to "observe the strict decree / Of my dear
God with all my power & might" with which "The Holdfast" begins,
confession, even of one's total indebtedness, entails the prospect of
impertinent self-assertion.

Confession, furthermore, is all the more insidious because it so
easily parades as pious accomplishment. Luther warns his followers
to "beware of the great error of those who approach the Sacrament of
Eucharist leaning on that frail reed—that they have confessed . . . for
by these things they do not become worthy and pure, but rather they
become defiled through that trust in their purity."[90] Confession de-
files in proportion to the confidence it inspires in its purgative capaci-
ties. By abolishing sacramental confession, Protestantism intended
to dismantle the institutional and individual control bestowed upon
the auditor of such utterances. But by making God rather than an ec-
clesiastical authority the audience of confessional discourse, Protes-
tantism actually exacerbated the political conflicts implicit in the
structure of confession. By enjoining one to speak, to put a self into
language, confession empowers one to fashion a self.[91] It endows the
subject with the tools necessary to envision its own authority. Al-
though the project outlined at the end of "The Reprisall" is a far less
inappropriate response to divine sacrifice than the occasionally ludi-
crous imitation proposed in "The Thanksgiving," confession offers
not so much a resolution to the problem of "dealing with" God as it is
a new aspect of the problem. The power structure it inhabits disputes
the hierarchical relationship it intends.

The act of confession, furthermore, may have more to do with dis-
possession than expression, fabrication than revelation. Rather than
making the self in the image of another, confession makes the imita-
tive self into another, "The man, who once against thee fought." Un-
like the Catholic priest, the Protestant God can see the inner reality
that perpetually recedes from the language that struggles to reveal it.
In doing so, as the following quotation from Archbishop Bramhall
suggests, the divine audience of Protestant confession throws into re-

lief the manner in which confession continually objectifies, and so displaces, the very self it aims to divulge:

> Our Protestant Confessions are for the most part too general and a little too presumptuous . . . And a little too careless, as if we were telling a story of a third person that concern'd not us: We confess light Errours willingly . . . but greater crimes, . . . we conceal and cover with as much art as maybe. Lastly, even while we are confessing, we have too often a mind to return *with the dog to his vomit*, and with the *sow to her wallowing in the mire;* what is this but a plain mocking of God? . . . we rather cover our sins, or forbear rather than forsake them; wee desire rather to make a Truce with God, than a Peace . . . we do not desire to take an everlasting farewell of our sins, . . . but onely a Coversen [sic], to hide them in an heap of Devotions.⁹²

Confession, Bramhall proposes, is a form of narrative self-fashioning, always in peril of objectifying the sinning self as "the story of a third person," or, in Herbert's terms, "the man who once against thee fought." Bramhall trenchantly observes that confession may conceal more than it reveals. He sees, moreover, the potentially insidious nature of confessional utterance, proposing that the verbal rehearsal of one's sinfulness can rekindle the very sins confession purports to forsake. Punning (somewhat heavy-handedly) on "conversion" and "cover," Bramhall suggests that confessional utterance may convince the confessing self that its sins are converted when in fact they are only covered.

Bramhall's suspicions of the potentially fictionalized nature of the attempt to verbalize inwardness correspond to the comments of Jacques Lacan on psychoanalysis, the twentieth-century version of secular confession:

> Does the subject not become engaged in an ever-growing dispossession of that being of his, concerning which—by dint of sincere portraits which leave its idea no less coherent, of rectifications which do not succeed in freeing its essence, of stays and defenses which do not prevent his statue from tottering, of narcissistic embraces which become like a puff of air in animating it—he ends up by recognizing that this being has never been anything more than his construct in The Imaginary and that this construct disappoints all his certitudes? For in this labor which he undertakes to reconstruct this construct *for another,*

he finds again the fundamental alienation which made him construct it *like another one,* and which has always destined it to be stripped from him *by another.*[93]

Inevitably, confession is self-construction masquerading as self-revelation, alienating the very subject it intends to express. Because of what Stephen Greenblatt describes as "the dependence of even the innermost self upon a language that is always necessarily given from without and upon representation before an audience," confessional discourse suffers the same distortions and interference that disrupt speech and motives in the political world.[94] The two selves at the end of "The Reprisall"—"The man, who once against thee fought" and the man who pledges to fight against this figure—can be (and are, in the course of *The Temple*) subdivided *ad infinitum* precisely because they are so inextricably linked. Where imitation attempts to fashion a self in the image of authority, confession, by contrast, endeavors to reveal a self to authority. Yet even this endeavor entails an act of fabrication, the construction of a self in the image authority demands. It is an image, moreover, which is always receding from the language used to contain it. As "The Thanksgiving" shows how imitation of superiority blends into appropriation of power, so does "The Reprisall" suggest how confession dissociates rather than subjugates the sinning self.

Like Bramhall and Lacan, Herbert was profoundly aware of the resistance of the self to language. For Herbert, this resistance was intimately related to the reluctance of selves to submit to authority. Rather than abandoning the hope of ever apprehending in language an elusive self or settling for the glib solutions of a formulaic orthodoxy, Herbert chose to make poetry out of these two parallel acts of resistance. "Onely an open breast," Herbert asserts in the poem called "Confession," "doth shut [God's afflictions] out." Yet the poems of *The Temple* chronicle not the pellucid declarations of an open breast but the roiled utterances of a suffering soul. "Fiction," concludes Herbert in "Confession," "Doth give a hold and handle to affliction." To his artistic and spiritual credit, there are no "true confessions" in Herbert, only sincere and compelling fictions. By quarrying rather than concealing the gap between the self and the language of self-presentation—a gap he necessarily learned to exploit in the political realm—Herbert attains in "The Thanksgiving," "The Reprisall," and in the series of reprisals that constitute the remainder of *The Temple* a stunning record of the obstacles erected by the self in its efforts to

53

submit to divine authority. As the following chapters will show, "The man who once against thee fought" continues to bear arms against the God he attempts to worship.

The Temple, it is important to remember, was not an easy book to get licensed for the press. As Walton relates, "when Mr. *Farrer* [Nicholas Ferrar] sent this Book to *Cambridge* to be Licensed for the Press, the *Vice-Chancellor* would by no means allow the two so much noted Verses,

> Religion stands a Tip-toe in our land,
> Ready to pass to the *American* Strand.

to be printed; and Mr. *Farrer* would by no means allow the Book to be printed, and want them."[95] It is only "after some time, and some arguments," that the Vice-Chancellor consents to license the book, "hop[ing] the World will not take [Herbert] to be an inspired Prophet." Written on the title page of the Bodleian manuscript is "The Original of Mʳ George Herbert's Temple; as it was at first Licensed for the presse," followed by the signature of the Vice-Chancellor of Cambridge and four other academic authorities.[96] The poems thus bear the literal inscription of the kinds of political authority they metaphorically address. These authorities, moreover, may have had good reason to be nervous about the volume of poems they were licensing. Three of the signers—Benjamin Laney, Vice-Chancellor; Matthew Wren, Master of Peterhouse; and William Beale, Master of Jesus—were appointees of Archbishop Laud and frequently acted as his agents.[97] The lines from "The Church-Militant" that made the Vice-Chancellor particularly anxious—certainly written early, since they are in the Williams manuscript, but neither erased nor revised by the mature Herbert—were genuinely inflammatory, particularly from a Laudian perspective. William Prynne records that in 1635, two years after the first edition of *The Temple* was published, Samuel Ward was imprisoned

> for preaching . . . against Bowing at the name of Jesus, the Booke of sports on the Lords day, and saying, that the Church of England was ready to ring the Changes, and insinuating unto his Auditory, that there was cause to fear an Alteration of Religion; saying, that *Religion and the Gospel stood on tiptoes ready to be gone.*[98]

The Vice-Chancellor's fear that Herbert would be taken for a prophet is indeed fulfilled in the Puritan Ward's echoing of Herbert's words to attack the authority of the church Herbert had served and defended.

In the next chapter, " 'My God, My King': Socializing God," I will explore the degree to which Herbert's imagination of God was infused by the concept of royal authority. The conflation of divine and political authority that "The Thanksgiving" inaugurates served disparate ideological ends in the seventeenth century: it could be used to inculcate obedience to the state or to license disobedience; it could be used to defend the liturgy of the Church of England or to attack it. Herbert's handling of the monarchical metaphor shows a similar flexibility, at once echoing and critiquing absolutist claims, and praising and manipulating God. Throughout *The Temple*, Herbert investigates the coincidences and conflicts that arise between a social hierarchy based on wealth and birth and a spiritual hierarchy in which the first shall be last. The lyrics express a worldly and sophisticated courtliness even as they engage in a powerful and revolutionary attack on courtly distinction. Where this chapter has been concerned with the opposition between the subject and authority, the next chapter will explore Herbert's abiding need of authority to supply the parameters of the subject.

"Despite the differences in epochs and objectives," observes Michel Foucault, "the representation of power has remained under the spell of monarchy. In political thought and analysis, we still have not cut off the head of the king."[99] Herbert died sixteen years before he would have had the chance to relish or reject cutting off the head of King Charles. It is impossible to guess how Herbert would have responded to this opportunity. By deliberately situating himself in the country in the letter to Anne Clifford and in the title of *The Country Parson*, Herbert implicitly aligned himself with a region whose longstanding cultural antipathies to the court have been viewed as a contributing factor to the Civil War.[100] His familial connections, moreover, suggest Parliamentary inclinations. While his younger brother Henry, Master of the Revels until the closing of the theaters, took up arms on Charles's behalf, his elder brother Edward became a reluctant Parliamentarian after neutrality ceased to be a viable option. Philip Herbert, the fourth earl of Pembroke, to whose patronage George Herbert owed his appointment at Bemerton, eventually joined the Parliamentary cause. Sir Robert Harley, Herbert's cousin and the recipient of his gossip-laden epistle, was a committed Parliamentarian and Presbyterian. Sir John Danvers served as a colonel in the Parliamentary Army and signed the death-warrant of the king.[101] Yet legend suggests that "Herbert's divine Poems," along with the sermons of Lancelot Andrewes and Richard Hooker's *Laws of Ecclesiastical Polity*, constituted the reading of the imprisoned Charles I.[102] Gentle George Herbert might have recoiled in horror from the opportunity to act upon the aggression and resentment towards monarchical authority that his lyrics and orations whisper; but he might also, like so many of his relatives, have entertained the chance to trumpet the social frustration the monarch had come to represent. We can never know. But by tracing the unexpected and intersecting vectors of political and divine authority throughout *The Temple*, we can gauge the hold that monarchy possesses on Herbert's conception of the sacred, and perhaps begin to come to terms with the control that monarchy still exerts on our own conceptions of power.

2
"My God, My King": Socializing God

A sonne honoureth his father, and a servant his Master. If
then I be a father where is mine honour? and if I be a
master, where is my feare, saith the Lord of hostes.
—Malachi 1.6

Where the word of a king is, there is power.
—Ecclesiastes 8.4

In the foreground of Gentile da Fabriano's splendid *Adoration of the Magi* (1423), an old Magus bows to kiss the foot of the Christ child. Just to his right a servant kneels in order to remove the spurs of his dazzlingly dressed lord. So similar in structure and so different in direction, the two gestures of obeisance trace the axis of social and sacred reverence in the Renaissance. In this remarkable parallel between worship of the Christ child and the submission demanded by figures of the political hierarchy, Gentile brilliantly exposes the tensions and correspondences between the sacred and secular hierarchies, limning the moment when God becomes human in terms of a rich but dizzying interpenetration of spiritual and political authority.

As court painter to Pope Martin V, Gentile must have been painfully aware of the homologies between political and religious obeisance. Yet in this picture executed for the Florentine merchant and humanist Palla Strozzi, Gentile seems concerned not only with the similarity between these two acts of kneeling but also with their differences. The old Magus is viewed in profile, while the squire is glimpsed in foreshortened obscurity, pointing directly at the viewer (perhaps implicating the wealthy patron in the desire to have such obeisance done to him). Their similar gestures are nevertheless

Figure 2.   Gentile da Fabriano, *The Adoration of the Magi* (1423). Florence, Uffizi. Alinari/Art Resource, New York.

pointed towards very different objects. The richness of the worshipping Magi and the worshipped young lord contrasts with the sartorial simplicity of the Christ child and the submissive squire, aligning Christ with the socially dispossessed, and suggesting perhaps that the meek will inherit the earth. Relatedly, the two monkeys perched on a camel in the background hint at a criticism of cavalier pretension. Yet the gilt halos of the child and of the bowing Magus (his

crown is cast at the feet of the virgin) parallel the aureate crowns of
the other two Magi, aligning Christ's majesty with the powers of this
world. Lacking both halo and crown, the squire seems in this align-
ment less akin to the Magus kneeling to his left than to the greyhound
kneeling to his right—just another beast kept for the amusement of
royalty. Despite the humble circumstances of his birth, perhaps this
God is the savior of the aristocracy.

Herbert's poetry exploits the same rich set of correspondences be-
tween sacred and secular power. Gestures of social reverence furnish
Herbert with a repertoire of actions to convey his devotion to God.
Like Gentile's *Adoration*, furthermore, Herbert's poems are imbued
with a courtly magnificence which they seem partially to reject. Fas-
cinated by the striking similarities and telling differences between
behavior towards God and king, both Herbert and Gentile allow their
gestures of devotion to oscillate between these two kinds of adora-
tion. The effect may be at times perplexing, but the sound produced
by this oscillation truly is, in Herbert's words, "musick for a king"
("Sion," line 24).

In "Jordan (I)," for example, one of Herbert's troublingly opaque
pleas for simple poetry, Herbert both contrasts and conflates secular
and sacred power. The poem opens with a pair of rhetorical questions
about the relationship of truth and art to which no one would dare
answer in the affirmative: "Who sayes that fictions onely and false
hair / Become a verse? Is there in truth no beautie?" Such disarm-
ingly easy questions, though, quickly modulate into political terms
whose answers are less obvious: "May no lines passe, except they do
their dutie / Not to a true, but painted chair?" The issue here is no
longer the union of truth and beauty but the need to perform the ap-
propriate obeisance before one's poetic "lines" are allowed to "pass."
The verses refer to the pressure that political authority continually
exerts upon utterance, requiring all statements to bow to the powers
that be. Moreover, by identifying this authority with an item of furni-
ture, and a painted one at that, Herbert hints at a critique of the vacu-
ousness and superficiality of the very authority whose pull he records.
We need to remember, moreover, that the lines in "The Church-
Militant" predicting that "religion stands on tip-toe in our land, /
Readie to passe to the *American* strand" (lines 235–36), made the li-
censing authorities at Cambridge so nervous that they almost did not
allow Herbert's lines to pass. With a requisite and discreet indirec-
tion, "Jordan (I)" assesses the pressures of authority on speech. It at
once deliberates upon and participates in what Annabel Patterson has
termed "the hermeneutics of censorship," the way that utterance was

shaped in a variety of ways by the exigencies of political existence.[1]

Herbert does not in the least question the need of lines to "do duty" to authority. But he does leave open the question of what is designated by the "true" and the "painted chair." Should one copy Gentile's squire and bow to secular power, or imitate the aged magus and bow to sacred authority? Following Anthony Low's subtle reading of the poem as a criticism of the court masque, Marion Singleton suggests that the painted chair "is the throne of the earthly ruler."[2] By implication, then, Herbert is exposing earthly monarchy as a "fiction," a "painted chair" in contrast to the throne of God. The concluding line, in which Herbert declares that he, unlike other poets, will "plainly say, *My God, My King,*" would reveal God as the true king, compared to whom earthly sovereigns are only a pale imitation. Devotion to God, then, would contain a component of political insurrection. "Praise can serve as a kind of dispraise," asserts Kenneth Burke, "Augustine's praise of God was a way of *not* praising the emperor."[3] Indeed, the Puritan critique of mortal kingship often derived precisely from the claim that kingship was the prerogative of God. In 1576, Archbishop Edmund Grindal disobeyed Elizabeth's order to suppress prophecyings by setting his duty to his heavenly king against his duty to his mortal monarch, writing: "Bear with me, I beseech you, Madam, if I choose rather to offend your earthly Majesty than to offend the heavenly Majesty of God."[4] In its declaration of devotion to God in monarchical terms, then, "Jordan (I)" seems to be just the kind of utterance that authority might have reason to censor. Rather than doing "duty" to political authority, Herbert exposes that authority's illegitimacy.

Yet the last stanza further complicates the poem's covert critique of political authority:

> Shepherds are honest people; let them sing:
> Riddle who list, for me, and pull for Prime:
> I envie no mans nightingale or spring;
> Nor let them punish me with losse of rime,
>   Who plainly say, *My God, My King.*

This plea for simple poetry is terribly abstruse. *Prime* is another word for the pastoral *spring* that inspires the shepherds' song as well as a reference to the courtly card game of primero.[5] The apology, moreover, is disingenuous; the poet does not lose his "rime" because of his purportedly "plain" devotion to God. Indeed, the concluding utterance that Herbert offers as representative of his own unaffected poetic practice—"My God, My King"—is not a work of plain saying at all.

As Wilbur Sanders remarks, "The whole point about these words is that they say nothing plainly; and it is only by a sentimentality about the rough honest speech of his 'shepherds' that Herbert can pretend they do."[6] The shepherds can be construed both as "honest people" who sing in the plain unaffected way to which Herbert aspires, and as a model for the kinds of subterfuge that authority forces upon all who open their mouths to speak. "No matter what its pretensions to simplicity of form or matter," remarks Edward Tayler, Renaissance pastoral poetry "proves on inspection to be highly stylized and carefully calculated."[7] Like the game of primero to which it is contrasted, pastoral literature is an aristocratic pursuit, deeply implicated in an ornamental discourse of "enchanted groves," "sudden arbours," and "purling streams," where all is "vail'd." Moreover, as George Puttenham relates, the genre of pastoral is specifically intended "under the *vaile* of homely persons, and in rude speeches to insinuate and glaunce at greater matters, and such as perchance had not bene safe to have beene disclosed in any other sort."[8] The singing of honest shepherds, then, is not just an alternative to a discourse in which "all [is] *vail'd*, while he that reades, divines, / Catching the sense at two removes" but also a common vehicle of such discourse. It is, moreover, an important tactic for dodging the need to do overt duty to authority with which the poem began, allowing one to discuss issues otherwise dangerous to whisper. This fear of authority creeps back into the poem's penultimate line, where the speaker hopes he will not be "punish[ed] . . . with losse of rime." Phoebe Sheavyn suggests that in Renaissance England, "any utterance construed as a reflection upon political topics was apt to be regarded as seditious and treasonable, and to be accused of these offences was to be liable, before conviction, to imprisonment and torture."[9] Herbert circumspectly sublimates the immense anxiety aroused by the unpredictable capacity of writing to incur the displeasure of authority into a disingenuous fear that he will be "punish[ed]" by being forced to miss a rhyme. The attack on "vail'd" poetry seems nevertheless to practice the kind of duplicity it deplores. As Patterson maintains, the ambiguity we so value in works of Renaissance literature—and that Herbert in "Jordan (I)" both exercises and demeans—was produced by the pressures that authority exerted upon utterance.[10]

Furthermore, the phrase "My God, My King," is deeply unstable. Are the two nouns to be read as designating alternative objects, or as different names for the same being? If the latter, which is tenor and which vehicle? Is God being represented as a king, or is the king being likened to a God? As we saw in the last chapter, James himself was a major proponent of the ideology of divine right kingship. Herbert in turn often flattered the king by appealing to his delusions of godlike powers. The fusion of divine and earthly kingship could lead to such utterances as Buckingham's clever closing in a letter to King James: "I ame now goeing to give my redemer thanks for my maker."[11] In a world governed by an absolutist monarch, "My God, My King" cannot be a piece of plain speech. The conclusion of "Jordan (I)," then, could be construed as an act of devotion to God, the true king, at the expense of attention to James I, or as a flattering reiteration of the very ideology of absolutist kingship that James promulgated. Herbert deftly manages to have it both ways: stylistically, he writes a roiled plea for pellucid poetry, and politically, he both criticizes and praises the earthly king. He does duty to both chairs. In "Jordan (I)," as in Gentile da Fabriano's *Adoration*, the lines of analogy between earthly and heavenly power continue to become entangled.

Recognition of the migratory nature of authority tracked in "Jordan (I)" gives point to Herbert's plea in the previous poem, "The Temper (II)," for God to "fix thy chair of grace, that all my powers / May also fix their reverence." Herbert wants God to identify the true chair of grace so that he can bend his reverence in the proper direction. Herbert complains that without proper evidence of the true chair, his "powers . . . grow unruly." As in "Humilitie" and "The Familie," the site of political power is removed from the court to the self. He compares himself to a miniature court, suggesting in part the degree to which courtly values have been internalized, absorbed as a code of conduct for regulating the self. "Like their courts," argues Frank Whigham, "courtiers' minds were peopled with crowds of retainers and servants—a doubt police, marginal forebears of Foucault's surveillance orders."[12] Herbert's poems on the court of the self represent just this process. Yet as the pun on "unruly" implies, the comparison is not for Herbert simply a matter of internalizing modes of totalitarian surveillance; rather, he longs for a stable authority that will provide him with the tools for shaping and controlling a frighteningly unstable interiority. Without such an authority, he has no power over his mutinous powers; subjection is required for manageable subjectivity. "The prohibitions supported by social sanctions are reproduced in the individual as self-controls," argues Norbert Elias; "the social code of conduct so imprints itself in one form or another on the human being that it becomes a constituent element of his individual self."[13] "The Temper (II)" demonstrates the enfranchising aspects of this internal civilizing process. The poem concludes by asking God to "Let not thy higher Court remove, / But keep a standing Majestie in me." Psychological peace is imagined as the internalization of political power. While the deferential litotes of Herbert's prayer align the utterance with a suit addressed to earthly power, the request explicitly identifies its object as God's "higher court." Unlike the situation of "The Thanksgiving" explored in the last chapter, where the inimitability of Christ's beneficent sacrifice precipitates mortal aggression against authority, here authority is welcomed as the principle by which a mortal achieves control over his own subjectivity.

The language that enables Herbert to collate internal, political, and heavenly kingdoms was a felicitous by-product of Herbert's historical situation. Both theologically and politically, the elision of the differences between secular and sacred authority served a range of social and rhetorical ends. The translation of the Bible into the vernacular fused the language of social hierarchy with the biblical terminology for God, thus making available a matrix of contemporary social referents for God. In its prayer for the monarch, the *Book of Common Prayer* addresses a typically politicized divinity: "O Lord, our heavenly father, high and mighty king of kings, Lord of Lords, the only ruler of princes, which doest from thy throne behold all the dwellers upon earth."[14] God's behavior was socialized in terms of the characteristic conduct of a king, a lord, a master, and a father. Consequently, the language and gestures used in diurnal conversation with social superiors were assimilated into discourse with the divine. Indeed, as Keith Thomas observes, behavior towards superiors and conduct towards God were part of the same liturgy of deference:

> In church [people] took off their hats and knelt down, just as they uncovered their heads and knelt before their social superiors. God was "the great landlord," as one preacher called him; or he was an authoritarian father whose attributes were those of fathers men themselves knew. His ordinances were those of society itself.[15]

Stefano Guazzo is only ventriloquizing a cultural commonplace when he declares that "Princes" are "Gods on earth."[16] Because of the divinity that hedges kings, "to reason of and call into question their dooinges, is nothing else but with the Gyants to lay siege to heaven." To Guazzo, the analogy extends into a frightening omniscience, so that "like Gods they knowe not only what men say, but what men thinke." The exercise of their power is also remarkably like the divine: "Princes partake with the divine power, being able to pull downe the mighty and set up the weake."[17]

Guazzo deploys these linkages between divinity and monarchy to determine the conduct proper to earthly superiors, authorizing the social uses of ceremonial behavior by analogy to its efficacy in the divine realm:

> as the sacred Ceremonies, which are voide of superstition, are not displeasant in Gods sight, and stirre up to devotion the mindes of the ignorant people . . . so these worldly ceremonies purchase us the good will of our friendes and superiours, to whom they are addressed, and make us knowne for civile people, and from rude countrie loutes.[18]

For Guazzo, an analogous decorum governs behavior in social and sacred spheres. Ceremonious behavior not only fulfills the function of social differentiation, allowing us to distinguish ourselves from "rude countrie loutes," but also wins the good will of God and superiors.

The analogy, moreover, works both ways. George Downame terms the verse from Malachi that serves as epigraph to this chapter "Malachi's rule," arguing it enjoins us to "examine our selves whether we be as carefull to speak unto the Lord as we would be unto a Prince: and herein also let us shew that reverence which we ow unto the Lord."[19] Daniel Featley likewise uses courtly criteria for devotional purposes: "What Courtier presumeth to come into the Kings presence in stinking and nastie cloathes, or with his hands and face all besemared with dirt, or spotted with inke? How dare we then appeare before *God* with a foule and nastie conscience?"[20] The demands of social decorum shaped, and were shaped by, behavior towards God. The circuit connecting obeisance to "My God" and "my King" allows current to flow in both directions. Debate about the proper liturgical form of the English church, for example, continually boils down to the question of the appropriate behavior before political authority. By attending briefly to this discourse—one that Herbert almost certainly knew since he joined in the controversy with his *Musae Responsoriae*—we can more fully apprehend the cultural weight and polemical force behind Herbert's use of political terminology in his portrait of his relationship to God.

The Puritan Thomas Cartwright inaugurates the controversy by criticizing the *Book of Common Prayer*'s method of "mingling lessons and prayers" by analogy to the decorum of petitioning an earthly king:

> If a man should come to a prince, and having very many things to demand, after he had demanded one thing, would stay a long

time, and then demand another, and so the third: the prince might well think that either he came to ask before he knew what he had need of, or that he had forgotten some piece of his suit, or that he was distracted in his understanding, or some other such like cause of the disorder of his supplication.[21]

Cartwright assumes that behavior towards God is commensurate with behavior towards social superiors. Praying to God and petitioning a king, he argues, are part of the same universe of discourse, and to both the same strategies of supplication apply. A liturgy which violates the decorum of secular supplication, Cartwright claims, is deeply inappropriate to the ends of worship.

The Conformist response is polemically predictable but politically surprising—to bifurcate the two realms which Cartwright's analogy conjoins. Archbishop Whitgift begs the question, but in profoundly significant terms: "As much difference as there is betwixt man and God, so far is your similitude from proving your purpose."[22] He asserts that an unbridgeable gulf differentiates humanity from divinity, rendering Cartwright's anthropomorphic analogies inappropriate. Moreover, Whitgift insists, Cartwright's analogy impinges upon the dignity of God's omniscient majesty by comparing him to a far lesser being:

And here you do injury to God, to compare him to an earthly prince, especially in this behalf. For what prince would not think himself abused if a man should daily and hourly sue unto him? But it is not so with God; for we have a commandment to pray continually.[23]

The strategies of petitioning an earthly king, Whitgift maintains, are irrelevant to the occasions and forms of prayer. God's omniscience and patience render him a very different audience from an earthly monarch. To compare God to an earthly king does "injury" to him by implicitly limiting his power and patience to that of a mortal sovereign.

Whitgift, however, does not declare whether the analogy between divine and earthly authority is to be surrendered completely (as he seems to imply), and if so, what rationale of behavior towards God is to take its place. But Richard Hooker, in Book 5 of his *Laws*, explicates at much greater length the distinction between conduct towards God and behavior before earthly superiors. Even as he tries to undercut its implicit endorsement of nonconformist liturgy, Hooker shows himself unwilling to relinquish completely the monarchical metaphor for God:

> Our speech to worldly superiors we frame in such sort as serveth best to inform and persuade the minds of them, who otherwise neither could nor would greatly regard our necessities: whereas, because we know that God is indeed a King, but a *great* King, who understandeth all things beforehand, which no other King besides doth, a King which needeth not to be informed what we lack, a King readier to grant than we to make our requests; therefore in prayer we do not so much respect what precepts art delivereth touching the method of persuasive utterance in the presence of great men, as what doth most avail to our own edification in piety and godly zeal.[24]

God's foreknowledge, Hooker claims, makes him a totally different audience of supplicatory utterance from an earthly king. Echoing the *Venite* of the *Book of Common Prayer* (Ps. 95.3)—"For the Lord is a great God: and a great king above all gods"—Hooker argues that God is "indeed a King, but a *great* King," one who knows a request before it is uttered.[25] God's greatness, moreover, is a cause not of terror but of confidence: unlike a mortal monarch, God is "readier to grant than we to make our requests," and is unmoved by the methods of artful persuasion so important in suing to an earthly king. As a result, the divine supplicant becomes the primary audience of his own request, speaking not what has the best chance of altering favorably the conduct of his monarch but "what doth most avail to [his] own edification in piety and godly zeal."

Because the audiences of sacred and secular utterance differ so utterly, it would be absurd, Hooker argues, to "frame a rule that what form of speech or behavior soever is fit for suitors in a prince's court, the same and no other beseemeth us in our prayer to Almighty God."[26] Hooker does not completely banish the decorum of social supplication from the realm of divine behavior. But he does wish to preclude its definitive use in critiques of English liturgy. To fix God by comparison to an earthly sovereign, Hooker insists, is to delimit the power and majesty of a being whose only constraints are the inscrutable laws he freely places on himself.[27]

Herbert's own portrait of God thrives on the tension exposed in these theological disputes between the conception of God as a social superior and the realization that God surpasses any earthly referent. Like Cartwright, Herbert continually orients his behavior towards God as if he were a political superior. Yet like Whitgift and Hooker,

Herbert confronts how absolutely this God differs from even the most politically exalted mortals. The poems of *The Temple* repeatedly incur the risks of imagining and responding to a God who is "indeed a King, but a *great* King," exceeding in power and majesty the very terminology used to describe those traits.

The issue of the relevance of social imagery for God is, then, linguistic as well as political and theological. In *The Country Parson*, Herbert discovers in the parabolic method of Christ a hierarchical model for human discourse about the divine. Christ, he observes, "was the true householder, who bringeth out of his treasure things new and old; the old things of Philosophy, and the new of Grace; and maketh the one *serve* the other" (my italics; p. 261). The social metaphor of service that so informs Herbert's sense of his relationship with God also determines Herbert's sense of the proper relationship between human language and its divine object. The things of this world can function as metaphors for the divine as long as they remain properly subordinate to it. Herbert expresses great admiration for the "skill" of Holy Scripture, "when it condescends to the naming of a plough a hatchet, a bushell, leaven boyes piping and dancing; shewing that things of ordinary use are not only to *serve* in the way of drudgery, but to be washed, and cleansed, and *serve* for lights even of Heavenly Truths" (p. 257). With the proper degree of linguistic subordination, nearly anything may serve as a vehicle of divine praise. As "The Elixir" contends,

> A man that looks on glasse,
> On it may stay his eye;
> Or if he pleaseth, though it passe,
> And then the heav'n espie.

Herbert here imagines a way of glimpsing heavenly affairs via earthly phenomena that does not, in the words of "Jordan (I)," "catch the sense at two removes."

Yet figurative language does not provide a transparent window on the divine. At best, it allows us to see through a glass darkly, thriving on the imbrication between likeness and difference. The unstable blend of similarity and disparity that separates metaphoric language from mere reiteration or distant allegory contains a danger for the divine poet that is at once linguistic and political. For metaphor, assert Michael and Marianne Shapiro, "is defined as that trope in which the (simultaneously) established hierarchy of signata is either reversed or neutralized."[28] Divine metaphorics, then, even those intended to induce a sense of awe, have the potential to level or even reverse the hierarchy that should obtain between signifier and signified, and so between earth and heaven. It is this potential that accounts for the attractions of negative theology, "the idea that God cannot and should not be described in positive terms, but only in negative ones."[29] But Herbert rarely if ever succumbed to these attractions; he was instead fascinated by the way that "in any created thing, whether infinitely large and complex or infinitesimally small and neat, he could read the paradoxes of totality and multiplicity implied in the notion of the divine *logos*."[30] Because divine metaphors, like the relationship between heaven and earth they express, at once assert and subvert hierarchy, the devotional writer must exercise great care that the figures used to describe God are not allowed to define, and so delimit, his power. As Donne warns, "If thou be tempted to worship God in an Image, be able to answer God something to that, *To whom will yee liken God, or what likenesse will yee compare unto him*? There can be no example, no patterne to make God by: for that were to make God a Copy, and the other, by which he were made, the Originall."[31] To metaphorize God is potentially an act of political insurrection, inverting the proper relationship between original and imitation. Activity in the linguistic hierarchy and behavior in the political realm run on parallel tracks. Like the attempt to imitate God explored in the last chapter, the rivalry between divine tenor and mortal vehicle is, finally, a political battle.

This volatile relationship between political metaphor and divine subject informs "To all Angels and Saints," Herbert's paradoxical poem to the heavenly court about his refusal to address any heavenly audience but God. The poem is deeply uneasy about the relationship of a graduated hierarchy to the absolute power at its pinnacle. It opens with an appeal to those "glorious spirits" who, unlike earthbound mortals, see God "without a frown or strict commands." In heaven, Herbert imagines, "ev'ry one is king, and hath his crown, / If not upon his head, yet in his hands." But as he explains his reasons for failing to address his suits to these various monarchs, Herbert's vision of an egalitarian heaven evaporates before the extensive prerogative of the principal sovereign. He "dare not" address Mary or the angels because "our King . . . Bids no such thing." As Richard Strier remarks, "The opening vision of heaven as a democratic realm . . . has given way to a vision of a single absolute monarch reigning equally over both heaven and earth."[32] To address anyone besides this monarch would be to "steal" a flower from his "rich crown" of royal "prerogative" in order "To make a posie for inferiour power"—something that Herbert says he "dare not" do.

Yet the referent of "our King" is not exclusively the heavenly God, as Strier implies. The same ambivalence that infiltrates the conclusion of "Jordan (I)" suffuses Herbert's portrait of the political structure of heaven. As Louis Martz asks, "Isn't there at the same time a lurking suggestion of another, earthly King, who *now, alas,* 'bids no such thing' for the Anglican? It is hard to avoid the implication."[33] The pronoun "our" is ambiguous; it can be construed as either including or excluding the angels he addresses (our king, not yours, on the model of the "we on earth" in the final stanza). "Prerogative," moreover, was a term charged with profound political significance in the early seventeenth century. As Perez Zagorin asserts, "the constitutional issue between [the king] and his opponents centered on the nature of his prerogative and his powers under it."[34] The royal prerogative entailed theoretically a sovereign right over subjects that superceded both common law and Parliamentary privilege—a power possessed by a monarch "from whom lyes no appeal" on earth, if not "At the last houre." The attributes that Strier associates with the Puritan deity reverberate with the appurtenances of Jacobean absolutism. Troublingly, the poem glosses over the differences between an earthly king who demands that all worship God in the way he prescribes and a jealous deity who will allow none but himself to receive petitions. For Herbert, the angels and saints cannot be addressed because absolute power, whether divine or mortal, will not abide it.

Herbert's attitude is in clear contrast to that of Donne, who dismisses invocation of the saints not by recourse to divine command but by reference to the refreshing ease with which God, unlike an earthly monarch, makes himself available to his inferiors:

> Certainly it were a strange distemper, a strange singularity, a strange circularity, in a man that dwelt at Windsor, to fetch all his water at London Bridge: So is it in him, that lives in Gods presence, (as he does, that lives religiously in his Church) to goe for all his necessities, by Invocation to Saints . . . If any man have tasted at Court, what it is to speake to another to speake for him, he will blesse that happiness, of having an immediate accesse to God himselfe in his prayers.[35]

Mediation and intercession were unavoidable facts of courtly life; much of the royal largesse, declares Whigham, "was distributed by courtiers and functionaries, who formed a many-layered matrix of mediation and themselves demanded wooing, from below as well as from above."[36] It is just this system which both Donne and Herbert consider but finally reject as a model for the processes of divine supplication. But where Herbert bemoans the injunction not to petition saints as an extension of royal prerogative which he greets with fear ("dare not"), Donne rejoices in the immediate access and lack of intercessionary interference it represents. "The absence of the sacrifical Christ," contends Strier, renders the poem uncharacteristic of Herbert, for whom "mercy rather than 'jealousy' is the dominant attribute of deity."[37] But the nervous apology to figures he dare not petition betrays an attitude towards authority that is profoundly characteristic of Herbert. The poem limns, albeit marginally, the portrait of a God whose characteristic attitude to his earthly creatures is one of "frowns" and "strict commands." The ideological strain between a stratified and an egalitarian heaven is paralleled by the unresolved nature of the monarchical power whose jealous commands Herbert somewhat reluctantly obeys.

In "To all Angels and Saints," then, Herbert quietly records the fear and trembling with which he approaches a monarchical God who begrudges petitions directed to any but himself. But in "Affliction (I)," the difficulties arising from the confusion of secular and sacred sovereignty become far more ominous. In this troubling poem, Herbert deploys the appurtenances of absolutist kingship to reveal the immense difficulty of maintaining a posture of absolute devotion towards God. With "a remarkable lack of censorship," the poem allows the God of "frowns" and "strict commands" inferred in "To all Angels and Saints" to surface.[38] The poem demonstrates how the failure to subordinate the things of this world to their divine referents becomes for Herbert a linguistic version of the speaker's refusal to submit himself fully to God. It releases the potential energy of confusion and rebellion latent in the complete fusion of social and divine service, and forces reader and speaker to confront the manner in which God is, in Hooker's phrase, "a King, but a *great* King," not bound by the decorum of earthly political behavior in his dealings with his subjects.

"Affliction (I)" is a poem which at once invites and frustrates biographical speculation.[39] Many of the details of the experience narrated tempt one to interpret them autobiographically—e.g., the references to illness, the anxiety about usefulness, the "lingring book" and academic "gown." The overall shape of the poem, moreover, seems to reflect the curve of regal favor followed by apparent disfavor limned by Herbert's career. Yet the rebellious and accusatory energies directed at God tempt one to distance the speaker from the poet, and to segregate such bitter utterances from the "sweet singer of the Tem-

ple." I do not want to read the poem as overt autobiography. I do, how-
ever, want to explore the deeply uneasy consonance between the
spiritual experiences the poem narrates and the political experiences
we know Herbert had. By playing out the multifarious and sometimes
clashing aspirations of Herbert's career, the poem deploys the politi-
cal as a model for the spiritual even as it calls into question the pro-
priety of such deployment.

The speaker relates that his initial reasons for entering the service
of his sovereign were secular and superficial:

> When first thou didst entice to thee my heart,
>   I thought the service brave.
> So many joyes I writ down for my part,
>   Besides what I might have
> Out of my stock of naturall delights,
> Augmented with thy gracious benefits.

The "joyes" of serving this monarch seem to blend the realms of na-
ture and grace, as the speaker describes his "stock of *naturall* de-
lights / Augmented with thy *gracious* benefits." Yet even in this
relatively innocent phrase designating God's benefits lurks the possi-
bility of insubordination; rather than making nature serve grace, as
does Christ, Herbert suggests here that grace only supplements na-
ture. The implicit hierarchical inversion whispers the insurrection
the poem will later shout. The speaker reveals himself as one fasci-
nated with the trappings of power. As Ilona Bell remarks,

> Enthralled by his own "pleasures," "joyes," and "hopes," Her-
> bert confused God's "gracious benefits" with social graces and
> physical allures . . . Herbert's lavish, carefree affluence, devot-
> ed to a "King" of "pleasures," confused God's heavenly grace
> with "gracious benefits" offered by fine society.[40]

The confusion Bell astutely notes is precisely the conflation of earth-
ly and heavenly service sought by the young Herbert in his desire to
join the "earthiness" of secular employment to the divinity of heav-
en. "*Both* heaven and earth," remarks the speaker of "Affliction (I),"
"payd me my wages in a world of mirth." The young Herbert praised
the orator's post as "the *finest* place in the University"; the speaker of
"Affliction (I)" declares to his monarch: "I looked on thy furniture so
fine / And made it *fine* to me" (my italics). Enchanted by the gran-
deur of their respective employments, both ambitious youth and lyr-
ic speaker reveal a fascination with glamorous surfaces.

Underlying this concern with surfaces, however, is a subtle accusation of his king for seducing him with this pleasurable facade: "Thy glorious houshold-stuffe did me entwine, / And 'tice me unto thee." Such verbs as "entice" and "entwine" (the Williams manuscript even has "bewitch") underscore this beguiling power. Herbert's portrait of an enthralling courtly environment not only functions as tacit accusation of God but also contains a cogent historical dimension; "an alluring court," maintains Lawrence Stone, operated in the kingdom "as a stabilizing political factor" by "attracting the nobility to court by the lure of office and rewards." In "Affliction (I)" we see Herbert succumbing to the attractions of the court even as he expresses his deep resentment of the mendicancy that such surrender thrust upon him. His stance of passivity in this seduction is a subtle modulation of those devotional postures of submission and quiescence that Herbert continually attempts to achieve and sustain.

The speaker describes himself as "argu'd into hopes," as if a habitual caution evaporated under the light of such intense royal favor:

> my thoughts reserved
> No place for grief or fear.
> Therefore my sudden soul caught at the place,
> And made her youth and fiercenesse seek thy face.

He attempts to exercise an intimacy the sovereign's favor seems to encourage. Yet Lorenzo Ducci, author of the *Ars aulica*, advises the vigilant courtier that the way to retain a prince's favor is "not one jot to diminish the reverence and duty towards the Prince, nor because of speciall confidence to presume to use familiaritie."[41] In desiring a face-to-face encounter with his sovereign, the speaker of "Affliction (I)" is guilty of precisely this presumption. Denys de Refuges warns against responding to royal favor with familiarity because princes "attribute all familiaritie to disdaine."[42] In the complex symbology of courtly conduct, even a familiarity bred by favor can imply a contempt which hastens the loss of that favor. Rather than the "respective boldnesse" Herbert counsels in "The Church-porch," the speaker of "Affliction (I)" practices here unmitigated boldness. Such boldness, however, only precipitates the afflictions of the title. Like so many courtiers who lost royal favor by mistakenly presuming on it, the speaker watches helplessly as his king of pleasures evolves into a king of grief.

Like the monarch Herbert served in his secular career, the sovereign of "Affliction (I)" does not dispense reward equitably. Rather, he entices the speaker into his service and then precludes the act of service:

When I got health, thou took'st away my life,
And more; for my friends die;
My mirth and edge was lost; a blunted knife
Was of more use than I.

Narration here swerves into explicit accusation. Much of the energy of the poem's diatribe against God underwrites the wisdom of one of the *Outlandish Proverbs* Herbert collected: "Service without reward is punishment" (p. 354, no. 1015). The speaker accuses his sovereign not only of failing to reward him but also of afflicting him with illness and of killing off his acquaintances and courtly connections: "my friends die." Loss of such figures would be not only emotionally devastating but also politically ruinous, for "advancement in all worlds," observed one Elizabethan, "be obtained by mediation and remembrance of noble friends."[43] The headstrong monarch of the poem, then, prevents the speaker's employment by foreclosing all avenues of possible advancement. Without the protection of patrons and friends, he becomes "thinne and lean without a fence or friend . . . blown through with ev'ry storm and winde." The cruel combination of physical and social afflictions leaves the speaker in a state of political and somatic paralysis: "I came where / I could not go away, nor persevere."[44] Like so many disgruntled Renaissance courtiers, the speaker portrays himself as a victim of the capricious will of an inscrutable monarch who rewards devout service with needless suffering.

The speaker complains that

Whereas my birth and spirit rather took
The way that takes the town;
Thou didst betray me to a lingring book,
And wrap me in a gown.

The profound division between his innate desire for "the way that takes the town" and the "lingring book" and "gown" to which his sovereign directs him probably represents in some form the tension in Herbert's own career between courtly and academic employment. The accusatory force of the verb designating his monarch's action towards him—"betray"—should not be underestimated. Even the speaker's success in the academic hierarchy is viewed as an act of treachery by his king. Indeed in the next stanza, the speaker accuses his monarch of using "Academick praise" to "Melt and dissolve my rage." These lines encompass a complete reversal of normative sovereign-courtier relations; rather than the courtier offering his monarch the "sweetned pill" of praise, here the monarch flatters his courtier to quell his anger.

Yet the suggestion of empowerment on the part of the speaker implicit in such a reversal is quickly silenced in his lament that

> Yet lest perchance I should too happie be
> > In my unhappiness,
> Turning my purge to food, thou throwest me
> > Into more sicknesses.
> Thus doth thy power crosse-bias me, not making
> Thine own gift good, yet me from my wayes taking.

His monarch will not even allow him to become habituated to his suffering to the point where his bitter purge might taste like food; rather, the monarch "throws" him "into more sicknesses." The violence of his monarch's action towards him evolves into an image of the subject as a ball in a game of bowling. God "throws" him into afflictions, and puts enough spin on him (the meaning of "crosse-bias") to ensure that he swerves from his own "wayes." Perhaps we are meant to hear a criticism of the speaker's egotistical emphasis on "my wayes." But that criticism does not mute the cruelty by which he characterizes God's conduct. Like Gloucester in *King Lear*—"As flies to wanton boys are we to th' gods, / They kill us for their sport" (4.1.36–37)—Herbert considers, if only briefly, the terrifying possibility that humans are merely playthings for the amusement of an antagonistic divinity.

The speaker refuses to respond to these experiences by "simpring all mine age," that is, by smiling through gritted teeth at the invidious actions of his sovereign. "Simpring," insists Herbert in "The Church-porch" (lines 123–24), "is but a lay-hypocrisie," that is, both an "unlearned form of hypocrisy" and "a layman's (courtier's) form of hypocrisy, with an agreeable appearance covering corruption."[45] By characterizing stoic sufferance as "lay-hypocrisie," he attempts to invest accusation with moral authenticity. Rather than hiding behind a cowardly and insincere simper, the speaker daringly chooses to present his sovereign with a catalog of the injustices he has experienced.

Despite his clever attempts to render complaint the only authentic response to such unfair treatment, the speaker's decision to arraign his superior involves a remarkable rupture of social decorum. The degree of this rupture can be gauged in some manner by the prescriptions of Angel Day, author of *The English Secretarie*. In one of the sample letters Day offers, the writer reveals himself to be in a situation very much like that outlined in "Affliction (I)." He complains to his superior that he has "neither skill to use that little you gave, nor will to raise my selfe after my fall"; furthermore, he laments that his "friends [are] decayed and dead."[46] Day warns that

> this kind of expostulating falleth most with persons of equalitie, for though it is scarce thought good manners, and sometimes held perilous to dispute of offenses with one far above us in authoritie . . . yet is the force thereof manie times carried from an inferiour to his better, neverthelesse with a kinde of aunswerable submission always respective to the other's reputation or greatness.[47]

Yet Herbert explicitly engages in this "perilous" discourse "with one far above in authoritie," and without the cloak of "aunswerable submission" Day recommends. Antony de Guevara likewise warns the courtier to

> shewe no countenaunce to the king of insatisfaction, neyther to be passioned in casting his service in the prynces teeth, saying all others have been recompensed save only him, whom the prince hath *cleane forgotten*. For princes will not that wee onely serve them, but that we also (at their willes and pleasures) tary for recompence.[48]

Herbert, however, does not hesitate, even in the poem's penultimate line, to assert that he has been "clean forgot" by his prince. In the last chapter we examined Herbert's epistolary anecdote of the Frenchman who complained about the size of the reward James had given him. Despite his intimate awareness of the dangers of such utterance—the Frenchman was banished from the court and ultimately committed to prison—Herbert here engages in a far more profound critique of the conduct of his sovereign, complaining not so much about the meagerness of his reward as the intensity of his suffering. James had admonished Parliament that "as to dispute what God may do is blasphemy . . . so is it sedition in subjects to dispute what a king may do in the height of his power."[49] Herbert, though, willingly accepts the danger of disputing the conduct of his "king" of "pleasures." By interrogating an authority both political and divine, he verges at once on blasphemy and sedition.

In the last two stanzas the present tense uncomfortably breaks through the narrative distance the poem attempts to achieve: "Now I am here."[50] The speaker claims his sovereign's past and future actions are completely unintelligible to him: "what thou wilt do with me / None of my books will show." He retreats temporarily into the wish for a natural, vegetative form of service: "I reade, and sigh, and wish I were a tree; / For sure then I should grow / To some fruit or shade." He attempts to convert his vegetative paralysis into a stoic acceptance of the status of subordination: "Yet though thou troublest me, I must be meek; / In weakness must be stout." But this stance is immediately obliterated by an explicit statement of the rebellion implicit in the accusatory mode of his narrative: "Well, I will change the service, and go seek / Some other master out." Herbert here gives full and frightening voice to the intense frustration bred by the perpetual experience of submission and prostration at the Jacobean court. The resentment seething just under the surface of Herbert's epigram on James's love, of his gossip-laden letter on the French writer, and of his oration on Charles's return from Spain, erupts here undiluted by ritual encomium. Remarkably, Herbert shouts at his divine monarch a degree of insurgence he could not even whisper in the presence of a Stuart king.

In doing so, Herbert exercises what Strier has shown to be one of the central tenets of Reformation theology: that "the regenerate . . . are entitled and encouraged to address God boldly and familiarly."[51] In "Affliction (I)," though, Herbert betrays a profound uneasiness with the furthest reaches of this privilege, and immediately recoils from the implications of his bold expostulation. The speaker mistakenly supposes that there is some other master worth serving, and that he could escape at will this former master's power. But contemporaneous English law, as well as societal mores voiced by Herbert, weigh heavily against this supposition. In *The Country Justice*, a work endorsed by Herbert in *The Country Parson*, Michael Dalton observes: "If a servant shall depart from his master, his master may take him againe, and reteine and keepe him whether he will or no."[52] Furthermore, in his final extant letter, written on the occasion of Arthur Woodnoth's contemplating withdrawal from the service of Sir John Danvers, Herbert reminds Woodnoth that "to Change [service] Shewes not well . . . Constancy is [of good report] & of great esteem wᵗʰ all" (p. 380). Yet it is precisely this powerful legal and consensual support for the constancy of a servant, despite the slender rewards of service, that the speaker of "Affliction (I)" proposes to ignore. In a sermon Donne praises David, who, though sorely afflicted, "changes not his Master but still applies himselfe to the Lord . . . He is not weary of attending the Lord, he is not inclinable to turn upon any other then the Lord."[53] But the speaker of "Affliction (I)," by contrast, considers at least briefly the possibility of serving another, more rewarding, master.

The image of a "slave who ran away from his master and chased a shadow instead" supplies Augustine with a prototype of the sinning self.[54] In considering another master, the speaker of "Affliction (I)" is likewise fleeing from his God. As if the perilous implications of his threat to serve another master occur to him in the moment of voicing it, the speaker immediately gasps: "Ah my deare God! though I am clean forgot, / Let me not love thee, if I love thee not." Paradox supplants paralysis. Because the phrase "though I am clean forgot" lacks an agent, it could be either a passive or a reflexive construction. As Ilona Bell asserts, the phrase "can be read either as a final criticism of God (though I have been completely forgotten and betrayed by you) or as a final confession (though I completely forgot myself, when I rebelled against you)."[55] The same words, then, function as apology and accusation. The conflation of such opposed intentions demonstrates the spiritual and political instability engendered by the inability to distinguish between heavenly and earthly service.

The final line nurtures such ambivalence into paradox. At once a request to be liberated from devout subservience to a figure of authority and a prayer to be made able to serve sincerely and without grudging, the final line fuses submission and opposition in a single syntactically and ideologically conflicted utterance.[56] Its deferential but confusing litotes seek both surrender to deity and release from servitude. 1 Cor. 16.22 reads: "If any man love not the Lord Jesus Christ, let him be Anathema Maranatha." The phrase "if I love thee not," then, considers the chilling possibility of the speaker as abomination to his God. The final line contains at once the devout wish to be blessed with the sincere love of God and the terrifying possibility of a self-imposed curse. Furthermore, the grammar of the two clauses in the final enigmatic line suggests two very different modes of being towards God. The if-clause posits a human ontology separate from divine will, while the let-clause entails an ontology of total dependence upon God. Syntactically and politically, the line vibrates between autonomy and contingency.

Louis Martz nevertheless finds in these lines a "sudden submission" which "demolishes the rebellion" that the poem contains.[57] Bell likewise argues that "these lines are the most trustworthy assertion: the speaker has never been forgotten by God's Providence, and he knows it . . . My rebellion was dastardly, he admits, but even when I forgot myself you remembered me; but I cannot bear the way I feel when my love makes me regret my behavior, so please, let me not love thee if I am going to act as if I love thee not."[58] Yet to read the poem in this morally optimistic way requires the rewriting of the poem's tortured close. "Affliction (I)" is not "Love unknown," where the voice of a friend tells the speaker that the afflictions imposed by his master show "more favour then you wot [know] of." Although vestiges of the speaker's language hint at the possibility of a salutary suffering—e.g., "sweetned pill" (line 47) and "crosse-bias" (line 53)— the poem refuses to collect such hints into a coherent account of the human experience of God. It explicitly resists the possibility of its own theological resolution. Donne remarks that "even afflictions are welcome, when we see them to be [God's]."[59] Herbert's poem briefly considers this attitude to affliction—"I must be meek"—but cannot sustain it. The poem concludes not by affirming the human capacity for love of God but rather by questioning it ("if I love thee not"). As Helen Vendler asserts, "Herbert has not so much resolved as ended his poem."[60] The haunting power of the poem derives from its refusal to be meek in the confrontation with an apparently adverse divinity. The double negatives of the final line register, as Barbara Harman maintains, "a resistance to closure, to complete and coherent self-representation, to knowledgeable statement."[61] Suspended uncomfortably between rebellion and submission, autobiography and art, politics and prayer, the poem confronts the chilling possibility of a malevolent divinity.

"Thou thoughtest that I was altogether such a one as thy selfe," declares the God of David in Psalm 50.21, "but I will reprove thee . . . " Beginning with the fusion of divine and earthly kingship and ending in complete spiritual confusion, "Affliction (I)" traces the savage direction of such reproval. The poem discloses the violation of attempting to socialize divine behavior, and the retribution with which God answers such attempts. Herbert's poetry, argues Strier, underscores "the difference between God's values and behavior and those of earthly lords." Strier emphasizes the manner in which poems like "Affliction (I)"—a poem he discusses only briefly— discover the immense differences between God and earthly superiors. "The notions of decorum in art and in social behavior," insists Strier, "are specialized applications of the concept of justice, of things or persons receiving their due." "The doctrine of faith alone," he argues, "outrages the demand for justice."[62] I would stress, however, that the impact of this divine disregard for courtly decorum hinges upon the powerful expectation that earthly standards of behavior do apply to heaven. The likenesses, that is, are frequently as striking as the differences to which they add force. Courtly decorum may be revealed as inadequate, but, as we saw with Hooker, it is not discarded entirely. If the behavior of his monarch at times "outrages the demand for justice," the theological knowledge that such outrage is inappropriate does not preclude Herbert's venting it. Throughout *The Temple* Herbert avails himself of the analogy between heavenly and earthly power in order to investigate the striking similarities and glaring differences between them.

Like "Affliction (I)," "Redemption" explores the manner in which God eclipses the social metaphors mortals generate about him. In this poem, however, such eclipse is disclosed as a beneficent, not a maleficent, gesture. "Redemption" also features an inferior who feels he is being treated unfairly by a superior. In this poem, however, the inferior never even gets to make his case. Because of the crucial difference between God and a mortal superior identified by Hooker—that is, his foreknowledge—the speaker's suit is granted before it is made. This gift enriches the speaker, allows him to thrive, but also impoverishes his primary mode of assertion toward the divine: petition. Where "Affliction (I)" chills because its penetrating cries are never answered, "Redemption," by contrast, disquiets because its urgent suit is never uttered. While tracing the movement from the Old to the New Testament, from the covenant of law to the covenant of grace, the poem also uncovers the rupture of social decorum inherent in human traffic with God.

The speaker presents himself as a "tenant . . . to a rich Lord." The adjective clues us in to the materialistic concerns of the speaker. By making a point of his lord's wealth, the speaker expresses some undue pride in the resources of his lord even as he suggests that this lord ought to be able to afford what he is about to ask of him. Discovering that he is "not thriving," the speaker resolves "to be bold, / And make a suit unto him, to afford / A new small-rented lease, and cancell th'old." Such a resolution involves a degree of boldness difficult for us to appreciate. Richard Baxter remarks on the subjugation of seventeenth-century tenants that "I believe that their great Landlords have more command of them than the King hath."[63] Renaissance tenants normally had a "choice" between paying steadily increasing rents or starving. Those occasions where they dared to complain about rent increases required extreme deference to defuse charges of presumption or rebellion.[64] The speaker of "Redemption," though, boldly seeks not to halt a rent increase but to decrease his current rent. His brazen desire for a "new small-rented lease" would have seemed a shocking violation of a divinely ordained social hierarchy.

He seeks his lord "in heaven at his manour" (a line only Herbert

could write, so effortlessly fusing the homely and the celestial),
where he is told that his lord is on earth "to take possession" of some
land "which he had dearly bought." Like a good Renaissance
magnate, this "rich lord" is busy consolidating his vast holdings. The
speaker, a "commonsensical character" in Strier's phrase, assumes
from his Lord's "great birth" that he would frequent the "great re-
sorts" of "cities, theatres, gardens, parks and courts," and accordingly
seeks him there.[65] The speaker supposes that his lord, like other
members of the gentry, has left the country for the joys of city life.[66]
But "at length," hearing "a ragged noise and mirth / Of theeves and
murderers," he unexpectedly spies his lord, "who straight, *Your suit
is granted*, said, & died." His lord was not inhabiting the "great re-
sorts" frequented by those of "great birth" but rather was surrounded
by "theeves and murderers." As Chauncey Wood asserts, "Now ten-
ant and lord have changed places. The 'rich Lord' dies in low worldly
surroundings, making the speaker richer than he had hoped."[67]

But is the speaker really "richer than he had hoped"? His suit is
granted, but at the cost of his expectations of socially decorous be-
havior on the part of his lord. As Strier remarks, "The conception of
the most glorious and powerful Being in the universe, the King of
Kings, dying a humiliating death among 'theeves and murderers'
violates decorum in a fundamental way."[68] What is more, the fore-
knowledge of his Lord prevents (in both senses, as in "The Thanksgiv-
ing") the speaker from the self-assertion that the act of suing would
effect. The beneficent omniscience the lord displays is indeed com-
mendable. As orator, Herbert praised Bacon for granting requests be-
fore they were uttered: "Thou indeed art always our patron, even
when we are silent; how much more when we make a request."[69] But
for one who has finally worked up the courage to address his superior
boldly, there is something slightly humiliating about having his suit
granted before it is spoken. The poem, then, underscores divine
power and human impotence even as the event it leads up to—the sac-
rifice of Christ—emphasizes the power, albeit temporary and illu-
sory, that humans exert over God. In Isaiah 65.24, God promises:
"And it shall come to passe, that before they call, I will answere, &
whiles they are yet speaking, I will heare." "Redemption" cogently
displays both the magnanimity and the deprivation implicit in the
fulfillment of this promise.

Richard Hooker defends "endowments and tithes" by arguing
"that unless by a kind of continual tribute we did acknowledge God's
dominion, it may be doubted that in short time men would learn to
forget whose tenants they are, and imagine that the world is their own

absolute free and independent inheritance."[70] For Hooker, tithes function as a symbolic rent which mortals pay to God in order to remind them of their dependence upon and subordination to him. But for Herbert, this economic model for divine-human relations is inadequate, even presumptuous. The title of the poem, as John Mulder observes, "is derived from the Latin *redimere*, 'to buy back.'"[71] The actual agent of the purchase is not the speaker, but Christ, "dearly buying" with his death not just the property for which the speaker wants a better lease but also the speaker himself. For Herbert, to pay rent to one's owner is not, as Hooker claims, a reminder of one's dependence but rather a sign of overweening *in*dependence. The speaker's wish for the relative independence of a renter vanishes in the discovery of his status as the unilateral recipient of God's benefits.

The poem, then, seems to support the view, put forward most powerfully by Lewalski and Strier, of Herbert's profoundly Protestant theology, in which mortals can neither oblige nor repay their God. Herbert, as Strier proposes, rejects the implicitly rationalistic bent of both Arminianism and Puritan covenant theology.[72] As the head of an inherently monopolistic enterprise, Herbert's God acts as the ultimate landlord, beneficently forcing mortals to abandon the possibility of a rational economic model for their own devotional gestures. But in "Redemption," the rejection is not as absolute as Strier contends. Even as "Redemption" reveals the complete inadequacy of the speaker's rational and economic expectations, it also suggests that the lord grants rather than repudiates the speaker's initial wish for a "small-rented lease." Although he has been wrong about everything else, the speaker's desire to imagine divine-human relations as an economic transaction is tacitly endorsed by the last words of his dying lord: "Your suit is granted." Even as the opportunity for human supplication is precluded by divine omniscience, then, the possibility of significant human activity towards the divine is reasserted in the notion of a lease, however "small" the rent. I do not want to overemphasize the importance of the granting of the lease; but it is a moment when Herbert quietly reintroduces an economic decorum between God and mortal whose larger structures he has repudiated. In doing so, Herbert glances at the possibility—generally denied in his poetry—of human activity separate from the divine. Perhaps it is just a further aspect of the divine benevolence the poem emphasizes that God occasionally indulges the misguided legal fictions of his befuddled creatures.

Where "Redemption" emphasizes the failure of earthly standards of decorum to encompass divine behavior, "Unkindnesse" applies the same standards to mortal conduct towards God, and likewise finds them wanting. In "Redemption," however, the gap between courtly expectation and divine behavior is a product of God's baffling mercy and willing condescension to his undeserving inferiors. In "Unkindnesse," by contrast, the gap results from the human inability to value God's benefits correctly. The poem begins by stating a principle of courtesy towards friends:

> In friendship, first I think, if that agree,
> Which I intend,
> Unto my friends intent and end.

Although he always considers the effect upon his friends before acting, the speaker fails to employ such thoughtfulness towards his greatest benefactor: "I would not use a friend, as I use Thee." The poem requires us to remember that friendship in the Renaissance was more involved in the world of political favors than we assume. As Lawrence Stone remarks, "the word did indeed often mean a loved one, . . . But it was also frequently used to mean not a person to whom one had some emotional attachment, but someone who could help one on in life, with whom one could safely do business, or upon whom one was in some way dependent."[73] The courtliness of the situations described in the poem, and the recurrence of the verb *use*, invigorate the utilitarian and materialistic meanings of the word.

After establishing the comparison between divine and mortal friendship that structures the poem, the speaker proceeds to catalog a variety of courtly situations in which he behaves unselfishly on behalf of a friend. Realizing the importance of reputation in his status-conscious culture, the speaker defends his friend's honor "from the least spot or thought of blame." Showing both his profound awareness of the increasing delicacy of Renaissance manners and his gracious willingness to overlook the indelicate conduct of those less aware, the speaker agrees to lend his friend money even after the friend has "spit upon my curious floore."[74] Finally, instead of "working the heads" to gain employment, as the young Herbert had done, the speaker withdraws from consideration for a "place" the friend seeks. In each case he opposes the "use" of mortal friends to the "use" of God. "Yet can a friend what thou hast done fulfill?" asks the speaker of the divine figure who has given all "onely to purchase my goodwill." Although his unselfish conduct towards undeserving mortal friends supplies a secular version of the sacrificial friendship practiced by God, the speaker behaves thoughtlessly towards his supremely deserving benefactor: "Yet use I not my foes, as I use Thee."

"The question of why the speaker fails to treat God as a friend," asserts Strier, "fades before the recognition that he treats Him worse than an enemy." Yet this does not mean, as Strier argues, that "the notion of 'friendship with God' has been shown to be an ill-conceived and fanciful speculation."[75] For friendship still supplies the standard against which both the speaker's discourteous conduct and the lord's essentially courteous behavior are gauged. The conduct of God is seen as the epitome rather than the repudiation of friendship.[76] It is the acquaintance who spits upon the speaker's floor that violates the decorum of friendship, not the God who dies for his creatures.

"Prayer (II)" similarly aligns courtly and heavenly activity, imagining God as a monarch who listens from his "throne" to the requests of his supplicants. Herbert praises God for the "easie quick accesse" he grants his subjects; God is a ruler whose "state dislikes not easinesse." As Strier declares, "anyone familiar with the protocol of the Elizabethan and Stuart English court will realize how sharp the implied contrast is."[77] Yet the admittedly sharp contrast does not preclude Herbert's frequent recourse to comparisons between the courts of earth and heaven. "As Princes are Gods," remarks Donne, "so their well-govern'd Courts, are Copies, and representations of Heaven."[78] In "H. Scriptures (I)," Herbert terms the Bible "heav'ns Lidger here, / Working against the states of death and hell." The Bible thus fulfills the role of heaven's resident ambassador to earth, a position akin to that held by Herbert's brother Edward in France from 1619–24; where Edward worked largely against the Catholic state of Spain, the Bible battles the dual states of death and hell. In "The Banquet," Herbert declares that God "found me on the ground," "low and short, / Farre from court," and "rais'd me to look up" via the Eucharist. Like some new favorite, Herbert is elevated and brought to court by his monarch. "The Starre" likewise envisions, in Elizabeth Stambler's phrase, a "very courtly heaven."[79] Herbert implores a falling star to take him "unto the place where thou / Before didst bow" and "get me a standing there, and place / Among the beams, which crown the face" of God. The star here fulfills the function of courtly mediator, like those "friends" in "Affliction (I)" whose loss the speaker laments, and those "heads" that Herbert pledges to "work" in the letter to his stepfather describing his search for employment. Employment at this court, Herbert reassures the star, will profit both of them; not only will it supply him with a position at court but also will provide the "joy" to the star of "gaining me / To flie home like a laden bee / Unto that hive of beams." Courtly position here functions as a vehicle of divine favor. The supplicatory tactics by which one acquires divine favor echo the manipulations of the patronage system that the young Herbert practiced.

Licensed by the preponderant imagery of service in the Bible, Herbert frequently deploys the model of service to a superior in his relations with divinity.[80] "Indeed mans whole estate / Amounts (and richly) to serve thee," remarks Herbert in "Mattens." Fascinatingly, a term denoting wealth and status ("estate") is yoked to a term denoting subordination ("serve"). Yet the difficulties of discovering the proper mode of serving God are not dissipated by such acts of translation. As Herbert remarks in "Miserie," "Man cannot serve thee; let him go, / And serve the swine." The immense differences between God and his creatures disable the metaphor of service for divine-human interactions. "How shall infection / Presume on thy perfection?" asks the speaker of "Miserie." The immense ontological difficulty of serving a being who is omnipotent, and so has no need of servants, is explored by George Ryley, Herbert's early eighteenth-century annotator, in his notes to "The Crosse":

> when Josue had told the people they must *fear the Lord and Serve Him*, & brought them to this Resolution *we will Serve the Lord, for He is our God*. Then he teaches them that they *Cannot Serve the Lord* Josh: 24:14, 18, 19. This our Author Calls a Cross.[81]

For Herbert, this contradictory imperative must have been particularly troubling. As a younger son on an apparently insufficient and often tardy annuity, Herbert necessarily experienced acute anxiety about his own employability. As we saw in our discussion of "Affliction (I)," the possibility of his own utter uselessness—"a blunted knife / Was of more use then I"—seems to have engendered some of Herbert's deepest fears. In a letter written to his mother ostensibly to comfort her in her illness, his own obsession with usefulness diverts Herbert from his appointed task: "For my self, *dear Mother*, I alwaies fear'd sickness more than death, because sickness hath made me unable to perform those Offices for which I came into this world" (p. 373).

Throughout *The Temple*, then, Herbert feels himself divided between the injunction to serve God and his inability to do so—a division which rehearses many of Herbert's own social anxieties relating to employment. The longing for employment, and the spiritual and political favor employment would represent, receives frequent and vehement articulation. I do not think, however, that the theme of employment in any way resolves itself into a "vocational sequence," as

Diana Benet and Marion Singleton have recently argued.[82] Rather, it recurs regularly as a model for Herbert's devotional hindrances and aspirations. Even the final offer of the speaker of the last lyric in *The Temple*—"My deare, then I will serve" from "Love (III)"—voices this wish for employment. Yet once more, this wish is repudiated by the impoverishing grace of divinity: "You must sit down, sayes Love, and taste my meat."

The speaker of "Employment (I)" desires to serve his God, wishing that "as a flowre doth spread and die, / Thou wouldst extend me to some good." Like a clever courtier, he appeals to the self-interest of his superior, showing that they both have much to gain by such employment:

> The sweetnesse and the praise were thine;
> But the extension and the room,
> Which in thy garland I should fill, were mine.

As in so many asymmetrical relationships in the Renaissance, the speaker promises to supply praise in return for employment. The situation seems so clearly in both of their interests that the speaker cannot comprehend why God has not yet hired him:

> Let me not languish then, and spend
> A life as barren to thy praise,
> As is the dust, to which that life doth tend . . .

Supplication, however, quickly modulates into lament, as the speaker complains of his unnecessary idleness:

> All things are busie; onely I
> Neither bring hony with the bees,
> Nor flowres to make that, nor the husbandrie
>   To water these.

> I am no link of thy great chain
> But all my companie is a weed.
> Lord place me in thy consort; give one strain
>   To my poore reed.

The Great Chain of Being is here revealed as a Great Chain of Service—a chain the speaker senses he is no part of.[83] Rather than the flower he hoped to resemble at the beginning of the poem, he is but a "poore reed," surrounded by weeds. Divine favor, he feels, would be manifested by gainful employment, being "place[d]" in God's "consort."

"Employment (II)" uses the botanical metaphor of the previous poem to utter a similar lament. The speaker wishes that he were

> an Orenge-tree,
> That busie plant!
> Then should I ever laden be,
> And never want
> Some fruit for him that dressed me.

Herbert feels his own inutility sinks him lower than the vegetable substratum of the natural world. "Even in Paradise man had a calling," remarks Herbert in *The Country Parson*, arguing "the necessity of a vocation" for all (*Works*, p. 274). One goal of *The Country Parson*, as Cristina Malcolmson argues, is to "create an identity out of a profession."[84] It is precisely this close connection between identity and profession that precipitates the overwhelming fear of uselessness haunting his social and spiritual existence.

In the poem "Providence," which celebrates "the wonderful providence and thrift of the great householder of the world" (*Works*, p. 241; the phrase is from *The Country Parson*), Herbert seems to discover a vocation for humanity in the Great Chain of Service:

> Of all the creatures both in sea and land
> Onely to Man thou hast made known thy wayes,
> And put the penne alone into his hand,
> And made him Secretarie of thy praise.

Our linguistic and conceptual gifts, Herbert suggests, render us the only species capable of praising God. As God's "secretarie," one enters into a relationship with God modelled closely on the social. It was common for an ambitious youth to serve a great lord as secretary on the way to a career at court. John Donne, for example, served as secretary to Sir Thomas Egerton before his infelicitous marriage to Egerton's young niece. Furthermore, the two University Orators at Cambridge prior to Herbert—Sir Robert Naunton and Sir Francis Nethersole—used the position "as 'a stepping-stone' to a career as a secretary of state."[85] The title Herbert bestows upon humanity, then—"Secretarie of Praise"—has powerful personal resonance, apparently answering his urgent need for spiritual and social employment.[86]

Yet towards the end of the poem, after a lengthy praise of God's ingenious husbandry, Herbert asks:

> But who hath praise enough? nay, who hath any?
> None can express thy works, but he that knows them:

> And none can know thy works, which are so many,
> And so complete, but onely he that owes them.

Understanding "owe" in its Renaissance sense of "own," one realizes that only God is qualified to offer his own praise because only he can "know and own" his works. The property of creation, as "Redemption" and "Obedience" make clear, belongs exclusively to God. But in the Renaissance, "owe" also conveyed its modern meaning of "debt" or "obligation"; and this debt accrues to mortals despite their inability to pay it. Praise, then, is an eternal obligation, a debt humanity owes but cannot requite. As Herbert remarks in "Miserie":

> My God, Man cannot praise thy name:
> Thou art all brightnesse, perfect puritie;
> The sunne holds down his head for shame,
> Dead with eclipses, when we speak of thee.
> How shall infection
> Presume on thy perfection?
>
> As dirtie hands foul all they touch,
> And those things most, which are most pure and fine:
> So our clay hearts, ev'n when we crouch
> To sing thy praises, make them lesse divine.

This is not the job description of an ideal "secretary of praise."

Yet, as Herbert adds, "either this, / Or none, thy portion is." God must take what he can get. "There is," asserts Stein, "a grim confrontation between 'My God, Man cannot praise thy name' and the bond [of praise] which God will not release."[87] As a consequence, the primary form of praising God is manifested as the expression of inadequacy for that office. Yet this was a tactic of praise used with some frequency by Herbert in the role of University Orator. Herbert begins a letter to James, for example, by proclaiming that "your infinite kindnesses to us not only exhaust all words, but even our thoughts," and closes by apologizing for the fact that "our acknowledgments scarcely answer to the greatness of (thy) kindnesses."[88] In the conclusion of "Providence," Herbert conjoins this rhetorical topos of inexpressibility with a theological sense of human inadequacy to produce a mode of praise which magnifies its divine object by demeaning the mortal subject.[89] Perhaps humanity is granted the office of "Secretary of Praise" because it is the only species capable of uttering its unworthiness for the position. The anxious assignment of accomplishing a task one is by definition incapable of performing precipitates the urgency of so many Herbert poems.

"The Odour, 2 Cor. 2.15" begins by relishing with a remarkable sensuality a language denoting subordination, and connoting serviceability, to God:

> How sweetly doth *My Master* sound! *My Master*!
> As Amber-greese leaves a rich sent
> Unto the taster:
> So do these words a sweet content,
> An orientall fragrancie, *My Master*.

Yet the biblical figure on which the poem is based—"we are unto God a sweet savour of Christ"—is as Chana Bloch observes "boldly reverse[d]" by Herbert "so that it is he, not God, who is breathing incense."[90] The reason for such boldness with the Bible, however, is not Herbert's spiritual confidence but rather his social insecurity. The speaker fears it would be presumptuous to imagine himself as pleasing to God. Indeed, as the third stanza makes clear, he longs for but is not yet involved in a relationship of service with his lord. God may be his master, but he is not God's servant:

> *My Master*, shall I speak? O that to thee
> *My servant* were a little so,
> As flesh may be
> That these two words might creep & grow
> To some degree of spicinesse to thee!

The speaker deeply desires to be sweet and serviceable to God, but this is made contingent not upon any action of his own but upon God's yet unannounced acceptance of him into his service. The speaker attempts to appeal to God's self-interest, but disguises this design partially through effusive deference ("shall I speak?"). He argues that God's accepting him as "my servant" would

> with gains by sweetening me
> (As sweet things traffick when they meet)
> Return to thee.
> And so this new commerce and sweet
> Should all my life employ, and busie me.

But this promised "commerce" of sweetness between him and God is in fact unilateral action on the part of God. God makes something sweet and then smells it. The optative mood of this last stanza, furthermore, reveals that the speaker must maintain the status of "a pretender, not a bride" ("The Size," line 36), hopeful but uncertain of being accepted into God's service. The poem may represent, as Bloch contends, Herbert's "freedom in the handling of biblical texts," but it also displays his trepidation about the mortal capacity to serve God.

"Submission" is a poem often cited to demonstrate Herbert's relinquishment of the desire for secular advancement, and his acceptance of the humbler mode of divine service. Leah S. Marcus, for example, argues that

> by the time he wrote "Submission" Herbert had clearly given up his earlier implicit belief that English church and state were part of [a] single unity: the Kingdom of God and the kingdom of James I and Charles I were not one organic whole, but two distinct realms serving contradictory ends.[91]

Perhaps. The poem is not in the Williams manuscript, and so we can presume that it was not written early in Herbert's career. Furthermore, the poem does exhibit far more tension between sacred and secular promotion than most of the poems we have been examining. Nevertheless, "Submission" continually oscillates between the unconditional surrender represented by the poem's title and a conditional negotiation with authority very much like that practiced in the courtly realm it aspires to relinquish. In *The Country Parson*, Herbert suggests that "ambition, or untimely desire of promotion to an higher state, or place, under colour of accommodation, or necessary provision, is a common temptation to men of any eminency" (p. 238). "Submission" shows just how seductive, and insidious, this temptation could be.

The poem's simple, common meter (remarkable in a volume so self-consciously filled with metrical ingenuity) represents formally the farewell to courtly tastes the poem intends to signal. But the fascinating thing about the poem is its insight into the way that every gesture of submission entails an equal and opposite reaction of insurrection, a process never fully achieving equilibrium. The first stanza, though, speaks as if rebellion were a possibility only in the past, before Herbert adopted his lord's perspective:

> But that thou art my wisdome, Lord,
>   And both mine eyes are thine,
> My minde would be extreamly stirr'd
>   For missing my designe.

Yet the donation of his eyes to God is premature. The memory of what he might feel precipitates what he does feel:

> Were it not better to bestow
>   Some place and power on me?

89

> Then should thy praises with me grow,
> And share in my degree.

As in "Employment (I)," Herbert seeks promotion via appeal to the self-interest of his superior. Raise me, he promises, and your praise will grow with the honors you give me.

The next stanza recoils from the implications of this courtly negotiation, labeling the premises on which it is based as "pilfring" and "Disseiz[ing] thee of thy right." He concedes that the terms of his promise may have been misleading:

> How know I, if thou shouldst me raise,
> That I should then raise thee?
> Perhaps great places and thy praise
> Do not so well agree.

Although these lines do acknowledge that secular and sacred employment may not automatically coincide, they do not indicate such careers are inevitably opposed. I would want to emphasize, furthermore, the force of the "perhaps" that introduces Herbert's hypothetical division of "great place" from the duty of praising God. It may be ironic understatement;[92] but it nevertheless suggests that Herbert is unwilling to separate unequivocally his own desire for place from the divine injunction to praise. "Do not so well agree," moreover, is an exceedingly roundabout way of saying "disagree," registering in its periphrasis the recalcitrance with which the message is being internalized. The rhythms of reluctance infiltrate the utterance of submission.

Even in the final stanza, where the speaker gets extremely close to the unadulterated submission he seeks, the kind of negotiation he claims to relinquish lingers amid the language of acceptance:

> Wherefore unto my gift I stand;
> I will no more advise:
> Onely do thou lend me a hand,
> Since thou has both mine eyes.

He promises to stop counselling his lord, yet he uses the prestative leverage implicit in the image of submission with which he began ("both mine eyes are thine") as a tool for continuing to counsel his lord. He sustains the fiction that his submission is a "gift" to God. Since I have given you both mine eyes, the speaker advises, the least you can do is "lend me a hand." With "onely," he signals that he is placing conditions on a submission he claims is unconditional.

Blending submission and stipulation, the request is much more humble than his initial imprecation, but not structurally different from it. Before he pleaded for help in getting a "great place," but here he seeks guidance from the God to whom he has donated both his eyes. Even in its quiet close, the poem teeters between the bargaining with which it began and the blind obedience to which it aspires.

The opening gambit of "Praise (I)" is to offer a far less disguised version of the delicate negotiations performed in "Submission":

> To write a verse or two is all the praise,
> > That I can raise:
> Mend my estate in any wayes,
> > Thou shalt have more.

The speaker promises God enhanced praise if God will only enhance the speaker's social situation. Yet even as his desire for increased status seems to endorse hierarchical aspiration, the poem curiously urges a vision of the social world where the very distinctions that anchor questions of "estate" are rendered irrelevant:

> Man is all weaknesse; there is no such thing
> > As Prince or King:
> His arm is short; yet with a sling
> > He may do more.

In its sketch of universal human debility, the poem considers the politically subversive possibility that "there is no such thing / As Prince or King." Compared with the divine monarch, the lines suggest, mortal royalty is a sham. Yet even then, human activity does not collapse into divine omnipotence; mortals are weak, but "with a sling . . . may do more." The poem shows how the power of God may be used both to reinforce and to level the gradations of the social hierarchy.

"God and Kings," remarks Donne, "are at a near distance, All *gods*; Magistrates, and inferiour persons are at a near distance, all *dust*."[93] "Praise (I)" provides a similarly divided perspective on the relationship between the earthly and celestial hierarchies. In "Praise (I)," the impulse to use the power of God to criticize all human pretension ultimately evaporates before the primary rhetorical goal of asking God for "more" (the word that ends each stanza). The poem is torn between its vision of human impotence and the rhetorical force it wishes to exercise. At other moments in *The Temple*, however, Herbert carefully nurtures this dual perspective on the relationship between divine and secular power into a powerful critique of all earthly distinction. "Praise (I)" is, like *The Temple* itself, an ideologically conflicted work. The image in "Praise (I)" of David—a lowly shepherd, but soon, of course, to become a king—defeating Goliath with a sling epitomizes the division in Herbert between the compelling ambition for earthly promotion, and the gripping fantasy of wielding the power of God to level and mock human social distinctions. As different as these two visions are, in both the weak are empowered, while "strength," in the words of "The Crosse," "doth sting."

Richard Strier has argued cogently for "the anti-elitism of the doctrine of faith alone"—a doctrine to which he demonstrates Herbert's allegiance.[94] This anti-elitism often assumes forms which are politically radical, and which rest uncomfortably next to the unmistakable elitism we have traced. The poem "Faith," as Strier maintains, praises its titular subject for its democratic capacity to level all social distinctions. Faith, Herbert asserts, is accessible to all, regardless of status or strength, so "now by Faith all arms are of a length; / One size doth all conditions fit." Faith accomplishes this by elevating the humble and humbling the proud:

> A peasant may beleeve as much
> As a great Clerk, and reach the highest stature.
> Thus dost thou make proud knowledge bend & crouch,
> While grace fills up uneven nature.

Although nature, Herbert concedes, is "uneven," grace counterbalances such advantages. "Content" likewise envisions the irrelevance of social distinction; in this poem, however, death and decay rather than grace and faith are the agents of social levelling:

> The brags of life are but a nine dayes wonder;
> And after death the fumes that spring
> From private bodies make as big a thunder,
> As those which rise from a huge King.[95]

This grisly reminder of the dissolution of all flesh—akin to Hamlet's tracing Alexander's remains to the loam that plugs a bunghole—offers a striking vision of the ultimate equality exposed by our common mortality. The careerist corollary to this vision is the poem's idealization of

> the pliant minde, whose gentle measure
> Complies and suits with all estates;
> Which can let loose to a crown, and yet with pleasure
> Take up within a cloisters gates.

The poem's vision of decay also dissolves the distinction between aiming at (the meaning of "let loose to," a term from archery) a crown and retreating from the world to find pleasure in a cloister.

In "The Sacrifice," the suffering Christ reveals that "mans scepters," the image of his monarchical power, "are as frail as reeds" (line 177). "Peace," by contrast, exposes not the impotence but the rottenness just beneath the surface of symbols of sovereignty. The speaker looks for peace at the root of "a gallant flower, / The Crown Imperiall," only to discover "a worm devour[ing] / What show'd so well." Sidney Gottlieb appropriately calls attention to "the stunning irony and critical force of Herbert's use of the 'Crown Imperiall' to suggest that the royal powers in England were not capable of bringing the country to true peace."[96] Such tacit censure of monarchical power gives moral force to the enigmatic prayer of "Church-musick," "God help poore Kings." Even "The Sonne," Herbert's sonnet in praise of the English language for giving "one onely name / To parents issue and the sunnes bright starre," importantly ignores the connotations of royal magnificence present in its central image in order to focus on "our Lords humilitie." By rejecting the politicization of this symbol, Herbert tacitly resists the encroachment of absolute monarchy.

Although the poems of *The Temple* carefully align their motives and concerns with courtly practices, then, they also record a sporadic but striking series of anti-hierarchical and anti-authoritarian sentiments. For a younger son, prevented by the custom of primogeniture and an accident of birth from inheriting the family fortune, there must have something psychologically satisfying in utterances such as *Lucus* 17, "On a Proud Man," where Herbert reminds a haughty aristocrat "That thou possessest the same flesh and blood / As artisans; that cobbler, if you choose, / Who for your humblest serving-boy makes shoes!"[97] "The Quip" similarly pokes fun at a figure infatuated by the appurtenances of courtly pretension and scornful of all inferiors:

> Then came brave Glorie puffing by
> In silks that whistled, who but he?
> He scarce allow'd me half an eie.

The supercilious half-glance of this figure records the not-so-hidden injuries of class, while his clothes exhibit the social privilege that encourages such disdain.

Yet Walton records that the young Herbert "kept himself too much retir'd, and at too great a distance with all his inferiours: and his cloaths seem'd to prove, that he put too great a value on his parts and

Parentage."[98] If so—and Walton is a bit more reliable when dealing with Herbert's flaws than he is when constructing his legend of Herbert's saintliness—Herbert was at least in his youth implicated in the forms of social pretension that he mocks in his caricature of "brave Glorie." In *The Country Parson*, Herbert ventriloquizes in order to mock the sentiments of "the Gallant," who, when told he must not be idle, "is ready to ask, if he shall mend shoos, or what shall he do?" (p. 275). But as Malcolmson remarks, "the parson attacks Herbert's own 'gallant' proclivities here, that attraction to wit, fashion, and social rank recorded in 'The Pearl' and his early letters."[99] Likewise, the volume of poems that reviles social pretention is, as Ivan Earle Taylor has argued, "concerned to a remarkable degree with interests generally associated with the cavaliers: wine, game, women, sophisticated conversation, dress, and the like."[100] Herbert's style, declares L. C. Knights, involves "the well-bred ease of manner of 'the gentleman.'"[101] *The Temple* is not *Hesperides*; but the poems of *The Temple* practice to a surprising degree the social biases they castigate. In "Avarice," for example, the aristocratic speaker snobbishly disdains money because its "parentage is base and low." Likewise, "Hope," as Empson asserts, draws its structure "from the life of secular ambition, since the notion of exchanging presents suggests Court ceremonial and modes of obtaining preferment."[102] Even those poems that attempt to turn from the court do so in courtly terms. In "The Priesthood," Herbert restates and revises his own aristocratic disdain for the lowborn in his amazement that "wretched earth," ground "Where once I scorn'd to stand," can be used to make dishes "for the boards of those / Who make the bravest shows." "The Pearl," a poem about exchanging the apparent riches of this world for the authentic opulence of heaven, is filled, in Joseph Summers's phrase, with "courtly boasting";[103] moreover, the vehicle by which God leads Herbert from earth to heaven is a "silk twist"—the same fabric worn so loudly by "brave Glorie" in "The Quip." Even the stanza from "The Elixir" that is so often marshalled to show Herbert's antielitist work ethic—

> A servant with this clause
> Makes drudgerie divine:
> Who sweeps a room, as for thy laws,
> Makes that th' action fine.

—represents, as Christopher Hill contends, "a point of view more common among employers and independent craftsmen than among employees."[104] The poems of *The Temple* keep swerving towards the class-consciousness of the social hierarchy even as they try to turn away from it. The court, that lodestone of power and ambition explored in "Affliction (I)," continues to exercise its pull on Herbert's poetic.

In the postscript to an elaborately deferential letter written by Herbert in 1618–19, when he was deeply engaged in "working the heads," to Lancelot Andrewes, a powerful social superior as well as an important member of the religious hierarchy, the lines of force drawing the young Herbert towards and away from the court can be traced.[105] Herbert tries to have it both ways, distancing himself from courtly pretension by means of gestures whose elegance is the essence of courtliness. "Forgive, most illustrious lord," begins Herbert, "that my pronouns move along so boldly in this epistle: I could have stuffed the lines full of 'honours, magnificences, highnesses'; but, as it seems to me, Roman elegance does not suffer it."[106] Herbert apologizes so profusely for his lack of bombast that the apology itself becomes the kind of bombast it rejects. "I preferred to do service to thine ears," explains Herbert, "than to indulge the extravagance of the age and the excrescence of ambition, not so far cured by our most excellent King but that it swells and exalts itself every day." The letter both engages in and reproves a concern with titular distinction and political aspiration, flattering its addressee's indifference to the pomp it practices.

In the letter of comfort to his ailing mother, written just a few years later in 1622, while he was deeply engaged in his duties as University Orator, Herbert far more blatantly attacks a preoccupation with social distinction. Under the pretext of comfort, Herbert comes very close to reproaching his mother for being too concerned with her "Estate":

> For those [afflictions] of Estate? of what poor regard ought they to be, since if we had Riches we are commanded to give them away: so that the best use of them is, having, not to have them.—But perhaps being above the Common people, our Credit and estimation calls on us to live in a more splendid fashion?—but, Oh God! how easily is that answered, when we consider that the Blessings in the holy Scripture, are never given to the rich, but to the poor. I never find Blessed be the Rich; or, Blessed be the Noble; but, *Blessed be the Meek*, and *Blessed be the Poor*. (*Works*, p. 373)

Strier finds in this letter "a great breath of moral and religious clarity, of true ingenuousness" when compared with the worldly "Churchporch."[107] The letter throws into relief the inevitable contradictions between a social hierarchy which values wealth, birth, and privilege and a spiritual hierarchy which the poor and the meek shall inherit. "Gold and grace did never yet agree," remarks Herbert in "The Church Militant," "Religion alwaies sides with povertie" (lines 251–52). "He that hath little is the less durtie," observes one of Herbert's proverbs, inverting the conventional Renaissance linkage between cleanliness and social status (no. 436, p. 336).

The *Memoriae Matris Sacrum*, the long Latin and Greek poem of mourning Herbert writes on his mother's death in 1627 (it is published that year with Donne's funeral sermon), betrays the sense of strain between a Christian and a social self that emerges in the epistle of comfort to his mother. Herbert remembers his mother as one who contained "the fiery contention / Of lord and commoner alike"; she was, he asserts, "Proud / And meek at once."[108] In her death, then, Herbert can idealize Magdalene Herbert as one who unified the social forces that seem so contrary in the epistle. The relationship between these forces, however, is not imagined as a harmonious blending but rather as a "fiery contention." The *Memoriae*, moreover, signals the immense difficulty Herbert has in linking his own subjectivity to the world of politics. "We weep / And mourn," he writes, "While . . . The king equips a fleet for great / Enterprise. Yet we weep . . . Tilly pursues the Danes, / The French pursue the sea; we / Pursue tears. Those royal with us / Have only these for code and sign / Among themselves."[109] As in the gossip-laden letter to Harley, Herbert records political events. But here such recounting signals not a tacit negotiation between self and world but rather a frightening separation between interior experience and worldly affairs. The edges of the hierarchy begin to blur through Herbert's grief-stricken perspective, as national events and religious wars are reduced to "codes and signs" among "those royal with us." This last phrase quietly presupposes another world of monarchy whose power mocks the purportedly grand schemes of this one.

Many of the *Outlandish Proverbs* Herbert collected encompass an outright attack on the exploitation built into the social hierarchy. Perhaps because their provenance is by definition so common, so far from the centers of power and status at court, proverbs supply Herbert with an alternative to and critique of courtly discourse.[110] "The dainties of the great are the teares of the poore," remarks one, suggesting, like the Lady in Milton's *Comus*, that the luxury and excess of the rich are achieved at the expense of the indigent (no. 937, p. 352). "The great," observes Herbert in another proverb, "put the little on the hooke," implying that the socially powerful only use the underprivileged as bait; the great do not even condescend to consume the little, but only use them to angle for fish more worthy of their refined palates.[111] The social version of the natural hierarchy celebrated in "Providence" was certainly not always benign for Herbert.

Another of his proverbs envisions social relations as an unending class struggle: "The great would have none great and the little all little" (no. 946, p. 352). The exclusivity of the rich and the levelling tendencies of the poor are perceived to be in perpetual conflict. Indeed, in *The Crucifying of the world*, Richard Baxter invokes Herbert as an authority for his own criticism of the gentry: "Some we have of our Nobility and Gentry that are Learned, Studious and Pious . . . But Oh how numerous are the sensual and prophane which provoked that heavenly Poet, of Noble extract (Mr. *G Herbet* [sic], *Ch. porch*) to say,"

> O England! full of sinne, but most of sloth;
> Spit out thy flegme, and fill thy brest with glorie:
> Thy Gentrie bleats, as if thy native cloth
> Transfus'd a sheepishnesse into thy storie:
>> Not that they all are so; but that the most
>> Are gone to grasse, and in the pasture lost.[112]

This stanza from "The Church-porch" (lines 91–96) functions for Baxter as a criticism of the indolence of the gentry—an indolence produced by the practice of enclosing common lands for the raising of sheep to supply the burgeoning English cloth industry. The citation is all the more effective because, as Baxter points out, Herbert himself was "of Noble extract." Baxter admires the audacity Herbert displays in admonishing the gentry in "The Church-porch," prefacing his quotation of several stanzas of this hortatory poem by remarking that Herbert "was so bold with the English gentry (when, they say, they were much wiser and better than they are now) as to bespeake them thus."[113] Yet Herbert's criticism of country privilege does not of course preclude his casting a deprecatory eye on court life. A proverb collected by Herbert identifies the strange sense of claustrophobic isolation that the omnipresent treachery of court life breeds: "So many men in Court, and so many strangers" (no. 874, p. 350). "Dotage" mocks "the folly of distracted men" who mistakenly prefer "a lothsome den / Before a court, ev'n that above so cleare." Perplexingly, the line momentarily seems to endorse court over country life before identifying earthly courts with the den to which they are initially contrasted.

Malcolmson argues that *The Country Parson* "was born in the disjunction between Herbert's need for clear, identity-defining boundaries, and the inability of the hierarchical class structure to provide them."[114] Nevertheless, the terms by which *The Country Parson* inscribes religious identity are derived precisely from the hierarchical class structure. A country parson, Herbert remarks, is the "Viceregent" of Christ, and "may do that which Christ did, and by his auctority" (p. 225). "The pulpit," remarks Herbert, is the parson's "joy and throne" (p. 232). The parson is to use "exhortations" to his congregation, a rhetorical strategy which "he cals his privy purse, even as Princes have theirs, besides their publick disbursments."[115] "The Countrey Parson," observes Herbert, "is in Gods stead to his Parish . . . Wherefore there is nothing done either wel or ill, whereof he is not the rewarder, or punisher" (p. 254). The parson, then, assimilates unto himself the very structures of authority that his presence is supposed to reprove. By "the stupifying and deading of all the clamorous powers of the soul," the parson becomes "an absolute Master and commander of himself" (p. 227). In doing so, the parson performs the activity for which the speaker of "The Temper (II)" seeks divine assistance—ordering the unruly powers of the self. The parson, Herbert remarks, "counts it the art, and secret of governing to preserve a directnesse, and open plainnesse in all things" (p. 240). Wittily fusing Machiavellian cunning with Christian virtue, Herbert locates the *arcana imperii* in the covert deployment of openness.[116] Remarkably, the parson's complete submission to divine authority bestows upon him great authority in the community: "The Countrey Parson desires to be all to his Parish, and not onely a Pastour, but a Lawyer also, and a Phisician" (p. 259). The parson is to avoid sin not only because of its moral depravity but also because of its social consequences; by sinning, the parson "disableth himself of authority *to reprove*" sinners. Sin is to be resisted because "sins make all equall," eradicating the regal power the post confers (p. 227).

This assimilation of social power licenses a kind of boldness towards superiors unavailable to others. Country parsons

> are not to be over-submissive, and base, but to keep up with the Lord and Lady of the house, and to preserve a boldness with them and all, even so farre as reproofe to their very face, when occasion cals, but seasonably and discreetly. They who do not thus, while they remember their earthly Lord, do much forget their heavenly. (p. 226)

Obedience to the heavenly lord enables and indeed requires a kind of arrogance towards earthly lords which the young Herbert could only dream of acting out. The exercise of boldness towards social superiors is an exorcism of the aggression that lingers among Herbert's gestures of submission to divine authority.[117] A Herbert all too familiar with the attention-mongering of the aristocracy advises that "if there be any of the gentry or nobility of the Parish, who somtimes make it a piece of state not to come at the beginning of service with their poor neighbours, but at mid-prayers," the parson is to present them to the bishop for discipline because "the debt and obligation of his calling" is "to obey God rather then men" (p. 232). Conversely, the parson "welcomes to his house any Minister, how poor or mean soever, with as joyfull a countenance, as if he were to entertain some great Lord" (p. 253). The parson is to overcome "the generall ignominy which is cast upon the profession" by "a bold and impartial reproof, even of the best in the Parish, when occasion requires: for this may produce hatred in those that are reproved, but never contempt either in them, or others" (p. 268). Where boldness towards authority was a kind of insurrection in "Affliction (I)," in *The Country Parson* Herbert translates such boldness into an act of obedience to a higher authority.

Yet at Bemerton, Herbert's activities are not as different from those of the courtly youth as most readers have supposed. As Malcolmson asserts, "Herbert may have understood his transition from urban gentleman to country parson as primarily a shift from a social to an ecclesiastical elite."[118] A close reading of his will suggests that Herbert had at least four maids and two male-servants in his employ.[119] Life in the country was certainly no retreat from the hierarchical distinctions on which life at court thrived. Nor was it even that far from the centers of power. Bemerton is walking distance to Wilton House, inhabited by his kinsman Philip Herbert, the fourth earl of Pembroke, to whose patronage Herbert probably owed his parsonage.[120] Throughout *The Country Parson* Herbert imposes upon his congregation a regulation of body and behavior that is continuous with courtly self-control. The parson, for example, "having often instructed his people how to carry themselves in divine service, exacts of them all possible reverence, by no means enduring either talking, or sleeping, or gazing, or leaning, or halfe-kneeling, or any undutifull behaviour in them, but causing them, when they sit, or stand, or kneel, to do all in a strait, and steady posture" (p. 231). Likewise, their answers are "to be done not in a hudling, or slubbering fashion, gaping, or scratching the head, or spitting even in the midst of their answer, but gently and pausably." This close attention to manner suggests that Herbert viewed his mission in the country as part of a larger "civilizing process."

In the writings from Bemerton, moreover, we see Herbert still "working the heads," just as he had in order to be elected University

Orator eleven years earlier. Herbert's translation of Luigi Cornaro's *Treatise of Temperance and Sobrietie* was accomplished "at the request of a Noble Personage."[121] Herbert writes to Lady Anne Clifford, wife of the earl of Pembroke, to thank her for "admitting our poor services" (p. 376). He corresponds with his brother Henry—now Master of Revels—to express his joy that he "used" Henry (the verb that recurs in "Unkindnesse" for action towards "friends") in petitioning the duchess of Lenox, and to suggest that "your offering of yourself to move my Lords of Manchester and Boollingbrook is very welcome to mee" (p. 377). A postscript to a letter to Nicholas Ferrar praises the work of Henry Herbert in "moving the Duches's heart, to an exceeding cheerfulness, in signing 100 *lib.* with her own hands (& promising to get her Son to doe as much)" (p. 379). The goal of such manipulation of the patronage network is no longer great place but rather the rebuilding of the decayed church at Leighton Bromswold. Courtliness, though, is not repudiated; like the images of regal authority with which Herbert conveys the parson's power, it is appropriated for sacred ends.

In "The Forerunners," though, Herbert records not his appropriations of royal power but rather the force with which royal power finally appropriates him. Like "The Temper (II)," "The Forerunners" is about, in the words that Herbert used to praise Valdesso's *Considerations,* the "observation of Gods Kingdome within us, and the working thereof" (*Works,* p. 305). But where "The Temper (II)" had celebrated God's entry into the self as the principal of order that made subjectivity bearable, "The Forerunners" bemoans the great costs of entertaining a monarch whose omnipresence necessarily occupies every chamber of the self. The poem begins colloquially and informally: "The harbingers are come. See, see their mark; / White is their colour, and behold my head." As Hutchinson notes, "Harbingers were sent in advance of a royal progress to purvey lodgings by chalking the doors."[122] The white hair of the poet is rendered as the mark by which the servants of a monarch scouted accommodations. The signs of old age are the harbingers of approaching death, a state which will finally unite the speaker and his king. Yet as the next lines demonstrate, this visit from his monarch is not for the poet a consummation devoutly to be wished but rather a usurpation of his individual rights:

> But must they have my brain? must they dispark
> Those sparkling notions, which therein were bred?
> Must dulnesse turn me to a clod?
> Yet have they left me, *Thou art still my God.*

The marks signal not only the approach of death but also the onset of senility, and the incumbent loss of poetic power. Rather than engaging in the inherently authoritative act of writing, the poet must become the sheet for receiving another's mark. The poet's brain must ruefully be emptied to accommodate the approaching king. Daniel Featley prays after receiving communion, "Enter high Lord of heaven and earth; take possession of all my inner roomes."[123] Herbert, by contrast, dreads total annexation by his king, and wants to keep at least one room to himself. In *Lucus* 15, "Martha; Mary," Herbert imagines welcoming Christ in terms of bustling household activity: "Christ is here. Sweep up the rooms, / Shake out the curtains, let a fire / Light the hearth. All should be clean . . . "[124] But in "The Forerunners," the approach of his king means for Herbert the literal and metaphorical death of the self.

Herbert, then, imagines himself as potential host to a monarch on a royal progress. The regret he feels at the approach of his king resembles the trepidation with which Renaissance English nobles greeted their monarch. Both Elizabeth and James loved to circulate with their vast trains about the English countryside in the summer, visiting homes of the nobility. As Lawrence Stone shows, it was very costly to entertain these monarchs, who "expected to be richly feasted and elaborately amused, and to be sent on their way with expensive parting gifts."[125] Fearing such exorbitant expenses, many "noblemen abandoned their homes and fled at the mere rumour of [the monarch's] approach." "In 1608," Stone relates, "King James threatened a descent upon Northamptonshire 'as unwelcome as raine in harvest,' and the prudent Lord Spencer promptly fled to Kent."[126] Although anyone seeking favor at court could ill afford to be inhospitable, few nobles could afford the high price of royal entertainment. The ambivalence Herbert feels at the approach of his divine monarch is akin to what a Renaissance noble must have experienced at the approach of a mortal sovereign. Although a mark of royal favor, visitation by a monarch also entailed a loss of power and a diminution of resources. Just as nobles could be bankrupted by the vast costs of entertaining a sovereign, so will Herbert's mental and lyric resources be impoverished by the visit of his king.

The tone of the second stanza changes from regret at what is being conscripted to gratitude for the one room that this monarch's servants have left him.

> Good men ye be, to leave me my best room,
> Ev'n all my heart, and what is lodged there:

> I passe not, I, what of the rest become,
> So *Thou art still my God*, be out of fear.

Although they have marked his brain for royal habitation, they have left him his heart, and the italicized profession of trust in and devotion to God that inhabits it. While the "sparkling" notions of his brain will be "disparked" to make room for this king, Herbert reassures the prosaic expression "Thou art still my God" that its habitation in the heart will be left untouched. Locating lyric and moral value in the heart rather than the head, Herbert praises the royal servants as "Good men" for leaving him his "best room."

Yet the poem does not really privilege the heart over the head in the way these lines seem to suggest. Of the expression "Thou art still my God," Herbert writes:

> He will be pleased with that dittie;
> And if I please him, I write fine and wittie.

The intentionally dreadful lyric quality of these lines—two of the most jangling Herbert ever wrote—not only suggests that the process of mental enfeeblement the speaker dreads may have already begun but also identifies the ultimate arbiter of aesthetic judgment as the approaching king. Richard Strier likens these lines to the situation of "A true Hymne," where the phrase *My joy, my life, my crown* can, "If truly said, . . . take part / Among the best in art."[127] But in "A true Hymne," the sincerity of the speaker rather than the judgment of authority determines the "finenesse" of an utterance: "The finenesse which a hymne or psalme affords, / Is, when the soul unto the lines accords." In "The Forerunners," though, "finenesse" is solely a product of pleasing divine authority. Perhaps what pleases such authority is sincerity, but that is not what Herbert says in "The Forerunners." Rather, by stressing the need to please authority, Herbert identifies the divide between aesthetic judgment and political authority that frustrated so many Renaissance writers. As the eccentric or bad taste of one in authority could (and did) make or break the career of a poet in the Renaissance court—one thinks of Spenser and Burleigh—so in "The Forerunners" does Herbert suggest the absolute power of his monarch to arbitrate aesthetic quality.

The two middle stanzas on the erotic origins of his devotional terminology (which I explore in more detail in the final chapter) sustain the tone of regret initiated in the first two, converting the poet's farewell to his poetic powers into a scenario of amorous leave-taking. "But will ye leave me thus?" asks Herbert of the "sweet phrases, love-

ly metaphors" to which he had devoted so much effort, echoing Wy-
att's famous song of sexual betrayal. The arrival of his king also
signals the parting of something very dear to him. The absoluteness
of the encroachment of divine power upon the self is measured in the
speaker's declaration that "My God must have my best, ev'n all I
had." Although the forerunners leave Herbert his "best room," his
God must ultimately have his "best," even "all." The sexual scenario
quickly evolves into a question of the relationship between language
and its subject—a relationship which for Herbert, as "Jordan (I)"
makes clear, is always political.

> True beautie dwells on high; ours is a flame
> > But borrow'd thence to light us thither.
> Beautie and beauteous words should go together.

The philosophical vision is similar to that expressed in "Love (II),"
where Herbert imagines the unification of immortal love and the
conventions of secular love poetry as a political restoration and an act
of social submission: "Thou shalt recover all thy goods in kinde, /
Who wert disseized by usurping lust: / All knees shall bow to thee."
But instead of the powerful prophecy of "Love (II)," "The Forerun-
ners" can only suggest tentatively that this unification *should* occur.
Ironically, the approach of the truly beautiful king whom beauteous
words should praise evicts the beauteous words from the poet's vo-
cabulary.

In the final stanza, Herbert's welcome of his approaching monarch
is manifested as a final farewell to his poetic powers:

> Yet if you go, I passe not; take your way:
> For, *Thou art still my God*, is all that ye
> Perhaps with more embellishment can say.
> Go birds of spring: let winter have his fee;
> > Let a bleak palenesse chalk the doore,
> So all within be livelier then before.

Yet the resignation is tinged with regret. As Louis Martz remarks:
"But what a world of reservation lies in that one word, so emphati-
cally placed: 'Perhaps'!"[128] Like the crucial "perhaps" in "Submis-
sion" ("Perhaps great places and thy praise / Do not so well agree"),
the word here leaves ajar the door the poem intends to close abso-
lutely. "Does it qualify 'all that ye can say' or 'with more embellish-
ment'?" asks Fish. "In one reading, the claims made for lovely lan-
guage are revived, in the other they are further diminished since even
the *ornamental* value of language is questioned."[129] The poem's con-

cessions, like its farewells, linger fondly over the material they should reject outright. Furthermore, even the gestures of acceptance are uttered as *fiat*'s, in the syntactic form through which regal and divine power most commonly makes known and exercises its will. Strier remarks on the "contrast between outdoor cold and indoor coziness" in these lines, but does not question whether this contrast belies the harmony of appearance and reality, of "beautie and beauteous words," for which the middle stanzas long.[130] The opportunity for such coziness, moreover, would be fulfilled only under a sovereign who does not demand "all." But Herbert's God "must have my best, ev'n all I had." Even interiority is his territory.

The tone of wistfulness with which the speaker meets this territorial claim is amplified in the poem's reference to another occasion on which doorways are marked: the Passover, when the mark of blood diverted the plague of God from the children of Israel. In a locution peculiar to this poem, Herbert twice uses the word "passe" meaning "care" ("I passe not," lines 9 and 31) to solidify this connection. Herbert does this because he wishes in some ways that he too could be passed over by his God. So careful to record the deep psychological and political costs of the entry of his king, Herbert registers his ambivalence about this moment by implicitly aligning it with an occasion when divine favor was demonstrated not by entry but by disregard. Part of him would like to be, in the words of "Affliction (I)," "clean forgot," for only by being passed over by his king could all within him really be livelier than before. The "resolute uneasiness" Fish locates in his fine account of the poem is fulfilled in its typological confusion of heavenly blessing and divine plague.[131] With Herbert's God, it is sometimes difficult to distinguish between them.

Unlike the restless oscillation between acceptance and resignation in "The Forerunners," "The Collar" successfully moves from a sense of violent frustration to a statement of genuine submission. The poem begins where "Affliction (I)" ends, with a gesture of vehement rage against an authority at once social and spiritual: "I struck the board, and cry'd, No more. / I will abroad." In "The Collar," however, the authority is not addressed directly until the final two words of the poem. The desire to escape the hold of an oppressive and unrewarding superior is translated into a wish to leave the country. "Ambition," maintains Francis Bacon, "is like choler."[132] "The Collar" investigates the relationship between these two dispositions, showing how frustrated ambition precipitates choleric rage. The speaker imagines that he possesses the capacity for a kind of speech unencumbered by the authoritarian pressures shaping "Jordan (I)," "To all Angels and

Saints," and "Affliction (I)": "What? shall I ever sigh and pine? / My lines and life are free; free as the rode, / Loose as the winde, as large as store." As most readers have noted, the lines themselves seem to participate in the freedom the poet imagines. Yet the word "store" signals the first rhyme of the poem, designating the implicit order encompassing the speaker's rebellion. For Herbert, there is no truly free speech. As Joseph Summers remarks, the poem offers "a formalized picture of chaos."[133] It allows the energies of freedom and rebellion to play themselves out in order to produce the authentic recoil of the poem's close. The speaker may never go abroad, but he does push the devotional lyric into unexplored territory.

The speaker's social and spiritual frustrations come to a head in his bitter question: "Shall I be still in suit?" The word "suit," contends Geoffrey Hart, "carries the sense of enforced attendance, the attitude of a courtier who has little to hope for."[134] The experience of a frustrated courtier blends here with the attitude of a disappointed religious supplicant. Both situations infer the presence of the authority the poem refuses, until its final two words, to address. For Hart, however, the word "still" indicates that "the speaker . . . is not in suit before a secular prince: his suit is before a supernatural king, and is to be decided by transcendent laws."[135] The distinction between secular and supernatural kingship, however, is not so easily established. The primary meaning of "still" is "always." In this sense, Herbert's question restates his earlier query, "shall I *ever* sigh and pine?" The situation of one who must continually petition a superior without satisfaction is far from unique to the spiritual realm; indeed, in *Mother Hubberd's Tale*, Spenser finds such apparently endless supplication to be the essence of his own courtly experience:

> What hell it is, in suing long to bide:
> To loose good dayes, that might be better spent;
> To wast long nights in pensive discontent
> To speed to day, to be put back to morrow;
> To feed on hope, to pine with feare and sorrow . . .
> To fawne, to crowche, to waite, to ride, to ronne,
> To spend, to give, to want, to be undone.[136]

The speaker of "The Collar" knows too well "what hell it is in suing long to bide." He impatiently wishes to break free of a system, both political and spiritual, which requires perpetual and unrequited supplication.

The word "still," of course, can also mean "silent," suggesting the meek patience with which he must accept the failure of his suits. To be silent and to be always in suit are equally tortuous and equally fruitless options. Silence, moreover, would demand finally the erasure of the creative self, the self that wants at least to hang onto the fictive activity of "making" unsuccessful suits. The speaker is not silent but chooses rather to speak as if in a private space where even God could not overhear. In so doing, the speaker demonstrates the depth of his despair even as he unearths the deep divisions within himself. The poem is an act of self-interrogation, a series of rhetorical questions in which the speaker queries the very terms on which he has organized his life:

> Have I no harvest but a thorn
> To let me bloud, and not restore
> What I have lost with cordiall fruit?
> > Sure there was wine
> Before my sighs did drie it: There was corn
> > Before my tears did drown it.
> Is the year onely lost to me?

The colloquy, as many readers of the poem have remarked, is imbued with sacred imagery. "Rode," for example, suggests not only the open highway but also the "rood" cross. Likewise, words such as "board," "harvest," "thorn," "bloud," "fruit," and "wine" carry a striking amount of religious baggage. Yet it is difficult to know just what to make of this phenomenon. For Louis Martz, the speaker uses such imagery as a conscious "blasphemy," intentionally accomplishing a "worldly perversion" of religious imagery.[137] Other readers, though, interpret the sacred overtones as a manifestation of the divine capacity to circumscribe the energies of rebellion. Hart, for example, asserts that

> Part of the brilliance of the poem lies in the fact that it expresses rebellion and atonement in the same vocabulary, and by so doing epitomizes its central idea: that rebellion necessarily entails, because of God's justice and mercy, atonement.[138]

The poem, I think, swerves indecisively between both possibilities, allowing the terrifying possibility of blasphemy to supply the vehicle for submission. The imagery of atonement suffusing the language of rebellion is another manifestation of Herbert's fascination with the process by which both the opposition of the proud and the submission of the poor function ultimately to praise might. Like the poem's formal formlessness, these images both vent anger and infer order.

The speaker represents himself as one totally ignored by those who bestow the rewards of earthly fame and glory:

> Is the yeare onely lost to me?
> Have I no bayes to crown it?
> No flowers, no garlands gay? all blasted?
> All wasted?

Rather than the crown of thorns he currently wears, the speaker wants a crown of poetic glory, composed of bays and flowers. He proceeds to answer his questions with a *carpe diem* which ominously echoes the Fall: "Not so, my heart: but there is fruit, / And thou hast hands." For Herbert, desire for independence is the original sin. Rather than the sense of *fruit* as a token of dependence offered to a superior that Herbert uses in "Dedication" and the "Employment" poems, the word here designates pleasures to be seized despite moral and societal injunctions against such action. The speaker wants to make up for lost time and gratification:

> Recover all thy sigh-blown age
> On double pleasures: leave thy cold dispute
> Of what is fit and not.

Paradise will be regained not by submission but by redoubled self-gratification. The speaker characterizes the priggish self he intends to abandon as quibbling not over what is morally right and wrong but rather over questions of decorum—"what is fit and not." The poem's own ruptures of decorum, beginning with the initial violent striking of the board and continuing with the accumulating violence of the speaker's questions, suggest that this self has already been relinquished.

The poem continually imagines freedom in the possibility of escape, of going abroad, of leaving or forsaking some prior self or oppressive superior. Resituating the initial urge to go abroad in psychological rather than geographical terms, the speaker tells himself to

> Forsake thy cage
> Thy rope of sands,
> Which pettie thoughts have made, and made to thee
> Good cable, to enforce and draw,
> And be thy law,
> While thou didst wink and wouldst not see.

The "rope of sands" represents both the island of England (ringed by sandy coastline) and shackles which have no power to bind except through the cooperation of the prisoner—what Milton terms "idle cordage."[139] The speaker has mistakenly construed as "law" ties that do not bind. He desires to turn the tables on these "mind-forg'd manacles": rather than being willingly bound by an insubstantial rope of sands, he tells himself to "tie up thy fears." Likewise, the question of supplication and reward is inverted and internalized; instead of unsuccessfully suing a superior, the speaker imagines a world in which one gets one's "wish and way" (the phrase is from "Affliction [I]") only by aggressively grabbing it:

> He that forbears
> To suit and serve his need,
> Deserves his load.

Rather than being "still in suit" to a superior, the speaker imagines a political and spiritual world in which one suits his own needs. Instead of serving a superior in hope of reward, Herbert broaches the possibility of people serving only their own urges. Like the poem itself, which is directed not to another but to himself, the speaker here imagines a solipsistic and isolated social economy. As one of Herbert's proverbs on court life contends, "At Court, every one for himself" (no. 795, p. 347). In such an individualistic world, to refuse to gratify oneself is in some sense to deserve whatever burdens one accrues.

It is precisely at this moment of the most pessimistic view of social intercourse that narrative frame and divine voice both intervene. Returning to the "cold dispute / Of what is fit and not" he attempted to forsake, the speaker passes judgment on the behavior of this past self, and restores sociability to the increasingly isolating experience of the poem. At the same time, his uncertainty about the nature of this voice ("Me thoughts") records a lingering solipsism, where inner and outer, imagination and reality, are difficult to distinguish:

> But as I rav'd and grew more fierce and wilde
> At every word,
> Me thoughts I heard one calling, *Child!*
> And I reply'd, *My Lord.*

Unlike "Affliction (I)," a colloquy addressed to a silent God, "The Collar" is a soliloquy interrupted by God. The interruption is also a restoration of the sort of unequal, dependent social relation the poem tries to repudiate. "When God is made master of a family," observes one of Herbert's proverbs, "he orders the disorderly" (no. 983, p. 353). The poem makes God the master of Herbert's internal family, and imposes order upon the chaotic impulses it voices. It dramatizes the process described in "The Temper (II)," where the "unruly" powers of the self are subdued by God's return. The meter and rhyme of "The Collar," so intentionally choppy and uneven up to this point, can likewise be heard falling into their proper place, like the tumblers on a combination lock.

By addressing himself rather than God, the speaker tries to establish a territory upon which authority has not yet encroached. His colloquy infers the possibility of privacy and independence, a region where speech does not have to do duty to either a true or painted chair. He hopes for an escape from the claustrophobia Stefano Guazzo identifies in conversation with princes: "in their companie a man cannot utter his minde freely nor doe any thinge contrarie to their pleasure . . . [it] bringeth us into a certaine kinde of bondage, which we cannot like of long."[140] Yet the surveillance of the heavenly monarch cannot be escaped. Mortals may forget "That thou within his curtains drawn canst see" ("Miserie"), but as Herbert advises in "The Churchporch," "Think the king sees thee still; for his King does" (line 122). "Sunday" suggests that "there is no place so alone, / The which he doth not fill." In "The Collar," the voice of God dispels the stultifying illusion of independence and privacy, resulting in a genuinely gratifying claustrophobia. As in "Prayer (II)," divine omniscience—"Thou canst no more not heare, then thou canst die"—is comforting, not stifling. God enters the poem, as he enters the self in "The Forerunners," to reclaim both as his possession. Rather than the profound ambivalence suffusing the approach of God the king in "The Forerunners," though, the "call" of God in "The Collar" is psychologically and formally welcome. The speaker discovers that his God offers not only chastisement but also love in a time of choler.

The terms by which God and speaker recognize each other are commonplace, yet their interaction is politically and spiritually intricate. "Child," for example, functions at once as a rebuke of the speaker, a reminder of his hierarchical inferiority, and an expression of divine love for him.[141] The speaker has been behaving childishly, God tells him; yet God also reminds him that he is the child of God, adopted in spite of his childish behavior. In *The Country Parson*, Herbert declares that the parson is "a father to his flock," and behaves "as if he had begot his whole Parish" (p. 250). What this social figuration means to Herbert is that "when any sinns, [the parson] hateth him not as an officer, but pityes him as a Father: and even in those wrongs which . . . are done to his owne person, hee considers the offender as a child, and forgives." The word "child," then, is a seal of forgiveness. Furthermore, it functions to socialize the speaker, proffering a pattern of submissive conduct to constrain his apparently uncontrolled behavior. As in "Dialogue" ("What, Child, is the ballance thine?"), God's term of address to humanity fuses love and judgment, coercion and endearment.

The speaker answers, however, not with the anticipated and corresponding term "My Father" but rather with "My Lord." The *Book of Common Prayer*'s epistle for the Sunday after Christmas—Galatians 4—proclaims that with the coming of Jesus, "now, thou art not a servant, but a son."[142] But the speaker of "The Collar" retreats into the role of servant from which Christ's death and God's words release him. Rather than accepting the characteristically familiar terms by which God greets him—God's "state," we remember fron "Prayer (II)," "dislikes not easinesse"—he displays the completeness of his submission by making himself lower than God allows.

Yet the speaker may also find some psychological comfort in the greater hierarchical distance between himself and this all-hearing deity that a lord-servant relationship allows. The last line of defense against such a beneficently intrusive deity, as "Love (III)" makes abundantly clear, is the observation of deferential distance.[143] The slight mismatch between divine call and human response, like the probable slant rhyme "Lord" makes with "word," suggests a lingering asymmetry between human and divine expectations. The human voice that has been aggressively wanting to seize the day humbly accepts far less than God offers. But the same words that register the degree of his submission, then, also supply a final tack for putting distance between himself and his superior. Although they are the only two words in the poem addressed to God, they assimilate and redirect the momentum of rebellion generated in the poem's previous thirty-five lines.

In the Renaissance, furthermore, the authority of a father was often integrated into that of a lord. As Gordon Schochet has persuasively demonstrated, paternal and political authority were inextricably linked throughout the English Renaissance.[144] The etymology linking "patron" and "paternity" bore a deep political truth. Indeed, Herbert's own comments on children and servants in *The Country Parson* suggest remarkable consonance between them. The parson, Herbert advises, "keeps his servants between love, and fear, according as hee findes them; but generally he distributes it thus, To his Children he shewes more love then terrour, to his servants more terrour

then love; but an old good servant boards a child" (p. 241). Children
and servants both experience terror as well as love; only the propor-
tions differ. Herbert's greatest aspirations ("The Odour") as well as
his worst nightmares ("Affliction [I]") were fulfilled in the blend of
terror and love that constituted the master-servant relationship.

Such a blend takes on great personal poignance when we remem-
ber that Herbert's father died when he was three, and his mother did
not re-marry until he was sixteen, and then to a man the age of her
eldest son. In the letters to his stepfather, Herbert addresses Danvers
as "Sir," not "Father," and signs himself "Your most obedient Ser-
vant," "Your faithfullest servant," "Your humblest Servant," and
"Your Extreme Servant."[145] The affectionate yet deferential tone of
the letters suggests that Danvers was more a beneficent patron than a
surrogate parent to Herbert. When Herbert talks about paternal be-
havior, then, it is largely secondhand. Both the political ideology of
his time, and the circumstances of his biography, conspire to elide the
differences between lordship and paternity.

In *The Country Parson*, Herbert suggests that God behaves towards
his creatures

> as a Father, who hath in his hand an apple, and a piece of Gold
> under it; the Child comes, and with pulling, gets the apple out of
> his Fathers hand: his Father bids him throw it away, and he will
> give him the gold for it, which the Child utterly refusing, eats it,
> and is troubled with wormes. (p. 272)

"But there is fruit, / And thou hast hands," the speaker of "The Col-
lar" tells himself, failing like this child to value correctly the gifts of
God. Herbert uses this passage to exemplify "how Gods goodnesse
strives with mans refractorinesse." But it also uncomfortably holds
out the possibility of God as the tempter, extending the wormy apple
to his creature before telling him that he should have taken the piece
of gold underneath it. It demonstrates the curious blend of terror and
love, familiarity and awe, that imbues Herbert's relations with the di-
vine throughout *The Temple*. From the attack on God licensed by the
political imagery of "Affliction (I)" through the restoration of a so-
cial relationship between humanity and divinity in "The Collar,"
Herbert filters his devotional experience through the patterns and
practices of social power.

Herbert's poems register the difficulty, if not impossibility, of ac-
cepting the Protestant ontology of complete dependence upon abso-
lute divine power. They translate Herbert's social anxiety about em-

ployment into the contradictory imperative to serve an all-powerful monarch, and record the corollary linguistic anxiety about addressing an ineffable deity. Negotiation with absolute political power provides a model for dealing with divinity as well as a standard against which to measure such interactions. Yet divine authority, these poems show, is constituted not only by those forces against which the self must rebel but also by those principles of order on which the self must build. The vectors of social and sacred power intersect and conflict throughout *The Temple*. When Herbert in "Jordan (I)" asserts that he, unlike secular poets who indulge their poetic faculties in "fictions onely and false hair," will engage in a simpler and more authentic kind of poetry which "plainly say[s], *My God, My King*," he implies that this poetry will be easy to compose—perhaps as easy as the process of "Copying out" the "sweetnesse readie penn'd" of "love" proposed by a "friend" in "Jordan (II)." To his credit, however, Herbert never rested in this seemingly simple metaphoric act, but continued to explore relentlessly the ramifications of saying "My God, My King," of addressing God as a social superior. His sense of the poetic promise and theological problems inherent in the identification of social and divine authority gives to his poems an aesthetic power and spiritual cogency far surpassing what would be achieved by plainly saying "My God, My King." Like Gentile's magnificent *Adoration* with which we began, *The Temple* transforms its intuitions about the parallels and contrasts between earthly and heavenly power into a work of worship and awe.

In this chapter we have seen just how necessary the patterns of political authority are to Herbert's construction of a devotional self. The nervous splendors of the Jacobean court supplied Herbert with an appropriate vehicle for divine glory. Divine power, in turn, provided the leverage for a profound critique of the social hierarchy. In the next chapter, we will see how the bleaker and more destructive aspects of the exercise of political power also furnished Herbert with a language for representing the divine. We will explore the surprising consonance between the afflictions God imposes on his creatures and the physically devastating tortures employed by figures of political authority in Herbert's day. Because they are so often slighted in accounts of Herbert, we will emphasize the elements of fear in that curious compound of terror and love by which Herbert defines the hierarchical relationship of masters and servants, and of fathers and children. This fear, and the physical pain that reinforces it, functions to underscore the absoluteness of divine power. By exercising the royal prerogative of torture in order to inflict excruciating pain on the body and soul of his creature, Herbert's God engages in the naked practice of power. In the arresting image of God punishing the bodies and souls of his creatures, Herbert represents the immense terror that divine love finally counter-balances. The love cannot be fully appreciated without attention to the terror it offsets.

II

"I Live to Shew His Power"

3

"Storms Are the Triumph of His Art": The Politics of Affliction

God may be subtle, but he is not malicious.
—Albert Einstein

A recent fundraising letter from John G. Healey, Executive Director of Amnesty International, begins with the rubricized words of some prison "guards" as they prepare to torture a captive: "We are God in here . . . "[1] The ultimate psychological terror, the words suggest, is the imagination of divine power in malevolent hands. In *The Body in Pain*, a work which has taught us to read rather than recoil from such utterances, Elaine Scarry investigates the political calculus which makes possible "the conversion of absolute pain into the fiction of absolute power" epitomized by the guards' threat.[2] Because torture is, in the words of Pierre Vidal Naquet, "nothing other than the most direct and most immediate form of the domination of one man over another, which is the very essence of politics," it supplies the logical if often-suppressed endpoint of the modes of political coercion explored in the last two chapters.[3]

Herbert's poems, I want to argue, chillingly reverse the guards' threat, imagining God as wielding various instruments developed by Renaissance culture specifically for the imposition of pain. Throughout *The Temple* Herbert betrays a preoccupation with the imposition of pain as an instrument of power. The infliction of pain on the body of a subject, and the imagined penetration of mortal flesh, offer gruelling physical manifestations of the encroachment of divine power on the interior self. In their meticulous portrait of the suffering that God imposes upon his creatures, though, Herbert's poems push the conversion identified by Scarry one step further, using the mortal agony they record not only to register the immense political distance that

117

separates God from his creatures but also to gauge the remarkable love that bridges this distance. "Intense pain," asserts Scarry, "is world-destroying."[4] For Herbert, however, it is also the necessary occasion for composing the self in the terms demanded by his God. "Mans medley" suggests that "Happie is he, whose heart / Hath found the art / To turn his double pains to double praise." Throughout *The Temple* Herbert attempts to discover the "art" by which the redoubled pains imposed by God can be converted into redoubled praise of God. His efforts are as manifold and discrepant as the apparently erratic behavior of the God they intend to laud.

"Josephs coat," the poem that supplies the title of this section ("I live to shew his power"), is a sonnet deploying the linguistic violence of Petrarchan oxymoron to investigate the distinctive blend of representation, power, suffering, and devotion that constitutes *The Temple*. In its not fully successful attempt to characterize the apparent cruelty of God's behavior towards humanity as the imposition of salutary suffering, the poem provides a place from which we can begin to admire the heroic effort required to comprehend the God of power as a God of love. The opening quatrain sounds very much like a resigned version of "Affliction (I)" in its portrait of an autocratic and injurious divinity:

> Wounded I sing, tormented I indite,
> Thrown down I fall into a bed, and rest:
> Sorrow hath chang'd its note: such is his will,
> Who changeth all things, as him pleaseth best.

Significantly, lines 1 and 3 fail to rhyme; the speaker cannot make his indictment of divine behavior rhyme with God's exercise of "will." As in "Deniall" and "Grief," Herbert indicates the resistance of suffering to formal expression by means of intentionally incomplete rhymes, quietly exposing a tension between mortal complaint and divine will which the poem never fully resolves.

A related tension emerges in the notable difference between what the titular image represents in the Bible and what it designates in the poem. In Genesis 37.3, Joseph's coat of many colors is a sign of paternal favor: "Now Israel loved Joseph more then all his children, because he was the sonne of his old age: and he made him a coat of many colours." But for Herbert, the coat of many colors represents neither paternal fondness nor patriarchal protection but rather the agonizingly variegated behavior of God towards him. "Without the title," asserts Joseph Summers, the poem "might be construed as an acknowledgment of a powerful and inexplicable Fate."[5] Even with the title, I would argue, the poem confronts the incomprehensibility and cruelty of the practices of divine power. Herbert portrays in this poem a willful deity who acts "as him pleaseth best." God knows, Herbert declares, that his frail creature would be unable to sustain "even one grief and smart" that "had his full career." Therefore, God has "giv'n to anguish / One of Joyes coats, ticing it with relief / To linger in me, and together languish." God makes him suffer, in other words, but cleverly halts before the affliction is fatal. In *An Humble Supplication to Her Majestie*, the Jesuit Robert Southwell complains that when Elizabethan torturers see that "the soule, weary of soe painfull an harbour, is ready to depart, they apply Cruell Comforts, and revive us, only to Martyr us with more deaths."[6] In "Josephs coat," Herbert imagines his God as the master of such cruel comforts, carefully preventing the death of the creature whose suffering he causes. The coat is a gift not to Herbert but to his anguish, and is the means by which God entices that anguish to linger in his creature. The present that signifies paternal love in the Bible functions in *The Temple* as an instrument for extending the speaker's suffering.

The poem concludes not with a revelation of the affection implicit in the biblical notion of Joseph's coat but rather with a reiteration of the divine power whose practices its mottled pattern at once designates and disguises: "I live to shew his power, who once did bring / My *joyes* to *weep*, and now my *griefs* to *sing*." A poem in some sense without an audience, speaking of its almighty divinity only in the third person, "Josephs coat" tries, with little success, to translate the phenomenon of divine affliction into the terminology of divine love. "The extraordinary mixture of joy and sorrow in the Christian's life is a particular sign of God's love," remarks Summers.[7] But the word *love*—one of Herbert's favorites—does not appear in the poem. Moreover, the concept of singing with which the poem begins and ends is not so much an avowal of mortal creative power as it is the anguished cry of one who is "wounded," in "grief," injured by the God whose power he shows but whose love he cannot discern.

"Josephs coat" is not one of Herbert's finest poems. But it is one of the best poems in *The Temple* at laying bare the complex nature of Herbert's devotional and artistic project. How does one "live to shew his power?" The poem holds out two possibilities: by suffering and by singing. God's power, the poem suggests, is exhibited by means of the afflictions he imposes, and the songs of suffering that result. In this chapter I will investigate the image that recurs throughout *The Temple* of Herbert's deity as a God of storms and torture, imposing upon his creatures a terrifying and painful if ultimately therapeutic

119

turbulence which Herbert declares to be "the triumph of [God's] art" ("The Bag"). "Power," contends Foucault, "is tolerable only on condition that it mask a substantial part of itself. Its success is proportional to its ability to hide its own mechanisms."[8] Much of the value of Herbert's poems lies in the coruscating clarity with which they investigate the mechanisms of divine power.

In the most sustained account of Herbert's poems of suffering, Richard Todd proposes that these poems should be understood "less in terms of God's deafness to Herbert's entreaties than in terms of our realization that Herbert is blind to God's response."[9] But to read the poems in this way is to vault over the troubling human experience they portray in order to arrive at a comforting theological truism. The impact of Herbert's poems of suffering lies not in their revelation of mortal blindness (although this is frequently present) but rather in their courageous willingness to confront the possibility of divine deafness. It would be easy, Herbert knows, to follow the cue of Job's comforters and declare salutary and justified a capricious and apparently senseless agony. But Herbert rejects such simplistic solutions to the problem of mortal suffering, focusing instead on the resistance of the experience of agony to the constructions by which mortals attempt to make sense of it. He limns a divinity who is not just a God of sweetness and light but also one of tempests and torture. The latter traits lend force to the former.

This deity is present in remarkably undisguised form in a passage in *The Country Parson* exploring God's "threefold power in every thing which concernes man"—sustaining, governing, and spiritual. Herbert suggests that because "God delights to have men feel, and acknowledg, and reverence his power," he "often overturnes things, when they are thought past danger; that is his time of interposing" (*Works*, p. 271). He then proceeds to characterize in chilling detail the violent interventions by which God exercises the power he wants his subjects to revere.

> As when a Merchant hath a ship come home after many a storme, which it hath escaped, he destroyes it sometimes in the very Haven; or if the goods be housed, a fire hath broken forth, and suddenly consumed them. Now this he doth, that men should perpetuate, and not break off their acts of dependance, how faire soever the opportunities present themselves. So that if a farmer should depend upon God all the yeer, and being ready to put hand to sickle, shall then secure himself, and think all cock-sure; then God sends such weather, as lays the corn, and destroys it: or if he

depend on God further, even till he imbarn his corn, and then think all sure; God sends a fire, and consumes all that he hath: For that he ought not to break off, but to continue his dependance on God, not onely before the corne is inned, but after also; and indeed, to depend, and fear continually. (*Works*, p. 271)

The God that emerges from these lines is one who destroys in order to ensure the reverence and dependence of his creatures. "There are but two devouring elements, fire, and water," remarks Herbert in another part of *The Country Parson*, and God "hath both in him" (p. 234). Herbert's God defeats the plans and devours the products of his servants in order to prompt their recollection of his power and to enforce their total dependence upon him.

Throughout *The Temple* Herbert tries to come to terms with this fiercely jealous deity, what he calls a "great God, and terrible" (p. 234). His corollary interest in the overwhelming love and mercy of this being should not preclude attention to his fascination with this being's terrifying power. When we read a line like that which concludes "Repentance"—"Fractures well cur'd make us more strong"—we are apt to forget that the image includes a God who breaks bones as well as one who heals them. *Outlandish Proverb* no. 315 remarks that "God strikes not with both hands, for to the sea he made havens, and to rivers foords" (p. 331). Herbert's God nevertheless strikes with one hand, and it is attached to an arm of immense strength: "Of what supreme almightie power / Is thy great arm, which spans the east and west" ("Prayer [II]").

Herbert's God exercises this arm with surprising frequency in the act of torturing his creature. In Herbert's day, of course, the capacity of the monarch physically to punish disobedient subjects was unquestioned. Malefactors were continually made to live (and suffer and sometimes die) to show the power of the the sovereign. In England, though, unlike much of the continent, the Common Law had no specific provisions relating to torture. As William Harrison remarks, in lines that richly demonstrate the social violation implicit in physical punishment:

> To use torment, also, or question by pain and torture in these common cases [e.g., felony, manslaughter, robbery, murder, rape, and piracy], is greatly abhorred . . . choosing rather frankly to open our minds than to yield our bodies unto such servile halings and tearings as are used in other countries . . . [We] cannot in any wise digest to be used as villeins and slaves, in suffering continually beating, servitude, and servile torments.[10]

121

Sir Edward Coke likewise writes in the *Third Institute* that "there is no law to warrant tortures in this land, nor can they be justified by any prescription, being so lately brought in."[11] Despite this proud English resistance to "servile" torment, torture was practiced throughout the English Renaissance. Coke himself warns Richard Weston, one of the Overbury murderers, that if he does not confess, he will "be extended, and then to have weights laid upon him, . . . which were by little and little to be increased."[12] Indeed, the very absence of torture from Common Law regulation meant that it was above the law, part of the royal prerogative, to be exercised at the sovereign's absolute discretion. "We have," declares John Langbein, "record of more than eighty cases from the century 1540–1640 in which the Privy Council or the monarch ordered torture (or the threat of torture) to be used against criminals or suspected criminals." Such numbers are perhaps unremarkable until one realizes how narrowly Langbein defines torture. The legal definition of torture, Langbein insists, must involve coercion used to extract information; it thus excludes other forms of the systematic infliction of pain—what he terms "afflictive sanctions"—because "punishment is not directed to extracting evidence or information." The chillingly common spectacle of suffering imposed by the state, by which "traitors were still being castrated, disembowelled, and quartered, felons hanged, heretics burned at the stake" while "lesser offenders were regularly whipped, their ears shorn, their noses slit," is thus relegated to the realm of punishment.[13] "Torture in England," contends Langbein, "remained a very exceptional practice of the highest central authorities."[14] But the imposition of pain upon the body of the governed was remarkably unexceptional.

The variety of available methods for inflicting pain—the rack for stretching the body to the point of dislocation, the "scavenger's daughter" for compacting the body to the point where it began to crush itself, iron gauntlets for suspending one by one's wrists, boots for crushing leg bones, suffocating iron collars, the pressing to death with which Coke threatens Weston, amputation, hot iron brands, and thumbscrews, to name just a few—testifies to the importance placed upon the technology of cruelty.[15] Even when not actually used, the very existence of such machinery was an act of governmental coercion. Indeed, in the Conciliar records of torture warrants, the torturer is normally ordered first to show the victim the instrument, as if the very sight thereof would precipitate the victim's cooperation.[16]

Such coercive governmental practices are not perhaps to be expected in a work like *The Temple*, designed as an act of divine praise.

Yet torture is the underside of the courtly world we have found so fully to infuse Herbert's sacred devotions. Fear of the physical suffering a monarch could impose can be heard, however distantly, in the modes of elaborate praise demanded by life at court. Torture provides in undisguised form the absolute end-point of the methods of political coercion we have been examining. As Nicholas Eymeric, papal inquisitor in Aragon during the latter half of the fourteenth century, writes in his influential handbook, *Directorium Inquisitorum*: "One must not resort to the question [torture] till other means of discovering the truth have been exhausted. Good manners, subtlety, the exhortation of well-intentioned persons, even frequent meditation on the discomforts of prison are often sufficient to induce the guilty ones to confess."[17] Remarkably, good manners and physical pain are imagined as part of the same continuum of imperious conduct.

The phenomenon of the incarnation, moreover, warrants the body as a site of sacrificial pain which enables Christian salvation. As John N. Wall asserts, "because of the centrality of the wounded Christ in Christian imagery, sites of wounding become the place of Christ in the world, making suffering the way of the cross, the way to be with Christ."[18] The second lyric in *The Temple*—"The Sacrifice"— ventriloquizes the immense suffering experienced by the God who becomes human. Yet for Herbert pain is not only an experience he shares with Christ but also a phenomenon that alienates him from his God. Unlike those who praise God for the cure but forget that the illness must also have had divine origins, Herbert knows his God is behind the deep agony he experiences. Furthermore, the concept of the physical body as the location of religious activity is highlighted by the title of Herbert's collection of divine poems—*The Temple*. Both a medical name for the sides of the skull and a Pauline metaphor for the body as a whole ("Knowe yee not that yee are the Temple of God"), "temple" identifies the body, not exterior architecture, as the field on which Herbert's devotional exercises occur.[19]

There was in the Renaissance, moreover, a calculated consonance between rituals of execution and religious ceremonial, between the sacrifice of the criminal for the good of the state and the sacrifice of Christ for the benefit of mankind. Because of "a desire to translate a public execution into a positive religious experience, into a reflection of the Mass, in which the death of the criminal bore symbolic resemblance to the sacrifice of Christ and the salvation of mankind," argues Samuel Edgerton, "the scaffold came to be regarded as a sort of altar."[20] The disciplinary institutions of Renaissance governments, then, were saturated by religious imagery. The exercises of religion, in

123

turn, were often literally penetrated by the pressures of governmental coercion. Foxe's extremely popular *Acts and Monuments*—a copy of which was placed in every English church beside the Bible—established a firm link between physical suffering and religious commitment. Recently described as that "popular sixteenth-century encyclopedia of torture, persecution, and violent death," Foxe's *Book of Martyrs*, as it was commonly called, appropriated the narrative structures and harrowing iconography of Catholic martyrology for profoundly Protestant ends.[21] Conversely, many of the most prominent sufferers of torture under Elizabeth were Catholics, since a proclamation of 1582 "pronounced all Jesuits and seminary priests to be, *ipso facto*, traitors."[22] In the first lines of poetry we have from Herbert—"My God, where is that ancient heat towards thee, / Wherewith whole showls of *Martyrs* once did burn, / Besides their other flames"—we can hear the immense impact the images of religious suffering contained in Foxe must have had on the imagination of the young George Herbert. The heat was not as ancient as Herbert's lines suggest. Indeed, Herbert reminds his ailing mother that her own "afflictions of the Body" are mild compared to those of "the holy Martyrs of God . . . [who] have been burnt by thousands, and have endur'd such other Tortures, as the very mention of them might beget amazement" (*Works*, pp. 373–74).

Physical punishment, then, was intimately linked to the proscription by political authorities of certain religious practices. Such punishments were not, however, limited to an outlawed religion, but could include a variety of offenses, often difficult to anticipate. "Many trespasses," remarks William Harrison, "also are punished by the cutting of one or both ears from the head of the offender, as the utterance of seditious words against the magistrates."[23] Such severe penalties made all utterances about magistrates that were not unadulterated flattery a terribly risky business. Yet speech was not only the cause but also the result of the authoritarian imposition of pain. Unlike simple punishment, torture was intimately connected to the extraction of confession, a kind of utterance with political as well as religious overtones. Pain was inflicted by power to generate a discourse of the subject's own guilt. In Shakespeare's *Othello* (5.2.305), Gratiano admonishes Iago: "Torments will ope your lips." Herbert brilliantly coordinates the practices by which sovereigns require such utterances of their disobedient subjects with the demands of the Protestant God that all confess their sinfulness and unworthiness. In tracing the connection between confession and suffering, between religious utterance and political submission, Herbert clarifies the etymological linkage of penitence and the penitentiary, of penitential practices and penal institutions, that would be manifested in the eighteenth-century prison.[24]

The very genealogy of judicial torture in Europe underscores its close connection to divine power. As Langbein points out, judicial torture displaced the ordeal in European law. Abolished by the Fourth Lateran Council in 1215, the ordeal had theoretically offered a way for divine omniscience to intervene in human affairs. As Europe abandoned the notion of God as the fact-finder on which the ordeal was based, legal theory turned to torture as a way of pretending to the god-like omniscience of interior states that the ordeal had claimed.[25] Vestiges of this genealogy linger in Martin Luther's endorsement of the right of rulers to punish and torture: "The hand that holds the sword and strangles is no longer a human hand, but the hand of God. It is not man but God who hangs, tortures, beheads, strangles, and makes war . . . "[26] By translating the punitive actions of sovereigns into the will of God, Luther espouses a principle for legitimizing the fiercest and most repressive regimes. He also daringly confronts the fact that an omnipotent God must in some sense be behind all mortal suffering.

Like Luther, Herbert refuses to ignore the fact that his God imposes the suffering he feels. His task as religious poet is to make sense of the intense pain he suffers without censoring it or disguising its divine source. In a political world replete with the diurnal cruelties of imprisonment, punishment, and torture, physical pain supplied an unbearably real metaphor for the exercise of power. Thus when Herbert in "The Temper (I)" complains that God is stretching him between heaven and hell, the apparition of the rack on which criminals were tortured in Renaissance England looms large. The poem traces a rapid downward spiral (like the career of the courtly Frenchman Herbert mentions in the letter to Harley explored in chap. 1), from negotiating with the superior it would praise to suffering penal constraint at his hands:

> How should I praise thee, Lord! how should my rymes
> Gladly engrave thy love in steel,
> If what my soul doth feel sometimes,
> My soul might ever feel!

> Although there were some fourtie heav'ns, or more,
> Sometimes I peere above them all;
> Sometimes I hardly reach a score,
> Sometimes to hell I fall.

> O rack me not to such a vast extent;
>> Those distances belong to thee:
>> The world's too little for thy tent,
>>> A grave too big for me.

> Wilt thou meet arms with man, that thou dost stretch
>> A crumme of dust from heav'n to hell?
>> Will great God measure with a wretch?
>>> Shall he thy stature spell?

As Fish asserts, "The stated wish to praise God . . . is a thinly disguised accusation of him" for being unfaithful and inconstant.[27] The disguise quickly drops away, as the baffling mutability that Herbert lamented in "Josephs coat" is imagined as an actual instrument of torture: the rack, the most frequently used engine of pain in Jacobean England. Significantly, the speaker does not request that God stop racking him, only that he not do so "to such a vast extent." Pain, the lines suggest, mediates the diurnal experience of God. The God of these stanzas, as Strier remarks, "does not seem in any way lovable. He seems a tyrant and a bully." In calling himself a "crumme of dust," Herbert in turn adopts "an aggressive, even militant, humility" which couches a plea that God pick on someone his own size.[28] The relations between mortals and God that these lines depict are characterized by suffering and strife.

The end of the poem recoils somewhat from this agonistic and agonizing portrait of divine-human relations, but not by denying the pain present in the previous stanzas. Even in its close the poem maintains the spectre of God painfully stretching his creature, but reinscribes the outlines of this image into a therapeutic musical metaphor:

> Yet take thy way; for sure thy way is best:
>> Stretch or contract me, thy poore debter:
>> This is but tuning of my breast,
>>> To make the musick better.

> Whether I flie with angels, fall with dust,
>> Thy hands made both, and I am there:
>> Thy power and love, my love and trust
>>> Make one place ev'ry where.

"God's actions as torturer," remarks Strier, "are ascribed to His role as temperer."[29] Indeed, by emphasizing God's power to contract as well as stretch his subject, Herbert may be quietly invoking another instrument of torture, the Scavenger's Daughter which, according to

Robert Southwell, made a particularly cruel tandem with the rack: "What unsufferable Agonies we have bene put to upon the Rack, it is not possible to expresse, the feeling soe farr exceedeth all speech. Some with Instruments have been rowled up together like a ball, and soe Crushed, that the blood sprowted out at divers parts of their bodies."[30] God's stretching and contracting the body of his creature involve the extremities of mortal agony. Yet for Herbert, as the title suggests, the process of breaking the body and spirit by means of such tortures is ultimately a constructive and invigorating experience in the hands of his God. As steel is strengthened by rapid heating and cooling, and as musical instruments are tuned by varying the tension upon their strings, so is Herbert confirmed by the extreme manipulations of his God.[31] To understand suffering as tuning, however, does not mute the pain emphasized in the earlier stanzas; rather, it amplifies the close relationship between the activities of suffering and singing announced in "Josephs coat" (which begins "Wounded I sing," and concludes with the remark that God has made "my griefs to sing").

Strier emphasizes how "the final stanza of 'The Temper (I)' replaces ontological and spatial terms with personalistic and qualitative ones."[32] But to bracket the conclusion in this way is to act as if the poem has truly left behind the agony with which it begins. The human activities in this stanza, moreover—flying and falling—take place upon the spatial grid supposedly replaced. The image of God's omnipresence that concludes "The Temper (I)" yields genuine comfort in the thought that whatever extremes one experiences, God is indeed there. Yet it also reminds one that whatever pain one suffers, God is there also. In its discovery that God's "hands made both" heaven and hell, the poem has come a long way from its agonistic depiction of God "meet[ing] arms" with his creature. Yet the image of God as the creator of hell, a place of eternal torture, quietly questions the reassurance the lines assert. Syntactically, the poem balances God's "power and love" with the speaker's "love and trust." Although "love" is the profoundly significant term that mediates between God and his creature, mortals must greet all exercises of divine power with a necessary but excruciating "trust," which Strier translates (correctly, I think) as faith. But because the poem yields far more evidence of power than of love or trust, it shows the difficulty of attaining the absolute faith its resolution demands. The love the speaker initially wanted to engrave in steel must be taken on trust amidst the unmistakable suffering that God imposes.

In "The Temper (I)," then, Herbert renders therapeutic but does not deny the image of God as a torturer. "Affliction (IV)" likewise imagines God placing his creature on the rack, but also superimposes a range of other modes of suffering to which God subjects him:

> Broken in pieces all asunder,
>> Lord, hunt me not,
>> A thing forgot,
> Once a poore creature, now a wonder,
>> A wonder tortur'd in the space
>> Betwixt this world and that of grace.
>
> My thoughts are all a case of knives,
>> Wounding my heart
>> With scatter'd smart.

Externally, he is shattered, hunted, stretched in the abyss separating earth and heaven, while internally he suffers the wounds of his own knifelike thoughts. The agony is so intense it is a "wonder" he is still alive, but God, as in "Josephs coat," knows just when to ease the pain. The speaker is not sure whether he is "a thing forgot" or the object of intense and frightening attention. As in "Affliction (I)," it is difficult to know whether the worse fate lies in being forgotten or in being remembered only to be "broken," "hunted," and "tortur'd."

Because the infliction of pain was so often intended to elicit confession in Herbert's culture, it is appropriate that Herbert's poem entitled "Confession" focuses on God's expertise in inflicting pain. Herbert imagines his God as terribly "cunning" with the internal tortures mentioned in "Affliction (IV)," and shows him practicing what Foucault would call the "art of unbearable sensations."[33] Not without some aesthetic pride, the speaker describes the elaborate workmanship by which he transformed himself into a literal chest of drawers:

> within my heart I made
>> Closets; and in them many a chest;
>> And, like a master in my trade,
> In those chests, boxes; in each box a till.

Strier emphasizes how "the imagery of craftsmanship here expresses the intensity and ineradicability of the 'natural' human desire to withdraw or withhold from God, to establish and maintain a place in the self apart from Him. Ingenuity is equated with egotism, and, most of all, with the attempt at evasion."[34] In his desire to render the speaker theologically culpable, however, Strier dodges the issue of the duress with which God responds to such activity. The stress on mortal workmanship in the first stanza only functions to enhance our aesthetic admiration for "grief," a "cunning guest," which God imposes on his creatures:

> No scrue, no piercer can
> Into a piece of timber work and winde,
>   As Gods afflictions into man,
>   When he a torture hath design'd.
> They are too subtill for the subt'llest hearts;
> And fall, like rheumes, upon the tendrest parts.

God's afflictions penetrate the flesh of his creatures more efficiently than an awl or screw pierces wood. This penetration, furthermore, is both a cause of pain and a manifestation of inwardness. "Herbert as often uses *grief* of physical as of mental pain," notes Hutchinson.[35] As pain itself is experienced in the body but felt in the mind, so do God's tortures afflict body and soul. Far more distressingly than thumbscrews, God's "subtill" tortures "fall, like rheumes, upon the tendrest parts," where they will cause the greatest pain.[36] The egotistical pride in painstaking workmanship the speaker expressed in the first stanza is translated into the grievous pain caused by God's carefully "design'd" afflictions. "Onely an open breast / Doth shut them out," remarks the speaker, suggesting the purgative function of the confessions God's tortures are designed to elicit. But in the context of this gruelling attention to the imposition of physical pain, the "open breast" not only invokes images of absolute sincerity but also may hint at the grisly spectre of the disemboweled traitor—the ultimate physical manifestation of exhumed interiority.[37]

In their extreme focus upon the body as the site of power and suffering, Herbert's poems have more in common with the contemporaneous phenomenon of Jacobean tragedy than one might anticipate. The grotesque activities that mark this theatre are, as Francis Barker argues,

> not instances of the arbitrary perversity of single dramatists . . . but the insistence in the spectacle of a corporeality which is quite other than our own. The visibility of this body in pain . . . is systemic rather than personal; not the issue of an aberrant exhibitionism, but formed across the whole surface of the social as the locus of the desire, the revenge, the power, and the misery of this world.[38]

In Herbert's poetry, we can watch the process by which the spectacle of these external cruelties is beginning to be absorbed into the arena of the self. As the body mediates the subject's relation with the sovereign in Jacobean tragedy, so in Herbert's poetry does it mediate the soul's relation with the absolute power of God. The process of interiorization that Barker locates in the Restoration *Diary* of Samuel Pepys is already at work in Herbert's poetry, as the internal kingdom, not the material stage, becomes the site for playing out the conflicting cultural forces that intersect in the body. In Herbert's poetry, we can track the internal migration of authority that produces the modern subject. What Barker calls "the glorious cruelties of the Jacobean theatre" are rendered in Herbert as the desires and terrors of the Christian interior life.

Even when Herbert does not explicitly imagine God as a torturer, pain mediates the relationship between divinity and humanity throughout *The Temple*. As "The Glimpse" suggests, the proportion of suffering to solace that God doles out is alarmingly uneven: "For many weeks of lingring pain and smart / But one half houre of comfort to my heart." The speaker of "Home" complains that his "head doth burn," that God's "long deferrings wound me to the quick." The speaker of "Longing" likewise asks God to

> Look on my sorrows round!
> Mark well my furnace! O what flames,
> What heats abound!
> What grief, what shames!

He apprehends divine absence as excruciating, burning pain. Both "Longing" and "Home" investigate what Macbeth terms "the torture of the mind" (3.2.21). In "Love unknown," the speaker's heart is violently "thr[o]w[n]" into a "font" and then a "scalding pan"; the punishment for traitors in Renaissance England—to be "quartered alive," after which "their members and bowels are cut from their bodies and thrown into a fire provided near-hand, and within their own sight"—cannot be far from Herbert's mind.[39] Even when he tries to sleep, the speaker of "Love unknown" finds his bed "stuff'd" with "thorns." The agony is revealed to be spiritually salutary by the speaker's friend, but the pain is not denied or eased. Even the title of "The Collar" may refer both to the physical suffering caused by the disease *choler* and to a burdensome instrument of penal restraint.[40]

Herbert's close attention to the pain he feels is very different from the masochism of Donne or Crashaw. Donne begs God to "Batter my heart," to "o'erthrow mee . . . to breake, blowe, burn and make me

new" (Holy Sonnet 14); "I turn my back to thee," says Donne in
"Good Friday, 1613. Riding Westward," "but to receive / Corrections
. . . O thinke me worth thine anger, punish mee." Herbert, by con-
trast, is not seeking the pain but lamenting it. "There are no ecstasies
of 'sweet pain' in Herbert," argues Strier, contrasting Herbert to
Crashaw's "Hymn to the Name and Honour of the admirable Saint
Teresa"; "Herbert never courts pain for the purpose of self-immo-
lation. His acceptance of pain is hard-won, and he always reserves his
right to complain."[41] Unlike Donne and Crashaw, who long to be vio-
lently seized by God, Herbert fears such abduction and detests the
pain. In "Sighs and Grones" he pleads with God not to punish him,
however much he deserves it: "O do not bruise me! . . . O do not
scourge me! . . . O do not grinde me! . . . O do not kill me." "Dis-
cipline" implores God to "throw away thy rod, / Throw away thy
wrath," not to use it upon him. Although the request itself, as Ed-
mund Miller maintains, "assumes a predisposition to wrath on the
part of God," it also affirms the speaker's refusal to accommodate
himself to this divine predisposition.[42]

By focusing on the image of the rod, an instrument of discipline
and punishment, Herbert engages in the process identified by Elaine
Scarry as "the translation of all the objectified elements of pain into
the insignia of power, the conversion of the enlarged map of human
suffering into an emblem of the regime's strength."[43] Yet it is pre-
cisely by means of this translation that Herbert is able to discover
a mode of affliction that is genuinely salutary. In the power and
strength represented by the rod of punishment he fears, Herbert finds
the possibility of the order he so craves. "Affliction (III)" praises God's
capacity to "guide and govern" the very grief he precipitates, "making
a scepter of the rod." The instrument of punishment is converted into
the sign of royal power. "Charms and Knots" likewise remarks that
"a poore mans rod, when thou dost ride, / Is both a weapon and a
guide." In the poem "Time," "Christs coming" transforms the brutal
"hatchet" of "Time" into a gentle "pruning-knife," and promotes
Time himself from "an executioner at best" to "a gard'ner" and "an
usher to convey our souls / Beyond the utmost starres and poles"; in
consequence, "length of dayes lengthen[s] the rod." A truly capital
punishment, the poem suggests, lies not in imminent death but in
extended life.

By focusing not on God but rather on the instruments through
which he makes his wrath known, then, Herbert succeeds in render-
ing that wrath beneficent. In Herbert's translation of "The 23d

Psalme," all vestiges of punishment have been purged from the rod of comfort:

> Yea, in death shadie black abode
> Well may I walk, not fear:
> For thou art with me; and thy rod
> To guide, thy staffe to bear.

Herbert wants God not to throw away this rod but to use it as a tool to uphold and sustain his subject.

As the flexibility of the image of the rod would suggest, Herbert is indeed fascinated by the dual valence of divine power, its capacity to wound and to heal, to make and to unmake, the same object. "Sighs and Grones" tactfully reminds God that he is "both *Judge* and *Saviour, feast* and *rod, / Cordiall* and *Corrosive.*" Where the speaker of "Affliction (III)" rejoices in God's capacity to make a scepter of the rod, the speaker of "Justice (I)" confesses absolute incomprehension at the extreme treatment he receives from his God:

> I cannot skill of these thy wayes.
> *Lord, thou didst make me, yet thou woundest me;*
> *Lord, thou dost wound me, yet thou dost relieve me:*
> *Lord, thou revivest, yet I die by thee:*
> *Lord thou dost kill me, yet thou dost reprieve me.*

He does manage to find some "justice" in this baffling behavior by linking it to his own fickleness:

> But when I mark my life and praise,
> Thy justice me most fitly payes:
> For, *I do praise thee, yet I praise thee not:*
> *My prayers mean thee, yet my prayers stray:*
> *I would do well, yet sinne the hand hath got:*
> *My soul doth love thee, yet it loves delay.*
> I cannot skill of these my wayes.

Despite the assertion of "fit" justice and the formal symmetry between divine and human action, some sense of inequity lingers in rewarding a mortal's straying prayers and delaying love with wounding and killing. Like so many aspects of the Renaissance penal code, the punishment seems a bit extreme for the crime.

"Bitter-sweet" explores the same mystery of the extremes of divine behavior, but reverses the process of explanation. Where "Justice (I)" finds divine variability to result from human frailty, "Bitter-sweet" argues that mortal fickleness takes its pattern from the incomprehensible patterns of divine conduct:

> Ah my deare angrie Lord,
> Since thou dost love, yet strike;
> Cast down, yet help afford;
> Sure I will do the like.
>
> I will complain, yet praise;
> I will bewail, approve:
> And all my sowre-sweet dayes
> I will lament, and love.

It is tempting to elide the acts of violence recorded in this unpretentious poem—striking, casting down in anger. Yet to do so is to enervate the love and help that counterbalance the anger and aggression. Like a good courtier, the speaker proposes to imitate the actions of his lord: "Sure I will do the like." Yet as we saw in our discussion of "The Thanksgiving" in chapter 1, imitation of the divine king only registers the ultimate disparity in power between God and his creature. In "Bitter-sweet," this disparity is recorded in the considerable difference between the verbs designating divine and human action: striking versus bewailing, casting down versus lamenting. As in "The Temper (I)," which balances God's "power and love" against the speaker's "love and trust," a single common term bridges the abyss opened up between divine and human action—love. In "Bitter-sweet," the word mysteriously circumscribes both the violence of divine aggression and the vehemence of human lament. The trick is to see both furious complaint and ferocious casting down as manifestations of love.

Like Herbert, Donne was fascinated and troubled by the pressing need to translate divine power and mortal suffering into evidence of love. For both Donne and Herbert, fear and love are ultimately interdependent emotions. "If you take away due Fear" of God, remarks Donne, "you take away true Love. Even that fear of God, which we use to call *servile fear*, which is but an apprehension of punishment, and is not the noblest, the perfectest kinde of fear, yet it is a fear, which our Saviour counsels us to entertain; *Fear him that can cast soul and body into hell*; even that fear, is some beginning of wisdom."[44] "The fear of Gods punishments," continues Donne, "disposes us to love him . . . as there is no love without fear, so there is no fear without power."[45] Fear and love, emotions so apparently opposed, are ulti-

133

mately interdependent. As Herbert's country parson shows "more terrour then love" to his servants and "more love then terrour" to his children, so are Herbert's relations with God interwoven of these contrary threads (p. 241). The fear of God's punishments—recorded so acutely by Herbert—supplies the ground for loving him.

Indeed, God's terrifying power can produce not only love but also comfort. "Lest any man in his dejection of spirit, or of fortune, should stray into a jealousie or suspition of Gods power to deliver him," Donne prescribes an extended meditation upon the awesome puissance of an almighty God:

> As God hath spangled the firmament with starres, so hath he his Scriptures with names, and metaphors, and denotations of power. . . .
>
> The Names of God, which are most frequent in the Scriptures, are these three, *Elohim*, and *Adonai*, and *Jehovah*; and to assure us of his Power to deliver us, two of these three are Names of Power. . .
>
> No Act of God, though it seeme to imply but spirituall comfort, is without a denotation of power, (for it is the power of God that comforts me . . .).[46]

Comfort, Donne realizes, is inextricably linked to power. Donne's God requires immense might to alleviate the tremendous anxiety he arouses. Yet for Donne, as for Herbert, it is not always easy to let the fear such a being inevitably produces to evaporate amidst the comfort attained by contemplation of his strength. In "The Search" Herbert begs God to "Be not Almightie, let me say, / Against, but for me." The power of God is a two-edged sword, terrifying and comforting with equal facility.

In "Nature," Herbert implores God to exercise his power militaristically, by invading the realm of the internal self:

> O tame my heart;
> It is thy highest art
> To captivate strong holds to thee.

By tactically praising God's "highest art" in his request that God tame him, the speaker himself practices a high art which he hopes will tame God. The poem thus imagines the possibility of internalizing the military power of God. "Mattens" also explores the way that God's powerful art is aimed at the heart of his creature. Herbert expresses his amazement that God "wooe[s]" a heart, "Powring upon it all thy art, / As if that thou hadst nothing els to do?" The image of the great God courting his creature strikingly reverses the normative politics of divine-human relations, while the play on pour/power reminds us of the immense power this deity nevertheless possesses.

In his defense of feasting and fasting, Richard Hooker explores the similar interdependence of the corollary emotions of joy and grief: "The affections of Joy and Grief are so knit unto all the actions of man's life, that whatsoever we can do or may be done unto us, the sequel thereof is continually the one or the other affection."[47] As the rod of punishment can be hammered into a staff of comfort, so can the pattern of violent change that was torturous in "Josephs coat" and "The Temper (I)" be rendered salutary. "There is but joy and grief," remarks Herbert in "Affliction (V)"; "If either will convert us, we are thine." Even when God is at his most cruel, the possibility of his turning from joy to grief is always at hand. As the speaker of "Repentance" asks:

> Sweeten at length this bitter bowl,
> Which thou hast pour'd into my soul;
> Thy wormwood turn to health, windes to fair weather.

Neither the bitterness of the liquid nor the fact of divine agency is denied. But as a child is forced to take a bad-tasting medicine for his own good, so does Herbert suggest that repentance, however distasteful, functions as a medicinal purgative. In "Providence," Herbert asserts that "Even poysons praise thee . . . Since where are poysons, antidotes are most: / The help stands close, and keeps the fear in view" (lines 85–88). Herbert never forgets that his God is the maker of poisons as well as the antidotes they contain, deserving of fear even when offering help. "Feare," observes one of Herbert's proverbs, "keepes the garden better then the gardiner" (no. 268, p. 330).

Herbert, then, is terrified and fascinated by the double-edged force of God. This fascination extends to his concern for the power implied by God's omniscience. "The Church Militant" opens with an image of God as a ruler whose vision and power encompass all levels of creation:

> Almightie Lord, who from thy glorious throne
> Seest and rulest all things ev'n as one:
> The smallest ant or atome knows thy power,
> Known also to each minute of an houre.

God's power here is a function of his sight as much as it is his strength. Seeing is a tool of control. "Think the king sees thee still," advises Herbert in "The Church-porch," "for his king does" (line

122). In doing so, he extends the political paranoia bred by the excruciating visibility of Jacobean social life into a religious world in which every action is policed by God.

To the best of his ability, the country parson functions as the representative of God's surveillance: "The Country Parson, where ever he is, keeps Gods watch; that is, there is nothing spoken, or done in the Company where he is, but comes under his Test and censure" (p. 252). Parsons are to perform, in the words of King Lear, as "God's spies" (5.3.17), serving as the unnecessary but visible eyes of an invisible but omniscient deity. Moreover, as the country parson reminds his congregation, God's omniscience, like his afflictions, penetrates to the interior of his creatures, eradicating any possibility of concealment, and providing a continual check not just on behavior but even on thought: "Oh let us all take heed what we do, God sees us, he sees whether I speak as I ought, or you hear as you ought, he sees hearts, as we see faces: he is among us" (p. 234). God, then, possesses the knowledge of interior states that torture tries to bestow upon the agents of the state; as Southwell complains, "we are by the extreamest tortures forced to reveale our very thoughts."[48]

Indeed, the poem "Miserie" imagines the complete dissolution of privacy in the gaze of a God who peers both behind the bed-curtains, and inside the brains, of his creatures: "No man shall beat into his head, / That thou within his curtains drawn canst see." Herbert contemplates here a God who sees all and is monarch of all he surveys. Michel Foucault has suggested that pastoral power, "a form of power whose ultimate aim is to assure individual salvation in the next world, . . . cannot be exercised without knowing the inside of people's minds, without exploring their souls, without making them reveal their innermost secrets. It implies a knowledge of the conscience and an ability to direct it."[49] God's omnipresent vision, and its objectification in the parson, epitomizes the operations of this pastoral power. In his compelling account of *Measure for Measure*, a play deeply involved in the processes of pastoral power, Steven Mullaney argues that James I's "intrusive display of sovereign authority" in sentencing a cutpurse to death without a trial "suggests a monarch who does not recognize limits to his power or his domain, who might pass judgment as readily on his subjects' thoughts and intentions as on their deeds." Such actions, Mullaney asserts, "raised the specter of Jacobean rule as a sort of *psychotyranni*," a specter to which Shakespeare in *Measure for Measure* gives "a local habitation and a name."[50] Herbert's inquiries into the operations of divine and pastoral power locate the apotheosis of such a *psychotyranni* in the intrusive activi-

ties of the God whose eyes the parson represents. The entire system
operates like an extremely efficient version of the eighteenth-century
panopticon described by Foucault, inducing "a state of conscious and
permanent visibility that assures the automatic functioning of
power."[51] The poems of *The Temple* record the sometimes comfort-
ing, sometimes excruciating, experience of total visibility before
God's gaze. *The Country Parson* assimilates the power implicit in po-
litical surveillance to religious goals.

Like the imposition of pain upon the body of his subjects, then, the
unseen but omnipresent gaze of God is an exercise of power. This per-
petual surveillance, however, is for Herbert both ominous and prom-
ising; it is the source at once of paranoia and of reassurance. Indeed, in
"The Glance," we can see just how comforting the notion of being
seen by God could be for Herbert:

> When first thy sweet and gracious eye
> Vouchsaf'd ev'n in the midst of youth and night
> To look upon me, who before did lie
>   Weltring in sinne;
>   I felt a sugred strange delight,
> Passing all cordials made by any art,
> Bedew, embalme, and overrunne my heart,
>   And take it in.

The speaker emphasizes the remarkable power of God's mere glance.
The verb used to designate the political direction of this glance—
"vouchsafe"—is for Herbert, as Strier maintains, "always a word that
indicates gracious and utterly unimaginable condescension."[52] Like
a courtier catching the eye of his monarch, the speaker rejoices in his
visibility before authority. Penetrating directly to the speaker's
"heart," and so laying bare his interior states, the glance is presented
as "not only [as] transcendently 'sweet' but also as transcendently
powerful."[53] Indeed, as the next stanza suggests, the sweetness that
infuses the gaze is a direct product of the power it bears:

> Since that time many a bitter storm
> My soul hath felt, ev'n able to destroy,
> Had the malicious and ill-meaning harm
>   His swing and sway:
>   But still thy sweet originall joy,
> Sprung from thine eye, did work within my soul,
> And surging griefs, when they grew bold, controll,
>   And got the day.

The memory of the initial divine glance functions not just as nostalgia for a rarely experienced intimacy but also as a principle of regulating the self. By internalizing the power of this gaze, Herbert discovers a method for controlling the "bold" and "surging griefs" lurking within him. The poem concludes by looking forward to the time "when thou shalt look us out of pain," that is, when the immense power of "thy full-ey'd love" will not just control but ultimately banish from Herbert's internal kingdom the tempestuous and destructive grief whose operations the poem records. Herbert imagines the "light" and "delight" of such complete visibility will be "More then a thousand sunnes"; the speaker will be light-years from the "youth and night" in which God originally found him.

Both God's gracious condescension and his military power are brought into focus in "Discipline." Describing himself as one who "creep[s] / To the throne of grace," the speaker tries to convince God to turn from wrath to love. Fusing a classical Cupid with biblical imagery of a vengeful God (Exod. 15.3 describes God as "a man of warre," while the God of Deut. 32.23 threatens: "I will heape mischiefes upon them, I wil spend mine arrowes upon them"), the speaker praises the superior offensive capacity of Love:

> Love is swift of foot;
> Love's a man of warre,
>   And can shoot,
> And can hit from farre.

This divine artillery, moreover, has a nearly infinite range. "Who can scape his bow?" the poet asks, arguing that "that which wrought on thee, / Brought thee low, / Needs must work on me." "Love," the speaker assures his divine audience, "will do the deed" better than wrath, "For with love / Stonie hearts will bleed." The poem, then, emphasizes the ferocity of love in order to dissuade God from anger; it tells God that there is far more true "discipline" in the arrow of love that pierces the heart than in the rod of punishment that strikes the body.

Like the punitive rod that becomes a comforting staff and the penetrating gaze that becomes a favorable glance, the bow can be turned from a weapon of aggression into an instrument of consolation. Indeed, the rhyme between *bow* and *low* in "Discipline" hints at a relation between the "bow" that is the essence of courtesy and the "bow" that intends injury—a relation that underscores the ideological rhyme we have been exploring between politeness and truculence. In "Affliction (V)," we can watch the process that "Discipline" longs for, by which the bow that launches God's arrows evolves into a sign of the bond between God and humanity. The speaker prays that God will "so temper joy and wo, / That thy bright beams may tame thy bow." The bow here is not just the weapon deployed in "Discipline" but also the rainbow set in the sky as a token of God's covenant with Noah after the flood.[54] The alternation of joy and woe, a source of torture in "Josephs coat" and "The Temper (I)," here becomes the means by which the threatening bow is refashioned as a favorable meteorological omen. In "The Bag," too, Herbert tells how the "God of power" willingly descended to earth and vulnerability, "undressing all the way," and offering "the cloud his bow, the fire his spear." Next to "spear," the bow is a weapon for inflicting pain; but next to "cloud," the bow designates the rainbow assuring humanity that no flood will ever again overtake the entire earth. The very object that menaces also promises.

In the bow, then, Herbert finds an image expressing not just "the decrees of power, but [also] the bands of love" ("The Church Militant," line 10). Like the rod that is made a sceptre in "Affliction (III)," the threatening bow is recast as the rainbow of the covenant. In the turbulent weather that produces the auspicious rainbow, moreover, Herbert discovers a repertoire of images for describing the bafflingly various fronts God presents to humanity. Aldous Huxley has suggested that in Herbert, "the climate of the mind is positively English in its variableness and instability. Frost, sunshine, hopeless drought and refreshing rains succeed one another with bewildering rapidity. Herbert is the poet of this inner weather."[55] Like Shakespeare in *King Lear* and *The Tempest*, Herbert is fascinated by the power that tempests ventilate. Imaging both natural chaos and directed wrath, both disorder and tyranny, they represent two equally terrifying possibilities: that of God's anger towards his creatures and that of God's indifference to them. "We want our God all love, our Jesus meek and mild," remarks Stephen Orgel, "but Herbert's God is, like Prospero, a god of storms and power too."[56] Like Shakespeare's magus, Herbert's God is one for whom "storms are the triumph of his art" ("The Bag"), a "god of power" who enjoys the salutary flailing of those figures he will shipwreck and then save.

Herbert frequently imagines both physical and spiritual distress in terms of storms. A Latin poem entitled *"Afflictio"* prays:

> Those waves you walked upon,
> My Lord, and which come up to
> Your feet, pound and leap above

> My head. Christ, if I can't go
> On top of the water, let me at least,
> I beg you, pass through the waves.[57]

In the *Memoriae Matris Sacrum*, storminess offers a metaphor for the desolating grief Herbert feels. He laments that "now bare to chance, / without a mother, / To storms defenseless, mercurial, / More fluid than the open sea, am I."[58] The speaker of "Affliction (I)" likewise describes himself as "without a fence or friend, . . . blown through with ev'ry storm and winde." Like Lear on the heath, the speaker meets the full brunt of the storm lacking the shelter of either nature or culture.

Tempestuous weather supplies Herbert with a metaphor for the devastating experience of God's apparent absence in "A Parodie": "No stormie night / Can so afflict or so affright, / As thy eclipsed light." The haunting possibility that God has abandoned his earthly creatures—a possibility Herbert dares to consider in "The Search" ("Lord, dost thou some new fabrick mould, / Which favour winnes, / And keeps thee present, leaving th' old / Unto their sinnes?") and "Longing" ("Hast thou left all things to their course, / And laid the reins / Upon the horse?")—is in "A Parodie" likened to the terrifying isolation and vulnerability exposed on a stormy night. In *The Country Parson*, Herbert describes the necessity and difficulty of maintaining "perfect patience, and Christian fortitude in the cold and midnight stormes of persecution and adversity" (p. 237). Storms encapsulated for him the related catastrophes of spiritual despair, social ostracization, and divine abandonment.

In "Miserie," the image of a boat in a storm is used to convey a sense of mortal instability and self-destruction. "Man" is represented as "A sick toss'd vessel, dashing on each thing; / Nay his own shelf: / My God, I mean my self." The God of storms here watches as his poor creature runs aground on a shelf of his own making. "The Size," by contrast, employs the same nautical metaphor to demonstrate that life bends inevitably towards heaven. What Petrarch and Wyatt imagine as a voyage of helpless despair "thorough sharp seas," " 'tween rock and rock," guided by "mine enemy, alas, / That is my lord," becomes in Herbert's hand a trip "to th' Isle of spices," a region to which mortals "art heir."[59] Rather than subjection to forces beyond his control, Herbert imagines a voyage of colonial enrichment like that of the Virginia Company, in which many of his friends and relatives were involved. The conclusion of the poem allegorizes the globe on which such voyages are plotted: "Call to minde . . . An earthly globe, / On whose meridian was engraven, / *These seas are tears, and heav'n the haven.*" Suffering is included in the poem's vision, but it is rendered liminal, a territory to be traversed.

"Affliction (V)" also attempts to construe as therapeutic a terrifying turbulence. The poem begins with a statement of the paradoxical "firm[ness]" of "thy floting Ark; whose stay / And anchor thou art onely, to confirm / And strengthen it in ev'ry age, / When waves do rise, and tempests rage." "We are the trees," concludes the speaker, "whom shaking fastens more, / While blustring windes destroy the wanton bowres." Herbert's Latin poem in response to Donne's gift of one of his seals—whose subject was the cross of suffering becoming an anchor of stability—likewise uses the violence of tempests to discover the firmness of the cross: "Let the world reel, we and all ours stand sure, / This holy Cable's of all storms secure."[60] Storms destroy the wanton but confirm the devout.

In "Affliction (III)," Herbert internalizes the tempests he undergoes, likening a sigh—thought by contemporaneous physiology to shorten life—to "A gale to bring me sooner to my blisse."[61] Rather than unleashing its violence against God, Herbert envisions the force of his sighs—caused by spiritual suffering—as a powerful wind that impels him to God and heaven. "The Pulley," too, imagines storms as instruments of salvation, alluding in its conclusion to humanity as a ship "pulled" by tempests towards God. Although bestowing a wealth of blessings on his creature, God withholds "rest" in the hope that "if goodnesse leade him not, yet weariness / May tosse him to my breast." As in Prospero's tempest, salutary exhaustion drives one towards the authority in control of the wearying storm.

Herbert's emphasis upon God's ability to control the elements uses imagery that was the common coin of monarchical praise in the Jacobean masque. In the masques, remarks Stephen Orgel, "the king is allegorized in ways that imply intellect, control, power: as Neptune, tamer of the elements, or Pan, the god of nature, or the life-giving sun."[62] The anti-masque often represented an elemental chaos that is brought under the absolute control of the monarch. *Pan's Anniversary* (1620), a celebration of King James on his birthday, describes the monarch as a Pan who "keeps away all heats and colds, / Drives all diseases from our folds, / Makes everywhere the spring to dwell." In *News from the New World* (1620), James is represented as a sun whose light and heat "alone [are] able to resolve and thaw the cold" his worshippers "have presently contracted."[63] *Neptune's Triumph* (1624), a masque M. C. Bradbrook suggests George Herbert may have seen in one of his many visits with his younger brother Henry (who super-

Figure 3. Jacopo Tintoretto, *Christ at the Sea of Galilee* (1575–80).
Washington, D.C., National Gallery of Art, Samuel H. Kress Collection.
Canvas, 1.170 × 1.685.

vised the costumes for it), addresses King James as "great lord of
waters and of isles."[64] Anthony Low has argued that "Jordan (I)" is
directed against the court masques of the Stuart monarchs.[65] In
Herbert's frequent recourse to the imagery of tempests and elements,
we can hear Herbert absorbing the panegyrical and political energies
of the Stuart masque. In his efforts to represent divine power, then,
Herbert adopts the appurtenances of Stuart rule not only at its most
physically cruel but also at its most gloriously idealized.

Tintoretto's splendid painting, *Christ at the Sea of Galilee* (Na-
tional Gallery of Art in Washington, D.C.), expresses visually the
same blend of threat and comfort, turbulence and control, that im-
bues Herbert's spiritual climatology. The driven clouds and storm-
tossed waves conspire to impel the boat to shore, where the resur-
rected Jesus stands. Like the sigh in "Affliction (III)," this storm is "a
gale to bring me sooner to my blisse." A sailor tries vainly to control
the sail loosened by the storm. In contrast, Simon Peter, thrilled at the
vision of his Lord, prepares to fling himself into the choppy sea in or-
der to reach shore even sooner. On the right side of the painting, and
parallel to the resurrected Jesus, is a tree which, like those "trees

whom shaking fastens more" that Herbert praises in "Affliction (V)," represents the firm foundation Christ offers "when waves do rise, and tempests rage." Christ holds out his hand in a gesture which seems either to encourage the storm that drives his disciples towards him or to calm the threatening sea. Either meaning of the gesture inscribes his elemental power. As Herbert's "Providence" contends, "tempests are calm to thee; they know thy hand" (line 45).

The opening stanza of "The Bag" envisions a Christ like that in Tintoretto's painting, one who guides by means of the turbulence he imposes:

> Away despair! my gracious Lord doth heare.
> Though windes and waves assault my keel,
> He doth preserve it: he doth steer,
> Ev'n when the boat seems most to reel.
> Storms are the triumph of his art:
> Well may he close his eyes, but not his heart.

Like Tintoretto, Herbert converts a deity of turbulence and power into a God of rest and love. Storms are the triumph of God's art because of the immense power they both unleash and control. In *Lucus* 12, *"Tempestas Christo dormiente"* ("The storm, while Christ sleeps"), Herbert also imagines a God who closes his eyes:

> While you sleep the sea arises:
> When, Christ, you rise up again,
> The sea slumbers. How well
> You master things![66]

Without continual divine control, the Latin epigram suggests, the chaos of tempests bursts forth. But in Tintoretto's painting, and in the tempestuous lyrics of *The Temple*, we get a more compelling if more disturbing portrait of the God who creates the storms he leads his creatures through. The question asked twice by the desperate, storm-tossed voyagers in the first scene of *The Tempest*—"Where's the master?" (1.1.9–10, 12)—is answered in the second scene, with Prospero, a "god of power," reassuring his daughter that despite the violence she has just witnessed, "There's no harm done" (1.2.15). Like Shakespeare, Herbert and Tintoretto succeed in showing us both the alarming chaos of the storm and the comforting master who is in charge.

Herbert's spiritual meteorology is not perpetually stormy, but tempests seem always to be approaching or departing. "Nothing but drought and dearth, but bush and brake, / Which way so-e're I look, I see," remarks the speaker of "Home." The speaker of "The Glance" suggests that his soul has felt "many a bitter storm . . . ev'n able to destroy." In "Vanitie (I)," Herbert praises a God who "mellow[s] the ground / With showres and frosts, with love & aw." Like the bow that is both weapon and promise, the God who brandishes it sends nourishing rain as well as killing frost. Such extremes provide a meteorological version of the maddeningly variable behavior lamented in "Josephs coat" and "The Temper (I)." Yet in "Even-song," variability provides evidence not of divine cruelty but rather of God's love. "Which shows more love," Herbert asks, "The day or night: that is the gale, this th' harbour." He concludes not by resolving but by suspending the debate: "My God, thou art all love." Like the alternation of night and day, the gale and harbor are interdependent and mutually defining experiences. Together, they show forth the constant if dynamic love of God for his creatures, however hard this love may be to perceive amidst the stormy clouds, killing frosts, and baffling variations that express it.

"The Crosse" and "The Flower" are Herbert's most satisfying attempts at coming to terms with the contradictory and sometimes frightening love this deity shows. The poems courageously confront the suffering that God imposes upon his creature. Moreover, they succeed in converting this suffering into evidence of God's love without deleting reference to the immense pain that results. Synthesizing the God of thunder and rainbows, of torture and succor we have been examining, these contiguous poems wrest theological and experiential sense from the meteorological variety and excruciating agony represented throughout *The Temple.*

"The Crosse" begins in the contemplation of the tumultuous emotions the speaker experiences when confronting the central symbol of Christian suffering:

> What is this strange and uncouth thing?
> To make me sigh, and seek, and faint, and die,
> Untill I had some place, where I might sing,
>   And serve thee; and not onely I,
> But all my wealth and familie might combine
> To set thy honour up, as our designe.

The cross, a "strange and uncouth thing," agitates the speaker, stirs within him a storm of contradictory emotions. Moreover, it instigates the ostensibly pious desire for a place from which to serve God and sing his praises. By service, though, the speaker means, as Fish insists, "an opportunity to exercise personal power rather than an admission of dependence or an acknowledgment of weakness."[67] In consequence, the devout desires that the cross awakens are defeated by the gift of the God whose sacrifice the cross symbolizes:

> And then when after much delay,
> Much wrastling, many a combate, this deare end,
> So much desir'd, is giv'n, to take away
> My power to serve thee; to unbend
> All my abilities, my designes confound,
> And lay my threatnings bleeding on the ground.

The agonistic relationship between God and humanity recorded in so many poems results here only in the total defeat of the speaker, as his "threatnings" are left bleeding on the battlefield. "Underlying the complaint about giving and taking away," remarks Chana Bloch, "is a verse from Job that is intoned in the Anglican Order for the Burial of the Dead: 'The Lord gave, and the Lord hath taken away, blessed be the Name of the Lord' (Job 1.21)."[68] Yet in Herbert's rendering, God is not blessed but accused. Moreover, it is the gift itself that takes away; giving and taking are not two temporally separate gestures but excruciatingly intermingled motives. Even the "much desir'd" gift of God subtracts from the "power" the speaker seeks, "unbend[ing]" his abilities and "confound[ing]" his designs.

A sickness both physical and psychological temporarily supplants military aggression as a metaphor for the afflictions God imposes:

> One ague dwelleth in my bones,
> Another in my soul (the memorie
> What I would do for thee, if once my grones
> Could be allow'd for harmonie):
> I am in all a weak disabled thing,
> Save in the sight thereof, where strength doth sting.

Paul's God reassures his infirm mortal followers that "my strength is made perfect in weaknes" (2 Cor. 12.9). The speaker of "The Crosse" perverts this Pauline conflation of strength and weakness. He confesses a requisite debility in everything but the sight of the cross, where he feels an absolutely unproductive, even agonizing, strength. He discovers the strength and power he seeks only when confronting an object to which weakness is the only appropriate response. The sight of the cross makes mortal strength "sting" body and soul.

As the agony exposed in the first three stanzas is given an agent in
the last three—God—the poem grows increasingly accusatory:

> Besides, things sort not to my will,
> Ev'n when my will doth studie thy renown:
> Thou turnest th' edge of all things on me still,
> Taking me up to throw me down:
> So that, ev'n when my hopes seem to be sped,
> I am to grief alive, to them as dead.

> To have my aim, and yet to be
> Further from it then when I bent my bow;
> To make my hopes my torture, and the fee
> Of all my woes another wo,
> Is in the midst of delicates to need,
> And ev'n in Paradise to be a weed.

The speaker cannot comprehend why God would want to frustrate
his devout intentions. We are meant to hear in a line like "things sort
not to my will" a suggestion of the rampant egotism of the speaker.
The cross, that "strange and uncouth thing" with which he began,
has been displaced by his frustration at the conflict between "things"
and his "will." Yet his smug incapacity to comprehend his failings
does not ameliorate our sense of the severity of God's actions towards
him. In an image suggesting the violence of sword-play, God "turns
the edge of all things" back upon the speaker. Startlingly reversing
Donne's "that he may raise the Lord throws down" ("Hymne to God
my God, in my sicknesse"), Herbert suggests that his God "tak[es] me
up to throw me down." God only lifts his creature so that he will have
better leverage when he chooses to hurl him down. Promotion en-
ables the imposition of greater affliction. Certainly, self-pity echoes
through the speaker's assertion that the only sign of life in him is the
grief he feels. Moreover, the image of "bending his bow," although in-
tended only to describe his long-range goals (*The Country Parson*,
Herbert maintains, was written "as a mark to aim at"), hints at the
aggression against God that suffuses the poem. God, for his part, inge-
niously creates a new art of suffering, transforming even the speaker's
hopes for an end to his suffering into a furtherance of his "torture."

Such intense and apparently unending agony erupts in a prayer that
God will relieve his pain:

> Ah my deare Father, ease my smart!
> These contrarieties crush me: these crosse actions
> Do winde a rope about, and cut my heart.

Overwhelmed by the contradictions of trying to serve an omnipotent God, the speaker cries out for his divine torturer not to stop his suffering but only to ease it. He is lacerated by the rope that constrains him; as in so many Renaissance tortures (e.g., the manacles, the collar, the Scavenger's Daughter), severe constriction is a mode of suffering. Like the speaker of "Affliction (I)," whose God "cross-bias[es]" him, the speaker of "The Crosse" experiences God's actions towards him as a kind of crucifixion. The poem concludes not with this cry being heard and the pain being relieved but rather with an acceptance of such acute pain as the lot of all Christians:

> And yet since these thy contradictions
> Are properly a crosse felt by thy Sonne,
> With but foure words, my words, *Thy will be done.*

The speaker resigns himself to the poem's brutal contradictions as the mortal version of Christ's sacrifice. The "strange and uncouth thing" whose contemplation initiated the poem comes to represent not just some distant act of suffering but the speaker's own acute agony. Moreover, as Fish remarks, the words "thy Sonne" contain a "precise ambiguity," referring both to "the speaker who is, as we all are, a son of the Father" and to "the crucified Christ."[69] His ventriloquizing Christ's four words as if they were his own completes the identification of his suffering with that of his saviour. In place of the frequent attention to "my will" and what it desires to accomplish is an absolute acceptance of "thy will." The four words themselves—resembling in number the branches of a cross—are a kind of cross, painfully difficult to accept.

"Every man hath afflictions," remarks Donne,

> but every man hath not crosses. Onely those afflictions are crosses, *whereby the world is crucified to us, and we to the world.* The afflictions of the worldly exasperate them, . . . The afflictions of the godly crucifie them. And when I am come to that conforming with my Saviour, as to *fulfill his sufferings in my flesh,* . . . then am I crucified with him . . . I put my mouth upon his mouth, and it is I that say, *My God, my God, why hast thou forsaken me?* and it is I that recover againe, and say, *Into thy hands, O Lord, I commend my spirit.*[70]

"If one can see pain as love," argues Debora Shuger in her discussion of Donne's "absolutist theology," "if one can, that is, mystify power, then one belongs to the elect."[71] By translating his afflictions into the image of the cross on which his savior suffered, the speaker of "The

Crosse" likewise transforms suffering from a manifestation of divine anger to a sign of his own godliness. The momentary eroticism of Donne's placing his mouth upon his saviour's mouth in order to utter his words with him fulfills the dream of equalling Christ's suffering that Herbert expresses in "The Thanksgiving." Like Herbert, Donne finds the mouthing of Christ's words to constitute a gesture of absolute conformity with the divine will.

"The Crosse," asserts Bloch, "is about anguish pure and unalloyed."[72] The poem struggles to discover the propriety of the afflictions God imposes upon his creatures while never denying the force or frequency of these afflictions. The following poem, "The Flower," is likewise concerned with wresting sense from the experience of misery. In the latter poem, Herbert places suffering in a meteorological and seasonal continuum which both contains and explains the violence God directs against his creatures. The poem conveys the difficulty and the urgency of understanding the God of power and frosts as the Lord of love and rain.

"The Flower" begins not in a moment of suffering but with a cogent sensual appreciation of God's "returns": "How fresh, O Lord, how sweet and clean / Are thy returns!" Yet the very praise of God's return implies a prior absence like that which terrified the speakers of "Longing" and "The Search." The frost that kills spring flowers, however, is momentarily dispelled by the elation of the vernal moment, and viewed as subordinate rather than threatening to the flowers:

> ev'n as the flowers in spring;
> To which, besides their own demean,
> The late-past frosts tributes of pleasure bring.
> Grief melts away
> Like snow in May,
> As if there were no such cold thing.

But in the next stanza, the speaker remembers that frosts bring not tributes but death to flowers, that indeed there is such a cold thing—and that such weather is the norm to which this day of rebirth is the exception.

> Who would have thought my shrivel'd heart
> Could have recover'd greennesse? It was gone
> Quite under ground; as flowers depart
> To see their mother-root, when they have blown;
> Where they together
> All the hard weather,
> Dead to the world keep house unknown.

The speaker begins by likening his own spiritual torpor to the apparent deadness of perennial flowers in winter. Like the flowers in the first stanza, his "shrivel'd heart" has "recover'd greennesse" by means of God's "return." Incomprehensibility about frosts is supplanted by the speaker's equally incredible spiritual recuperation. Yet as he describes in detail his experience of spiritual deadness, the bleak atmosphere of a naturalistic winter gives way to a communitarian season of snug domestic comfort. "We are," argues Strier, "miles away from . . . the perspective from which the speaker's heart felt 'shrivel'd' and then miraculously reborn . . . What makes the stanza particularly unsettling is that it nowhere acknowledges that it has ended in a realm entirely 'unknown' to its beginning."[73] Moreover, when one remembers the intensity of Herbert's bond with his mother, and the desolation he felt at her death, one might expect the metaphor of the "mother-root" to function as a vehicle for divine restoration rather than for apparent spiritual desolation. The complete dislocation between the beginning and end of this stanza replicates the experience of baffling change the poem is trying to fathom. The poem keeps resisting the interpretive constructs the speaker generates to assess his experience. Like the violent discontinuity with which it begins, the poem finally requires its reader, as God requires its speaker, to suffer a maddening inconsistency.

The extreme alterations between frost and flowers, between pleasure and grief, function for the speaker as evidence of God's absolute power.

> These are thy wonders, Lord of power,
> Killing and quickning, bringing down to hell
> And up to heaven in an houre;
> Making a chiming of a passing-bell.

The opening line of this stanza, as Vendler proposes, "may be translated 'These are thy tyrannies.'"[74] God's terrifying ability to give and take life, to save and to damn, implies a political absolutism that defies mortal capacities to praise or comprehend:

> We say amisse,
> This or that is:
> Thy word is all, if we could spell.

When humans speak of God, these lines suggest, they invariably "say amisse," making distinctions that falsify God's potent and multifaceted being. God's word is all, Herbert proposes, *if* only we could spell; but there is much virtue in that *if*. The poem itself is about the

149

impossibility of spelling God's word, of rendering legible the justice of God's bewilderingly variable treatment of his creature. Even the illumination recorded at the beginning of the poem is ephemeral and partial, expunging rather than including the darkness and frost that surround it.

The speaker wishes to escape from the mutability that serves as indisputable evidence of God's power: "O that I once past changing were, / Fast in thy Paradise, where no flower can wither!" The seasonal pattern of growth and decay makes little sense to the speaker except as the action of an angry and jealous God:

> Many a spring I shoot up fair,
> Offring at heav'n, growing and groning thither:
> > Nor doth my flower
> > Want a spring-showre,
> My sinnes and I joining together.

> But while I grow in a straight line,
> Still upwards bent, as if heav'n were mine own,
> Thy anger comes, and I decline:
> What frost to that? what pole is not the zone,
> > Where all things burn,
> > When thou dost turn,
> And the least frown of thine is shown?

Surprisingly, the greenness that the opening stanzas celebrated as spiritually regenerative is now linked to sinfulness.[75] The frost and grief that the initial lines could hardly imagine are theologized as the frown of a wrathful God towards an insolent creature. Herbert has, as Vendler contends, "been presumptuous in growing upwards as if heaven were his own, and therefore he has drawn God's terrible cold wrath upon himself."[76] But in this construction of his experience, frost, which had seemed to signal divine absence, is revealed instead as evidence of the enervating glare of an angry God. The speaker's "shooting up" and "Offring at heaven" are not signs of spiritual regeneration but implicitly aggressive actions akin to those explored in "The Crosse." Yet the battle is terribly uneven; where God's arsenal allows him to kill and quicken, the speaker can only grow and groan.

Despite the identification of greenness and sinfulness in the previous stanza, the speaker proceeds to celebrate his current rebirth as a form of vegetative growth, and to link it with the activity of writing. Even if it is only "saying amisse," or even "offring at heaven," writing is in stanza 6 relished as a sensuous and animating activity:

> And now in age I bud again,
> After so many deaths I live and write;
> I once more smell the dew and rain,
> And relish versing.

Vendler remarks on the "unearthly relief of this stanza."[77] The affirmation of the joy of creation certainly comes as a welcome alleviation of the poem's severe tone. But it does so at the cost of the theological order the poem asserts. As Strier remarks, "we do not know whether to connect the budding of stanza 6 with the shooting upwards of stanza 4 or the proud swelling of the ending."[78] Either way, an activity that is being affirmed in "the actual present" is placed in a historical and theological framework that would deny it value.[79] Although budding has been revealed as a sinful activity deserving of divine anger, the speaker will nevertheless celebrate the budding that writing designates. The theology and the experience go in totally opposite directions. Writing, saying amiss, is equated with living itself; the exhilarating smells of dew and rain are associated with the delicious sensations of versing. The mortal proceedings the poem's theology questions are trumpeted with a fervor unmatched in Herbert's corpus. The resulting incomprehensibility, like that with which the poem begins, obliterates the speaker's apprehension of God's seasonal and meteorological patterns:

> O my onely light,
> It cannot be
> That I am he
> On whom thy tempests fell all night.

As the love of writing overpowers the negative charge he gives it, so the burst of green life experientially overwhelms the memory of the tempests the speaker knows he has just suffered.

The final stanza opens with a reprise of the line proclaiming the wonders of the "Lord of power" (line 15), but the speaker substitutes *love* for *power* as the object of his worship: "These are thy wonders, Lord of love, / To make us see we are but flowers that glide." The tempests and frosts to which God subjects us, the speaker insists, are not just acts of arbitrary power but also manifestations of deep if inscrutable love. The variability of divine behavior is intended to enforce the transitory nature of mortal existence—exactly what the speaker continues to forget. Paradoxically, one escapes such torturous alteration not by bemoaning change and longing to be "Fast in thy Paradise" but rather by assenting to the ephemerality of one's existence:

> These are thy wonders, Lord of love,
> To make us see we are but flowers that glide:
> Which when we once can finde and prove,
> Thou hast a garden for us, where to bide.
>> Who would be more,
>> Swelling through store,
> Forfeit their Paradise by their pride.

Like the God of "Vanitie (I)," who "mellow[s] the ground / With showres and frosts, with love & aw," the God of "The Flower" imposes upon his creatures an ultimately salutary if apparently arbitrary alterability in order to remind them of their weakness and his power. In *"Justus quidem tu es,"* Gerard Manley Hopkins prays that the "lord of life" will "send my roots rain." But for Herbert, true regeneration demands both frost and rain, drought and flood. Strier proposes that the garden to which these lines refer is "certainly a 'paradise within,' a state of mind which attains stability and comfort through accepting what the 'natural' consciousness would flee from."[80] But the insight the poem wishes to enforce entails not internal stasis and comfort but rather of the necessary ephemerality and restlessness of mortal existence. The locus of the apocalyptic stability to which the poem points is not within us but rather in the possession of Herbert's maddeningly mutable deity: *"Thou* hast a garden for us." Like the deity of *The Country Parson,* who "delights to have men feel, and acknowledg, and reverence his power," and so "often overturnes things, when they are thought past danger," the God of "The Flower" uses tempests and frosts to shatter any misconceptions his creatures may have of their own permanence or independence (p. 271).

In his poem "To the Queene of Bohemia," Herbert attempts to comfort the unfortunate Winter Queen, caught in the middle of early seventeenth-century political intrigue, by reminding her that "afflictions are / A foyle to sett of worth, and make it rare."[81] But the poems of *The Temple* develop a far more complex, and less comforting, notion of the function of mortal suffering. In them, the imposition of pain is a primary practice of divine power, weaning the agonized mortal from any illusion of self-sufficiency. "Thou art my grief alone, / Thou Lord conceal it not," the speaker of "Affliction (II)" continues. The value of Herbert's poems of mortal suffering rests not only in the impressive precision with which they present pain but also in Herbert's valiant refusal to conceal the divine source of his suffering. Yet pain enters *The Temple* not just to measure the discrepancy between God and mortal but also to supply the medium of their kinship. The

physical tortures of "The Crosse" and the torturous changeability of
"The Flower" demonstrate the inextricable linkage between afflic-
tion and affection, between intense suffering and Christian salvation.
Like the speaker of "The Crosse," the speaker of "Affliction (III)"
comes to realize the relationship that obtains between his own pain
and the past agony of his savior. "Thy life on earth was grief," he re-
lates, "and thou art still / Constant unto it, making it to be / A point
of honour, now to grieve in me." The jocular reference to Christ's con-
cern with "a point of honour"—so different from the punctilious ob-
sessions of George's brother Edward, who challenged men to duels
over stolen hair ribbons and insufficently respectful salutations—
nevertheless reveals that the agony of inconstancy lamented by Her-
bert is in the larger scheme of Christian salvation a higher form of
constancy. "Kill me not ev'ry day, / Thou Lord of life," implores the
suffering speaker of "Affliction (II)." His God, he realizes, is a "Lord of
life" who nevertheless kills daily. But he also dies daily; "They who
lament one crosse," observes the speaker of "Affliction (III)," "Thou
dying dayly, praise thee to thy losse." The God who causes pain, Her-
bert remembers, also felt pain. As we will see in the next chapter, the
willingness of his God to suffer extends beyond the original act of sac-
rifice to include the process of attending to the piercing petitions of
his mortal subjects. Although Herbert's God has recourse to most of
the instruments of cruelty invented by Herbert's culture, Herbert, as
we will see, is well stocked with devices of rhetorical violence. He
does not, moreover, hesitate to use every trick in the Orator's book in
his attempts to manipulate divine behavior. Herbert lives to show
God's power not only by suffering but also by singing.

4

"Engine against th' Almighty':
The Poetics of Prayer

You can't pray a lie.
                              —Mark Twain

In "Justice (II)" Herbert offers an arresting image of the God explored
in the previous chapter, who has recourse to the machinery of torture
in his dealings with his creatures. In "Justice (II)," however, Herbert
wishes to displace this imminently threatening God into a distant
pre-Christian past:

> The dishes of thy ballance seem'd to gape,
> > Like two great pits;
> > The beam and scape
> > Did like some torturing engine show;
> > Thy hand above did burn and glow,
> Danting the stoutest hearts, the proudest wits.
>
> But now that Christs pure vail presents the sight,
> > I see no fears:
> > Thy hand is white,
> > Thy scales like buckets, which attend
> > And interchangeably descend,
> Lifting to heaven from this well of tears.

Historical distance and mistaken perception, however, do not fully
assuage the horror the initial image arouses. The "terror," as Coburn
Freer contends, "has a considerable reality" which quietly suffuses
the poem's optimistic close.[1] The poem depends, as Rosemond Tuve
has shown, on the common patristic image "of the Cross as a balance,
the scales of God's judgement."[2] "Christ's pure vail," the medium

that reveals justice as benign, is, according to Hebrews 10.20, "his flesh." What alters between these two stanzas, then, is not the phenomenon but rather the direction of violence: the flesh of Christ on the cross, rather than the bodies of mortals subjected to the burning hand of a sadistic judge, becomes the site of suffering. The cross is in fact the true engine of torture that the scales of justice mistakenly appeared to be.

The purpose of this chapter is to explore the processes by which the violence that God directs against mortals is, as "Justice (II)" suggests, converted into the aggression that mortals direct against God; the way, in other words, that God's "torturing engine" becomes an "engine against th' almighty." Where the poems explored in the last chapter record in excruciating detail a variety of connections between mortal suffering and divine power, using the prerogative of corporal punishment and the spectacle of cataclysmic tempests as vehicles for God's distressing if salutary actions towards his creatures, the subject of this chapter will be the parallel process by which Herbert's attempts to represent and petition God continually entail the mortal appropriation of divine power. As God exercises the privilege of a monarch to torture his creature, Herbert deploys the tacitly aggressive techniques of a courtier to supplicate a sovereign. Devotional utterance is never for Herbert simply the impotent outpouring of mortal desire into the vacuum of divine omnipotence. Rather, it is prayer, a mode of deeply rhetorical speech that intends to move its auditor to a particular course of action. By directing this speech to God, and always foregrounding this being's omnipotence, the poems of *The Temple* engage in a profound investigation of the rhetorical duress of mortal supplication.

In turning the supplicatory energies of courtly utterance to his unearthly monarch, Herbert investigates the dilemma of courtly conduct identified, but never fully resolved, by Castiglione: the immense difficulty of converting the meager authority bestowed by submissively pleasing one's monarch into courtly influence without subverting the monarch's authority or losing his favor. The perfect courtier, remarks Castiglione's Ottaviano, "ought to goe about so to purchase him the good will, and allure unto him ye mind of his Prince, that he may make him a free and safe passage to commune with him in every manner without troubling him"; he must "understand how to behave himselfe readily in all occurrents to drive into his Princes heade what honour and profit shall ensue to him and to his by justice, liberallitie, valiantnesse of courage, meekenesse, and by the other vertues that belong to a good prince."[3] Yet the very force demanded by such activities

155

("driv[ing advice] into his Princes heade") ultimately defeats them. As Ottaviano cynically remarks, "If I had the favour of some Prince that I know, and should tell him franckly mine opinion (I doubt me) I shoulde soone loose it."⁴ Unlike mortal monarchs, however, Herbert's God views favorably not just a potentially alienating frankness on the part of his subjects but even their most forceful endeavors to coerce his conduct. His unchallengeable rule welcomes violent attempts upon his person and transforms them into further manifestations of his beneficent reign. God's willingness to be assaulted by mortal petition lends further meaning to the conflation of submission and opposition at the end of "The Priesthood": "Lest good come short of ill / In praising might, the poore do by submission / What pride by opposition." Allowing himself to be wounded by supplicatory weaponry, Herbert's God replays daily his original act of sacrificial suffering; petition, in turn, reenacts the torment which mortals inflicted upon him. Throughout *The Temple* Herbert invests the art of supplication with a violence that approaches the art of torture practiced by his God. Prayer, Herbert shows, is an "Engine against the almighty" for which the almighty provides the blueprints and materials ("Prayer [I]").

"The words of man in the mouth of a faithfull man, of *Abraham*," asserts Donne,

> are a Canon against God himselfe, and batter down all his severe and heavy purposes for Judgements. Yet, this comes not, God knows, out of the weight or force of our words, but out of the easinesse of God. God puts himselfe into the way of a shot, he meets a weak prayer, and is graciously pleased to be wounded by that: God sets up a light, that we direct the shot upon him, he enlightens us with a knowledge, how, and when, and what to pray for; yea, God charges, and discharges the Canon himself upon himselfe.⁵

At once endowing human petition with the cannon-like power to batter God and revealing that such power is ultimately an illusion bestowed by a gracious, self-wounding God, Donne, like Herbert, is fascinated by the blend of rhetorical force and necessary impotence that makes up prayer. For both, a vision of mortals bombarding God ultimately surrenders to the image of God's condescending to be wounded by our weak and impotent utterances. The power of prayer circulates from the God it wounds; he loads the cannon, and fires it at himself. Even when petition is successful, we should remember that it is not "out of the weight or force of our words, but out of the easinesse of God." God's "state," remarks Herbert in "Prayer (II)," "dislikes not easinesse."

Corollary to Herbert's fascination with the punitive measures God takes towards his creatures, then, is a preoccupation with the manipulative powers of human art. Herbert imagines the self not just as the suffering object of divine power but also as the director of artful aggression against God. Throughout this chapter we will track Herbert's profound uneasiness with the practices of human art and courtly craft in relation to an omnipotent deity. In a range of poems he asks what it might mean to "show God's power" in singing artful song rather than in suffering direful torture. Does the attempt to manifest divine power invariably include the wish to appropriate divine power? Does one show forth divine power as perpetrator or as victim, as subject or as object?

The second poem of "The Church"—"The Sacrifice"—confronts many of these issues by means of the voice of Christ as he is tormented by the very creatures on whose behalf he suffers. The only poem spoken entirely by God, and the poem most deeply saturated by the liturgy, "The Sacrifice" has always seemed something of an anomaly, if not an outright anachronism, in *The Temple*. Ilona Bell asserts that the poem "force[s] us to ask what role this traditional, Catholic reenactment of Christ's suffering is meant to play in 'The Church' as Herbert envisioned it," and argues that "ultimately 'The Sacrifice' undermines the traditional meditative goal of communal suffering."[6] If, however, we attend to the poem in light of the bilateral violence that suffuses the entire volume, we realize that the poem functions not only as the generic representation of an outmoded devotion but also as the origin and end-point of extant mortal aggression against God. The punishing God of the last chapter is not absent from the poem; Christ describes himself as one "who grasps the earth and heaven with his fist, / And never yet, whom he would punish, miss'd." Moreover, as Empson has argued, the final lines contain an excruciating ambiguity that divides between the merciful words of a God who does not want his creature to suffer as he has, and the terrifying threat of a vengeful deity who will punish his insubordinate tormentors: "Onely let others say, when I am dead, / Never was grief like mine."[7] Nevertheless, the majority of the poem emphasizes the violence mortals direct against their God: "They use that power against me, which I gave," Christ complains; "they condemne me all with that same breath, / Which I do give them daily" (lines 11, 69–70). Like Donne's self-wounding God, Herbert's vulnerable Christ bestows the power his creatures turn against him. The bitter physical suffering of Christ—"They buffet him, and box him as they list," "They strike my head," "Shame tears my soul, my bodie many a wound; / Sharp nails pierce this, but sharper that confound" (lines 129, 170, 217–18)—functions not only to contextualize the mortal agonies explored in the previous chapter but also to literalize the implicit violence of human supplication that will be the subject of this chapter. Indeed, as "The Banquet" makes clear, the "sweetnesse" of the eucharistic feast commemorating Christ's sacrifice demands the reenactment of the original sacrificial violence:

> But as Pomanders and wood
> > Still are good,
> Yet being bruis'd are better sented:
> God to show how farre his love
> > Could improve,
> Here, as broken, is presented.

The full sensual pleasure of Christ's love is released only by bruising and breaking the eucharistic bread and the flesh it represents.

In its expressed desire to turn back upon God a power akin to God's control over tempests, "The Storm" exemplifies such mortal violence. The speaker begins by comparing the physical aspiration of mortal sighs with the metaphysical turbulence of divine tempests:

> If as the windes and waters here below
> > Do flie and flow,
> My sighs and tears as busie were above;
> > Sure they would move
> And much affect thee, as tempestuous times
> Amaze poore mortals, and object their crimes.

He longs for a mode of conduct which would genuinely "affect" God, which would "amaze" him as the tempests suffered in "The Flower" bewilder its mortal speaker.[8] Strier glosses these lines by remarking that "God can be as powerfully moved by the speaker's sighs and tears as men are moved by storms to thoughts of Judgment."[9] Yet this misses the hypothetical mood of the lines (they are introduced by an "if"). It is difficult to imagine, furthermore, what might be the equivalent response on God's part to the repentant terror storms arouse in mortals. The sighs and tears of the speaker are more likely be the product than the precipitant of divine action.

The next two stanzas nevertheless proceed to explore the attenuated power over God that God allows mortals to exercise:

Starres have their storms, ev'n in a high degree,
As well as we.
A throbbing conscience spurred by remorse
Hath a strange force:
It quits the earth, and mounting more and more
Dares to assault thee, and besiege thy doore.

There it stands knocking, to thy musicks wrong,
And drowns the song.
Glorie and honour are set by, till it
An answer get.
Poets have wrong'd poore storms: such dayes are best;
They purge the aire without, within the breast.

The "strange force" of a "throbbing conscience" does offer a diminished version of the violence the speaker had longed for in the first stanza. Herbert uses unmistakable military terminology to convey the vehemence of the activity: "assault" and "besiege." This brazen conscience will not take no for an answer; rather, "it stands knocking, to thy musicks wrong, / And drowns the song." "Herbert adds the contrast with the 'normal' music of heaven," proposes Strier, "in order to emphasize further the rudeness of the importunity."[10] Yet Strier also maintains that "Herbert presents God as putting aside all the concerns of His majesty in order to give the 'throbbing conscience' what it needs." This reading depends on a particularly optimistic construction of the subsequent lines: "Glorie and honour are set by, till it / An answer get." Herbert significantly uses the passive voice for this violation of decorum, thus skirting the question of agency that Strier's construction begs. One can imagine either the brazen sigh continuing its rudeness by casting aside the glory and honor of the superior it approaches, or the great God graciously condescending to attend to the wishes of his clamorous subject. Although less comforting, the former seems far more likely, since the poem up to this point has been about mortal violations of decorum, not divine ones. Moreover, the conclusion of the poem celebrates not the outward rhetorical power of its tempestuous activity but rather its internal cathartic function: "Poets have wrong'd poore storms: such dayes are best; / They purge the aire without, within the breast." Where Donne suggests that "those are my best dayes, when I shake with feare" ("Oh, to vex me"), Herbert's "best" days are spent in a tempest that blends internal suffering with external aggression.

"The Storm," then, concludes not by recoiling from the violence it yearns to direct at God but rather by celebrating the purgative application of its turbulence. Although they cannot "amaze" God, the clamorous sounds of mortal suffering may steal some of the thunder of the figure they address. Prayer is, as "Prayer (I)" insists, "Reversed thunder." If "The Storm" longs to turn back on God the tempestuous violence he often directs at his creatures, "The Agonie" recounts the historical moment of "The Sacrifice," in which mortals used upon their incarnate God the kinds of physical duress he often aims at them. The poem allows the representation of Christ as the Man of Sorrows to epitomize the workings of Sin:

> Who would know Sinne, let him repair
> Unto Mount Olivet; there shall he see
> A man so wrung with pains, that all his hair,
> His skinne, his garments bloudie be.
> Sinne is that presse and vice, which forceth pain
> To hunt his cruell food through ev'ry vein.

As Hutchinson notes, the principal metaphor is based on Isaiah 63.3–4, in which the voice of God threatens: "I have troden the winepresse alone, and of the people *there was* none with me: for I will tread them in mine anger, and trample them in my furie; and their blood shall be sprinkled upon my garments, and I will staine all my raiment. For the day of vengeance *is* in mine heart" (*Works*, p. 488). Also relevant, as Wilson Engel asserts, is Revelation 19.15: "he treadeth the winepresse of the fiercenesse and wrath of Almighty God."[11] Herbert, though, takes these frightening images of divine vengeance and converts them into a pathetic vision of divine suffering. Even more remarkably, he uses the contemporaneous method of execution by *peine forte et dure*, also known as pressing to death, to convey the violence of God's creatures against him. Originally a method to coerce defendants who refused to plead, it evolved into a legal loophole by which a defendant could ensure that his estate would not be forfeited to the crown, as it was for all convicted felons, upon his death. William Harrison describes the procedure with precision: "Such felons as stand mute and speak not at their arraignment are pressed to death by huge weights laid upon a board that lieth over their breast and a sharp stone under their backs, and these commonly hold their peace, thereby to save their goods unto their wives and children, which, if they were condemned, should be confiscated to the prince."[12] Because of the intense agony of such a death, and the concern over inheritance the willingness to endure it suggests, the image is particularly appropriate for the death of Christ, whose last thought, as "Redemption" makes clear, is to provide for his heirs. The bitter pun on "vice" ("Sinne is that presse and

160

vice, which forceth pain"), blending a word for mortal depravity with another method of torture—the screw-press, which used spiraling gears to apply pressure to parts of the body—reinforces the connection between human sinfulness and divine agony that is the poem's primary subject.[13] Despite the emphasis on acute suffering, Herbert finds in this image not only evidence of the cruel power of mortal sin but also a manifestation of divine love:

> Who knows not Love, let him assay
> And taste that juice, which on the crosse a pike
> Did set again abroach; then let him say
>   If ever he did taste the like.
> Love is that liquour sweet and most divine,
> Which my God feels as bloud; but I, as wine.

Like the wine-press, which "forceth pain / To hunt his cruell food through ev'ry vein" in order to produce the wine of the eucharist, the spear that penetrates God's side makes possible the taste of love. Prayer is, as "Prayer (I)" maintains, a "Christ-side-piercing spear." In the final line, which is as Hutchinson notes "a kind of inversion of the doctrine of transubstantiation," Herbert again emphasizes the disparity between the agony of the wounded Christ and the mortal joy his suffering makes possible. Christ experiences as a painful wound what is for Herbert the taste of a "liquour sweet and most divine."

"The Altar," the first work of verse in "The Church," explores the role of mortal agency in commemorating the event celebrated in "The Sacrifice" and "The Agonie." The poem is not so much about the overt deployment of mortal violence against God as it is about the dangers of covert usurpation of divine authority implicit in devotional action. As it looks for a way of marking the violent death of Christ that does not re-enact the aggressive energies vented in this historical moment, the poem uncovers the difficulty of transforming the self into a site which will properly display the sacrifice being observed. If Herbert's project is truly to "live to shew his power," "The Altar" exposes the lingering gap between the claims of the mortal subject and the prerogatives of its divine object. It takes up this issue of representation and power in terms which at once question and affirm human creative abilities.

In "The Altar," the reader confronts a poem whose shape and opening lines broadcast the abilities of its human maker. The first two lines of the poem—"A broken ALTAR, Lord, thy servant reares, / Made of a heart, cemented with teares"—further emphasize the agency and power of the poet through a language of architectural con-

struction: "reares," "Made," "cemented." Yet the next couplet, sacri-
ficing one poetic foot per line, also sacrifices the claims for human
craftsmanship made in the opening pentameter couplet: "Whose
parts are as thy hand did frame; / No workmans tool hath touch'd the
same." The architectural skill advertised in the first two lines is dis-
placed by an acknowledgment of God's fashioning power. If "no work-
mans tool" has touched this altar, then the human agent cannot
claim credit for having made, cemented, and reared it.

The substance of this altar, however, is not material stone but
rather a hard human heart. As a result, the altar falls exclusively with-
in the provenance of God's power:

> A HEART alone
> Is such a stone,
> As nothing but
> Thy pow'r doth cut.

Because it "endow[s] interior physical events with an external non-
physical referent," asserts Elaine Scarry, the Old Testament altar "is a
turning of the body inside out."[14] In its emphasis upon the substance
of the heart, Herbert's poem in the shape of an altar externalizes an
interiority vulnerable only to the keen-edged power of his God. Yet
this very vulnerability supplies the occasion for praise rather than
complaint:

> Wherefore each part
> Of my hard heart
> Meets in this frame,
> To praise thy Name.

God exercises his power by cutting and breaking the heart—the im-
age of the internal body—in the shape he desires. God's wounding
power—often manifested, as we saw in the last chapter, in the act of
torturing his creature—is here rendered as a praiseworthy capacity
for fashioning mortal hearts in the image of a sacrificial altar. The lac-
erating weapon is transformed into a surgical instrument.

"The Altar," then, aspires to show God's power by relinquishing all
claims for its artful shape to the provenance of God. As a number of
readers have noted, the phrase "no workmans tool" derives from
God's detailed instructions for the altar he desired the Israelites to
build: "And if thou wilt make mee an Altar of stone, thou shalt not
build it of hewen stone: for if thou lift up thy toole upon it, thou hast
polluted it."[15] Herbert, however, converts the biblical injunction

against using hewn stones into the occasion for investigating the problems of composing devotional poetry. Should one only rearrange the biblical phrases that God's power has already shaped? Or should one struggle for an original and artful expression of one's sincere desire to present to God something of value? Should one make an altar of self-immolation from elements in which the self invests much energy and effort, or should one avoid at all costs the self-display inherent in such a practice?

In a sermon consecrating the Chapel of Epping in Essex (1623), the Puritan Jeremiah Dyke meditates on these dilemmas implicit in the Old Testament directions for the altar:

> What? an Altar of earth for the God of heaven? How suite they, what proportion betweene the glorious God of heaven, and a homly Altar of earth?[16]

Yet the apparent indecorum of such an exalted being's preference for plainness is explained by reference to the enhanced sense of divine glory that mortal meanness conveys:

> The lesse glory in the Altar, the more glory to God, who perfects his power in weaknesse, his glory in outward meannesse, and gets himself great glory in convaying heavenly blessing by earthly instruments.[17]

God's power is revealed not by the craftsmanship of his servants but rather in inverse proportion to their creative power. Mortal debility supplies a field on which God may exercise his omnipotence unencumbered by the pretensions of human accomplishment. The result of God's particular manner of showing his power, declares Dyke, is a complete inversion of normal aesthetic standards:

> Thus that which in mans judgment would have been polition [polishing], Gods law makes pollution, that which men would count finenesse, God counts filthinesse.[18]

Mortal attempts to polish (the form "polition," although unrecorded by the OED, seems a variant spelling of "polishing" intended to heighten the contrast with "pollution"), to adorn with art and skill the altar upon which sacrifices are made to God, are only acts of pollution; by attempting to refine the altar of God, one "alters" and defiles it. As another Puritan, John Cotton, remarks in his preface to the *Bay Psalm Book* (1640), "God's Altar needs not our polishing."[19]

Yet this does not mean that all mortal effort is to be surrendered.

The attempt to avoid the pollution of the "workmans tool" does not license mortal quiesence:

> I pleade not for idle negligent and slubbering handling of the Word, I condemne not Art, diligence, learning, painfulnesse, and substance. *For cursed is every one that doth the worke of the Lord negligently* . . . God would not have his Ministers idle, he would not have them only poure the oyle out of the Jarre, to be translators and transcribers, but would have them *beat* their heads, and *beat* their brains thoroughly, to prepare for light in the ministery of the Word.[20]

Devotion, argues Dyke, requires a kind of sacred *sprezzatura*, a studied nonchalance which would allow its practitioners to avoid at once negligence and affectation. While shunning the pollution of the workman's tool, mortals must somehow engage in strenuous effort, "beating their brains" to find a language appropriate to the already written Word. One cannot just transcribe Christ's "fair, though bloudie hand" ("The Thanksgiving"); one must grapple for a language proper to such an elevated subject.

But the process by which humans may perform devotions appropriately artful yet unpolluted by the polishings of human art is never described by Dyke. Nor is it ever resolved finally and satisfactorily by Herbert. Rather than reconciling this dispute between divine and human agency, "The Altar" aggravates it, exposing the tension at the heart of all devotional effort between the finely wrought work of submission and the self-immolation that submission intends to induce. Indeed, the second tetrameter couplet juxtaposes the two competing accounts of human agency, stressing both the necessity of human silence before its inscrutable divine object and the equally urgent necessity of praising God: "That if I chance to hold my peace, / These stones to praise thee may not cease." As many readers have suggested, Herbert is here playing upon the traditional "claim for the immortality of poetry."[21] The poem and altar composed of the stones of his heart will continue to praise God even after the speaker falls silent. Herbert thus affiliates his own devotional motives with the social incentives of literary composition in Renaissance England, offering to God what so many poets promised their patrons in return for favor: eternal praise.[22] But however appropriate such promises are with a mortal patron, they are impertinent in relation to God. To wish to rescue the eternal God from devouring Time is both hubristic and ludicrous. The lines, however, may be read as expressing not a sequential but a consequential relationship between the two clauses, so that the praise manifested by the stones is contingent upon the speaker's silence, not his utterance. In *The Country Parson*, Herbert uses the phrase in just this way while exemplifying the parson's use of apostrophes to God: "Oh my Master . . . let me hold my peace, and doe thou speak thy selfe" (p. 233). Within this construction, praise of the speaker's Lord is produced by the speaker's silence, so that God in some sense composes his own praise. In "Aaron," Herbert suggests that "Christ . . . lives in me while I do rest," implying that God's presence can only be manifested by means of the self's inactivity. "A true Hymne" likewise imagines utterance that requires the muffling of the subject in order to be heard: "As when th' heart sayes (sighing to be approved) / *O, could I love!* and stops: God writeth, *Loved.*" As Richard Todd proposes, "Perhaps that possibility, when the heart 'stops,' is only achieved with the death of the speaker."[23] In "The Altar," Herbert uses the highest claims about the cultural import of poetry to display its absolute limitations in relation to an absolute God. Like the phrase "no workmans tool," the speaker's effort to "hold his peace" places the question of mortal agency upon the altar he has built.

There is a deep propriety in the persistence with which "The Altar" asserts simultaneously the need to praise and to be silent, to shape and to acquiesce, for even as its lines are hewn to form an altar upon which the poet intends to sacrifice himself and his poems to the greater glory of God, the poem limns a giant capital "I."[24] The altar of self-immolation supplies the site of self-advertisement. Although absent from the poem (except in line 13, where it is negated by the context of holding peace, being silent), the speaker's "I" is at the same time overwhelmingly present. Joel Fineman has recently explored the process by which "the rhetorical magnification [that] praise accords its object also rebounds back upon itself, drawing attention to itself and to its own rhetorical procedure, drawing attention, that is to say, to its own grandiloquent rhetoricity."[25] Herbert's "Altar" demonstrates how difficult it is for panegyric to escape this process. The poet's carefully hewn lines declare freedom from the contaminations of the self in the praise of God. Yet the "I" that emerges from this declaration defies this freedom. Moreover, as it turns its attentions from mortal effort to the divine source of all effort, the poem implies that God not only authorizes, but also authors, his own praise. By oscillating between God's praise of himself and the speaker's self-reflexive praise of God, the poem records the inherently autistic energies of artistic panegyric.

In *The Arte of English Poesie*, Puttenham remarks that in poems such as "The Altar" whose form yields "an oracular representation" of the matter contained therein, "the maker is restrained to keepe him within his bounds, and sheweth not onely more art, but serveth also much better for briefeness and subtilitie of device."[26] As Puttenham suggests, the writing of pattern poetry is a way of displaying the art and subtlety of the poet, not of denying them. "He that contrived verses into the forms of . . . an Altar, and a paire of Wings," argues Thomas Hobbes, sought "glory from a needlesse difficulty."[27] The shape of "The Altar," then, is a curious choice for a poem intending to relinquish aesthetic claims. Indeed, "The Altar" resembles not the communion table of Herbert's day but rather a classical altar.[28] Among the examples of pattern poems supplied by Puttenham, "The Altar" shares an uncanny resemblance with a form called "The Piller." According to Puttenham,

> The Piller is a figure among all the rest of the Geometricall most beawtifull . . . In Architecture he is considered with two accessorie parts, a pedestall or base, and a chapter or head, the body is the shaft. By this figure is signified stay, support, rest, state, and magnificence.[29]

The form of "The Altar," in other words, can suggest not only the submission, sacrifice, and dependence that the language of the poem demands but also the contrary qualities of autonomy, uprightness, and magnificence. The sacrifice of the self and its abilities also provides the occasion for the display of the self and its abilities.

Herbert's "Altar," then both releases and reestablishes certain claims for the power of poetry. "The speaker's very effort to construct an altar, upon which to make his contrite offering," argues Donald Dickson, "thus appears to undermine his very intentions."[30] The poem is, in the apt phrase that William Nestrick borrows from Sir Thomas Browne, "a memorial unto me."[31] Because of the distressing tension the poem generates between the first and second couplets, between divine and human agency, between the need to praise and the need to be silent, between the desire to polish and the horror of pollution, critics have tried to construe the poem in a way which would make this tension only apparent, not actual. Stanley Fish argues that the assertion of divine agency cancels the claims for human craftsmanship made by the poem's shape and its opening lines:

> The poem concludes exactly as it began, by calling attention to its shape, but in the interim the responsibility for that shape and

for the art that produced it has been shifted to God and away from Herbert. In losing the poem Herbert also loses, happily, the prideful claims it made silently in his name.[32]

For Fish, the tension between divine and human agency is dissipated by the discovery of God as the true artificer of the poem. Richard Strier, in contrast, differentiates between "the perfectly shaped typographical altar, a product of human craft familiar as such . . . and the internal 'broken altar.'" This distinction allows Strier to dismiss the tension between human and divine art: "Herbert could hardly be confusing or equating his art with God's."[33] But this is precisely the point of the poem, making both the altar that God has fashioned out of the speaker's stony heart and the altar that the speaker has formed out of his biblically saturated language bear the same name and shape.

Rather than defusing the tension between the poet's act of devotion and the polluting act of self-display, the poem exposes the central paradoxes of Herbert's poetic project, making the altar of self-sacrifice shadow a pillar of self-praise. The claims for human agency are never completely relinquished, as Fish argues, nor are they put in their place, as Strier asserts. Rather than resolving the question of agency and art, the conclusion of "The Altar" highlights the primacy of this question in the devotional struggles that ensue:

> O let thy blessed SACRIFICE be mine,
> And Sanctifie this ALTAR to be thine.

Just as the penultimate line looks forward to the following poem, "The Sacrifice," and to the problems of appropriating the benefits of that sacrifice without re-enacting its violence, so does the final line of "The Altar" glance back upon the poem it concludes, showing the final gesture of his consummate art to be the acknowledgment of its need for divine sanctification. "The Altar," in this sense, does not conclude. Poised on the unsteady base of mortal supplication, the poem kindles the friction it generates between agency and quiescence into a flickering sacrificial flame which continues to burn throughout *The Temple*.

Like "The Altar," "Jordan (II)" grapples with the immense difficulty of using art to show God's power. The speaker takes as his project not the commemoration of Christ's suffering but rather the celebration of the "heav'nly joyes" this sacrifice makes possible. The opening three lines demonstrate how easily this project becomes the occasion for displaying not God's power but one's own artistic talents:

> When first my lines of heav'nly joyes made mention,
> Such was their lustre, they did so excell,
> That I sought out quaint words, and trim invention.

The relation between the poet's lines and their divine subject sounds a bit casual, even incidental; the lines only "make mention" of "heav'nly joyes," they do not concentrate exclusively upon them. Moreover, as Fish remarks, the poem "turns on the confusion in his thought of a concern for God with a concern for the art he would offer to God; and it is a confusion we share (momentarily) in the second line when the pronouns 'their' and 'they' refer indiscriminately to 'heav'nly joyes' and 'my lines.'"[34] As the altar of self-immolation delineates a capital "I," so do these lines blur the distinction between mortal accomplishment and the divine subject they profess. Like the quotation from Psalm 29.9 that graces the title page of the first edition of *The Temple* (1633)—"In his Temple doth every man speake of his honour"—unclear pronoun reference betrays the reflexive nature of praise. Theologically, both *his*'s must refer to God; but grammatically, God is not present. In speaking of another's honor, one also, and inevitably, speaks of one's own.

With far more elaboration than the epigraph from Psalms can supply, "Jordan (II)" discloses the self-glorifying tendencies of praise of another. Indeed, by line 3, the divine subject has been erased by the speaker's indulgent attention to his strenuous compositional effort.

> My thoughts began to burnish, sprout, and swell,
> Curling with metaphors a plain intention,
> Decking the sense, as if it were to sell.

> Thousands of notions in my brain did runne,
> Off'ring their service, if I were not sped:
> I often blotted what I had begunne;
> This was not quick enough, and that was dead.
> Nothing could seem too rich to clothe the sunne,
> Much lesse those joyes which trample on his head.

The desire to "deck" and "clothe" connotes an activity which covers rather than discovers—a connotation reinforced by the corollary impulse to "curl with metaphors a plain intention." Even when the Son is mentioned, he is obscured by the ingenious if common metaphor likening him to the astronomical sun. In the case of both sun and Son, though, embellishment clouds the subject it intends to clothe. These lines, furthermore, invert the relationship that obtains between God and humanity immediately after the Fall, where God clothes his naked and embarrassed creatures (Gen. 3.21). The desire to clothe the sun/Son, then, not only obfuscates its appointed subject but also inverts the hierarchy between God and mortal. In trying to show God's power, Herbert mistakenly appropriates its structures as a manifestation of his own creative authority.

Moreover, these lines contemplate, albeit tangentially, the relationship between poetry and the two markets available to a poet in early seventeenth-century England: the aristocratic and the popular. The "thousands of notions" that run through his brain, "Off'ring their service, if I were not sped," transform the speaker into a kind of patron to whom the notions themselves offer service in hope of reward. The author, in this model, internalizes the kinds of political authority his productions normally serve. Writing, this comparison suggests, is an authoritative and empowering act. Conversely, his urge to "deck the sense, as if it were to sell" implicates the speaker in the activity of writing to please the aesthetic taste of the popular literary market. Such writing does not necessarily empower, but it may enrich.[35] The marginal mention of both aristocratic and popular clientele betrays the ambition that lingers in the desire to write impressively.

Originally entitled "Invention," the poem is deeply anxious about discovering or creating (both available meanings of "invention") the right language to convey its ineffable divine subject. Its attention to the curling actions of metaphor, the propriety of innovation, the necessity of clothing, and the intention of selling, is anticipated in a strikingly similar passage from a medieval rhetorician, Albert of Monte Cassino:

> it is the function of metaphor to twist, so to speak, its mode of speech from its property; by twisting, to make some innovation; by innovating, to clothe, as it were, in nuptial garb; and by clothing, to sell, apparently, at a decent price.[36]

Like Albert, Herbert is fascinated by the way that metaphor compels the attention and admiration of the reader. For Herbert, however, the meretricious nature of metaphor must be censured as another attempt to display the talents of the mortal writer rather than the traits of his divine subject. The very innovation that Albert admires is for Herbert an act of obfuscation.

The notion of self-display implicit in the search for ingenious metaphor is exposed in the first two lines of the last stanza:

> As flames do work and winde, when they ascend,
> So did I weave my self into the sense.

The imagery of weaving picks up on the concept of clothing from the first two stanzas, and uncovers the true object of such effort—the self. The ascension that this working and winding have as their goal fulfills the political and mercantile ambitions implicit in the poem's brief invocations of the aristocratic and popular markets. Rather than placing his works in a sacrificial flame, Herbert here utters a desire for flame-like aspiration. As in "The Altar," the self becomes the primary subject of its own act of worship.

The final lines of "Jordan (II)" propose a mode of escape from the solipsistic praise registered in the first two stanzas:

> But while I bustled, I might heare a friend
> Whisper, *How wide is all this long pretence!*
> *There is in love a sweetnesse readie penn'd:*
> *Copie out onely that and save expense.*

Even as the previous compositional effort is mocked as "bustling," fussing unnecessarily, the voice of another, perhaps of the figure the speaker originally intended to praise, gently invades the poem. But is this really the voice of another? As in "The Collar," Herbert fudges the issue, framing it with "Methoughts" and "I might." The solipsistic aesthetic the poem intends to escape is partially replicated in its uncertainty about the source of this voice.

Moreover, although the compositional process proposed by this "friend" may serve as a check to the "long pretence" of bustling self-display recorded in the first two stanzas, it is unclear just what the recommended process involves. Where is the "sweetness readie penn'd" of love? What might it mean to "copie out onely that"? Would it entail an act of competitive imitation like that explored in "The Thanksgiving" ("How then shall I imitate thee / And copie thy fair though bloudie hand")? Or would it be the passive, uncreative work of an amanuensis?[37] We can see how "wide" of the mark the "long pretense" of self-reflective praise has been. But in telling the speaker how to "save expense," the "friend" appeals to the same economic sensibility that had been "decking the sense, as if it were to sell." Saving rather than selling becomes the primary means of accruing verbal capital.

One cannot help but feel, moreover, that the desire to "save expense" is in some ways a cheapening of the devotional motive. Daniel Featley, author of the *Ancilla Pietatis: Or, The Hand-maid to Private Devotion*, declares: "For my part, I am resolved with *David never to offer that to God which costeth mee nothing.*"[38] Yet as Stanley Fish observes, saving expense is also psychologically costly: "The price of this saving expense is very high, for the expense saved is the effort that would allow the self to justify its pretentions to independence and efficacy . . . By copying out what is already there one speaks in the words of another, and therefore, to the extent that speech is an assertion of self, does not speak."[39] To save expense, then, would be to veer towards the encomiastic silence produced by the death of the speaking subject imagined in "The Altar": "if I chance to hold my peace, / These stones to praise thee may not cease." Can one reconcile the desire to "save expense" with Herbert's promise in "Praise (II)" that "with my utmost art / I will sing thee"? Likewise, can his observation in "The Forerunners" that "my God must have my best" be harmonized with the folk wisdom of one of Herbert's proverbs: "Hee that makes a thing too fine, breakes it"?[40] Can one's praise of God accrue any value without an expense of spirit?

The poems of *The Temple* seem never fully able to resolve the tension between divine and mortal agency that "The Altar" inaugurates and "Jordan (II)" develops. Herbert remains deeply divided between the desire to devote to God the best of his abilities and the need to repudiate the self-display inherent in such an otherwise pious desire. "The ultimate method of reflecting God's glory," asserts Joseph Summers, "was the creation of a work of decency and order, a work of beauty, whether a church, an ordered poem, or an ordered life."[41] But Herbert remains profoundly anxious about the self-reflexive implications of such creations, interrogating by means of his art the very possibility of "reflecting God's glory" through artistic creation. As the creature of a jealous God, Herbert is enjoined to trace all his acts of creation back to their divine source. Such efforts often issue in dizzyingly regressive syntax; in *The Country Parson*, Herbert declares that he is "desirous (thorow the Mercy of God) to please Him, for whom I am and live, and who giveth mee my Desires and Performances," and recommends that we "apply our powers to the service of him, that gives them."[42] But in his desire to please God and to show God's power of creation, Herbert continually requires the exercise of the mortal version of that power. He must appropriate the prerogative of the figure he intends to praise.

This tension between divine and mortal agency is explored in "Sion," a poem which privileges, but not without regret, naked emo-

tion over crafted expression. The poem begins with a statement of
nostalgia for the glorious modes of Old Testament worship that the
New Testament renders obsolete:

> Lord, with what glorie wast thou serv'd of old,
> When Solomons temple stood and flourished!
>   Where most things were of purest gold;
>   The wood was all embellished
> With flowers and carvings, mysticall and rare:
> All show'd the builders, crav'd the seeers care.

Herbert feels more than a tinge of envy towards a devotion which
sanctions and encourages elaborate artifice. As Strier remarks, "we
are close here to the end of the first stanza of 'Jordan (II)' in which the
description of another past effort at elaborate art ('Curling with meta-
phors a plain intention') culminated in another subversive summary,
'Decking the sense, as if it were to sell.'"[43] Like the baroque aesthetic
"Jordan (II)" castigates, the ornate architecture of "Sion" serves to
show forth only the mortal builder's care, not the divine creator's
power. Jesus identified such devotional exhibitionism as the essence
of pharisaical ambition: "But all their workes they doe, for to be seene
of men" (Matt. 23.5). Herbert admonishes Arthur Woodnoth that
even "in things inwardly good to have an eye to ye world may be phar-
isaicall" (*Works*, p. 380). Although impressing its mortal audience,
"all this glorie, all this pomp and state / Did not affect thee much,
was not thy aim." The goal of the speaker's sighs in "The Storm"—to
"affect" and "amaze" God—is here translated into the hoped-for but
frustrated impact of aesthetic pomp and stately architecture: to influ-
ence the behavior of the being who should be its primary builder and
beholder. "Now," by contrast, the "Architecture" of God is directed
towards internal control rather than external glory: "For all thy frame
and fabrick is within."

In place of the aesthetic labor required to create the glorious embel-
lishments of Solomonic devotion emerges a very different kind of
spiritual effort: the struggle between God and a "peevish heart." A
deeply agonistic relationship between God and humanity supplants
the arduous tasks of artistic construction. In this interior domain,

> There thou art struggling with a peevish heart,
> Which sometimes crosseth thee, thou sometimes it:
>   The fight is hard on either part.
>   Great God doth fight, he doth submit.

Pomp and circumstance are replaced by struggle and surrender. The verb "cross" is wonderfully multivalent, meaning simultaneously to crucify, to meet adversely, and to contradict. Syntactically, it implies "the equality of power between the two contestants";[44] but it also underscores the all-important differences between divine sacrifice and mortal resistance. Likewise, the ambiguous "he" in the last quoted line represents the fiction of mutuality that God deigns to bestow on the creature with whom he struggles. Whether "Great God" or the "peevish heart" is the subject of the surrender (the nearest grammatical referent of "he" is "Great God," but the poem proceeds to celebrate the sound of mortal submission), the struggle itself is, in Strier's terms, a "celebration of condescension."[45] Ultimately, the external riches of Old Testament devotion are rendered of less real value than the garbled cries of mortal strife: "All Solomons sea of brasse and world of stone / Is not so deare to thee as one good grone." "Brasse and stone," the speaker continues, are "tombes for the dead, not temples fit for thee." But groans, by contrast, are ethereal, "quick," and "all their motions upward be." Like the flames that "work and winde as they ascend" in "Jordan (II)," groans aspire to the heavens. These groans, though, are not the ambitious product of the painstaking compositional processes depicted in "Jordan (II)" but rather the disordered emission of a heart struggling with its God. "Physical pain," remarks Elaine Scarry, "is not only itself resistant to language but also actively destroys language, deconstructing it into the pre-language of cries and groans."[46] "Sion" records the process by which God chooses to replace the articulate embellishments of the Solomonic edifice with pained utterances of his creature. The glorious temple of Sion is supplanted by the internal temple of sighing. In the final line Herbert tells us that "the note" produced by a mortal struggling with God "is sad, yet musick for a King." "The King's Music," notes C. A. Patrides, was "the official title of the *secular* musical establishment at court."[47] We are meant in part to admire the willing condescension of God, in whose gracious ears the inarticulate sounds of his afflicted creatures surpass the sensuous aural splendors of the Jacobean court. As Strier argues, the final phrase "makes us realize that throughout the poem Herbert has been redefining both the nature of service to God . . . and the meaning of God's kingly state."[48] But in "Sion," as in "The Temper (I)," it is difficult not to shudder at the spectre of a sovereign who prefers harsh shrieks of pain to harmonious notes of music.

"Decay" likewise begins with a wistful glance at a mode of devotion rendered obsolete because of the emphasis on the interior kingdom present in New Testament Christianity. But where "Sion" asserts that struggle is the result of God's migration from exterior edifice to interior heart, "Decay" suggests that God's internal migration precipitates the loss of the opportunity to struggle with God:

> Sweet were the dayes, when thou didst lodge with Lot,
> Struggle with Jacob, sit with Gideon,
> Advise with Abraham, when thy power could not
> Encounter Moses strong complaints and mone:
> Thy words were then, *Let me alone.*
> . . . .
> But now thou dost thy self immure and close
> In some one corner of a feeble heart.

Surprisingly, the obsolete modes of Old Testament devotion seem at once more powerful, and more intimate, than New Testament interiority. The Christian relocation of the site of devotion from "some fair oak, or bush, or cave, or well" to the heart feels very claustrophobic. Herbert longs for a God who would say to his creatures, as King James once declared to his importunate subjects: "I would you had first my doublet and then my hose, and maybe when I were stark naked you would leave me alone."[49] Not only the power of mortal supplication, but also the power of God himself, seems to wane under this new dispensation; in the heart, "both Sinne and Satan, thy old foes, / Do pinch and straiten thee." In "Sion" Herbert wants to emphasize what is gained in the shift from the Old Testament to the New, but in "Decay" he cannot help mentioning his fondness for what is lost. The poem concludes not with a realization of the greater intimacy God's habitation of the heart makes possible but rather with a desolate vision of universal conflagration:

> I see the world grows old, when as the heat
> Of thy great love, once spread, as in an urn
> Doth closet up it self, and still retreat,
> Cold Sinne still forcing it, till it return,
>   And calling *Justice*, all things burn.

"In the cruel ending of the poem," remarks Vendler, " 'Love' indeed returns, but only in vengeful guise, not as heat but as fire, consuming, with the aid of Justice, the whole world . . . The anger of God seems explicable only as a projection of Herbert's own anger against God for the abandonment of his creatures; but Herbert's speculation here does not extend to his own motives."[50] Because the apocalyptic Christianity the poem describes precludes the modes of proximate intimacy and overt aggression celebrated in the opening stanza, the constricted violence against God must be vented covertly, by means of the tacit anger Vendler attentively records.

The ambivalence that "Decay" expresses about the interior worship demanded by Christianity is translated into an irreconcilable aesthetic dilemma in "A Wreath." The speaker of this poem desires to present God with "a wreathed garland of deserved praise" but finds that he can only display his own "crooked winding wayes." Yet the elaborately interwoven form of the poem offers both a wreathed garland and a model of the speaker's "crooked winding ways." Affiliating human art with indirection, he declares God to be "more farre above deceit, / Then deceit seems above simplicitie." But the labyrinthine syntax of this utterance suggests how intertwined simplicity and complexity finally are. All the speaker can do is pray for the profound simplicity possessed by his God, and promise that if his prayer is granted, he will return "a crown of praise" rather than "this poore wreath." Even as the impressive formal accomplishment of the poem is demeaned, it is paraded.

The poems of *The Temple*, then, seem to direct their energies towards what Arnold Stein has oxymoronically termed "the art of plainness."[51] They marshal all the appurtenances of human art to aspire to the heightened simplicity towards which "A Wreath" can only point. "That is not good language which all understand not," observes one of Herbert's *Outlandish Proverbs*, suggesting that the value of an utterance depends on its perspicuity (no. 302, p. 331). But this is not a route often taken by Herbert's lyrics; rather, they achieve a kind of temporary solution to the problem of showing forth God's power in art by interrogating the richness they deploy, "mak[ing] art of the very artifice [they] disavow."[52] Richard Todd has recently analyzed the "significant opacity" of Herbert's poems, arguing that they exercise an obscurity which itself represents the humbling resistance of experience to glib resolution.[53] Todd does not, though, consider that the physics of obscurity make it at once mortifying to a reader and empowering to a writer. But John Donne, one of the most intentionally opaque of Renaissance poets, understood well the relations between the cultivation of lyric obscurity and the achievement of poetic authority. Those who taught "the people by Parables and darke sayings," remarks Donne, "were the powerfullest Teachers among [the Jews], for they had their very name (*Mosselim*) from power and dominion; They had a power and dominion over the affections of their Disciples, because teaching them by an obscure way, they created an admiration, and a reverence in their hearers."[54] Jesus, too, practiced the conversion of intentional obscurity into interpretive power:

> when it is said, *They were astonished at his Doctrine, for his word was with Power* [Luke 4.32], they refer that to this manner of teaching, that hee astonished them with these reserved and darke sayings, and by the subsequent interpretation thereof, gained a reverend estimation amongst them . . . For those Parables, and comparisons of a remote signification, were calld by the Jews, *Potestates*, Powers, Powerfull insinuations.[55]

Jesus, Donne suggests, was the first metaphysical poet, astonishing his auditors with "comparisons of a remote signification," and enhancing his homiletic power by means of the obscurity of his words.

Such cultivated obscurity is as effective in courtly as religious discourse. As Castiglione remarks in *The Courtier*, "if the words that the writer useth bring with them a little . . . covered subtilitie, and [be] not so open, as such as be ordinarily spoken, they give a certaine authority to writing."[56] Opacity, moreover, can also function to produce or enhance the desire of an auditor. George Puttenham, asserts Javitch, "encouraged indirection and ambiguity in language because he realized that the pleasures derived from poetry are related to the way it obscures and retards the disclosure of its meaning."[57] Indeed, as J. A. Mazzeo has argued, Augustine considered "the obscurities of Scripture" as "stylistic virtues which have the function of exciting our desire to know more."[58] In their professed desire to "make a bait of pleasure," to "turn delight into a sacrifice" ("The Church-porch," lines 4, 6), Herbert's lyrics wish to exploit the courtly and biblical virtues of obscurity. Rather than practicing the simplicity they opaquely praise, the poems of *The Temple* deploy the authority and pleasure that obscurity bestows. Even "claims of innocence carry the suggestion of knowledge," observes Frank Whigham in his discussion of the role of deceit in courtly conduct, "and the self can only be unveiled by veils."[59] The overall effect of Herbert's poems implies that the question asked in "Jordan (I)"—"Must all be vail'd, while he that reades, divines, / Catching the sense at two removes?"—may be answered with an unexpected "yes" rather than the resounding "no" the poem seems to solicit. Herbert's roiled pleas for plainness wish to have it both ways, acquiring the power of obscurity even as they assimilate the moral nature of the simplicity they praise but do not practice.[60]

Walton tells us that Herbert's first sermon at Bemerton was delivered "after a most florid manner; both with great learning and eloquence," at the end of which he told the congregation that such elegance "should not be his constant way of Preaching . . . but that for their sakes, his language and his expressions should be more plain and practical in his future Sermons."[61] The story may be apocryphal; it does, however, suit the desire we have noted in *The Temple* to possess both the political authority that obscurity bestows and the moral clarity that homiletics demands.

Although, as Leah S. Marcus contends, there may have been in the early seventeenth century an "Anglican plain style," the political connotations of plainness in the period are largely oppositional.[62] Neil Rhodes argues that "it is the Puritans who speak with an increasingly radical voice during this transitional period between Elizabethan and Jacobean, and it is the Puritans who abandon rhetoric in favour of the truthfulness of the plain style. As far as the Elizabethan establishment was concerned, it was the plain style which was subversive, not the exuberant troping of a Nashe, a Sidney or a Shakespeare."[63] By valuing a plainness they rarely practice, the poems of *The Temple* make space for an oppositional mode they never fully inhabit. Perhaps that is why in our discussion of "The Altar," a poem whose very title and shape advertise a liturgical furnishing rejected by many Puritans, the best glosses on the poem were nevertheless provided by two Puritans, Jeremiah Dyke and John Cotton. Moreover, just as he perceived clearly the pride that masquerades as humility, so was Herbert well aware of the way in which the plain style, in its deliberate attempt to show forth God's power rather than human craft, can be absorbed into the persuasive and artful discourse it purportedly repudiates. Stefano Guazzo, author of *The Civile Conversation*, perceives that those "who professe them selves mortall enemies" to ceremonies "openly detest them but secretly desire them." To use no ceremony, continues Guazzo, "is a certaine kinde of Ceremonie and behaviour, whereby they goe about to cover their ambition."[64] Daniel Featley castigates not only those who "court Almighty *God* with idle complements . . . [and] cast up Prayers with strong lines to heaven" but also those who "affect a kinde of *Rhetorike*, which weedeth out all flowers of Rhetorike."[65] Pietistic plainness, Featley apprehends, is as rhetorically affected as aesthetic embellishment. "Sighs," remarks Featley, "are the figures that move almightie God, and teares the fluent and most current Rhetoricke before him."[66] But once one has transformed the inarticulate cry privileged by "Sion" into a trope, one has detached it from the interior reality that gives it value. The fine line separating the anguished groans of "Sion" from the elaborate form of "A Wreath" requires much art to draw.

A similar impasse is reached in Herbert's poems investigating the role of the self in divine service. Just as the poet must shun the self-display of artifice even while giving God his best effort, so must the servant of God make himself the transparent vehicle of divine action, translating his own actions into evidence of divine power. The speaker of "The Elixir," for example, prays for the corollary capacities to see God in all things and to reveal God's presence in all that he accomplishes:

> Teach me, my God and King,
> In all things thee to see,
> And what I do in anything,
> To do it as for thee.

Like the country parson who "labours to reduce [his parishioners] to see Gods hand in all things" (p. 270), the speaker of "The Elixir" prays for a kind of x-ray vision by which the divine source of all action could be glimpsed:

> A man that looks on glasse,
> On it may stay his eye;
> Or if he pleaseth, through it passe,
> And then the heav'n espie.

Such transcendent vision is the elixir of the title, that "famous stone / That turneth all to gold." The alchemical project of purifying earthly matter is itself transformed into a metaphor for the effort to peer through fragile and impure earth to a pure and eternal heaven.[67] Yet the curious contingency attached to this process—"if he pleaseth"—designates both mortal intention and divine pleasure, showing the difficulty of separating the two perspectives the poem identifies. One may succeed if one only desires to, the line suggests, or only if one pleases God. In one perspective, then, the mortal gets credit for having attained the transcendent vision the poem advertises; in the other, such vision is exclusively the product of the will of a capricious God.

Even as it implies that this all-important capacity for transcendence may depend upon pleasing an absolute divine monarch, the poem proposes a vision of social democracy insulated from such hierarchical distinctions:

All may of thee partake:
Nothing can be so mean,
Which with his tincture (for thy sake)
Will not grow bright and clean.

A servant with this clause
Makes drudgerie divine:
Who sweeps a room, as for thy laws,
Makes that and th'action fine.

The phrase "for thy sake" functions as a kind of magical spell, instantly transforming the meanest object, person, or action into something bright, clean, and fine. As Herbert asserts in *The Country Parson*, it is "the greatest honor of this world, to do God and his chosen service; or as *David* says, to be even a door-keeper in the house of God" (p. 270). Unlike Donne, who in "To Mr. Tilman after he had taken orders" dubs the priest "embassadour to God and destinie," bestowing upon him the spiritual equivalent of a prized political position, Herbert derives the honor of divine service from the master one serves rather than from the title one is granted.

Fascinatingly, this poem arguing for a transparency which would reveal God's hand in all is one of the most heavily revised poems in *The Temple*.[68] The original title of the poem in the Williams manuscript is "Perfection," suggesting just the kind of emphasis on human accomplishment that the revised version of the poem repudiates. The unrevised manuscript version, furthermore, focuses not on the ability to perform *"as* for thee," to "sweep a room, *as* for thy laws," but promises that the perfection of the title is the endowment of one who *"does* ought for thee." The difference is only that of one short word— *as*—but in that word lurks the all-important difference between believing that one's actions genuinely serve God and peering through such illusions in order to show God's hand in all. The revisions, then, retreat from a claim for human accomplishment in order to display God's power behind all action. As Herbert remarks in "Providence," "All things have their will, yet none but thine" (line 32). Mortal agency is a necessary but misleading fiction under the rule of an omnipotent deity.

"The Windows" employs the imagery of light and glass used in "The Elixir" to query the fitness of humanity for the most literal form of divine service Herbert would know: the priesthood. The poem begins by contrasting mortal ephemerality with the permanence of that which it is the preacher's task to convey: "Lord, how can man preach

179

thy eternall word? / He is a brittle crazie glasse." But mysteriously, the absolute difference between mortality and divinity produces the elixir by which fragile and flawed glass becomes a window to the divine:

> Yet in thy temple thou dost him afford
> This glorious and transcendent place,
> To be a window, through thy grace.

The ambiguity of the final phrase demonstrates that God is the agent of this transformation as well as the object of the action. By means of God's grace, one becomes a window to God's grace.

For Herbert, then, the self is made fit to show God's power by transforming its incapacity into transparency. Not the roiled waters of "Jordan (II)" but the pellucid panes of "The Windows" offer a medium proper to its divine subject. Such transparency supplies a visual equivalent of the laudatory silence towards which "The Altar" inclines. For Herbert, the self is granted a "glorious and transcendent place," but a place which nevertheless necessitates absolute subordination in order to allow God's light and life to show through. The very flawed and fragile nature of the human medium makes "the light and glorie" of God grow "more rev'rend," helps it "win" "more."

Like "The Windows," "The Priesthood" explores the process by which unfitness becomes for Herbert a necessary qualification for the service of God. "The Priesthood," however, analyzes this dilemma in poignantly personal terms rather than the collective abstractions of "The Windows." The poem begins by contemplating what is for Herbert the most terrifying and attractive aspect of divine service— its power:

> Blest Order, which in power dost so excell,
> That with th' one hand thou liftest to the sky,
> And with the other throwest down to hell
> In thy just censures; fain would I draw nigh,
> Fain put thee on, exchanging my lay-sword
> For that of th' holy Word.

Yet the power and glory that so entice Herbert also make him draw back in awe:

> But thou art fire, sacred and hallow'd fire;
> And I but earth and clay: should I presume
> To wear thy habit, the severe attire

> My slender compositions might consume.
> I am both foul and brittle; much unfit
>   To deal in holy Writ.

He fears that his desire to join this "blest order" is an act of presumption for which the God he desires to serve will punish him. He also shudders at the possibility that the role and its robes will "consume" his "slender compositions" in its "sacred and hallow'd fire." As the country parson reminds his congregation (quoting Heb. 12.29), God "himselfe *is a consuming fire*" (p. 234). "Compositions," moreover, refers not just to "states of the body, or of body and mind combined," as Hutchinson notes (p. 533), but also to "the art of constructing sentences and of writing prose or verse" (OED 6b). In referring to his "slender compositions," then, Herbert invokes at once the notion of himself as created by God and the notion of himself as creator. By using the same word for each, he affirms the close relationship between self and poetry celebrated in "The Flower." He also reawakens the tension between mortal creativity and divine omnipotence explored in "The Altar."

Yet in a strategy similar to that deployed in "The Windows" and described in "The Elixir," Herbert converts the imagery denoting his unfitness into an element which shows forth God's power. The "fire" whose consumption he fears is juxtaposed with his own "clay"-like mortality to produce an image of human utility and divine creativity:

> Yet have I often seen, by cunning hand
> And force of fire, what curious things are made
> Of wretched earth. Where once I scorn'd to stand,
> That earth is fitted by the fire and trade
> Of skillfull artists, for the boards of those
>   Who make the bravest shows.

The biblical image of God as potter—Jeremiah 18.6 reads "as the clay is in the potter's hand, so are ye in mine hand"—emphasizes both the "force of fire" and the "cunning hand" of God. Indeed, the marginal gloss on this passage in the Geneva Bible makes clear that the thrust of the image is the terrifying power of God:

> As the potter hathe power over the clay to make what pot he wil, or breake them, when he hath made them: so have I power over you to do with you as semeth good to me.[69]

The image of God as potter conjoins the creative and destructive capacities of divinity; it suggests both God's care for his creatures and his disdain for them. Herbert's God is, like those South American Indian deities studied by Claude Lévi-Strauss, a "jealous potter."[70] As "wretched earth" can by "skilfull artists" be made to serve at the table of the great, so does the speaker of "The Priesthood" hope that he will be "fitted" by God for divine service.

Yet the image of clay in the potter's hand does not totally ameliorate the intense trepidation Herbert feels about entering the priesthood. "Th' holy men of God" are not just common dinnerware but

> such vessels . . .
> As serve him up, who all the world commands:
> When God vouchsafeth to become our fare,
> Their hands convey him, who conveys their hands.

The prestigious position of servant to the commander of the world intimidates Herbert with the responsibilities it entails. Furthermore, the fact that the same verb—"convey"—can be used for divine and human action suggests a danger of presumption which Herbert is unable to dismiss. Even as God handles them, they manipulate him. As a result, Herbert seems to decide against entering the ministry:

> Wherefore I dare not, I, put forth my hand
> To hold the Ark, although it seem to shake
> Through th' old sinnes and new doctrines of our land.

Herbert compares his desire to become a priest in this time of doctrinal dispute to Uzzah's attempt to steady the Ark of the covenant as the oxen transporting it stumbled. As Strier remarks, "a gesture could hardly seem either more natural or more pious."[71] But in one of the most terrifyingly arbitrary actions in the Bible, God strikes Uzzah dead (2 Samuel 6.6–7). The gloss in the Geneva Bible wrings some theological sense from the apparently senseless story, but only by generating immense and unending anxiety about the self-serving aspects of desiring to serve God: "Here we se what danger it is to followe good intentions, or to do anie thing in Gods service without his expresse worde." "In a world ruled by this God," asserts Strier, "one does not 'put forth' one's hand . . . unbidden—regardless of one's motives (or one's needs)."[72] For Herbert, the story of Uzzah represents the great danger of attempting "to do anie thing in Gods service." In "The Priesthood," Herbert tries to come to terms with serving a God who punishes with immediate death even the seemingly commendable desire to stabilize the unsteady Ark. At the same time, he anxiously inspects his own motives for any vestiges of presumption lurking within even the best-intentioned actions.

Yet just as he seems to have reached an impasse in his desire to serve God, Herbert returns to the image of the self as the vessel of God:

> Onely, since God doth often vessels make
> Of lowly matter for high uses meet,
>   I throw me at his feet.

Rather than the power of "throw[ing others] down to hell" that initially attracted him, Herbert here "throws" himself at the feet of the divine superior he hopes to serve. In this gesture of complete subordination, he offers himself as the clay on which God can exercise his shaping power:

> There [at his feet] will I lie, untill my Maker seek
> For some mean stuffe whereon to show his skill:
> Then is my time.

The speaker's very abjection supplies the consummate medium for an omnipotent being to show just what he can do unencumbered by the claims of human agency. Mortal depravity functions as an indirect mode of divine praise, by demonstrating how much God can do with so little.

Yet even as the poem seems to settle into a mode of divine service demanding the inactive Christian patience celebrated eloquently in the final line of Milton's Sonnet "On His Blindness"—"They also serve who only stand and wait"—it begins to interrogate the strategic aspects of such behavior. "Then is my time" echoes the tactical, opportunistic conduct the poem tries to repudiate. Such socially shrewd calculations are made even more explicit in the poem's close:

> The distance of the meek
> Doth flatter power. Lest good come short of ill
> In praising might, the poore do by submission
>   What pride by opposition.

In chapter 1 we discussed the unexpected return to social terminology at the end of this poem renouncing the social world. Equally remarkable is its exposure of the coercive nature of its own gestures of submission. The self-abasement the poem encourages is revealed to be a tactic for "flatter[ing] power." The success of the "good" in praising the might of God is gauged against the surprising standard of the "ill" in fulfilling this project. The deferential display of the distance separating mortals from God is exposed as another tactic for trying to close that distance. Even when hurling himself at the feet of his God,

Herbert suggests, one attempts to flatter divine power, and so, in some sense, to partake of it. The art and cunning required to represent divine power inevitably appropriate it.

A range of poems in *The Temple* explore the process exposed at the end of "The Priesthood," by which self-deprecation and praise become tools to use against the divine. As Herbert is fascinated by the way that God's wounding power is enacted as salutary surgery, so is he equally interested in the process by which his own sincere gestures of tribute and submission mask aggression and manipulation. In these poems, even the act of praise or the offering of gratitude becomes a kind of negotiation, a tactic for influencing and delimiting divine power. These poems make a point of their resistance to the transparency and subordination recorded in "The Elixir" and "The Windows."

"Gratefulnesse," for example, self-consciously publishes its own cleverness in making the utterance of an admirable gratitude into a technique for coercing the behavior of a benefactor. The poem begins with the speaker confessing his absolute dependence upon his divine patron—a dependence which covertly makes this patron responsible for the welfare of his client.

> Thou that hast giv'n so much to me,
> Give one thing more, a gratefull heart.
> See how thy beggar works on thee
>   By art.
>
> He makes thy gifts occasion more,
> And sayes, If he in this be crost,
> All thou hast giv'n him heretofore
>   Is lost.

Strier argues that in this poem "Herbert presents a textbook case of indecorum, of gross impoliteness—'He makes thy gifts occasion more'—as an image of the special privileges of a Christian."[73] I would argue on the contrary that the poem provides a consummate example of the coercive power of politeness. The confession of dependence supplies the occasion to display the "art" of the beggar, which is to offer thanks in a way that will encourage future beneficence. As Donne asserts in a letter to Henry Goodyer, "nothing doth so innocently provoke new graces, as gratitude."[74] Rather than pretending to the illusion of such innocence—a pretense which would be absolutely ineffectual in relation to an omniscient God—the speaker of "Gratefulnesse" proudly displays the strategic "art" he deploys upon

his beneficent superior. "In 'Gratefulnesse,'" observes M. C. Brad-
brook, "the skilful mendicant gives away his case to God as he never
did to King James."[75] Donne praises the art of the supplicant who can
"make his thanks for one blessing, a reason, and an occasion of an-
other; so to gather upon God by a rolling Trench; and by a winding
staire, as *Abraham* gained upon God, in the behalfe of Sodome."[76] It
is just this kind of supplicatory manipulation that the speaker of
"Gratefulnesse" practices, regaining in the process, as Donne sug-
gests, a measure of the Old Testament agon whose loss Herbert la-
mented in "Decay." Daniel Featley utters a superficially similar
request: "Give me yet more, O Lord. *What wilt thou give me?* Give
mee a thankfull heart for all these inestimable favours of thine infin-
ite love."[77] Unlike Herbert, however, Featley is not interested in un-
covering the supplicatory shrewdness of his request. The opening
gambit of "Gratefulnesse" is indeed an artful blend of two supplica-
tory strategies identified by Frank Whigham as commonly inhabiting
"the rhetoric of Elizabethan suitors' letters": a "negative self-charac-
terization" deriving from embarrassment at "the assumption of the
supplicatory stance," which "may arouse the other's protective tact
or charity"; and "the ubiquitous phenomenon of self-deprecation," a
technique which is both "disarming" and the occasion for "a con-
spicuous display of humanist awareness and noble affectation—
another form of desert by cleverness."[78] In seeking the "bountie or
largesse" of superiors, advises Puttenham, one should "remember
unto them all their former beneficences, making no mention of our
owne merites."[79] This is precisely the tack of the speaker of "Grate-
fulnesse." Rather than mentioning his own merits, he exults in his
lack thereof. The humorous threat—"If he in this be crost, / All thou
hast giv'n him heretofore / Is lost"—makes explicit the coercion im-
plicit in his supplicatory tactics. He warns God that all previous be-
neficence will be wasted if this gift too is not granted. Pivoting on a
resonant use of the word *cross*, the threat at once enforces and mocks
its manipulative orientation.

In his recent study of noncoercive generosity, *The Gift: Imagina-
tion and the Erotic Life of Property*, Lewis Hyde twice misquotes
"Gratefulnesse" in order to view the poem as escaping the cycle of
coercive reciprocity.[80] By changing "see how thy beggar works *on*
thee / By art" to "see how thy beggar works *in* thee / By art," Hyde
transforms Herbert's display of his manipulatory prowess into a work
of idealized benefaction. Hyde's act of unintentional textual violence
conceals the intentional rhetorical violence that Herbert exposes. By
turning his suppliant self into a third person ("thy beggar"), the speak-

er of "Gratefulnesse" at once distances himself from, and practices, the courtly manipulations that the poem highlights. As in "The Reprisall," where "the man who once against thee fought" objectifies the speaker's abiding competitiveness, the self-conscious beggarliness of the speaker of "Gratefulnesse" mollifies the covetousness the supplication represents. In *The English Secretary*, Angel Day offers the following "epistle petitorie" as exemplary of the strategies of supplicating a superior:

> Even as a bold begger, the more he is relieved, the more he still presseth forward upon the bounty of those whom he supposeth to favor him: so fareth it with mee, who having eftsoons enioied your travel to my no small benefit, am nevertheless so shameles as stil to importune you in the same.[81]

Like the writer of this letter, the speaker of "Gratefulnesse" knows the power that such displays of modesty and dependence can exercise over those in power. By preemptively confessing their own boldness and shamelessness, both petitioners critique the attitudes they practice. Both understand how the expression of gratitude "works on" its audience, binding it to continue its beneficent behavior.

The poem concludes not with a submissive recoil from its overtly manipulative tactics but rather with a threat to extend them in the form of a continuing tantrum. As we saw in "Sion," God prefers the cacaphonous sounds of his creatures to the finest music:

> Nay, thou hast made a sigh and grone
> Thy joyes.
>
> Not that thou has not still above
> Much better tunes, then grones can make;
> But that these countrey-aires thy love
> Did take.

Strier suggests that Herbert here "presents God as being whimsical in a way that many great lords are . . . in having, that is, an oddly powerful penchant for pastoral."[82] One might, though, want to remember what the breezy tone of the poem almost forgets, that sighs and groans are the sounds of suffering subjects, not singing shepherds. The speaker threatens to maintain the "noise" his God affects until his plea is granted.

> Wherefore I crie, and crie again;
> And in no quiet canst thou be,

Till I a thankfull heart obtain
> Of thee:

Not thankfull, when it pleaseth me;
As if thy blessings had spare dayes:
But such a heart, whose pulse may be
> Thy praise.

We cannot lose sight of the fact that the goal of Herbert's extortion is indeed admirable—a sincerely, even instinctively, grateful heart. But the tactic, as Herbert continually reminds us, is nevertheless extortion. The very distance between the genuine gratitude Herbert seeks and the manipulative gratitude he practices highlights the depth of his need.

As "Gratefulnesse" suggests, Herbert retains throughout his career the rhetorical orientation proper to a University Orator. He is preoccupied by the influence that writing exercises in the world, and in heaven. In *The Country Parson*, Herbert describes prophecy as "a letter sealed, and sent, which to the bearer is but paper, but to the receiver, and opener, is full of power" (p. 282). The transubstantiation of paper into power, of flimsy material into actual force, continues to fascinate Herbert. "Obedience," "Assurance," and "Judgement" imagine the negotiation between mortal and God in terms of writing in order to explore the power and authority that linger in the act of devotional composition. Each investigates the techniques by which the devotional subject attempts to accrue to himself some of the power of the being to whom he confesses his own utter impotence. "Obedience" opens with a hypothetical comparison between the contracts by which earthly titles are conveyed and the act of writing devotional poetry:

> My God, if writings may
> Convey a Lordship any way
> Whither the buyer and the seller please;
> Let it not thee displease,
> If this poore paper do as much as they.
> On it my heart doth bleed
> As many lines, as there doth need
> To passe itself and all it hath to thee.
> To which I do agree,
> And here present it as my speciall Deed.

With a subtle glance at the contemporaneous phenomenon of the sale of titles so often criticized under King James, Herbert imagines the possibility of a devotional writing that would be as powerful as those pieces of paper which bestow place and privilege in the social hierarchy. The hypothetical mood and deferential litotes ("Let it not thee displease"), however, suggest how uneasy he is with this model. As he proceeds to elaborate the terms of the agreement, the memory of Christ's "death and bloud," his "earnest" sorrows, invalidates the hypothesized contractual model:

> Where in the Deed there was an intimation
> Of a gift or donation,
> Lord, let it now by way of purchase go.

As Strier asserts, "the poet is taking back all suggestion that *he* had anything to do with God's possession of his heart . . . Through having been purchased by Christ is the only way a man's heart can be 'passed' to God."[83] The poem, however, does not conclude with this submissive retreat from its initial claims for the empowering nature of poetry but proceeds to transfer the coercive operations of poetry from its divine to its mortal audience:

> He that will passe his land,
> As I have mine, may set his hand
> And heart unto this Deed, when he hath read;
> And make the purchase spread
> To both our goods, if he to it will stand.
>
> How happie were my part,
> If some kinde man would thrust his heart
> Into these lines; till in heav'ns Court of Rolls
> They were by winged souls
> Entred for both, farre above their desert!

To Strier, "these stanzas seem to be an afterthought . . . They contradict the theological content and dramatic movement of the rest of the poem."[84] But this is I think to miss the subtle continuity that these lines achieve. They do not so much contradict the theology of the poem as indicate that the coercive power the poem wished to direct to God is far more appropriate when exercised upon mortal readers.[85] Although he cannot give himself to a God who has already bought him, the speaker can hope to influence the conduct of mortal readers by forcing upon them a similar recognition. Like the image of the deed with which it begins, the poem is engaged in a transfer of power; the transfer, however, is from divine to mortal audience.

"Obedience," then, traces the process by which the mortal desire to devote the self to God is undercut by the discovery that Christ has already bought the self. Language may be used to affect the behavior of its mortal readers, but it cannot be used to authorize the fiction that mortals have anything to give to God. The virtue of "Obedience" is epitomized not by signing the self over to God but by surrendering the illusion of independence on which such activity is based. "Assurance" develops this insight into a revelation of the absolute dependence of mortals upon God. Although Herbert laments in "Giddinesse," "Oh, what a thing is man! how farre from power," in "Assurance" it is the very distance from power that empowers the mortal, and so ensures the confidence broadcast by the title.

> O most gracious Lord,
> If all the hope and comfort that I gather,
> Were from my self, I had not half a word,
> Not half a letter to oppose
> What is objected by my foes.
>
> But thou art my desert:
> And in this league, which now my foes invade,
> Thou art not onely to perform thy part,
> But also mine; as when the league was made
> Thou didst at once thy self indite,
> And hold my hand, while I did write.
>
> Wherefore if thou canst fail,
> Then can thy truth and I.

"His first gesture," as Strier insists, "is to deny, in vehement terms, that he can find anything in himself on which to base his assurance."[86] Such denial, however, is the source of great comfort; it is because the relationship hinges not on mortal performance but on divine power that it is safe. God not only signed the papers himself but also held the hand of the speaker as he signed, and will perform the speaker's part as well as his own. This unearthly bargain is "totally one-sided," and so different from normative contracts as not to be a contract at all.[87] The speaker can only fail to perform, then, if God can—a prospect at once terrifying and inconceivable.

> but while rocks stand,
> And rivers stirre, thou canst not shrink or quail:
> Yea, when both rocks and all things shall disband,
> Then shalt thou be my rock and tower,
> And make their ruine praise thy power.

Even this frightening vision of apocalyptic destruction offers comfort in its affirmation of the power of the figure on whom the league exclusively depends.

Likewise investigating the encounter between God and human in terms of writing, "Judgement" provides a witty variation on the tack taken in "Assurance." The speaker is contemplating the terrifying prospect of the end of time with which "Assurance" ends, and wondering how mortals will stand up to it:

> Almightie Judge, how shall poore wretches brook
> Thy dreadfull look,
> Able a heart of iron to appall,
> When thou shalt call
> For ev'ry mans peculiar book?

The Last Judgment is imagined as a literary and economic activity, turning the book of one's life into God, the great accountant and critic. The speaker has heard that "some will turn thee to some leaves therein / So void of sinne, / That they in merit shall excell." Distrusting his own merit, however, the speaker chooses instead to "thrust a Testament into thy hand . . . There thou shalt finde my faults are thine." Where "Assurance" drew comfort from the fact that God held the speaker's hand as he wrote, "Judgement" confronts divine justice confidently by handing God's own writing back to him. In both cases, mortal debility imposes a claim on divine power. "He that made the mouth," declares Featley, "is not taken with words, unlesse they be such as proceed from his owne mouth."[88] In "Judgement," Herbert extends this principle one step further, turning God's words back upon him as a defense against divine judgment. Where in the refrain of "The Quip," Herbert appeals to God to respond on his behalf to a mocking world—"But thou shalt answer, Lord, for me"— "Judgement" asks God to answer his own demands for justice.

Self-deprecatory and laudatory tropes, then, can function paradoxically to empower the totally dependent mortal. The meek span the social distance they observe by exaggerating it. "The more / I am unworthy," observes Herbert in *Passio Discerpta* 2, "the worthier / You can be, coming to help me."[89] Throughout *The Temple* Herbert investigates the force possessed by the related activities of prayer and praise. "Prayer and Praise," remarks Donne, "is the same thing . . . Our Prayers besiege God . . . but our praises prescribe in God, we urge him, and presse him with his ancient mercies, his mercies of old; By Prayer we incline him, we bend him, but by praise we bind him . . . In Prayer we sue to him, but in our Praise we sue him himselfe; Prayer is as our petition, but Praise is as our Evidence; In that we beg, in this we plead."[90] The poems of *The Temple* look for ways to deploy the corollary coercions of prayer and praise to manipulate the almighty power of God for their own disparate ends. Prayer, declares Donne, offers a kind of political fantasy, allowing one to command not just a social superior but an omnipotent being: "It is an Honour to be able to say to servants, Doe this: But to say to God, *Domine fac hoc*, and prevail, is more; And yet more easie."[91] Like Herbert, Donne understands that prayer entails aggression towards the being it addresses. "Wee threaten God in prayer," remarks Donne, "prayer hath the nature of violence."[92] Throughout *The Temple*, Herbert's poems of divine petition deploy this violence to reveal the power that panegyric covets.

In "Discipline," for example, Herbert deviously flatters the imagined class-consciousness of his noble superior in order to encourage more lenient conduct. The poem begins with the request that God

> Throw away thy rod,
> Throw away thy wrath:
> > O my God,
> Take the gentle path.

In these lines he not only asks God to lay aside his weapons of punishment but also suggests that such angry behavior is not beseeming a truly "gentle" lord. The poem's conclusion continues such tactics:

> Throw away thy rod;
> Though man frailties hath,
> > Thou art God:
> Throw away thy wrath.

As Marion Singleton asserts, Herbert "fulfills the traditional courtly role of leading his ruler to virtue . . . he implies that God, as the occupant of the throne of grace, has no need of the wrath that a lesser ruler might be tempted to display and, furthermore, that the gentle path is more suited to His divine nature."[93] The surest way of dissuading a superior from a certain course of action, observes Angel Day, is to "shewe the indignitie, or ill beseeming of such a thinge unto him."[94] That is just what Herbert tries to do in "Discipline"; as "Gratefulnesse" used God's beneficence against him, so does "Discipline" turn God's own exalted status back upon him.

Prayer and praise, then, supply Herbert with a repertoire of tropes at once acceptable to and yet quietly manipulative of authority. "Praise," remarks Day, "(no doubt) in matter of exhortation or stirring up to well doing is of most singular force."[95] By flattering power, the meek acquire it. That is why "Prayer (I)" employs not only some of Herbert's most delightfully sensuous imagery ("The milkie way, the bird of Paradise") but also some of his most violent to define the act of divine supplication. Prayer is an "Engine against th' Almightie"; it is a "sinners towre, / Reversed thunder, Christ-side-piercing spear." It achieves communicative transcendence ("Something understood") by turning God's own astonishing violence back upon him. "The Bag" imagines the act of prayer as the welcome insertion of messages into the wound opened by this spear. "Prayer (II)" likewise envisions prayer as piercing, describing "how suddenly / May our requests thine eare invade." Preoccupied by the violence and power-structure that inhabit prayer, Herbert continually highlights the rhetoricizing tendencies of his most devout desires.

"Artillerie" is an extended meditation on the duress that imbues the words that pass between humans and God. In this poem, Herbert turns to a region for which he frequently expressed great abhorrence—the world of military armaments—to find a language able to convey both the violence that God directs at his creatures and the corollary aggression mortals direct at God. In *Lucus*, Herbert called the cannon "the engine / Most worthy of the sins of men," and lamented that "with but a shot, a thousand corpses lie / Prostrate on the field."[96] In "Artillerie," though, Herbert raids the grim world of munitions to find a model for the vehement negotiations that occur between mortals and God. At once playful and deadly serious, the poem begins in a kind of surreal situation comedy which belies the aggression the poem will explore:

> As I one ev'ning sat before my cell,
> Me thoughts a starre did shoot into my lap.
> I rose, and shook my clothes, as knowing well,
> That from small fires comes oft no small mishap.
> When suddenly I heard one say,
> *Do as thou usest, disobey,*
> *Expell good motions from thy breast,*
> *Which have the face of fire, but end in rest.*

The speaker's commonsensical fear of fire is revealed by this mysterious voice to be in fact a recoil from divine grace. God is, as we saw in "The Priesthood," a "sacred and hallow'd fire" which threatens to "consume" Herbert's "slender compositions." Instinct for survival is thereby manifested as habitual disobedience. The stanza encompasses, as Strier argues, an attack on the propriety of rationalism in the realm of religion: "The most natural of responses—self-preservation and the avoidance of pain—turns out to be opposition to God."[97] God's surprising means of approach to humanity may seem violent and frightening (they "have the face of fire"), but they point towards a peace and "rest" far more profound than the complacence they interrupt.

Realizing that the star is, like "all things," a "minister" of God, the speaker "turn[s]" to his superior to confess his customary stubbornness and express his willingness to seek pardon for it:

> If I refuse,
> Dread Lord, said, I, so oft my good;
> Then I refuse not ev'n with bloud
> To wash away my stubborn thought:
> For I will do or suffer what I ought.

Significantly, though, the speaker does not so much willingly accept the motions of his "Dread Lord" as negate his own refusal. The parallel syntax ("If I refuse . . . Then I refuse not . . . ") betrays the similarity between his desire for submission and his lingering resistance to it. Even the statement of his willingness to submit ("I will *do* or suffer what I *ought*"; my italics) is an affirmation of mortal action and a reinscription of the issue of desert—both elements which the poem's initial attack on rationalism wished to banish from the realm of devotion.

The ambiguous reference to "bloud" ("Whose blood?" asks William Nestrick, since "blood remains unmodified by 'my' or 'thy'") invokes at once the idea of military wounding present in the poem's title and the concept of sacrificial wounding at the center of the poet's religion.[98] The two meanings quickly merge, as the resistance implicit in the first two stanzas bursts forth in the next stanza. The speaker pulls out the heavy artillery against his God.

> But I have also starres and shooters too,
> Born where thy servants both artilleries use.
> My tears and prayers night and day do wooe,
> And work up to thee; yet thou dost refuse.

The stanza holds out the possibility of equality, even symmetry, between God and his creature. Where God has stars and shooters, the speaker has tears and prayers. As in "Sion" and "Gratefulnesse," Herbert imagines that the sounds of human suffering constitute a kind of artillery which humans aim at God.

The speaker proceeds to recoil from the presumption inherent in such parallels between divine and human activity, but he refuses to relinquish the parallel entirely:

> Not but I am (I must say still)
> Much more oblig'd to do thy will,
> Then thou to grant mine: but because
> Thy promise now hath ev'n set thee thy laws.

He confesses himself more obligated to *do* God's will than God is to *grant* his; the verbs underscore the hierarchy that the parallel syntax would disguise. The *must* of the parenthetical expression, further-more, infers the obligation to confess his inferiority that the speaker continues to forget. He nevertheless obligates God to live up to the terms of his own promise by translating this promise into a law. In the *Laws of Ecclesiastical Polity*, Richard Hooker likewise describes how God "is a law both to himself, and to all other things besides," but warns that "nor is the freedom of the will of God any whit abated, let, or hindered, by means of this; because the imposition of this law upon himself is his own free and voluntary act."[99] But the speaker of "Artillerie" attempts to turn God's will back upon him. He tries to transform God's voluntary act into an involuntary bond.

In "Justice (II)," the poem with which we began this chapter, Herbert tells the formerly terrifying figure of Justice that "Gods promises have made thee mine." There, divine promise mollifies the terror of divine judgment. But in "Artillerie," these beneficent promises are ham-mered into the weapons creatures aim at their God. Even as he draws misleading parallels between divine and mortal warmongering, the speaker recoils from the antagonistic relationship his terminology implies:

> Then we are shooters both, and thou dost deigne
> To enter combate with us, and contest
> With thine own clay. But I would parley fain:
> Shunne not my arrows, and behold my breast.

The speaker's own tactical imposition of obligation upon God results only in his longing for a treaty with God. The conclusion of the poem parodies such negotiations, demonstrating in its involuted syntax the ludicrous nature of the project.

> Yet if thou shunnest, I am thine:
> I must be so, if I am mine.
> There is no articling with thee:
> I am but finite, yet thine infinitely.

The speaker concedes his inability even to "article" with God, that is, to make a treaty with him. As Strier argues, "God is not to be conceived of as in any way bound or obliged to keep particular terms with men. There is all freedom on the one side and all obligation on the other."[100] The poem deploys a vocabulary of warfare and treaty to uncover at once the striking violence, and ultimate impotence, of human petition. It does battle with God in order to discover "the utter absoluteness of God's sovereignty."[101] Even the activity represented by the term embedded in both *artillery* and *article*—art—must, the poem suggests, be relinquished. Not only is there no "artillerie," no "articling" with God; as "Sion" and "Decay" make clear, there is no "art" with God, either, only the sighs and groans of human suffering. "Artillerie" develops, as A. L. Clements has shown, from the meditative tradition of the "Spiritual Combat" best known in Lorenzo Scupoli's work by that title.[102] But what is remarkable about Herbert's poem is the way he bends against his God the agonistic energies that this tradition directs at sin.

In the Epilogue to *The Tempest*, Prospero suggests that since he now lacks "Spirits to enforce, [and] art to enchant," the only power left him is that residing in "prayer, / Which pierces so, that it assaults / Mercy itself, and frees all faults." Like Herbert, Shakespeare clearly apprehends the unstable blend of power and plea, of mortal violence and divine condescension, that makes up prayer. Herbert never denies the aggression that suffuses the supplicatory process; he understands that the most devout petition nevertheless replays the scenario of the Passion, piercing and assaulting the figure of Mercy itself. But he does trace the crucial differences in emphasis between the human cruelty featured in "The Sacrifice" and the divine accessibility advertised in "The Bag." Although both poems depict the body of Christ as the site of mortal violence, the first ends in the ambiguous threat that Christ's torturers will someday say, "Never was grief like mine"; the latter concludes with the beneficent promise that "the doore" to heaven opened in his side "shall still be open." The wounded Christ further promises that he will "present" the mortal petitions that pierce him "and somewhat more, / Not to his hurt." In that last richly understated phrase resides the merciful irony of mortal violence and divine receptiveness. Prayer replays the terrible moment that makes divine supplication possible.

Herbert's poems, then, record in excruciating detail not only the suffering that God imposes on his subjects but also the aggression mortals direct at God. The mortal body is the site of a pain which both alienates and unites God and his creatures. Although God is frequently imagined as torturer and thunderer, placing his creatures on the rack, and surrounding them with terrifying storms and desiccating droughts, mortals in turn assault and batter God with their petitions, even capitalizing upon their inferiority as a tool of coercion. The rhetorical strategies of Renaissance courtly culture supply Herbert with a surprisingly effective medium for countering God's deployment of the spectacular cruelties of Jacobean England. In his unflinching portrait of the agony and turbulence with which God encompasses his creatures, and of the penetrating aggression of prayer, Herbert discovers the surprising relationship between God's terrifying power and his overwhelming love.

By investigating the remarkable force and ultimate impotence of human petition, the poems of *The Temple* tell us an immense amount about the manipulations and limitations of the language of social supplication in Herbert's day, and about Herbert's concept of the divine-human relationship. A lesser poet and soul would have censored or suppressed the often terrifying violence that mediates God's relations with his creature. But Herbert courageously depicts his God not as an insipid deity of pastel robes and flimsy mercy but rather as an omnipotent being whose power and love are to be feared and prized. Such power makes his willing condescension to be wounded by the petitions of his creatures all the more remarkable. As we will see in the next chapter, the weapons used by Herbert's God to kill his creatures include kindness as well as the rack, food as well as physic.[103] The fear bred by this being's awesome power explains in part the instinctive recoil from divinity that begins "Love (III)," the poem featured in that chapter: "Love bade me welcome: yet my soul drew back." Moreover, the love that motivates this God's condescension to physical vulnerability is fulfilled in the ravishing courtesy by which Love stoops to nourish his servant with the substance of his own body: "You must sit down, sayes Love, and taste my meat." The ultimate deed of violence, the poem suggests, occurs as an act of grace.

III
"Love Bade Me Welcome"

5
Standing on Ceremony:
The Comedy of Manners in "Love (III)"

Etiquette is a kind of dance, dance a kind of ritual, and worship a form of etiquette.
—Clifford Geertz

In the marginal notes to his personal edition of *The Temple*, Coleridge suggests that a complete appreciation of Herbert's poems requires "a constitutional Predisposition to Ceremoniousness, in piety as in manners."[1] In no poem is the conjunction of piety and manners more prominent than in "Love (III)," in which Herbert percolates a strenuous spirituality through the terrestrial politics of Renaissance hierarchical relationships. By representing God as an affable lord and humanity as an unworthy guest, Herbert amplifies the overtones of hospitality already present in Reformation discussions of the Eucharist.[2] But this act of amplification also implicates the discourse between humanity and divinity in the strategically submissive yet subtly coercive vocabulary of courtesy. When read as a part of this vocabulary, both the host's gracious invitation and the speaker's equally gracious refusals register an intense concern with propriety, precedence, and prestige. "Dining was but a pretext for a complex ritual and an occasion for social demonstration," argues Jacques Revel, building upon Norbert Elias's insights into the burgeoning fastidiousness of Renaissance commensal conduct:

Eating in company required self-control. A person had to forget about his body, with its indiscreet appetites, its functions, its noises, and its humors. But that alone was no longer enough. The diner had to learn how to conduct himself at table and how to consume his food. A meal became a kind of ballet, during which every gesture of every diner had to be controlled . . . it was only after the new rules had been learned that dining could fulfill its true function: to render visible the social relations among the diners.[3]

"Love (III)" is just such a ballet, transforming the occasion for satisfying primal hunger into an elegant aesthetic and communal form. In it, Herbert employs a situation fraught with social anxiety and political importance—dining with the great—not just to render visible his social relations with God but also to throw into relief the immense difficulty of responding properly to God's overwhelming beneficence.

"Love (III)" is based upon the prevalent Renaissance concept of the Lord's Supper as an actual meal to which one is invited by a lord. Heinrich Bullinger, for example, remarks that "as often as thou comest unto the supper of ye Lord, thou sittest down at the lords table, thou art made Christs guest."[4] The "Homily of the worthy receiving . . . of the Sacrament" likewise speaks of the Lord's "heavenly Supper, where every one of us must be ghestes," and compares the presumption of entering unworthily "into this presence of our Lord and Judge" to the behavior of servants who dare "presume to an earthly masters table, whom they have offended."[5] Herbert exploits this association of the Lord's Supper with earthly hospitality throughout "Love (III)." As Stephen Booth remarks, "the word 'host' never appears in the poem and is the common denominator on which its uneasy analogies turn."[6] By pivoting on a pun it never mentions, the poem supplies a metaphorical equivalent to its central event, incorporating the eucharistic host in a cordial and receptive superior, and disposing the discourse between divine and human according to the strategies and ceremonies of courtesy.[7]

The amenities of hospitality must have held particular personal significance for Herbert, since, as Amy Charles has shown, "From the time he left Cambridge until he settled into the rectory at Bemerton, Herbert had no habitation of his own."[8] Herbert's entire social existence in these six years was that of a guest, dependent on the bounty of relatives and patrons (categories which often overlapped) for sustenance and shelter. Yet the household in which Herbert was raised made a diurnal practice of lavish hospitality: "Seldom were the Herberts without guests at meals."[9] Edward Herbert remembers that his mother "had for many years kept hospitality with that plenty and order as exceeded all either of her countrey or time."[10] Significantly, the poems of *The Temple* often depict God as a generous magnate. "Whitsunday" recalls the days of apostolic Christianity as a time when God did "keep open house, richly attended, / Feasting all comers." Herbert's translation of "The 23d Psalme" declares that "the God of love my shepherd is, / And he that doth me feed"; this God "dost make me sit and dine." In "Providence," the whole of creation is depicted as a "feast, / Where all the guests sit close, and nothing wants" (lines 133–34), while in "Man" it is "either our cupboard of food, / Or cabinet of pleasure." In such passages, argues Leah Marcus, Herbert "re-create[s] for himself a near-extinct social institution," that of "the late-feudal household, with its scores of retainers, magnificent shows of hospitality, and great hall."[11] Yet Herbert's attraction to this vision may not have been so much nostalgia for a mode of life that has always been less visible in the present than in the past as it was profound insight into the power and prestige bestowed by the capability to feed others. As Felicity Heal has shown, the protocol of the age forged "an indissoluble link between gentility and household generosity"; "generosity," she argues, was "one of the methods by which the social, and even the political, power of the mighty was confirmed and sustained."[12] Licensed by a range of scriptural precedents, hospitality provides an appropriate vehicle for the exercise of God's beneficent power.

Indeed, even as they register the hospitality by which God confirms his power, the poems of *The Temple* record the inability and reluctance of mortals to accommodate God. Herbert is deeply troubled by humanity's indifference to a God who descends to visit his creatures as a guest. "Sepulchre" bemoans the fact that human hearts "can lodge transgressions by the score . . . yet out of doore / They leave thee." "Christmas" asks God to improve the earthly accommodations he seeks (and, by implication, the status of his mortal subject): "Furnish & deck my soul, that thou mayst have / A better lodging then a rack or grave." "Until he was past his mid-thirties," reminds Amy Charles, "Herbert was never head of his own house or of his own table."[13] Like the speaker of "Christmas," Herbert was able to exercise hospitality only by means of a prior act of grace from a superior. The contrast between divine hospitality and human poverty running throughout *The Temple* and culminating in "Love (III)" must have contained for Herbert a powerful social and biographical component. The situation of "Love (III)"—a superior's invitation to shelter and meat—presupposes a set of social conventions which Herbert's particular circumstances would have required him to know all too well.

The first line encapsulates the pattern of gracious invitation and polite deferral that these conventions demand: "Love bade me welcome: yet my soul drew back." Helen Vendler aptly compares the poem to "some decorous minuet . . . a pace forward, a hanging back, a slackening, a drawing nearer, a lack, a fullness, a dropping of the eyes, a glance, a touch, a reluctance, a proffer, a refusal, a demurrer, an insistence—and then the final seating at the feast."[14] By humbly withdrawing from Love's gracious approach because he feels "guilty of dust and sin," the speaker of "Love (III)" unfolds an etymological connection between his state and his behavior; the word "humble" comes from "humus," the Latin term for the ground that has begrimed him. Love counters the speaker's reluctance by asking the definitively hospitable question of whether his guest lacks anything. The speaker's rejoinder to this question—"A guest . . . worthy to be here"—wittily replicates his initial impulse to draw back from his Lord's threshold. In its depiction of a wavering speaker and a welcoming lord, the poem pulsates with the restrained rhythms and intentional understatements of polite conversation.

Within the guest-host metaphor, the speaker's protestation of unworthiness provides a prototypically courteous response to the offer of honor from a superior. Frank Whigham has identified the importance of such tropes of self-deprecation in the circulation of honor at court.[15] One of their uses was to disguise a "vulgar" ambition that would morally and socially devalue the recipient were it to be glimpsed by his courtly audience. As Stefano Guazzo remarks in *The Civile Conversation*, "it is the parte of him whiche receiveth these outwarde honours, first, modestly to refuse them, shewing thereby that hee looketh not for them, otherwise hee shall shewe to bee somewhat proude."[16] Yet the tropes of self-deprecation can also exert, in Whigham's phrase, "symbolic pressure" upon the superior who is bestowing the honor. Castiglione's *Courtier*, for example, suggests that one ought

> alwaies to humble his selfe somewhat under his degree, and not receive favor and promotions so easily as they be offered him, but refuse them modestly, shewing he much esteemeth them . . . that he may give him an occasion that offreth them, to offer them with a great deal more instance.
>
> Because the more resistance a man maketh in such manner to receive them, the more doth he seeme to the prince that giveth them to be esteemed, and that the benefit which hee bestoweth is so much the more, as he that receiveth it, seemeth to make of it, thinking himselfe much honoured thereby.[17]

Whigham describes well the complex politics of this passage: "The prescribed response does emphasize the gap between giver and recipient, thus flattering the giver. But at the same time, it extracts repeated offers, reiterations of the recipient's desert. . . . . refusal arouses wooing and compliment . . . this mechanism allows one to recycle an occasion of gain for further gain."[18] The modest denial of worth furnishes praise of the superior in the recognition that what one is about to receive has not been earned, but is instead a gift, an act of grace; at the same time, it expresses an ingratiating humility which quietly paves the way for future favors. The modest initial deferral of the speaker of "Love (III)" thus is not necessarily a rejection of his superior's judgment but can be viewed as an attempt to enhance his own, and his superior's, status. As James Cleland remarks in the *Institution of a Young Noble Man*, "I wish you who are honoured, to refuse it modestlie, and to refer it back againe unto the honourer: which shall encrease your honour the more."[19]

Indeed, because of the potential for inverted self-aggrandizement implicit in such tactically modest behavior, Giovanni della Casa is deeply suspicious of the motives of those who practice it:

> they that embase themselves thus beyond measure, refusing that worship and honor that is but duely their owne of verie right: shewe more pride in this contempte, then they that usurp those things that are not so due unto them.[20]

Pride is manifested not only in the attention-getting exhibition of one's own humility but also in the scorn of others that it implies:

> he that refuseth that which every man els doth hunt for: sheweth therin, he reproveth or contemneth the common opinion of men. And, to contemne the honour & renowne which other men gape for so much, is but to glorie and magnifie him selfe above other.[21]

We have come full circle from Guazzo's recommendation that the courtier initially refuse "outwarde honours" so that he will not "shew to bee somewhat proude." To della Casa, the modest refusal of deserved honor is as charged with arrogance as the impertinent acceptance of undeserved honor.

The speaker of "Love (III)," then, is placed in a complex and delicate political situation. If he defers too strenuously or accepts too eagerly the invitation, he will fail to manifest the requisite honor to his superior as well as the appropriate humility in himself. In a chapter of *The Arte of English Poesie* entitled "Of decencie in behaviour which also belongs to the consideration of the Poet or maker," George Puttenham narrates the story of Anaxagoras, a philosopher who received from Alexander the Great a rich gift "disproportionable both to his profession and calling and therefore indecent."[22] The indecorousness of the gift, however, is outweighed by the potential impertinence of refusal, which "had otherwise bene some empeachement of the kings abilitie or wisedome." Such impeachment, concludes Puttenham, "had not bene decent in the philosopher."[23] The refusal of an un-deserved and "indecent" gift from one's superior is more "indecent" than accepting it, because such refusal impugns the judgment of one's superior. One should eschew the potential insubordination of such refusal because "princes liberalities are not measured by merite nor by other mens estimations, but by their owne appetits and according to their greatnesse."[24] To refuse a superior's gift is to rebuff his authority.

So even the initial polite deferral of honor by the speaker of "Love (III)" is charged with the possibility of political presumption. I do not mean to suggest that the guest's initial response is necessarily as stra-tegic and calculated as the deferrals exemplified in the courtesy liter-ature we have been examining. I am arguing, however, that the political pressures of courtesy invade the socially determined recoil from a superior's invitation: "Love bade me welcome: yet my soul drew back." The speaker, furthermore, does not stop with this initial deferral, but continues to stand on ceremony, to cling to the issue of his inability to merit such an honor. To his host's assertion that "you shall be [a guest worthy to be here]," the speaker protests his own un-worthiness for the favor his superior has chosen to bestow upon him, replacing his general statement of human unfitness—"Guiltie of dust and sinne"—with a declaration of his own particular sinful-ness—"I the unkinde, ungratefull"—and a confession of the shame this sinfulness engenders in him—"Ah my deare, / I cannot look on thee." Love counters with a question—"Who made the eyes but I?"— which stresses his own prerogative of judgment derived from his sta-tus as creator of the speaker's eyes as well as his "I," his sense of an integral and independent self. The speaker concedes this point, but his concession only gives him material for a further deferral, as he proceeds to assert his own unworthiness on the grounds that he has corrupted these gifts from his Lord: "Truth Lord, but I have marr'd them: let my shame / Go where it doth deserve." Love responds to this deferral with another question—"And know you not . . . who bore the blame"—this time emphasizing not his creative but his re-demptive powers. The speaker then offers to meet his Lord half-way, entering into his house, but only as a servant, not as an honored guest: "My deare, then I will serve." In offering to serve, the speaker is still declaring his unworthiness to be served, still attempting to avoid the gracious invitation that his lord has extended. Love's final response cleverly appropriates the speaker's proffer of service; Love commands him, as one orders a servant, to behave as an esteemed guest: "You must sit down, sayes Love, and taste my meat." Realizing that he has been beaten at his own game, the speaker is compelled by his own tender of submission to submit to a position of honor. He finally surrenders, performs as he is told: "So I did sit and eat." The poem ends, as Strier argues, "with a vision of the speaker *actually doing* what he was told, and not with a vision of him *resolving* to do so."[25] In this profound nutritive silence, the speaker also demonstrates a rudimentary lesson of table manners: don't talk with your mouth full.[26]

The speaker of "Love (III)" obviously far exceeds the ceremony of first refusal recommended by Guazzo and Castiglione as the proper response to a superior's favors. What begins as a gesture of modest denial quickly becomes a "contest in courtesy and humility"[27] in which guest and host battle for the superiority inherent in the capacity to do someone service. The initially ingratiating gestures by which the speaker avows his unworthiness are supplanted by the speaker's stubborn insistence on the impropriety of his presence at his lord's table. Deference and submission, normally expressions of one's willingness to adapt to the will of another, are exposed as vehicles for self-assertion and intransigence. "Love (III)," observes James Merrill, is a work in which "two characters are being ravishingly polite to one another."[28] The impact of the poem derives from its rigorous investigation of the process by which the pendular rhythms of politeness mask the effectual operations of power.

The Mirror of Complements, a seventeenth-century courtesy book, discloses the manner in which such protracted displays of deference can become expressions of social aggression. The following dialogue, entitled "To entertaine a friend that comes to visit us," suggests that the contest of courtesy between the speaker and host of "Love (III)" is actually a battle for political superiority:

You are very welcome, good Sir, you honor me a thousand times above my merit . . .

Pardon mee Sir, it is I that have received the honour . . .

Sir, you oblige me too much, I have not merited these favors from you.

Sir, this is but a part of my respect, for I owe you much more in things of greater consequence.

Sir, there is no need that you should use these terms to your obliged servants . . . I wish to serve you in all that I am able, and I should more willingly expresse it in action than in speech.

Sir, you have already expressed it very amply, and I were worthy to be thought ingratefull if ever I should faile to make acknowledgement that I am much beholding to you . . .

I see that you will conquer me with courtesie, but if it please you to sit, wee shall discourse more at leisure.

I thanke you sir, it needs not; besides, it were undecent for mee to be first in place, but if it please you to sit, I shall keepe you company.

Then I pray you sit there.

It shall be then to obey you.

Sir, I am your servant.

Sir, it is I that am yours, and the most affectionate of all your servants.[29]

In this dialogue, the seemingly simple matter of inviting a friend to supper becomes charged (as it does in Jonson's poem of that title) with questions of social status and political power.[30] Like the guest and host of "Love (III)," the two interlocutors engage in an elaborate fencing match, employing expressions of deference, obligation, and service as foils. Victory is achieved not by mastery but by submission. He who wins is he who most effectively serves and obeys the other, since in doing so, he places the other in his debt.[31] Expressions of obligation, unworthiness, and respect thus function to exclude the self from further obligation, and to provide for the symbolic acquisition of real social power.

It is probably impossible for those of us in the twentieth century to hear the full range of political nuance in such an elegant if overstated dialogue. We do not regularly kneel, bow, doff our hats, and lower our eyes when meeting superiors. Yet as Norbert Elias remarks,

> in court society . . . the chance of preceding another, or sitting while he had to stand, or the depth of the bow with which one was greeted, the amiability of one's reception by others, and so on, were not mere externals—they are that only where money or profession are taken as the reality of social existence. They were literal documentations of social existence, notations of the place one currently occupied in the court hierarchy.[32]

Common courtesy supplied the idiom of social differentiation. "Each utterance of 'my lord' or 'dame' or 'sir,'" states Whigham, "ratified not only the place of the superior but that of the speaker as enfranchised witness in a coherent social universe."[33] In the attempt to register the all-important nuances of social difference, questions of precedence were codified to a nearly unimaginable degree in a number of treatises.[34] Rather than being simply indicators of the vanity and superficiality of Renaissance nobles, however, such questions involved at once a rehearsal of the divinely approved social hierarchy and an exhibition of one's place in it.

"One of the most decisive transitions" in the civilizing process of Western Europe, proposes Elias, "is that of *warriors to courtiers*."[35] Such a historical movement required the sublimation of the martial violence of a military aristocracy into the "status blood bath" of courtly behavior.[36] Lawrence Stone has commented on "the extraordinary amount of casual inter-personal and verbal violence" in seventeenth-century England.[37] "The issues men fought over were prestige and property, in that order," contends Stone. "A gentleman carried a weapon at all times, and did not hesitate to use it."[38] The exercise of force indigenous in issues of status seethed just under the rigidly controlled surface of this courtly world, waiting to erupt. In one such moment, Francis Norris, the first earl of Berkshire, was imprisoned "for brabling [quarreling] with the Lord Scroope that carelesly and unawares stept in at the doore before him."[39] Sir William Drury, the father of Sir Robert (Donne's famous patron), was slain in a duel with Sir John Boroughs over "the more honourable Place and Precedency."[40] The *Autobiography* of George Herbert's eldest brother Edward, a work replete with duels over issues of status, appropriately likens verbal exchange to physical sparring: "a mans witt is best shewed in his answer and his valour in his defence . . . as men learne in Fencing how to ward all blowes and thrusts which are or can bee made against him, Soe it will bee fitting to debate and resolve before hand what you are to say or doe upon any Affront given you, least otherwise you should bee surprized."[41] The rhetorical violence explored in the last chapter is simply the apotheosis of this attitude to social relations. Indeed, the dedicatory epistle to Henry Peacham's *The Garden of Eloquence* advertises the work as a manual of verbal self-defense:

> those figures and formes of speech conteined in this booke . . . are as martiall instruments both of defence & invasion, and being so, what may be either more necessary, or more profitable for us, then to hold those weapons alwaies readie in our handes, wherewith we may may defend our selves, invade our enemies, revenge our wrongs . . . for looke what the sword may do in war, this vertue may performe in peace, yet with great difference, for

that with violence, this with perswasions, that with shedding of blood, this with pearcing the affections.[42]

In a world demanding perpetual vigilance in arms and words, the line separating social affronts from martial challenges wore precariously thin. "Hee that strikes with his tongue, must ward with head," observes one of Herbert's *Outlandish Proverbs* (no. 313, p. 331). Because a scuffle over threshold precedence was also a battle for political preeminence, the symbolic violence of stratified behavior readily degenerated into physical strife.

The interlocutors in *The Mirror of Complements* and in "Love (III)" spar not by means of overt combat but rather through expressions of fierce humility and belligerent deference. The stakes, however, are just as high. Rather than quarrelling over the right to enter first, they contest the right to exert a supreme modesty. When confronted with an impasse in such an altercation, Guazzo recommends

the example of that discrete gentleman, who, after long strife betweene him and certaine of his friendes, who should first enter into the house, saith, You may nowe knowe well howe much I am at your commaunde, seeing I am ready to obey you in thinges which turn to my dishonor: which said, he entred in without strayning curtesie any longer.[43]

Torn like the speaker of "Love (III)" between the dishonor of accepting a position of undeserved honor and the dishonor of straining courtesy to the breaking point, Guazzo's "discreete gentleman" cunningly translates his acceptance of the dishonor of an undeserved precedence into an act of service and obedience. By doing so, he converts the potential liability of accepting favor from another into the acquisition of political superiority over that other. A gesture which could place him in debt to another issues in an enhanced sense of the other's obligation to him.

By truculently asserting his unworthiness and declaring his desire to serve rather than to be served, the speaker of "Love (III)" attempts with far less finesse than that shown by Guazzo's "discrete gentleman" to shun the acknowledgment of his complete dependence upon his superior. He rejects the political obligation his superior's beneficence imposes upon him, for in the symbolic capital of social prestige, to receive beyond desert, without having served, is to be humbled by a debt which can never be requited. As Denys de Refuges observes in his *Treatise of the Court*, "we are . . . shame fac'd before those [to] whom we are oblig'd and beholding, without having had the meanes to requite."[44] One can avoid such shame only by giving rather than receiving, serving rather than being served. "A high-minded man," remarks Aristotle in the *Nichomachean Ethics*,

> is the kind of man who will do good, but who is ashamed to accept a good turn, because the former marks a man as superior, the latter as inferior. Moreover, he will requite good with a greater good, for in this way he will not only repay the original benefactor but put him in his debt at the same time by making him the recipient of an added benefit . . . For the recipient is inferior to the benefactor, whereas a high-minded man wishes to be superior.[45]

Shame functions in the political world as guilt does in the spiritual world, at once producing and recording the debts of obligation.

In *The Country Parson*, Herbert shrewdly commandeers the political lessons of Aristotle and de Refuges in his battle for social esteem. The parson, Herbert remarks, knows "he must be despised"; nevertheless he should respond to the "contempt" in which his profession is held "by a courteous carriage, & winning behaviour . . . doing kindnesses, but receiving none . . . for this argues a height and eminency of mind, which is not easily despised" (*Works*, p. 268). Like Aristotle's high-minded man, the parson achieves prestige by putting others in his debt. The parson, moreover, is to deal with those who "hold strange Doctrins" by "finding out Courtesies to place on them" (p. 262). As Herbert's peculiar phrasing suggests, courtesies are not uninterested acts of beneficence but obligations imposed on others with the intention of influencing their conduct.

The speaker of "Love (III)" aspires to the same "winning behaviour," hoping to find courtesies to place on his gracious superior while dodging those courtesies his superior would impose upon him. By announcing his unworthiness and subordination, the speaker attempts, paradoxically, to avoid a recognition of his own complete unworthiness and subordination, and to hold out the possibility that he could be worthy, that he could serve and requite his lord. But as one of the *Outlandish Proverbs* collected by Herbert declares, "God, and Parents, and our Master, can never be requited" (*Works*, p. 348; no. 805). Erving Goffman defines "avoidance rituals" as "those forms of deference which lead the actor to keep at a distance from the recipient and not violate . . . the 'ideal sphere' that lies around the recipient."[46] "Love (III)" is in part an elaborate avoidance ritual, with the speaker attempting to maintain a comfortable distance between himself and his lord through a shield of deference. In "Love (III)," though, deference functions not to prevent his violation of the host's "ideal sphere" but rather to protect his own "ideal sphere" from violation by his host. The poem records the phemonenon that "The Forerunners" explored from the other side of hospitality, of the self's wish to sustain a space of inviolate privacy in the face of an encroaching deity. Stefano Guazzo apprehends clearly the process that Goffman describes and the speaker of "Love (III)" practices, by which deference masks a fear of intimacy:

> though in token of true friendship, you call your companion brother, perchaunce hee shall have no minde to tearme you so: and to take that custome from you, hee wyll call you Maister Guazzo. And that you may not use too familiar speeche to him hee will speake to your worship in suche sorte, that you shall bee faine to retyre one steppe backe, and use him rather Ceremoniously then lovingly.[47]

The speaker of "Love (III)" likewise hopes to use ceremony as a path of retreat from love. By "retiring one step back" from a familiarity his superior would grant, the speaker attempts to demarcate some part of himself as neither subject to nor dependent upon his superior.

Because of the subjugation inherent in accepting the favor of a superior, Henry Peacham recommends the complete avoidance of dining at the table of the great. When "a great man inviteth you to dinner to his table," Peacham observes, "the sweetness of that favor and kindness is made distasteful by the awe of his greatness."[48] For Peacham, the experience, although in itself an honor, is inherently humiliating:

> in his presence not to be covered, to sit down and to be placed where and under whom he pleaseth, to be tongue-tied all the while, though you be able to speak more to the purpose than himself and all his company . . . you must endure to be carved unto many times of the first, worst, or rawest of the meat. Sometime you have a piece preferred unto you from his own trencher, but then imagine his belly is full or he cannot for some other reason eat it himself.

Superiors, he perceives, revel in doling out scraps from their tables to subordinates, because "they love you should have a kind of dependency of them, that they might make use of you at their pleasure." Like Jonson in "To Penshurst," Peacham differentiates himself from those "faine to sit . . . At great mens tables," declaring: "I had rather dine even at a threepenny ordinary, where I may be free and merry, than to be a dumb tenant for two hours at a lord's table."[49]

210

Peacham's comments on dining with superiors expose the close correlation that obtains among concepts of feeding, dependency, and power in the English Renaissance. Lawrence Stone remarks that the "prime test of rank" in the period "was liberality, the pagan virtue of open-handedness. It involved . . . above all maintaining a lavish table to which anyone of the right social standing was welcome."[50] Because of its ability to obligate others, food supplies an index of social status. "The bit that one eates, no friend makes," observes one of Herbert's *Outlandish Proverbs* (*Works*, p. 325, no. 142), suggesting that food has greater value as the creator of social obligations than as the nourisher of physical bodies. Food is the medium of political power, the symbolic currency by which one displays the capacity to make and maintain dependents.[51] The word "Lord," advises Anne Williams, "is itself derived from the Old English word that means 'keeper of the bread.'"[52] One contemporary remarks on the symbiotic relationship between food and power: "The more resort he hath, the more is the Maister of the house honored, and the more authority a Gentleman hath in the shier, the more is the resort unto him."[53] And if feeding others is an exercise of power, then the algebra of political obligation demands that the acceptance of another's fare is a mark of submission. "That day the Courtyer graunteth to dyne with any man," warns Antony de Guevara in *The Diall of Princes*, "the same day hee bindeth himselfe to be beholding to him that bids him."[54] Or, as Herbert remarks in another of his *Outlandish Proverbs*, "Anothers bread costs deare" (*Works*, p. 332, no. 324).

The speaker of "Love (III)" attempts to elude with all his verbal resources the subordination inherent in the acceptance of his superior's invitation to supper. He hopes to dodge the "deare cost" of consuming "anothers bread." Yet his superior demonstrates even greater dexterity with the rituals of courtesy, countering every move of the speaker, and displaying a hospitality which is truly overwhelming. Like Peacham's lord, the host of "Love (III)" acts in a manner which emphasizes his guest's dependency upon him. By the prerogative of creation ("Who *made* the eyes but I?") and redemption ("And know you not, sayes, Love, who *bore the blame*?") as well as sustenance ("You must sit down, sayes, Love, and *taste my meat*"), the host of "Love (III)" asserts his authority to compel others to sit and be served in his house. But unlike Peacham's lord, the host of "Love (III)" does not carve the "worst of the meat" for his guest. Rather, like the hospitable magnate of Penshurst, Robert Sidney, Lord Lisle, he offers to his guest the "lords owne meate" ("To Penshurst," line 62), and even condescends to serve the meat himself. The mysterious invitation to cannibalism at the core of Christianity's central rite ("Take, eate: this is my body" [Mark 14.22]) is here rendered as the epitome of courteous conduct.[55]

Like the action of eating, the scenario of a superior serving an inferior engages a complicated set of political variables. Condescension by a superior can be used to reward an inferior. As Guazzo remarks, inferiors "are marvellous wel apaid when they see a Gentleman, notwithstanding the inequalitie, which is betweene them, to make him selfe their equall. Whereby they are induced to love him, to honor him, to do him service."[56] By deigning to approach their inferiors on ostensibly equal terms, social superiors repay their serviceable inferiors in the symbolic capital of prestige. "Such delightful condescension," asserts Whigham, "is joyful because inexplicable."[57] As such, it provides an appropriate social counterpart to the mysterious theological grace that "Love (III)" punctuates. Yet as Guazzo insists, such condescension can issue in a coercion more effective than outright commands, inducing the inferior to do his superior further service. Indeed, in the *Discoveries* Jonson discerns not delightful condescension but scheming compulsion in those moments when superiors stoop to serve their servants: "I *have* discovered, that a fain'd familiarity in great ones, is a note of certaine usurpation on the lesse. For great and popular men, faine themselves to bee servants to others, to make those slaves to them."[58] To Jonson, the act of social condescension accomplishes a kind of inverse usurpation which results in the covert enslavement of those who are ostensibly being rewarded by familiarity with the powerful. "When domination can only be exercised in its *elementary form*, i.e. directly, between one person and another," observes Pierre Bourdieu, "it cannot take place overtly and must be disguised under the veil of enchanted relationships, . . . in order to be socially recognized, it must get itself unrecognized."[59] Despite the great chronological gap between them, both Bourdieu and Jonson trenchantly perceive that the domination of those in power is all the more binding for the veil of beneficence it assumes. As Sabinus declares in Jonson's *Sejanus*: "When power, that may command, so much descends, / Their bondage, whom it stoupes to, it intends."[60]

By descending the social hierarchy in order to serve his dusty and unworthy guest, then, the host of "Love (III)" reinforces that hierarchy. He stoops to conquer. In asking if the speaker "lack'd any thing," the host uses the stock phrase of an Elizabethan storekeeper or peddler, whose traditional refrain was "What lack ye?" Leatherhead in *Bartholomew Fair*, for example, shouts: "What do you lack?

What is 't you buy? What do you lack? Rattles, drums, halberts, horses, babies o' the best?"[61] Yet this linguistic descent is also the source of the host's power. He makes himself a servant in order to make the speaker a kind of slave. When he says to the speaker, "You must sit down . . . and taste my meat," the coercive power of the Lord's submission is made manifest. He offers the finest fare from his table, but compels the speaker to accept. His attentive behest is a gentle version of the decree by which a host ends a dispute over seating arrangements in a sixteenth-century dialogue: "You shall sit there," he tells his guest, "have I not power to commaunde in my house?"[62]

Emphasizing either the courtesy or the coerciveness of divine behavior, readers of the poem divide on these dilemmas inherent in the operations of hospitality. Vendler, McCanles, Marcus, and Bloch, for example, focus on the sweetness of the reward the speaker receives and on the gentleness with which it is offered; all would endorse Bloch's description of Herbert's God as "tactful, fine-grained, sweetly insistent."[63] Stein and Fish, on the other hand, emphasize the host's coercive techniques and stress the psychological costs of accepting his beneficence; Fish in particular sees the host as "hard and unyielding."[64] Yet the force of the poem lies in its ability to encompass such apparently contradictory perspectives on the human relationship to God. As Strier argues, "Both Fish and Bloch are right—the divine voice does have an edge of toughness and the poem *is* truly sweet. The toughness makes for the sweetness."[65] Divine love is at once a demanding social superior and a gentle host.

Yet I would not endorse Strier's further attempt to find a theological resolution to the dilemmas of courtesy in the Reformation doctrine of the irresistibility of grace—an attempt that aligns him more with Stein and Fish than with Vendler, McCanles, Marcus, and Bloch. This would mean, as Strier himself concedes, that "the courtesy-contest of 'Love (III)' is ultimately no contest."[66] To read the poem in this way is to enervate both the speaker's gestures of resistance and the witty rejoinders of Love; it is to fold both mortal opposition and human surrender into the unilateral exercise of divine power. But as one of Herbert's proverbs remarks, "Curtesie on one side only lasts not long" (no. 809, p. 348). It is not just that "the polite form [of 'must'] is the thinnest of coverings for the naked command," as Stanley Fish observes.[67] Rather, the request constrains in proportion to the politeness through which it is expressed. "There is great force hidden in a sweet command," declares one of Herbert's *Outlandish Proverbs* (*Works*, p. 341; no. 589). Blending kindness and coercion, "sweet command" describes perfectly the benevolent domination the poem dramatizes. The courtesy framework, asserts Strier, "enabled [Herbert] to give a fully humanly acceptable account of [the doctrine of] irresistibility." But people do turn down invitations to supper; and humans do reject the gracious love of God. As Herbert remarks in *The Country Parson*, all sins but "the despising of Love" can be circumscribed by divine grace; "The thrusting away of his arme makes us onely not embraced" (p. 283). In Herbert's social and theological universe, humans possess at least the negative power to shun the welcoming arm of God. It is this power which invests the speaker's final gesture of silent submission with immense emotive force: "So I did sit and eat."

Don Quixote, that splendid satire of literary and social pretension, contains a scene which throws into comic relief the social and theological issues embedded in "Love (III)." Don Quixote and Sancho are dining with some goat-herds when Quixote, seeing his squire stand behind him while he sits, declares,

> That thou may'st understand, *Sancho*, the Benefits of Knight-Errantry, and how the meanest Retainers to it have a fair Prospect of being speedily esteem'd and honour'd by the World, 'tis my Pleasure that thou sit thee down by me, in the Company of these good People; and that there be no Difference now observ'd between thee and me, thy natural Lord and Master; that thou eat in the same Dish, and drink in the same Cup; For it may be said of Knight-Errantry, as of Love, that it makes all Things equal.[68]

Don Quixote's egalitarian pretensions are humorously exposed by the hierarchical terminology ("meanest Retainers," "thy natural Lord and Master") of his "gracious" offer. Even as he condescends to reward his servant by dining with him on equal terms, Don Quixote's language carefully registers the distance between them. Sancho has little choice but to feel grateful for this brief foretaste of equality as a reward for his dedication to "Knight-Errantry," a hierarchical system which somehow, like "Love," "makes all Things equall."

Because such gratitude enhances his inferiority without improving his fare, Sancho attempts to refuse graciously the privilege of dining on an equal footing with his master:

> I thank your Worship, cry'd *Sancho*; but yet I must needs own, had I but a good deal of Meat before me, I'd eat it as well, or rather better, standing, and by my self, than if I sat by an Emperor . . . Therefore, good Sir, change those Tokens of your Kindness, which I have a Right to by being your Worship's Squire, into

something that may do me more Good. As for these same Honours, I heartily thank you as much as if I had accepted 'em, but yet I give up my Right to 'em from this Time to the World's End.[69]

Sancho's rejection of the "Right" to feel grateful for such "Honours," however, is repudiated by his master: "Talk no more, reply'd Don *Quixote*, but sit thee down, for the Humble shall be exalted; and so pulling him by the Arms, he forc'd him to sit by him."

In "Love (III)" Herbert also imagines a scene in which a superior's act of condescension, refused by an inferior, at once erases and underscores a sense of inequality between them. In addition, "Love (III)" ends with a command by that superior to "sit and eat," a command whose very force reasserts the hierarchical distance apparently being spanned. "Love (III)" shows how "Love," like "Knight-Errantry," at once "makes all Things equal" and functions as a system of infinite stratification. But where Cervantes lampoons the tactical deployment of condescending behavior, Herbert uses the social anxiety that such behavior produces to investigate mortal resistance to an overpoweringly beneficent God. In the novel we laugh at Don Quixote's clumsy deployment of what is to the goat-herds the incomprehensible "Jargon of Knights-Errant."[70] But in the poem we smile somewhat nervously at the capacity of the lord's courtesy to out-flank the speaker's evasive actions.

In *The Country Parson*, Herbert displays great sensitivity to the emotive and manipulative power of such acts of social condescension. Like Don Quixote, the parson behaves in a way that induces his inferior "to love him, to honor him, to do him service." Because "love is his business, and aime," the parson "likes well, that his Parish at good times invite one another to their houses, and he urgeth them to it: and sometimes, where he knowes there hath been or is a little difference, hee takes one of the parties, and goes with him to the other, and all dine or sup together" (p. 284). The parson not only encourages the social bonding that develops among his parishioners from eating together but also deploys it himself towards individual parishioners. "The poor," Herbert observes, "are welcome also to [the country parson's] table, whom he sometimes purposely takes home with him, setting them close by him, and carving for them, both for his own humility, and their comfort, who are much cheered with such friendliness" (p. 243). A bit like Don Quixote, the parson makes a display of his own modesty, and rewards his inferiors by deigning to serve even "the poor." Through such hospitality and courtesy, the parson "mak[es] a book of his Charity," and "causeth [his poor parishioners] still to depend on him; and so by continuall, and fresh bounties, unexpected to them, but resolved to himself, hee wins them to praise God more" (pp. 244–45). The host of "Love (III)" likewise enforces dependence through gestures of humility, stooping to serve his subordinate, and surprising his guest with his unexpected bounty and hospitality. Such is the essence of courtesy: manipulating the behavior of others in words and gestures manifesting beneficence and declaring one's own subordination.

Such hierarchical condescension is also the essence of the sacrifice that the Lord's Supper commemorates: God becoming human, offering himself to and for all. After the Last Supper, Jesus asks his apostles: "For whether is greater, hee that sitteth at meat, or hee that serveth? Is not he that sitteth at meat? But I am among you as he that serveth" (Luke 22.27). Like the host of "Love (III)," Jesus consciously violates the principles of hierarchical decorum, making his inferiors "sit at meat" while he serves. In the Christian framework, normal status indicators such as the equation of service and subordination are inverted, so that "every one that exalteth himselfe, shall be abased; and he that humbleth himselfe, shall be exalted" (Luke 18.14). Just as the Son's greatness is measured by the degree to which he is willing to humble himself for humanity, so is humanity's ultimate greatness measured by the degree to which it is willing to be humbled before God: "Humble yourselves in the sight of the Lord, and he shall lift you up" (James 4.10).

This is exactly what the speaker of "Love (III)" attempts to do. He engages in forms of self-deprecation which allow his host the opportunity to perform the beneficent action of lifting him up. This conjunction of courteous self-deprecation and Christian humility is far from coincidental. In the passage from Castiglione advocating the initial refusal of honor from a superior, one of the interlocutors suggests that "me thinke ye have this clause out of the Gospel, where it is writen: When thou art bid to a mariage, goe and sit thee down in the lowest roome, that when he commeth that bid thee, he may say, Friend come higher, and so it shall bee an honour for thee in the sight of the guestes."[71] The Christian inversion of earthly hierarchies intersects the language by which a social supplicant addresses his superior. That is why Don Quixote can marshal scripture as a way of telling Sancho how to behave: "sit thee down, for the Humble shall be exalted." The Christian's response to God's grace enjoys a common language and a common set of behavioral imperatives with a social inferior's response to a superior's beneficence because they share

analogous political pressures. As Stefano Guazzo remarks, gentle-
men should behave "according to that *philosophical and Christian*
saying, That the more loftie we are placed, the more lowly wee ought
to humble ourselves: which is in deed, the way to rise higher."[72]

Herbert's portrait of the mortal relationship to God in terms of a
social transaction between an inferior and a superior releases the lin-
guistic energy inherent in this fusion of social and sacred behavior in
the Renaissance. As Joseph Summers asserts, "Herbert's poems make
clear the relations between the courtly virtue of courtesy and the
Christian virtue of humility."[73] But in clarifying this relation they also
expose the potential duplicity of any display of one's own humility. If
humility is indeed "the way to rise higher," can any expression of it
remain uncontaminated by the inverted forms of pride and self-exalta-
tion which it entails? Herbert's own sense of himself, we need to re-
member, was quite fully invested in the very forms of humility and
subordination by which the speaker of "Love (III)" attempts to avoid
divine grace. Barnabus Oley remembers Herbert as one who "lost him-
self *in a humble way*."[74] According to Nicholas Ferrar, Herbert's "mot-
to, with which he used to conclude all things that might seem to tend
any way to his own honour," was "lesse then the least of Gods mer-
cies." Ferrar also records that Herbert "in his ordinarie speech" would
refer to Jesus as "My Master" (*Works*, pp. 4–5).

Yet in "Love (III)" these same qualities—self-deprecation and sub-
ordination—are revealed to be impertinent and inadequate accounts
of the human relationship to God. It is as if in "Love (III)" Herbert is
exposing the incipient pride of his characteristic humility while re-
vealing the close relationship between insolence and submission that
the formulae of courtesy intend to conceal. In a sermon on Genesis
32.10 (the verse from which Herbert's motto is taken), Donne observes
that "we are not worthy as to profess our unworthiness . . . even hu-
mility it self is a pride, if we think it to be our own."[75] In stubbornly
professing his unworthiness and thus contradicting his Lord's declara-
tion that "you shall be he," the speaker of "Love (III)" asserts a kind of
worthiness and pride—the worthiness to judge his own unworthiness,
the pride of thinking humility to be his own.

In a letter to a friend, Coleridge suggests that he admires Herbert

because the folly of over-valuing myself in any reference to my
future lot is *not* the sin or danger that besets me—but a tenden-
cy to self-contempt, a sense of the utter disproportionateness of
all, I can call *me*, to the promises of the Gospel—*this* is *my* sor-
est temptation. The *promises*, I say: not to the *Threats*. For in

217

order to the fulfilment of these, it needs only, that I should be
left to myself—to sink into the chaos & lawlesss productivity of
my own still-perishing yet imperishable Nature—Now in this
temptation I have received great comfort from the following
Dialogue between the Soul & it's [sic] Redeemer.[76]

The poem that offered Coleridge such comfort in the midst of his des-
perate self-contempt is almost certainly "Dialogue," a poem closely
linked, as Ryley and Strier note, to "Love (III)."[77] What I find so in-
sightful and compelling about Coleridge's heart-felt comments is
their understanding that humility is in Herbert finally a temptation
rather than a virtue. The comfort the poems offer Coleridge derives
from their repudiation—voiced by divine authority—of the self-
contempt that masquerades as modesty.

Like "Love (III)," "Dialogue" records a conversation between God
and humanity around the issue of worthiness. In "Dialogue," how-
ever, the aggression implicit in the desire to earn salvation is high-
lighted rather than veiled. The speaker of "Dialogue" tells his
Saviour that because he "can see no merit, / Leading to this favour,"
he "disclaim[s] the whole designe." Only when the Saviour mentions
his own act of resignation—"That as I did freely part / With my glorie
and desert, / Left all joyes to feel all smart"—does the speaker recoil
from the conceit implicit in his desire to be saved on his own terms.
"Ah! no more: thou break'st my heart," exclaims the speaker, achiev-
ing emotionally what he could not fathom rationally—an acceptance
of the seemingly arbitrary nature of salvation. Somewhat more
quietly but far more powerfully, "Love (III)" depicts the dialogue be-
tween humanity and divinity as a dispute about the difficult politics
of the Christian dispensation. As Strier argues, in "Love (III)" Herbert
"dramatizes his awareness that the doctrine of faith alone can be un-
dermined not merely by assertions of merit and cooperation, but by
assertions of unworthiness as well."[78] The speaker wants to be a prof-
itable servant, one who earns his keep; but as Jesus tells his disciples,
all mortals are at best "unprofitable servants," unable to merit any-
thing of God.[79] Even the speaker's sincere offer to serve, then, is based
on the ultimately impertinent assumption that he has something of
his own which he may present to God. Like his pledge of service, the
speaker's desire to go where he deserves implies that service and
worth and desert are the criteria by which God dispenses his grace.
But such criteria defy the very essence of grace; as Edwin Sandys as-
serts, "It is called grace, because it is given gratis; freely and undeser-
vedly on our parts, to whom it is given."[80] In the mortal speaker's

polite resistance to the gracious heavenly host, the poem shows at once the psychological difficulty, and theological necessity, of accepting the human side of this deeply Reformation notion of grace.

"Love (III)," claims Marion Singleton, "harmonizes the grace which man can attain with the grace which only God can confer."[81] The behavior of the divine host does suggest a remarkable consonance between the amenities of hospitality and the operations of divine grace. But the conduct of the speaker excites rather than harmonizes the tension between these two kinds of grace, emphasizing the process by which the social graces can supply a pretext for the refusal of divine grace. In *The Saints Humiliation*, Samuel Torshell underscores the crucial difference between the unmerited grace of God and the acquired graces of humanity by revealing the theological pride inherent in the rejection of God's hospitality because of a conviction of unworthiness:

> Let not our unworthinesse discourage us, to maintaine these or the like Scruples: Will God looke upon such poore abject worthlesse Wretches? If I should offer any Service, would he not contemne both it and me? If I were more worthy, I would then draw neare him: as I am I dare neither sue for entertainment nor expect it. Away with such proud reasonings, such shewes of humilitie: would wee be challengers rather than beggars?[82]

For Torshell, the objections by which the speaker of "Love (III)" asserts his unworthiness are only "shewes of humilitie" which cloak "proud reasonings"; they are challenges to a God from whom we may only beg. A genuine awareness of our unworthiness, Torshell argues, would lead us not to dispute with or withdraw from God but to approach him and pray for acceptance.

In like manner, John Wing asserts in *Jacobs Staffe* that although you should judge yourself unworthy,

> if the Lord thinke you worthy it is well enough, you are bound to the one, he is free to the other, though it be your duty to account meanely of your self, yet it is his mercy to accept you as worthy of his best favours, and your estate must be conceived of, according to his, not your owne estimate . . . they who alledge [unworthiness] . . . doe make the favour and love of God farre inferiour to mans.[83]

To contend with God about one's unworthiness is to invert the very hierarchy that one's expressions of unworthiness are intended to assert. Although one must account oneself unworthy, one must also accept God's estimate of one's worth; to do otherwise is to elevate one's own judgment above God's. "To accuse my selfe of sin, after God hath pardoned me," warns Donne, "were as great a contempt of God, as to presume of that pardon, before he had granted it."[84]

At the moment of divine invitation, the speaker of "Love (III)" is torn between the necessary assertion of his own unworthiness and the duty that such unworthiness entails of yielding to the judgment of his superior. This dilemma is inherent in the two rubrics prefacing the service of the Eucharist in the *Book of Common Prayer*. When the parishioners have been negligent in attending the Lord's Supper, the minister is to beseech the congregation

> that ye will not refuse to come thereto, being so lovingly called and bidden of God himself. Ye know how grievous a thing it is, when a man hath prepared a rich feast . . . and yet they which be called without any cause most unthankfully refuse to come . . . When God calleth you, be you not ashamed to say you will not come? . . What thing can this be accounted else, than a further contempt and unkindness unto God? Truly it is a great unthankfulness to say nay when ye be called.[85]

The very language by which the speaker of "Love (III)" attempts to justify his refusal to partake of his Lord's meat ("I the unkinde, ungratefull," "let my shame / Go where it doth deserve") is here used to describe the effect of such refusal. Yet when the parishioners have been receiving the Eucharist negligently and without proper reverence, the minister's task is not to encourage them to communicate but to "exhort" them

> to consider the dignity of the holy mystery, and the great peril of the unworthy receiving thereof . . . so that in no wise you come but in the marriage garment, required of God in Holy Scripture, and so come and be received as worthy partakers of such a heavenly table . . . For otherwise the receiving of the Holy Communion doth nothing else but increase your damnation.[86]

It is an unkind and ungrateful act to refrain from partaking of the rich feast which the Lord has prepared; but it is a perilous venture to approach such a table unworthily. One cannot approach confident of one's own worth because to do so would be the worst form of presumption, and a sign that one was indeed unworthy. But to approach in full awareness of one's unworthiness is (in an ominous phrase) to "increase damnation." The rhythms of invitation and avoidance that Fish locates in catechistical literature, and in the series of threatening thresholds *The Temple* requires its reader to cross, also pervade the liturgy of the eucharistic service that structures "Love (III)": the speaker "must approach and taste if his soul is to receive its proper food; but if he approaches in a state of sin he will eat and drink damnation."[87] Access to the Eucharist, like the approach to figures of political power, is dangerous, full of great peril and potentially great rewards: "as the benefit is great, if with a truly penitent heart and lively faith we receive that holy Sacrament . . . so is the danger great if we receive the same unworthily."[88] Correspondingly, Guazzo observes of communication with princes: "though this conversation be daungerous . . . yet being well used, bringeth estimation and profit."[89]

A parallel sense of the simultaneous promise and risk immanent in the encounter between courteous divinity and diffident humanity can be glimpsed in several Renaissance representations of the Annunciation. The moment of Annunciation shares some striking similarities, as well as some notable differences, with the situation of "Love (III)." In the Annunciation, of course, it is an angelic messenger rather than God himself who condescends to honor his creature. Moreover, in "Love (III)" Herbert intends to portray the experience of all regenerate Christians, while the point of Mary's experience is its complete uniqueness in history. Nevertheless, both the annunciate Mary and the speaker of "Love (III)" will eventually contain God within their bodies, Mary by means of conception and the speaker by means of consumption. Furthermore, the epitome of heavenly courtesy mediates both encounters. Medieval legend suggests that the courtesy practiced by the host of "Love (III)" first arrived on earth with the angelic messenger; in *The Lytylle Childrenes Lytil Boke*, for example, we read that "clerkis that seven artes cunne [know], / Seyn that curtesy from hevyn come / Whan Gabryelle oure lady grette."[90] Although many painters portray Mary's placid acceptance of the divine message of love and honor, a number show her recoiling in fear (the angel in Luke 1.30 tells Mary to "feare not") from the graciously kneeling angel who bears the message.[91] Those paintings that emphasize Mary's understandable disquiet allow us to visualize at once the grace and terror, the love and awe, that permeate mortal relations with the divine in "Love (III)."

Simone Martini's richly gilded *Annunciation* (1315–44) in the Uffizi, for example, depicts a Mary deeply disturbed at, and shrinking from, the angelic greeting. Even as the messenger of divine love welcomes her to her distinguished role in Christian history, Mary's soul draws back in surprise and awe. The tension in her twisting body betrays a deep ambivalence about the honor she is being granted, and

221

Figure 4.   Simone Martini, *The Annunciation* (1315–44). Florence, Uffizi. Alinari/Art Resource, New York.

Figure 5.   Sandro Botticelli, *The Annunciation* (about 1490). Florence, Uffizi. Alinari/Art Resource, New York.

provides a potent contrast to the gentle serenity of the kneeling angel. The book whose place she retains with her left hand (tradition has her reading Isaiah 7.14, "Behold, a Virgine shall conceive and beare a Sonne, and shall call his name Immanuel") signals the astonishing interruption of her diurnal existence that the moment represents. Her right hand pulls her robes tight about her throat, as if afraid of any exposure before this heavenly being. Even as she averts her eyes from the messenger, however, she unintentionally turns her ear to the message the angel brings. As in "Love (III)," mortal recoil supplies divinity with the opportunity to welcome mortality.

Botticelli's Uffizi *Annunciation*, completed around 1490, manifests a similar sense of spiritual turbulence circumscribed by divine courtesy. Mary's dramatically crescent posture suggests her retreat from the kneeling angelic messenger; the angel, in response, seems about to arise in order to pursue further its fleeing audience across the canvas. Yet the angelic and virginal hand nearly touch, and echo one another's gesture, indicating a tacit consonance between heaven and earth which the moment will inaugurate. For Botticelli, the human recoil from divine honor, and the divine pursuit of the human, are movements in a kind of cosmic dance, betraying a formal harmony which the momentary distress of its mortal participant can neither comprehend nor escape.

Verbally rather than spatially, Herbert's "Love (III)" plays out a similar repertoire of responses to the divine. Like our two annunciations, "Love (III)" imagines a heavenly being graciously stooping to confer honor and love upon a mortal inferior. Both the poem and the paintings depict the mortal reaction to a courteous divinity to be a drawing back, an almost instinctive recoil. In both, diffidence is at once properly modest and problematically aloof as a response to the great honor being urged. The drama of attraction and repulsion delineated in these paintings of the Annunciation, and permeating Herbert's poem of divine invitation, seems to derive from a common sense of the concurrent danger and grace involved in the moment when humanity and divinity converge. Akin to these remarkable representations of the recoil implicit in the story of the Annunciation, Herbert's "Love (III)" manifests the astounding difficulty of responding properly even to the most courteous of divine figures.

This difficulty makes Herbert's country parson undergo "great confusion" about how to behave before his God. Discussing the much-debated point of the proper posture for the reception of the Eucharist, Herbert concedes that "the Feast indeed requires sitting, because it is a Feast" (*Works*, p. 259). This attitude aligns him with Puritan controversialists, who perceived elements of Catholic superstition and idolatry in the kneeling required in the *Book of Common Prayer*, and who argued that sitting was more appropriate because it signified "rest, that is, a full finishing through Christ of all the ceremonial law and a perfect work of redemption wrought, that giveth rest forever."[92] Herbert, though, immediately retreats from this view, asserting that although the decorum of a feast unquestionably requires sitting,

> man's unpreparednesse asks kneeling. Hee that comes to the Sacrament, hath the confidence of a Guest, and hee that kneels, confesseth himself an unworthy one, and therefore differs from other Feasters: but hee that sits, or lies, puts up to an Apostle:

224

Contentiousnesse in a feast of Charity is more scandall then any
posture. (*Works*, p. 259)

Paradoxically, one is to approach the Sacrament with "the confidence
of a Guest," but in a posture by which one "confesseth himself an un-
worthy one." Kneeling, a gesture embedded in that liturgy of de-
ference uniting church and state in the period, is used here to
establish the distinctively sacred nature of the occasion. By humbly
kneeling at the eucharistic feast, one achieves a kind of inverted so-
cial distinction in the display of how one "differs from other Feas-
ters." To sit with the confidence of a guest, Herbert suggests, without
the confession of unworthiness that genuflection entails, is to pre-
sume to the status of an apostle.

Yet the sweet command of the host of "Love (III)" requires the
guest to assume just this presumptuously apostolic posture: "You
must *sit down*, sayes Love, and taste my meat." Because such posture
is the norm at common meals but the exception in Herbert's discus-
sion of eucharistic reception, Strier argues that "the host-guest
framework is more central to the poem than representation of worthy
receiving"; "Love (III)," he concludes, is not "primarily Eucharistic in
reference."[93] But Strier fails to see how profoundly Herbert's complex
attitude to the Eucharist problematizes the issue of proper commen-
sal conduct in "Love (III)." The precise relationship between eu-
charistic feasting and common meals was a subject of some dispute
in Herbert's day—a dispute which allows us to consider just how
deeply intermingled the frameworks of social hospitality and eu-
charistic reception are in the poem. In his *Meditation Upon the
Lords Prayer*, King James I criticizes "Puritans," who "love to sit
Jack-fellowlike with Christ at the Lords Table, as his brethren and
camerades."[94] Daniel Featley likewise finds in the process of domes-
ticating the Lord's Supper a diminution of the sacral nature of the
event: "He that makes no more . . . of participating [in] the blessed
Sacrament, then taking a morsell of bread, or drinking a cup of wine,
can expect no blessing for the use, but rather ought to feare a curse for
the abuse of these meanes of salvation."[95] Featley attacks those who
sit "at the Communion as they doe at their ordinary table, without
expressing any thankfull humility, or giving testimony that they dis-
cerne the Lords body from common meat."[96] Like Herbert, Featley
and James stress the difference between the experience of the com-
municant and that of other feasters. The crucial aspect of the Lord's
Supper is its difference from, rather than its likeness to, common
meals.

Yet Herbert at the same time asserts a powerful sense of continuity between the two feasts. In the forceful manner that the Lord of "Love (III)" dismisses the liturgy of deference and unworthiness the speaker brings to the event, Herbert's account of the eucharistic feast anticipates in many ways that of John Milton. For Milton, the Lord's Supper was originally instituted as a "feast of free grace, and adoption to which *Christ* invited his Disciples to sit as Brethren, and coheires of the happy Covenant." But Roman Catholics and high church Laudians have converted this egalitarian "feast of love and heavenly-admitted fellowship" into a "subject of horror, and glouting adoration, pageanted about, like a dreadfull Idol."[97] Such pomp, Milton argues, "sometimes deceve's wel-meaning men, and beguiles them of their reward, by their voluntary humility, which indeed, is fleshly pride." For Milton, the rituals of modesty that Featley and James would encourage as a sign of the difference between this and common feasts are products of superstition and "fleshly pride." "Such was *Peters* unseasonable Humilitie," relates Milton,

> when *Christ* came to wash his feet; who at an impertinent time would needs straine courtesy with his Master, and falling troublesomly upon the lowly, alwise, and unexaminable intention of *Christ* in what he went with resolution to doe, so provok't by his interrpution the meeke *Lord*, that he threat'nd to exclude him from his heavenly Portion, unlesse he could be content to be lesse arrogant, and stiff neckt in his humility.[98]

Rituals of modesty, Milton suggests, betray a servility which the occasion—God dining with humanity—was designed to repudiate. At the same time, they arrogantly dispute the "lowly, alwise, and unexaminable intention of *Christ*."

For Herbert, the doctrinal and liturgical issues were not as clear-cut as they were for either Featley or Milton. Like Featley, Herbert finds the distinctions between this feast and common meals to be central: indeed, in *The Country Parson* the necessary qualification for receiving communion is not age but the capacity to discern the difference between this and other feasts: "When any one can distinguish the Sacramentall from common bread, knowing the Institution, and the difference, hee ought to receive, of what age soever" (p. 258). Like Featley, too, Herbert's speaker approaches this feast with a requisite trepidation, confessing his unworthiness. Yet like Milton, Herbert investigates the process by which such rituals of modesty can disguise mortal arrogance. Like Milton's God, moreover, Herbert's courteous divinity rebukes (albeit more gently) the behavior of a mortal who is "stiff neckt in his humility." Both Milton and Herbert suggest that the repetitive confession of unworthiness strains rather than exercises courtesy. Containing elements both of Featley's hierocratic service and of Milton's fraternal feast, "Love (III)" achieves an ambience homely yet ceremonial, lordly yet fraternal. Like the intentionally irenic conclusion to Herbert's discussion of the Eucharist in *The Country Parson*—"Contentiousnesse in a feast of Charity is more scandall then any posture"—the poem absorbs and muffles the theological disputes that produce it.

In the last chapter we analyzed the process by which mortal petition enacts a rhetorical version of the physical violence directed against Christ in "The Sacrifice." In "Love (III)," by contrast, we can see how the patterns of courtesy offer a beneficent manifestation of the violent political inversions explored in "The Sacrifice." In "The Sacrifice," the voice of the suffering Christ displays through bitter irony and cruel paradox the status reversal intrinsic to his suffering at the hands of his servants.[99] "Herod in judgement sits while I do stand," remarks the indignant king of kings; "I him obey, who all things else command" (lines 81–83). "Servants and abjects flout me," the tormented God complains. Human blindness is shown through the despicable manners of the soldiers: "The souldiers also spit upon that face, / Which Angels did desire to have the grace, / And Prophets, once to see" (lines 141, 181–83). "A King my title is prefixt on high," he protests, "Yet by my subjects am condemn'd to die / A servile death in servile companie" (lines 233–35). The indecorous servility he is made to undergo at the hands of inferiors seems to gall Christ as deeply as the acute physical torture he is forced to bear. "Love (III)" traces the same violations of social decorum. God stands while his human inferior sits. A king is subordinated to his servants. But where the inversions of "The Sacrifice" stress human hostility to God, the inversions of "Love (III)" emphasize divine hospitality to humanity. The social and cannibalistic violence of the moment when God and human unite is in "Love (III)" channeled into the amenities of courtesy.

In "Love (III)," remarks Chana Bloch, Herbert "explores, with sympathy and without censorship, the painful contradictions of the human condition."[100] The poem uncovers the pride inherent in the speaker's protestations of unworthiness; yet in doing so, the poem reveals the full nature of his unworthiness. The poem manifests God's overwhelming love for humanity, but at the same time it compels one to accept a theology of absolute dependence upon God. The thrust of the poem is to deny any possibility of reciprocity between God and mortal; yet the form of the poem—a dialogue between God and human—suggests at least the prospect of verbal reciprocity. The poem's tone is that of a playfully courteous social encounter. But the language of courtesy also provides the medium in which the two interlocutors maneuver for political power. "Love probably always includes a love for power," remarks Julia Kristeva; "no matter what it is, love brushes us up against sovereignty."[101] In "Love (III)," Herbert conjoins the ceremonies of piety and courtesy in order to explore this nexus of love and power. Set down with as much modesty as cunning, the poem displays the extreme anxiety and immense rewards of the Christian devotional life.

As we have seen, Herbert's various speakers struggle throughout *The Temple* to find a way to serve God, and by doing so to deserve the fruits of God's benefaction. From the initial attempt to "deal with" the beneficent and unique suffering of God in "The Thanksgiving," Herbert's intimate personae have been grappling with the radical difficulty of serving a distressingly generous superior. But here, in the last lyric of "The Church," the speaker is instructed not to serve but to "eat," to display his status as the undeserving recipient of God's unilateral beneficence. Although in "The Pulley" God sentences humanity to "repining restlessnesse," here the speaker is told by his God to "sit," that is, to adopt a posture of rest and repose. The poem concludes where *King Lear* begins, confronting the ineffability of human ardor amid ceremonial expressions of devotion: "Love, and be silent" (1.1.62). Such silence issues here, however, not in civil war but in heavenly peace. The poem is, finally, a comedy of manners, concluding the divine comedy of "The Church" on a note of gentle mirth. But like most good comedies, it is also a problem comedy, containing deep political tensions, and requiring coercion by a figure of superior power in order to achieve a successful resolution.[102] The poem's elementary diction and intricate politics reveal how astonishingly complex, and how unutterably simple, are the dynamics of the conjunction between God and his creatures. As it throws into relief the similarities and disparities between theological and social definitions of *grace*, "Love (III)" discloses the gentleness and the force of God's love for humanity, despite its unworthiness, and the necessity and presumption of humanity's protestations of unworthiness. It is a feast for which we are not worthy.

Our attempt to highlight the neglected political component of Herbert's negotiation with divinity in "Love (III)" has perhaps necessitated our overlooking the fact that the subject of the poem is not just a "Lord" of power but also the figure of "Love." The purpose of the next chapter is to remedy this oversight. In the following chapter we will explore Herbert's recourse to a vehicle for divine love and devotional desire at once more expected, and more surprising, than the social formulae we have been examining: that of human sexuality. Love is not simply a discourse of encoded politics in the Renaissance, as some recent work on the lyric would seem to suggest.[103] Rather, political utterance can supply a lexicon for describing the imperious urges of love. Herbert in particular discovers that his longing for the favor and love of God occurs at the nervous intersection of political, sexual, and religious courtship. Where the two previous chapters explored Herbert's investigation of the body as the site of salutary pain, the next will examine Herbert's representation of the body as the subject of anxious pleasure. As we will see, the poems of *The Temple*, and "Love (III)" in particular, constitute not only a profound inquiry into the politics of devotional conduct but also a subtle lesson in what one critic has aptly termed "erotic manners."[104]

6

"That Ancient Heat":
Sexuality and Spirituality in *The Temple*

Manners are love in a cool climate.

—Quentin Crisp

In a passage from the *Paragone* comparing the affective capacities of poetry and painting, Leonardo da Vinci includes a remarkable anecdote exploring the aesthetic conjunction of erotic and religious desire:

> It once happened that I made a picture representing a divine subject, and it was bought by a man who fell in love with her [*dall' amante di quella*]. He wished to remove the emblems of divinity in order to be able to kiss the picture without scruples [*baciare sanza sospetto*]. But finally conscience overcame his sighs of desire [*li sospiri e la libidine*] and he was obliged to remove the painting from his house.[1]

The viewer's confusion—relished by Leonardo as evidence of painting's emotive power—emblematizes the difficulty of mustering an adequate response to an object imbued at once with religious and erotic significance. Caught on the nexus of two parallel yet potentially opposed forces, Leonardo's patron desires to strip the artifact of all religious connotations in order to give free play to the concupiscence it arouses. Ultimately, however, he withdraws from the unsettling aesthetic experience altogether by having the painting removed from his field of vision.

The divine poetry of George Herbert does not provoke the kinds of libidinal desire that Leonardo's painting aroused in his patron. But like the viewer of Leonardo's painting, the reader of George Herbert's poetry confronts an aesthetic object poised on the cusp of erotic and spiritual longing. Rather than eliminating emblems of divinity in order to cultivate expressions of desire uncontaminated by religious scruples, however, most critics of Herbert have generally repressed elements of eroticism in order to worship without distraction. As Russell Fraser has recently remarked, "Cultural conditioning has sponsored a wheyfaced Herbert," denuded of the sexual intimations suffusing his poems.[2] Even when acknowledged, the erotic elements are typically discussed in footnotes, as if not quite worthy of full scholarly consideration. The purpose of this chapter is to give this vital phenomenon the importance Herbert grants it, and so to move sexuality from the margins to the center of scholarly discussion of Herbert. In "The Forerunners," Herbert announces that the substance of his sacred devotions is a language that "before / Of stews and brothels onely knew the doores."[3] He has, he tells us, "wash[ed]" it, and "brought [it] to Church well drest and clad"; but he does not claim to have broken this language of its habitual cupidity. Indeed, as he reluctantly admits, these "sweet phrases, [and] lovely metaphors" still desire to "leave the Church, and love a stie." In his passionate attachment to a vocabulary of affection he concedes is sullied, Herbert registers "the inconsistency between the Christian emphasis upon love as the chief reality . . . and the strong presence in Christian history of a negative attitude to sex."[4] As Herbert confusingly reminds himself in "The Size," "Thy Saviour sentenc'd joy, / And in the flesh condemn'd it as unfit." Enlisting a subtle but incandescent eroticism which chafes against the sacred urges it both contradicts and embodies, Herbert situates his reader on the visual and emotional axis occupied by Leonardo's bewildered patron. In failing to acknowledge this eroticism and the uneasiness it arouses, we make Herbert's poetry the subject of our own repressions.

The issue of sexuality may seem removed from the social and political conduct foregrounded in the previous chapters. For the Renaissance, however, the regulation of sexual conduct was a project continuous with the development of the codes of courtly behavior that we have been examining. As Norbert Elias's work has made abundantly clear, the "civilizing process" of western society involved the exercise of increasing discipline over all bodily functions. The proliferating proscriptions against physical activities formerly considered normative—e.g., spitting, farting, blowing one's nose, nudity—culminate in "a notable rise in the shame threshold" surrounding sexual behavior.[5] "The process of civilization of the sex drive," remarks Elias, "seen on a large scale runs parallel to those of other drives . . . The instinct is slowly but progressively suppressed from the public life of society."[6]

The conduct of the erotic life, then, is the culmination of the practices of courtesy. Developing the insights of Elias, Peter Stallybrass and Allon White have argued that manners, the rules and codes that regulate behavior, are intimately connected to

> the internal construction of the subject, to the historical formation of self, repudiating any possibility of a separation of the psychical and the social. Manners, regulations of the body, thus become the site of a profound interconnection of ideology and subjectivity, a zone of transcoding at once astonishingly trivial and microscopically important. Traversed by regulative forces quite beyond its conscious control, the body is territorialized in accordance with hierarchies and topographical rules which it enacts automatically, which come from elsewhere and which make it a point of intersection and flow within the elaborate symbolic systems of the socius.[7]

We have already seen in chapters 3 and 4 how for Herbert the body is made both the site of an excruciating and alienating pain imposed by God as evidence of his power and the locus of an ultimately salutary agony that unites God and mortal. In this chapter we will see how the incarnation also licenses the body as the source of a profoundly nervous pleasure that both divides and unites mortal and God.

The increasingly complex rules governing conduct that constitute Renaissance courtliness, then, were not just the product of an elite wishing to secure and dramatize its superiority by means of its refined behavior, as the work of Frank Whigham suggests.[8] Rather, by demanding intense scrutiny of all aspects of social conduct, these rules produced the discourse in which the modern subject could be delineated. As Foucault's later work on the history of sexuality has demonstrated, the regulation of sexuality does not negate desire but rather enables it; discipline does not erase subjectivity but rather produces it.[9] Sexuality is one among "a group of practices" which Foucault terms the "arts of existence"; these arts, he maintains, are "those intentional and voluntary actions by which men not only set themselves rules of conduct, but also seek to transform themselves, to change themselves in their singular being, and to make their life into an *oeuvre* that carries certain aesthetic values and meets certain stylistic criteria."[10] The "care of the self," Foucault argues, is "not an exercise in solitude, but a true social practice."[11]

In Herbert's own "Church-porch" we can see the intimate linkage between care of the self, sexual desire, and social practice identified by Foucault. "By all means use sometimes to be alone," Herbert advises; "Salute thy self" (lines 145–46). Self-scrutiny absorbs the social practice of offering respect ("salute") in order to supply the space within which a social self may be fashioned. The rules of conduct the work contains are intended to produce just the transformation of self that Foucault describes; they will "Ryme thee to good," and "turn delight into a sacrifice." Opening with the need to regulate sexual desire—"Beware of lust: it doth pollute and foul"—and concluding with conduct in church—"In time of service seal up both thine eies, / And send them to thine heart"—"The Church-porch" spans the continuum of sexual and religious behavior in its attempt to inculcate the requisite "arts of existence" in seventeenth-century England. The severe regulation of sexuality that Herbert endorses is at the junction of religious discipline and Renaissance courtesy. In Herbert we can see how these discourses normally linked to power and repression produce rather than reduce the arena of the self. For Herbert, finally, the self inhabits a space whose walls and flooring are constituted by the two discourses that ostensibly would suppress it. By mediating between the internalized demands of a culture and the socially structured urges of the self, manners formulate the very desires they regulate. The physical body, on which the corollary disciplines of social courtesy and religious devotion bestow so much attention, becomes the site not only of negation but also of affirmation, not only of intense anxiety but also of profound joy.

The issue of sexuality is linked to the patterns of courtesy and devotion, moreover, by means of the common verbal structures through which their respective desires are expressed: the formulae of courtship. At the conclusion of his provocative study of "The Rhetoric of Elizabethan Suitors' Letters," Whigham proposes that "the subtle turgid repetitions of [Sir Tobie] Mathew's politic petitions may teach us new things about the congruent realms of erotic and religious desire."[12] By assimilating political and erotic motives to the goal of religious supplication, the poems of The Temple ask us to learn such lessons in depth. Courtship, then, is the central discourse of sexual, political, and religious desire.[13] Castiglione's Courtier, we need to remember, allows its cunning advice on conduct at court to culminate in Bembo's ecstatic vision of the ennobling aspects of love. Later works of courtesy literature such as Cupids Schoole (1632), The Academy of Complements (1640), and The Mirrour of Complements (1650) intertwine, in the words of the subtitle of the last work, the

"practise" of "complementall and amorous expressions." Through-
out the seventeenth century, handbooks are written to convey, in the
wonderfully descriptive title of another work, *The Mysteries of Love
& Eloquence, Or, the Arts of Wooing and Complementing* (1658).
"Sexual courtship," argues Kenneth Burke, "is intrinsically fused
with the motives of social hierarchy."[14]

In a Latin poem attributed with some confidence to Herbert—
"*Aethiopissa ambit Cestum Diuersi Coloris Virum*"—we can watch
the author manipulate the parallel discourses of political and sexual
courtship in ways that prepare us to appreciate the erotic accomplish-
ment of *The Temple*.[15] The situation of the poem—a black woman
wooing a reluctant white male—at once inverts traditional gender
identifications and transgresses cultural and racial boundaries. Echo-
ing the female interlocutor in the Song of Solomon ("I am blacke, but
comely"), Herbert's speaker attempts to transform her blackness—
culturally encoded as a sign of undesirability and marginality—into
the occasion for her appeal:

> What if my face be black? O Cestus, hear!
> Such colour Night brings, which yet Love holds dear.
> You see a Trav'ller has a sunburnt face;
> And I, who pine for thee, a long road trace.
> If earth be black, who shall despise the ground?
> Shut now your eyes, and lo, all black is found;
> Or ope, a shadow-casting form you see;
> This be my loving post to fill for thee.
> Seeing my face is smoke, what fire has burn'd
> Within my silent bosom, by thee spurn'd!
> Hard-hearted man, dost still my love refuse?
> Lo, Grief's prophetic hue my cheek imbues!

The poem identifies erotic desire with a darkness for which Herbert's
culture had a great aversion, but it does so only in order to make dark-
ness precipitate rather than quell the desire of its intended audience.[16]
The emphasis on darkness, then, can be read as a kind of erotic de-
ference, by which the speaker, in calling attention to traits likely to be
viewed unfavorably, hopes to win favor.

The machinations of this erotic deference become more pro-
nounced in the accompanying English poem addressed to Francis
Bacon, Herbert's close friend.[17] Herbert identifies the poem as a com-
modity in a courtly gift exchange: "My Lord. A diamond to mee you
sent, / And I to you a Blackamore present" (*Works*, p. 209). As in Her-
bert's poem "Hope," as well as in his exchange of Latin verses with

Donne, poetry and generosity offer a mode of social negotiation. Arguing that "Gifts speake their Givers," Herbert proceeds to align himself with this female speaker, suggesting that "you may read in mee / (Whom Schollers Habitt & Obscurity / Hath soild with Black) the colour of my state" (*Works*, p. 209). His state is a negatively valued color, but it is also by implication a culturally subordinate gender. At the same time he cleverly affiliates the "hard-hearted man [*dure*]" with Bacon, who has given him a diamond, a gift proverbial for hardness.[18] Yet the diamond was also proverbial for favor; in *Timon of Athens*, a lord describes Timon's wild mood swings by remarking that "one day he gives us diamonds, next day stones" (3.6.120). Fascinatingly, erotic entreaty by a black woman provides Herbert both with a gift in his courtship of Bacon's favor and with a prototype for that act of courtship. He calls attention to the contrast between Bacon's "bright gift" and the sullied nature of his own. He implores Bacon to "shutt not the doore / Against this meane & humble Blackamore." Blackness and femininity, both disparaged by Herbert's culture, come to stand for the scholar's impoverished state, and to function as the vehicle of an ingratiating humility. Likewise, the speaker calls attention to his own "obscurity"—an obscurity which the bright favor of the Lord Chancellor should quickly disperse. Yet the adoption of blackness, like the donning of shepherds' weeds in pastoral, seems also to have been a popular courtly activity. Edward Herbert, George's elder brother, indulged in one of the period's literary vogues by composing a series of poems in praise of black beauty.[19] Jonson's first court masque, furthermore, *The Masque of Blacknesse* (1605), was performed by the Queen and her ladies in blackface. Herbert's assumption of a black persona demonstrates his awareness not only of his own social marginality but also of the court's fashions. He represents his position outside the court by means of a model sanctioned by the court.

Blackness, however, was often identified with a stereotype of sexual voracity by Herbert's culture. Bacon's own *New Atlantis* represents "the Spirit of Fornication" as "a little foul ugly Ethiop."[20] Herbert, by contrast, imagines sympathetically the discourse of a cultural other, transforming but not endorsing the negative connotations his culture placed on blackness. Like Shakespeare's *Othello*, Herbert's lyric contests the racial and sexual stereotypes it enlists. The erotic desire of a sexual and racial other ventriloquizes Herbert's own political aspirations. Sexual courtship remarkably provides Herbert with a surrogate for his own social desires. Eve Kosofsky Sedgwick has explored "the potential unbrokenness of a continuum between homosocial and homosexual" desire, between, that is, socially sanctioned patterns of male bonding and socially ostracized forms of homoeroticism. By identifying himself with a female speaker, Herbert translates homosocial desire into the terms of heterosexual longing; but this translation also allows him to voice a remarkably frank homoerotic sentiment.[21] Exploiting cross-racial courtship and gender inversion as models for social climbing, *"Aethiopissa"* exercises a remarkable degree of gender lability, and exposes the close association between political and sexual supplication.

The Galenic physiology inherited by the Renaissance made possible the conceptualization of the sexual mobility observed in *"Aethiopissa."* According to Galen, humans had the seeds of both sexes within them, and, as Stephen Greenblatt explains, "predominance, rather than the exclusion" of one gender, determined sexual identity. But this physiology also inscribed masculine anatomy as the ideal of which the feminine physique was understood to be an inverted or incomplete version.[22] The discourse that described this predominantly masculine sexuality imagined sexual identity as a blend rather than a prohibition of gender-specific traits. It also supplied Herbert and other Renaissance poets with a vocabulary fusing spiritual aspiration and swelling pride, devotional ardor and priapic aggression, corporeal lethargy and religious lassitude, carnal pleasure and physical death. William Harvey's description of the sexual behavior of the rooster— whose physiology was considered analogous to that of humans— exemplifies the ease with which this lexicon of sexual excitement could be translated into the terms of devotional experience:

> When males prepare themselves for coitus and, *swelling with desire*, are stimulated by the *fire* of venery, how wondrously does Cupid reigning within them *heighten* their *inflamed spirits*! how *proudly* do they parade themselves, bedecked with ornaments, how *vigorous* they are and how prone to do battle! But when this *office of life* is once ended, how suddenly does their vigor subside and their late fervour *cool*, their *swelling* sails hang *loose*, and they lay aside their late ferocity.[23]

The phallocentric vocabulary produced by this physiology invested the phenomena of heat and of rising with particular erotic significance. Shakespeare and Donne would exploit the available double entendres often and loudly. Herbert, by contrast, quietly taps into them. Throughout *The Temple* and culminating in the encounter between impotent mortality and amorous divinity in the volume's final lyric, Herbert discovers in the phallocentric discourse of Renaissance sexuality a vehicle for his ardent devotional desires.

Although the erotic elements are somewhat more explicit in *"Aethiopissa"* than in the majority of his sacred lyrics, the phenomena of gender lability and sexual energy continue to infiltrate Herbert's literary performances. Throughout his career Herbert remains preoccupied by the libidinal prototypes of his own social and devotional urges. Significantly, his first two extant poems—sonnets written as a "New years gift" to his mother when he was sixteen—deploy the terminology of carnal heat and heightened spirits exemplified in the passage from William Harvey to investigate the relationship between erotic and religious passion. In these poems, sexuality is not imagined as the repressed source of religious feeling but rather as the outgrowth of suppressed religious urges. Utilizing the sonnet form to excoriate its traditional amorous connections, these lyrics painstakingly oppose "those many Love-poems, that are daily writ and consecrated to *Venus*" to the "few [that] are writ, that look towards *God* and *Heaven*" (*Works*, p. 363). Yet the poems expressing this pious opposition engage in bawdy word-play which blurs its apparent borders. In asking, "Doth Poetry / Wear Venus Livery? Only serve her turn?" for example, the adolescent Herbert plays upon the Renaissance sense of "service": to "serve Venus's turn" intimates sexual intercourse.[24] Similarly, his question, "Cannot thy love / Heighten a spirit to sound out thy praise / As well as any she?" compares God's ability to arouse suitors to the point of an erection with the capacity of a mortal lover to excite carnal desire ("spirit" being a common Renaissance euphemism for "penis" as well as "semen").[25] In these poems, Herbert wants to impress his devout and clever mother with his verbal ingenuity and spiritual piety, perhaps by imitating the witty manner of Donne, his mother's good friend. But the curiously ribald puns Herbert makes begin to corrode the pious distinction he draws between the "ancient heat" of religious martyrs and the lascivious heat of secular lovers. If Herbert has washed this language, as he was to claim in "The Forerunners," the taint of carnal desire lingers.

One can perhaps dismiss the unresolved tension between bawdy word-play and pious intention in the two youthful sonnets as the product of a gifted, devout, but immature poet. In "Marie Magdalene," however, a poem not in the Williams manuscript, and so presumably written comparatively late in Herbert's career, we can see a similar conflict with regard to the relationship between feminine sexuality and religious devotion. Herbert's mother, the recipient of his youthful sonnets, must have been in the back of his mind as he wrote this poem, since her first name was Magdalene; Donne continually resorted to the Magdalene story in his discourse with and about

237

Magdalene Herbert.[26] The poem attempts to describe the uneasy moment when the incarnate Christ meets the woman who embodies the sinful pleasures he will suffer to redeem. Herbert highlights the paradoxes that suffuse the scenario of the repentant Magdalene washing the feet of her sinless lord:

> When blessed Marie wip'd her Saviours feet,
>   (Whose precepts she had trampled on before)
> And wore them for a jewell on her head,
>   Shewing his steps should be the street,
>   Wherein she thenceforth evermore
> With pensive humblenesse would live and tread:
>
> She being stain'd her self, why did she strive
> To make him clean, who could not be defil'd?
> Why kept she not her tears for her own faults,
>   And not his feet? Though we could dive
>   In tears like seas, our sinnes are pil'd
> Deeper then they, in words, and works, and thoughts.
>
> Deare soul, she knew who did vouchsafe and deigne
> To bear her filth; and that her sinnes did dash
> Ev'n God himself: wherefore she was not loth,
>   As she had brought wherewith to stain,
>   So to bring in wherewith to wash:
> And yet in washing one, she washed both.

The subject of the poem is, as Vendler observes, "social courtesy, so well suited to Herbert's mind and art"; yet "something went desperately wrong with the poem."[27] Vendler calls attention to the "shocking contradiction" present in the "grotesque verbal collocation" of the first two lines of the last stanza, where Herbert in a single sentence describes the Magdalene as "a 'Deare soul' full of 'filth.'"[28] Herbert consciously rejects a common mode of dealing with the Magdalene which would translate her erotic past into present religious desire; as Richard Strier asserts, "Herbert does not present Mary erotically in his poem; the single allusion which he makes to Mary's past is studiedly abstract."[29] The poem negotiates unsuccessfully between body and soul, between action and significance, between filth and ablution. This disjunction is matched by the unresolved tension between Herbert's description of the incarnate Christ as one "who could not be defil'd," and his account of the way that "her sins did dash" (which means both "to splash" and "to strike with violence") "ev'n God himself." "Caught between the wish to honor his mother and his own intractable response to sexual sin," proposes Vendler, Herbert "produced an uneasy poem."[30] Like the two sonnets to his mother, the poem represents an abortive attempt to locate religious devotion in relation to human sexuality.

The two sonnets entitled "Love" in *The Temple* mediate somewhat more successfully between the attendant demands of spirituality and sexuality. In these sonnets, Herbert complains, as he did in the two sonnets to his mother, that secular poets allow "mortall love" to usurp the prerogative of devotion due solely to "Immortall Love." Hinting at a pun on "wit" and "penis," the first sonnet remarks how "wit fancies beautie, beautie raiseth wit"; both poetic craft and phallic desire are castigated for their elevated attention to physical beauty.[31] "Herbert views his erected wit with alarm," remarks Strier, aptly capturing Herbert's wordplay.[32] In these poems, Herbert indeed seems to be responding to Sir Philip Sidney, particularly his discussion in the *Defense* of the applicability of secular love conventions for sacred poety:

> that lyrical kind of songs and sonnets which, Lord, if he gave us so good minds, how well it might be employed (and with how heavenly fruits both private and public) in singing the praises of the immortal beauty, the immortal goodness of that God who gives us hands to write and wits to conceive, of which we might well want words but never matter, of which we could turn our eyes to nothing but we should ever have new-budding occasions.[33]

Like Sidney, Herbert emphasizes the impropriety of devoting to "mortal love" language better suited to an "immortal" object. But for Herbert, even the erected wit, if not directed exclusively towards God, is the product of infected will. Yet the second sonnet looks forward to the prospect of rectifying this faculty in its prayer that the "greater flame" of God will "kindle in our hearts such true desires, / As may consume our lusts."[34] As a result of obeying the urges of such *"true* desires," Herbert promises that "all knees shall bow to thee; all wits shall rise." By bending poetic ingenuity and erotic energy to God, one can achieve the virtuously heightened spirit and genuinely purifying heat Herbert forecast in the sonnets to his mother.

"Dulnesse" likewise compares the activities of devotional and secular poets. In this poem, however, the comparison allows Herbert to

lash his own lyric torpor rather than the misdirected attentions of
secular lovers:

> Why do I languish thus, drooping and dull,
>> As if I were all earth?
> . . . .
> The wanton lover in a curious strain
>> Can praise his fairest fair;
> And with quaint metaphors her curled hair
>> Curl o're again.
>
> Thou art my lovelinesse, my life, my light,
>> Beautie alone to me:
> Thy bloudy death and undeserv'd, makes thee
>> Pure red and white.
> . . . .
> Where are my lines then? my approaches? views?
>> Where are my window-songs?
> Lovers are still pretending, & ev'n wrongs
>> Sharpen their Muse:
> But I am lost in flesh . . .

Herbert characterizes his devotional lassitude as a lack of physical vi-
rility ("drooping and dull") in contrast to the erotic vigor and "sharp-
en[ed]" muse of the "wanton lover." Moreover, the language used to
describe the activity of this lover has bawdy connotations which be-
tray his carnal goals. "Strain," for example, can designate not only the
secular lover's song of praise but also the close embrace he intends to
win through this song.[35] Similarly, "quaint" can suggest the female
pudendum, a meaning here underscored by its juxtaposition with
"curled hair."[36] Yet Herbert's explanation for his comparative in-
ability to offer appropriate praise to God wittily elides the distinction
he asserts between such carnal concerns and his own. The phrase
"but I am lost in flesh" weirdly designates the activities of the wan-
ton lover to whom he ostensibly contraposes his own devotional tor-
por. The poem appropriately concludes in the interrogative mode,
asking "to *love* thee, who can be, / What angel fit?" The initially glib
contrast between religious devotion and erotic affection dissolves
into a question of mortal (and even angelic) capacity for properly
cherishing God.

Other poems in *The Temple* explore the ways in which Herbert's
devotional motives are found as well as lost in flesh. In "The Pearl,"
Herbert proclaims that he

> know[s] the wayes of Pleasure, the sweet strains,
> The lullings and the relishes of it;
> The propositions of hot bloud and brains;
> What mirth and musick mean; what love and wit
> Have done these twentie hundred yeares, and more:
> I know the projects of unbridled store:
> My stuffe is flesh, not brasse; my senses live.

As Strier remarks, " 'Sweet strains' blends both realms [musical and
sexual] brilliantly."[37] Such carnal knowledge provides both a pattern
for, and the antithesis of, the statement of impassioned devotion to
God that concludes each of the first three stanzas: "Yet I love thee."
The conclusion of "Employment (I)" offers a similar pun on "strain,"
imploring God to "give one strain / To my poore reed." As Janis Lull
points out, the reed is a "symbol of male egotism—at once phallus,
musical instrument, and pen."[38] For Herbert, the unwanted phallic
self—"my poore reed"—represents the ultimate state of inutility the
poem bemoans.

Like "The Pearl," "Church-musick" links musical and sexual plea-
sure. In "Church-musick," furthermore, the rapture of divine song is
astonishingly compared with a visit to a brothel:

> Sweetest of sweets, I thank you: when displeasure
>   Did through my bodie wound my minde,
> You took me thence, and in your house of pleasure
>   A daintie lodging me assign'd.
>
> Now I in you without a bodie move,
>   Rising and falling with your wings:
> We both together sweetly live and love.

The intangible experience of music is expressed in terms of a lim-
inality that is corporeal as well as architectural—"in you," the
"sweetest of sweets." The entry into the edifice of the church, a true
"house of pleasure," is likened to the entry into another's body.
"Comfort, I'le die," declares the speaker, anticipating a death which
is both spiritual and sexual. The moment of physical consummation,
however, is also a disembodied experience: "Now I in you without a
bodie move." As in Donne's "Extasie," abandonment of the flesh oc-
casions abandonment to the flesh.

In "Sinnes round," by contrast, flesh is the site of sinfulness rather
than the element of spiritual rapture. Jonathan Goldberg has recently
suggested that the subtitle of *The Temple*—"Sacred Poems and Pri-

241

vate Ejaculations"—aligns the writing of devotional poetry and the "spurting forth of seed and fluid."[39] Although Herbert almost certainly had nothing to do with this subtitle (it appears in neither manuscript), Goldberg's suggestion nevertheless gets at a truth about Herbert's conception of certain aspects of the creative process. For in "Sinnes round," a poem Goldberg does not discuss, Herbert depicts the cycle of penitence and offence that produces self-condemning poetry in remarkably onanistic terms:

> Sorrie I am, my God, sorrie I am,
> That my offences course it in a ring.
> My thoughts are working like a busie flame,
> Untill their cockatrice they hatch and bring:
> And when they once have perfected their draughts,
> My words take fire from my inflamed thoughts.
>
> My words take fire from my inflamed thoughts,
> Which spit it forth like the Sicilian Hill.
> They vent the wares, and passe them with their faults,
> And by their breathing ventilate the ill.
> But words suffice not, where are lewd intentions:
> My hands do joyn to finish the inventions.
>
> My hands do joyn to finish the inventions:
> And so my sinnes ascend three stories high,
> As Babel grew, before there were dissentions.
> Yet ill deeds loyter not: for they supplie
> New thoughts of sinning: wherefore, to my shame,
> Sorrie I am, my God, sorrie I am.

As Hutchinson observes, the poem is almost certainly a development of Isaiah 59.5, where the wicked "hatch cockatrice eggs" (*Works*, p. 520). Part rooster, part snake, hatched by a serpent from an egg laid by a cock, and able to kill with a glance, the cockatrice consolidates images of masculine sexuality, aberrant generation, and spiritual peril.[40] "Cockatrice," furthermore, is also a slang term for a prostitute, thus suggesting an object of male sexual desire as well as the subject of male sexuality.[41] When this mythical creature is juxtaposed with the ejaculatory imagery of "the Sicilian Hill" (the volcanic Mount Etna), the phallic erection of Babel, the flames of concupiscence, the heightened respiration of sexual excitement ("by their breathing ventilate the ill"), and the remark that his "hands do joyn to finish" the "lewd intention" begun in the brain, the suggestion of masturbation is hard to avoid. The poem is an act of self-abuse (in both senses), rendering the clasped hands of penitential prayer as a potentially onanistic posture. Even as the speaker confesses his "sin of self-love," the poem's ophidian form completes the closed circuit of shame and desire he describes, turning back upon itself in auto-erotic repetition of the sins of the previous line or stanza.[42] "In Western literature—beginning with Christian monasticism—masturbation remains associated with the chimera of the imagination and its dangers," argues Foucault.[43] The poem is a meditation on the imagination's collateral corruptions of physical procreation and literary creation. "Akin," as Strier contends, to "Jordan (II)"—"both focus on the peculiar independence of thoughts from conscious direction, a phenomenon which Herbert found deeply disturbing"—"Sinnes round" traces the close relationship between self-involved writing and masturbatory desire.[44] Indeed, the two activities are so intertwined in "Sinnes round" that it is difficult to tell whether writing functions as a metaphor for masturbation, or masturbation a metaphor for writing. Playing on the assonance of "sin" and "ascend," and perhaps deploying an unstated pun on the "pen" of the poet and the "penis" of the speaker (since both are tools in the poem's depiction of perverse creation), Herbert links the "self-willed" product of his creative imagination to the erotic fantasies and barren tumescence of masturbation.[45]

A similar image of erection is explored in "The Flower." Rather than spilling his seed upon the ground, however, the speaker of this poem hopes to become a plant in God's garden. He observes that

> Many a spring I shoot up fair,
> Offring at heav'n, growing and groaning thither:
> > Nor doth my flower
> > Want a spring-showre,
> My sinnes and I joining together.
>
> But while I grow in a straight line,
> Still upwards bent, as if heav'n were mine own,
> > Thy anger comes, and I decline.
> What frost to that? what pole is not the zone,
> > Where all things burn,
> > When thou dost turn,
> And the least frown of thine is shown?
> > (lines 24–35)

Because the poem opens with a lament against barrenness ("Who would have thought my shrivel'd heart / Could have recover'd greennesse?"), one would expect the dilation announced in "many a spring

243

I shoot up fair" to be celebrated. Such virility, however, is revealed as
sinful, akin to the aggressive sexuality castigated in "Sinnes round,"
and wilting under the climatic "pole" of God's boreal glare. In the fi-
nal stanza, moreover, priapism is equated with "pride," a word desig-
nating, as Strier notes, both a period of heightened sexual desire and
an exaggerated sense of self-esteem:

> These are thy wonders, Lord of love,
> To make us see we are but flowers that glide:
> Which when we once can finde and prove,
> Thou hast a garden for us, where to bide.
> Who would be more,
> Swelling through store,
> Forfeit their Paradise by their pride.

"We cannot miss the tentative sexuality of his 'budding' and 'shoot-
ing up' and later 'swelling,'" remarks Helen Vendler.[46] This sexuality,
and the aspiration for upward mobility it represents, must be sacri-
ficed before he can be placed in God's garden, "where no flower can
wither."

In the poem "Church-monuments" Herbert prescribes a visit to a
tomb to curb such desires. Herbert directs his "deare flesh" to "take
acquaintance of this heap of dust" so that it may learn its "stemme /
And true descent." This lesson will be valuable, Herbert hopes, at
those moments when, as in "Sinnes round" and "The Flower," his
flesh "shalt grow fat, / And wanton in thy cravings." Concupiscence
and pride are represented in unmistakable images of tumescence.
"Mortification," too, describes the time "when youth is frank and
free / And calls for musick, while his veins do swell." As in "Church-
musick" and "The Pearl," musical pleasure is linked to physical in-
dulgence. In both "Church-monuments" and "Mortification," how-
ever, death and decay provide a check to the distension that such
indulgence produces. The "ashes" of corporeal dissolution, Herbert
reminds his body in "Church-monuments," are "tame," "free from
lust." Likewise, the music that accompanies the youth's swelling
veins in "Mortification" only "summons to the knell, / Which shall
befriend him at the houre of death." Such morbid thoughts, Herbert
hopes, will provide a sobering influence upon the wanton and unruly
urges of protuberant flesh.

"Frailtie" begins where "Church-monuments" and "Mortifica-
tion" conclude, with the speaker complacently enunciating the sort
of admirable *contemptus mundi* sentiments we expect in religious
poetry:

> Lord, in my silence how do I despise
> What upon trust
> Is styled *honour, riches,* or *fair eyes;*
> But is *fair dust!*
> I surname them *guilded clay,*
> *Deare earth, fine grasse* or *hay;*
> In all, I think my foot doth ever tread
> Upon their head.

Yet even as he rehearses this pious contrast between earthly and heavenly joys, his statement of contempt for the world dissolves into a striking image of his passion for it:

> But when I view abroad both Regiments;
> The worlds, and thine:
> Thine clad with simpleness, and sad events;
> The other fine,
> Full of glorie and gay weeds,
> Brave language, braver deeds:
> That which was dust before, doth quickly rise,
> And prick mine eyes.

The juxtaposition of *prick* and *rise* betrays Herbert's arousal by the resplendent world whose attractions he would piously dismiss. Augustine suggests that postlapsarian corruption is signaled by the inability of reason and will to control the penis; Herbert's mortal "frailty" is likewise indicated by an erection beyond his volition.[47] The poem concludes by imploring God to forestall this phenomenon by making the pleasures of his own regiment more apparent:

> O brook not this, lest if what even now
> My foot did tread,
> Affront those joyes, wherewith thou didst endow
> And long since wed
> My poore soul, ev'n sick of love:
> It may a Babel prove
> Commodious to conquer heav'n and thee
> Planted in me.

Like the spouse in the Song of Solomon, the speaker is truly "sick of love," and longs to be cured by being "wed" to God, that is, by establishing an amorous bond between God and his soul that would preclude his deep desire for the world. As in "Sinnes round," the rearing of Babel represents both a phallic excitement about earthly pleasure and a priapic threat to heaven. In "Frailtie," however, lust infiltrates the very pieties that aspire to deny its power.

As mortal frailty is betrayed by the erect penis, intellectual vanity is for Herbert imagined, as Strier notes, "in terms of aggressive sexuality."[48] In "Vanitie (I)," for example, Herbert envisions the misplaced pride and ultimate futility of human scientific pursuits in images of penetration which grow progressively sexual in the course of the poem. "The fleet Astronomer can bore," observes Herbert, "And thred the spheres with his quick-piercing minde." His impalement of these spheres does not preclude his engaging in a kind of ocular flirtation with them; he "knoweth long before / Both their full-ey'd aspects, and secret glances." Similarly, "The nimble Diver" incisively "cuts through the working waves, that he may fetch / His dearely-earned pearl" as a gift for a woman of "excessive pride." The actions of "the subtil Chymick," finally, consummate the forms of sexual violation implicit in the invasive work of astronomer and diver; the "chymick"

> can devest
> And strip the creature naked, till he finde
> The callow principles within their nest:
> There he imparts to them his minde,
> Admitted to their bed-chamber, before
> They appeare trim and drest
> To ordinarie suitours at the doore.

Chemistry is imagined as an act of rape which strips and invades the "callow principles" in their "bed-chamber."[49] In "Divinitie," Herbert likewise complains about the invasive violence of doctrinal dispute; theologians, he contends, use "the edge of wit" to "cut and carve" "divinities transcendent skie," and to "jag," or slash, the "seamlesse coat" of "wisdom." In contrast to such penetrating wit, "Faith needs no staffe of flesh." The latter phrase has, as Strier notes, an "uncannily literal phallic dimension."[50] Like astronomy in "Divinitie," astronomy, oceanography, and chemistry in "Vanitie (I)" are all imagined as versions of sexual assault. Both poems attack scientific inquiry by envisioning it in terms of a powerful phallic sexuality.

The frequent identification of the erect penis with sin, rebellion, and aggression in Herbert's poetry can be understood at least in part by reference to Renaissance discourse about the ritual of circumcision. John Donne, a figure whose fascination with the relations between sexuality and spirituality is perhaps more conspicuous than Herbert's (although not necessarily more profound), explains in a sermon that

God made the apparently curious choice of the penis, "so base and uncleane a thing," to seal his covenant with Abraham because *"that part of the body is the most rebellious part."*[51] Suggesting momentarily that man relates to his penis as God relates to his unruly creatures, Donne proposes that "to reproach Mans rebellion to *God, God* hath left one part of Mans body, to rebell against him." As an organ beyond the control of man, the erect penis represents the continual tendency of God's creatures to rise against him. Paraphrasing Saint Bernard, Donne claims that "the spawns of *Leviathan,* the seed of sinne, the leven of the Devil, abounds and reignes most in that part of the body; it is . . . the *Sewar* of all sinne." Because, reasons Donne, "this rebellious part, is the roote of all sinne, . . . therefore did that part need this stigmaticall marke of Circumcision."[52] As the penis becomes a synecdoche for mortal depravity, circumcision comes to represent the severing of our capacity for sin: "In this Circumcision, we must cut the *root,* the *Mother-sinne,* that nourishes all our sinnes . . . It is not the Circumcision of an *Excessive* use of that sinne, that will serve our turne, but such a circumcision, as amounts to an *Excession,* a cutting off the *root,* and *branch,* the *Sinne,* and the *fruits,* the *profits* of that sinne."[53]

In "Paradise," Herbert prays for just such a severance from an aggressive male sexuality similarly imagined in botannical terms. Unlike Donne, however, Herbert includes a vision of fructifying beneficence in his account of God's cutting action. The speaker begins by praising a God who prunes in order to produce fruit—"I blesse thee, Lord, because I GROW / Among thy trees, which in a ROW / To thee both fruit and order OW." Probably taking the cue from Old Testament injunctions about circumcision, which promise fruitfulness to those who are part of the covenant that circumcision signifies—"And the Lord thy God will circumcise thine heart, and the heart of thy seed, . . . And the Lord thy God will make thee plenteous in every worke of thine hand, in the fruit of thy body, and in the fruit of thy cattell, and in the fruit of thy land"—Herbert emphasizes the fecundity and discipline represented by God's careful truncation.[54] But in the body of the poem, excision gets as much attention as expansion:

> Inclose me still for fear I START.
> Be to me rather sharp and TART,
> Then let me want thy hand & ART.
>
> When thou dost greater judgements SPARE,
> And with thy knife but prune and PARE,
> Ev'n fruitfull trees more fruitfull ARE.

Such sharpnes shows the sweetest FREND:
Such cuttings rather heal then REND;
And such beginnings touch their END.

The act of "pare-ing" is at the linguistic and theological core of Herbert's "Par-adise." Unlike Milton's Eden with its lushly erotic vegetation, Herbert's paradisal garden is an orchard of neatly ordered, well-pruned trees. For fear that he will "start," or literally stand out among such plants, the speaker of "Paradise" asks to be circumscribed by his Lord's arm even as he is symbolically circumcised by his Lord's knife. The pun on "sharp" (used twice) punctuates the physical presence of this weapon. Furthermore, the rhyme words themselves produce meaning through amputation of letters, demonstrating the spiritual fruition that this salutary emasculation should foster.[55] In this Paradise, less really is more. Shorn of his potent and potentially aggressive sexuality, the speaker, like the "flowers that glide" at the end of "The Flower," approaches what Stanley Stewart terms a "blessed state of passivity."[56]

A related wish to find a mode of religious devotion walled off from refractory erotic passion emerges in "H. Baptisme (II)."[57] The speaker of this poem prays for the opportunity to recapture the pre-sexual purity of childhood:

O let me still
Write thee great God, and me a childe:
Let me be soft and supple to thy will,
Small to my self . . .
. . . .
The growth of flesh is but a blister;
Childhood is health.

Herbert links the burgeoning flesh of maturation with blistering, the sexual edema portrayed in "Sinnes round" and "The Flower," and contrasts that with his own salubrious desire to remain small. "The yearning for childhood and the antagonism to maturity (a 'blister'),"
proposes E. Pearlman, "suggest again the rejection of adult sexuality and the embrace of an earlier period of unequivocal security."[58] A corollary to the analogy linking hardness and sinfulness that recurs throughout *The Temple* (see, for example, "The Altar," "The Sinner," "Sepulchre," and "Love unknown") is the expressed intention in "H. Baptisme (II)" to become "soft and supple." Childhood is health be-

cause it integrates social subordination and carnal ignorance, and so does not threaten God with "shooting up," "offring at heaven."

Although Herbert imagines his own sinfulness in terms of an aggressive and largely masculine sexuality, he nevertheless attempts to comprehend the mystery of Christ's descent into vulnerable flesh as an adoption of tacitly feminine traits. "Throughout the Old Testament," remarks Elaine Scarry, "God's power and authority are in part extreme and continually amplified elaborations of the fact that people have bodies and He has no body."[59] In "The Bag," Herbert's uncharacteristically grotesque portrait of the wounded Christ forces his readers to comprehend the complete strangeness of the New Testament's reversal of this relationship. In a nursery-rhyme style that belies the latent eroticism and blatant violence of its treatment of Christ, Herbert tells how his "Lord Jesus, . . . The God of power," traveled to earth, "undressing all the way," confident that "he had new clothes a making here below." The *kenosis* of Christ is rendered as a kind of cosmic striptease. The disrobed God is wounded by a soldier's spear, transforming his body into the bag of the title, a receptacle for carrying messages "unto my Fathers hands and sight." Moreover, he invites his torturers to follow the spear in penetrating his body so they may "put [their messages] very neare my heart," and enticingly reminds them that "the doore shall still be open." Robert Graves perhaps overstates the case, but he is close to the truth when he suggests that "the Divine Figure in 'The Bag' is fused with the figure of the temptress and at the end of the poem subordinate to her, when it has distinct feminine characteristics."[60] The poem's details—the action of "undressing," the placement in an "inne," the emphasis upon pregnability, the seductive promise that "the doore / Shall still be open"—all connote a sexual scenario which never fully surfaces, but which suffuses the process by which the almighty God of power becomes a vulnerable and compassionate deity. The wound of "The Bag" functions as a kind of vaginal orifice, feminizing a traditionally masculine Christ.[61] Christ's willingness to assume a vulnerable body and be entered by all opens him up to the contamination of a fallen, and surprisingly feminine, sexuality.

Several Latin poems by Herbert also envision piercing the divine body and intimate the possibility of a feminized Christ. *Passio Discerpta* 4, "*In latus perfossum*," depicts the "remorseless steel . . . open[ing] up a path" in Christ, a path the speaker hopes his heart will follow.[62] *Lucus* 30, "*In Thomam Didymum*," begins with a striking image of a mortal penetrating the divine body—"The servant puts his fingers in you"—and sees Jesus' allowance of such penetration as a manifestation of his love:

> Do you, Redeemer, permit this sign?
> For sure you are all love, and the pith of it.
> You make a shelter and sweet rest
> For a grudging faith and a narrow mind.[63]

In contrast to the quiet femininity of "The Bag," a Latin poem by Herbert addressed "To John leaning on the Lord's breast" (*Lucus* 34) imagines an overtly female Christ, nourishing with milk and blood his mortal disciples. Based on John 21.20, in which John is described as "the Disciple whom Jesus loved" and as the one "which also leaned on [Jesus's] breast at supper," the poem envisions a relationship to the body of Jesus which is at once erotic and maternal. Like a jealous sibling, Herbert's speaker declares to John:

> Ah now, glutton, let me suck too!
> You won't really hoard the whole
> Breast for yourself! Do you thieve
> Away from everyone that common well?
> He also shed his blood for me,
> And thus, having rightful
> Access to the breast, I claim the milk
> Mingled with the blood.[64]

E. Pearlman rightly calls attention to this remarkable "vision of a female or bisexual Jesus whose breast is not only comforting but in fact a source of milk."[65] As strange as this figure may seem, however, it suits perfectly the widespread medieval image of "mother Jesus" recently explored by Caroline Walker Bynum. Bynum uncovers a remarkable number of representations of Christ as a nourishing mother, and argues that "What writers in the high Middle Ages wished to say about Christ the savior who feeds the individual soul with his own blood was precisely and concisely said in the image of the nursing mother whose milk *is* her blood, offered to the child."[66] Herbert's Christ exudes blood and milk at once, blending maternal and sacrificial capacities. As the subtly seductive femininity of "The Bag" consoles in its open absorption of sinful humanity, the outright maternity of "To John" reassures in its outpouring of feminine nurture. Whether inviting another into itself or nourishing another with its substance, the female body provides a conduit of heavenly grace.

Despite such surprising complicity between notions of divinity and images of femininity, *The Temple* is littered with conventional *contemptus mulieris* sentiments which make the final vision of an androgynous divinity in "Love (III)" all the more striking.[67] Among the worldly figures who gather to "geere at" the speaker of "The Quip" is a tempting female "Beautie," who "crept into a rose, / Which when I pluckt not, Sir, said she, / Tell me, I pray, Whose hands are those?" George Ryley, Herbert's eighteenth-century commentator, correctly views Beauty here as representing "the Lusts of ye flesh."[68] The speaker of "Home" wishes to dismiss such enticing femininity altogether, asking: "What is this woman-kinde, which I can wink / Into a blacknesse and distaste?" "Constancie" links "sick folks, women, those whom passions sway," while "Dotage" groups "foolish night-fires, womens and childrens wishes." Culturally understood as figures of feebleness and temptation, women supply Herbert with a repertoire of images for the allurements of the world and the frailty of the flesh.

Such disturbingly standard expressions of Renaissance misogyny, however, issue for Herbert in rather unconventional images of disgust at mortal sexuality. In "The Forerunners," Herbert depicts all desire not directed to God as devotion to a "stie" and "dung." "Filth" is the product of the sensuality represented by "Marie Magdalene" before her turn to God as well as the mortal matter lurking just under the surface of even "the best face" in Herbert's second sonnet to his mother. The speaker of "Miserie" asks, "What strange pollutions doth [man] wed, / And make his own?" Herbert seems to have had difficulty talking about sexuality without recourse to imagery of pollution, filth, and defecation. "Beware of lust," is the first lesson in conduct issued by the avuncular speaker of "The Church-porch," "it doth pollute and foul."

Indeed, "The Church-porch" expends much energy in the attempt to resist the stains of concupiscence. Herbert offers the youthful audience of this gnomic poem a commonplace choice of Pauline avenues for avoiding the pollutions of lust: "Abstain wholly or wed." Yet one should not "grudge" that "lust hath bounds and staies," because, insists Herbert, "continence hath his joy." This joy, Herbert asserts, is comparable to the carnal pleasures it repudiates. "If rottennesse have more" joy than continence, advises Herbert, then indulge the flesh, and "let Heaven go."[69]

An even deeper anxiety about sexuality arises in the poem's discussion of drunkenness. Excessive consumption of alcohol ("Drink not the third glasse" opines the sententious speaker three times in twenty-four lines) is to be avoided because it allows normally repressed desires to surface. In one of the strangest passages in all of Herbert, he imagines the liberating effects of alcohol on behavior:

> He that is drunken, may his mother kill
> Bigge with his sister: he hath lost the reins,
> Is outlawd by himself.
>
> (lines 31–33)

As Strier notes, this is "a completely arbitrary instance of drunken behavior that the young George Herbert would have found especially appalling and perhaps, in some Freudian depth, appealing."[70] In a phrase that chillingly blends incest and matricide, Herbert views the self as seething with turbulent desires kept under tenuous control by the internalized laws of society. Without such "reins," innate concupiscence seeks to satisfy its most violent and salacious drives. The natural gravity pulling one towards sensual dissipation must continually be resisted:

> Who keeps no guard upon himself, is slack,
> And rots to nothing at the next great thaw.
> Man is a shop of rules, a well truss'd pack,
> Whose every parcell under-writes a law.
> Lose not thy self, nor give thy humours way:
> God gave them to thee under lock and key.
>
> (lines 139–44)

This sense of a self necessarily maintained in a state of perpetual house arrest assumes profound misgivings about the body and its urges. Norbert Elias has traced the process by which "the prohibitions supported by social sanctions are reproduced in the individual as self-controls." Herbert's concept of humanity as a "shop of rules" powerfully dramatizes this internalization of social sanctions. Herbert's expressed nervousness about the body in "The Church-porch" records the procedures by which "the social code of conduct so imprints itself in one form or another on the human being that it becomes a constituent element of his individual self."[71]

In *The Country Parson*, too, Herbert subjects the body to intense scrutiny, and voices great anxiety about the individual and social implications of sexuality. The country parson, Herbert explains, "keeps his body tame, serviceable, and healthfull; and his soul fervent, active, young, and lusty as an eagle" (*Works*, p. 237). Subjugation of the body is the necessary condition of the soul's "lust[iness]." Distrust of the body extends to Herbert's endorsement of the assumption (atypical to Protestantism) that "virginity is a higher state then Matrimony"; as a result, declares Herbert, the country parson "is rather unmarryed, then marryed" (*Works*, pp. 236–37). "But yet," continues Herbert,

> as the temper of his body may be, or as the temper of his Parish may be, where he may have occasion to converse with women, and that among suspicious men, *and other like circumstances considered*, he is rather married then unmarried.

Herbert values marriage not as the glorious bond of "wedded Love, mysterious law, true source / Of human offspring" that Milton was to laud but rather as a convenient and efficient way of averting community suspicion (*Paradise Lost*, 4:750–51). Indeed, the unmarried country parson must go to great lengths in his daily life to remain free of the taint of scandal:

> If he be unmarried, and keepe house, he hath not a woman in his house, but findes opportunities of having his meat dress'd and other services done by men-servants at home, and his linnen washed abroad. If he be unmarryed, and sojourne, he never talkes with any woman alone but in the audience of others, and that seldom, and then also in a very serious manner, never jestingly or sportfully.

The passage exudes acute nervousness about female company. "Others" must always be around, as a check both on the parson's behavior, and on rampant community suspicion. Considering the rigor and inconvenience of such injunctions, it is not surprising that Herbert himself did marry one year before accepting the living at Bemerton. Even the parson's "choyce" of a wife, though, is "made rather by his eare, then by his eye; his judgement, not his affection."[72] Romantic love and erotic desire are suppressed as refractory and irreligious forces. Herbert never mentions the central Judeo-Christian argument for marriage: procreation. Perhaps significantly, his own short marriage, unlike that of his far more prolific contemporary John Donne, produced no offspring. Lust, termed by Herbert "impurity of heart," "carnall impurity," and "the pestilence that walketh in darkeness," is for the country parson both a personal and a social problem; the parson must not only control it within himself but also avoid any situation in which it could be imputed to him (p. 238).

Yet the domain of feminity about which Herbert expresses such misgivings also supplies him with the materials for representing the two institutions he served—the university and the church. In a letter to Robert Creighton, his successor as University Orator at Cambridge, Herbert advises Creighton to imagine the institution on whose behalf he writes as "a matron holy, reverend, of antique and august countenance," and warns him not to "apply to her crisping-pins, as to a young woman, introducing stainings of the eyes and paintings of cheeks," because in doing so "thou dost not adorn her so much as raise thy hand against her (proper) gravity."[73] For Herbert, the University truly was an *alma mater*, whose decorum was determined by her age and gender. In "Church-rents and schismes," likewise, Herbert employs the traditional topos of *mater ecclesia*.[74] Curiously, though, the poem depicts the church not only as a "mother" who blushes at the doctrinal disputes raging about her but also as a "brave rose" which has been invaded by "a worm." The juxtaposition of the worm and the rose functions—as in William Blake's "Sick Rose"—to underwrite an implicit if unmistakable image of sexual violation which rests uncomfortably next to the identification of church and mother.[75] Doctrinal dispute, Herbert seems to suggest, is a kind of incestuous rape, akin to the aggressive sexuality representing intellectual pursuits in "Vanitie (I)" and "Divinitie."

In "The British Church," by contrast, Herbert segregates sexual and maternal imagery in order to discover in his mother church a non-sexual, matriarchal edifice which transcends the erotic attractions of both Catholicism and Puritanism.[76] Rome, for Herbert, is a painted prostitute, seducing her followers with false promises and dazzling cosmetics:

> She on the hills, which wantonly
> Allureth all in hope to be
> > By her preferr'd,
> Hath kiss'd so long her painted shrines,
> That ev'n her face by kissing shines,
> > For her reward.

Geneva, by contrast, affects a modesty which paradoxically issues in an appearance nearly as salacious as Roman cosmetics—nudity:

> She in the valley is so shie
> Of dressing, that her hair doth lie
> > About her eares:
> While she avoids her neighbours pride,
> She wholly goes on th' other side,
> > And nothing wears.

Where Rome is erotically "painted," Geneva wears nothing at all. The misguided shyness of the latter produces a presence in total opposition to the modesty it affects: nakedness. The conduct of both breaches the accepted decorum of female behavior in the period. Like Donne in "Satyre 3" and "Show me deare Christ," Herbert converts religious choice into a question of sexual predilection. But where Donne is undecided, for Herbert the choice is clear; the "British Church," Herbert's "dear Mother," epitomizes the genuine allure Rome and Geneva imitate so unsuccessfully even as she repudiates their erotic enticements. Possessed of "perfect lineaments and hue," she is one in whom "beautie . . . takes up her place, / And dates her letters from thy face, / When she doth write." Unlike the meretricious availability of Rome and Geneva, Herbert's mother church is blessed with geographical and (by implication) sexual inaccessibility; God has chosen "to double-moat thee with his grace, / And none but thee."

Although it concludes by praising the British Church as "the mean" between Rome and Geneva, then, the poem emphasizes how the *via media* of the British Church is not so much an Aristotelian mean between their respective sensual claims as a "double-moat[ed]" island resting comfortably beyond them. At the same time, as Summers and Pebworth argue, the identification of mother and church "reflect[ed] a concerted Anglican strategy of advocating devotion and submission to the Church and its ceremonies by characterizing the Church as a maternal figure."[77] Summers and Pebworth cite in part Milton's profound glimpse into the ideological valence of the *mater ecclesia* topos in the *Animadversions*. In response to the accusation that "like ill bred sons you spit in the face of your Mother the church of *England*," Milton calls attention to "the crafty scope of the Prelates, [who] endeavour to impresse deeply into weak, and superstitious fancies the awfull notion of a mother, that hereby they might cheat them into a blind and implicite obedience to whatsoever they shall decree."[78] Milton finds it absurd that "we who by Gods speciall grace have shak'n off the servitude of a great male Tyrant, our pretended Father the Pope, should now, if we be not betimes aware of these wily teachers, sink under the slavery of a Female notion, the cloudy conception of a demy-Iland mother." Herbert, by contrast, has no difficulty with accepting "the slavery of a Female notion, the cloudy conception of a demy-Iland mother." For him the concept of mother church renders overt disobedience nearly unthinkable. As femininity subsumes both the whore of Babylon and the spouse of the Lamb in the book of Revelation, so for Herbert does it embody at once the whorish churches of Rome and Geneva and the maternal ideal of his English church.

In "Love (III)," the final lyric of *The Temple*, Herbert consolidates and reappraises the various strands of eroticism that we have been examining. If, as Elizabeth Stambler and others have argued, "*The Temple* as a whole resembles a volume of courtly love poetry," then "Love (III)" functions as a kind of epithalamion, consummating, like Spenser's *Epithalamion* appended to the *Amoretti*, a frustrating and difficult courtship.[79] Behind Herbert's portrait of his encounter with God in "Love (III)" are the biblical parable of the wedding feast and the sensuous imagery of the Song of Solomon.[80] Throughout the poem, Herbert awakens rather than represses the eroticism implicit in these biblical motifs to represent the full richness and complexity of the confrontation with divine love. Because God is in part represented as a social superior addressed as "Lord" as well as an innkeeper asking "What d'ye lack?" a majority of the interpreters of this remarkable poem have been able to sustain discussions of it without reference to the sexual.[81] The poem is probably the finest example of Herbert's ability to fold into a single text a variety of discourses and situations. "However we read it the poem is moving," remarks Joseph Summers, "but it gains immensely in richness when we recognize the relationships it establishes between this world and the next, between abstracted and incarnate Love."[82] To explicate the poem without attending to the sexual medium of Herbert's incarnate love is to dodge the disquiet it intends to enforce, and to miss some of its finest effects.

Even those readers who have begun to excavate the layers of eroticism in the poem have done so with some trepidation. Chana Bloch, for example, astutely notes "the suggestion . . . of a sexual encounter between an inhibited or impotent man and a gently loving, patient woman."[83] Yet "it is unlikely," she adds, "that [Herbert] would have intended an explicitly sexual scene," and suggests that he may have been "unconsciously guided by the memory or imagination of a human sexual encounter." Janis Lull also acknowledges the poem's eroticism, but argues that "it is only in the first lines of the poem that God is thus envisioned as a woman reassuring an inhibited and guilty male lover." The poem, contends Lull, "considers and rejects sexuality as an image of humanity's love relationship with God"; the speaker "must discard the sexual metaphor altogether."[84] Where Lull claims that Herbert intentionally rejects the sexual as a medium of devotion, Bloch asserts that he unintentionally adopts it.

Despite the sensitivity of their readings, both critics, in order to assuage the genuine discomfort that the eroticism of the poem generates, must deny that Herbert intended to express the meeting with divine love as an erotic situation. Yet the poem continually swerves towards the erotic in a way that must in some sense be intentional.

Together with the speaker's first and final term of address—"My deare"—the first four words of the poem—"Love bade me welcome"—stir the erotic meanings dormant in Herbert's devotional language, conjuring an image of sociable reception which shades into sexual invitation.[85] The initial epithet with which Love is described —"quick ey'd"—not only designates the animated and solicitous favor present in Love's gaze but also implies that Herbert's God of Love is no blind Cupid. The physical gesture by which Love responds to the speaker's statement of his inability to look on Love—"Love took my hand"—both signifies the decreasing physical distance between Love and the speaker and adumbrates the act of marriage, which is often expressed in the phrase "to take the hand of." This line shrewdly resuscitates the matrimonial imagery enveloping the theological occasion.[86]

Yet there is in "Love (III)" an even deeper eroticism than the phenomena we have been observing, phenomena which could simply be termed sacred parody.[87] Rather, as Malcolm Evans has recently argued, "the love figured in the Sacrament [is not] altogether separable from the more mundane construction of human love constituted by the colloquial scene and language of the poem. The relationship between the two is too close to dismiss, in the name of allegory, signifiers that bring together sacred and profane love."[88] Herbert's portrait of his encounter with divine love is invested with a physical referentiality which makes a purely spiritual or allegorical reading of the poem difficult to sustain. Herbert wants us to remember that the body is the anxious medium of the moment he describes. Herbert's concern for his own social power in relation to God—a concern we have traced throughout our study—is manifested in the poem's preoccupation with the physical manifestations of sexual potency. In the context of a sexual tryst, to "grow slack / From my first entrance in" indicates a loss of erection just after penetration.[89] Moreover, to "grow slack" is inherently oxymoronic, a phallic version of the proud humility highlighted in the last chapter. Similarly, Love's "sweetly questioning" if the speaker "lack'd any thing" plays upon the common Renaissance euphemism of "thing" for "penis."[90] If the speaker has grown sexually slack, he does indeed lack a proper thing, an erect penis. The apprehension the speaker feels about his own spiritual worth and social utility is translated into an anxiety about his sexual performance. Because of his slackness, he is a guest unworthy to be where he is—in the private chambers of Love.

The speaker protests that he is too abashed to "look on" Love, that even if Love did make his eyes, the speaker has "marr'd them." His

257

inability to look on Love brilliantly blends a gesture of social deference (averting one's eyes is a common sign of respect) with an expression of sexual shame. Moreover, as William Kerrigan explains, in the Renaissance "the activity of seeing was itself invested with sexual significance . . . The word 'propagation' referred to the multiplication of the visual image in the spatial continuum between the object and the eye—seeing was making love to the world . . . And certainly the Italianate love poetry of the sixteenth century had established gazing, glancing, glimpsing, peering, peeking, and peeping as a kind of sexual activity, a foreplaying near in effect to a consummation."[91] Furthermore, to "make eyes" is a gesture not only of divine creation but also of sexual invitation.[92] According to Renaissance physiology, erotic desire had ocular origins: "by often gazing one on the other, [lovers] direct sight to sight, join eye to eye, and so drink and suck in Love between them . . . the beginning of this disease [love melancholy] is the Eye."[93] The refusal to look on Love—and the implicit contrast with Love's "quick" eyes—are concurrently a product, and another version, of the speaker's inability to perform as he would like.

Because of this inability, the speaker requests that his "shame" be allowed to "go where it doth deserve." "Shame" here designates both what the OED terms "the privy member" (on the model of *pudendum*, the Latin word for "shame" and "genitalia") and the deep disgrace he feels at this organ's current incapacity.[94] Love responds by assuming full responsibility for the speaker's present state: "And know you not, sayes Love, who bore the blame." The sacrifice of Christ that engrosses human sinfulness and dismisses the theological question of worthiness is here portrayed in the kind words of one who understands a lover's incapacity and who willingly accepts the blame, however inappropriately, for it. The speaker's subsequent offer of service—"My dear then I will serve"—plays, as does Herbert's sonnet to his mother, upon bawdy and devout senses of "service." In offering to serve, then, the speaker expresses his desire to preserve some vestige of social and sexual sufficiency. Love answers with a command that both dismisses and fulfills this desire—"You must sit down, sayes Love, and taste my meat." Oral dependency supplants genital potency as an expression of love and union. Unable to stand or serve—both euphemisms for maintaining an erection—the speaker must "sit and eat." The final two sets of rhymes in the poem—"deserve/ serve" and "meat/eat"—are produced, as in "Paradise," by pruning, and represent the whittling away of the speaker's pretentions of social and sexual power.

"Herbert was notably interested in eating itself—the ritual act par excellence," remarks William Kerrigan of the activity that concludes "Love (III)." "The extrasensory *taste* of God had approximately the emotional centrality for Herbert that the similarly extrasensory *vision* of God had for Milton."[95] Yet Herbert's literary corpus also displays great anxiety about the mouth as an orifice allowing the world's contagion to enter. "Look to thy mouth," warns Herbert in "The Church-porch," "diseases enter there" (line 127). As translator of Luigi Cornaro's *Treatise of Temperance and Sobrietie*—a text whose thesis is that all illness derives from the ingestion of something either excessive or bad—Herbert demonstrates a profound concern with the regulation of substances entering the body. In *The Country Parson,* Herbert directs much attention to nourishment, fastidiously proposing "three rules" that "generally comprehend the faults of eating . . . men must eat neither to the disturbance of their health, nor of their affairs, (which being overburdened, or studying dainties too much, they cannot wel dispatch) nor of their estate, nor of their brethren" (p. 266). As if these rules were not enough to regulate the anxious activity of eating, Herbert proceeds to propose another "three rules" to keep parsons from eating

> so as to disable themselves from a fit discharging . . . of Divine duties . . . first, the custome, and knowledg of their own body, and what it can well disgest [sic]: The second, the feeling of themselves in time of eating, which because it is deceitfull; (for one thinks in eating, that he can eat more, then afterwards he finds true:) The third is the observation with what appetite they sit down. This last rule joyned with the first, never fails. (pp. 266–67)

"For Herbert," argues Terry Sherwood, "the truth of the body and its physiology required the dietary and penitential disciplines that he recommends so firmly."[96] Eating is an anxious activity not only because of the social implications explored in the last chapter but also because "an English body, and a Students body, are two great obstructed vessels . . . And obstructions are the cause of most diseases" (p. 243).

The poems of *The Temple* betray a surprising concern with the indigestion that such obstructions cause. The poem in praise of the "deare feast" of "Lent," for example, contrasts "the cleannesse of sweet abstinence" to the "sluttish fumes, / Sowre exhalations, and dishonest rheumes" of "fulnesse," gastronomical agonies which "reveng[e] the delight" of gluttony. "Even-song" laments that "thy diet,

care, and cost / Do end in bubbles, balls of winde." The final utter-
ance in *The Temple*, "L'Envoy," asks the "King of Glorie" to direct
such painful gastritis towards "Sinne," a creature who desires to "de-
voure thy fold" and who brags "that thy flesh hath lost his food":

> Choke him, let him say no more,
> But reserve his breath in store,
> Till thy conquests and his fall
> Make his sighs to use it all,
> And then bargain with the winde
> To discharge what is behinde.

Herbert's surprising recourse to "the material bodily lower stratum"
in his final words on sin nevertheless suits the fastidious Herbert we
have come to know; his wish that sin be sentenced to eternal flatu-
lence not only locates the obstructed body as the site of damnation
but also affiliates sin with a bodily activity—farting—that was just
beginning to be frowned upon by the truly courteous.[97] Sin is not only
immoral but also indecorous. Since overeating results in such flatu-
lence, earthly hunger is, as "The Size" suggests, an appropriate pre-
requisite for admission to the heavenly banquet: "To be in both
worlds full / Is more then God was, who was hungrie here . . .
Wouldst thou both eat thy cake, and have it?" Remarkably, that is just
what happens in "Love (III)"; the speaker gets to have his meat and eat
it too. The orifice about which Herbert felt such acute distress
proves the site of nutritive, spiritual, and sexual success: "So I did sit
and eat."

In the last two lines, terminology which is perfectly appropriate for
describing the experience of the Eucharist—"taste," "meat," "sit,"
"eat"—assumes striking venereal significance from the sexual sce-
nario suggested in the previous lines. "Eating" of course possessed
strong sexual connotations in the Renaissance (although not in the
modern American sense of specifically oral sex). Partridge, for ex-
ample, cites the bawdy jest of Apemantus in *Timon of Athens*—"O
they [ladies] eat lords; so they come by great bellies" (1.1.206)—and
Emilia's droll characterization of male sexual appetites in *Othello*:
"They are all but stomachs, and we all but food; / They eat us hungerly,
and when they are full / They belch us" (3.4.104–6).[98] "Meat," too, had
powerful venereal resonance. Robert Herrick's ribald epigram "Upon
Jack and Jill," for example, opens: "When *Jill* complaines to *Jack* for
want of meate; / *Jack* kisses *Jill*, and bids her freely eate."[99] Moreover,
as the following passage from Jacques Bossuet, a seventeenth-century

French theologian, suggests, an erotic interpretation of eucharistic feasting was available even to the devout:

> The Eucharist explains to us all the words of love, of correspondence, of union, which are between Jesus Christ and his Church, between the Bridegroom and the Bride, between him and us.
>
> In the ecstasy of human love, who is unaware that we eat and devour each other, that we long to become part of each other in every way, and, as the poet said, to carry off even with our teeth the thing we love in order to possess it, feed upon it, become one with it, live on it? That which is frenzy, that which is impotence in corporeal love[,] is truth, is wisdom in the love of Jesus: "Take, eat, this is my body": devour, swallow up not a part, not a piece but the whole.[100]

The Eucharist, Bossuet argues, perfects the incomplete incorporation of another that all seek in erotic experience. Love is a hunger for consumption of another, a hunger inevitably frustrated in mortal love but fully satisfied through the Eucharist, in which Christ, like a lover, offers the meat of his body to his beloved. As Theodoret, the fifth-century bishop of Cyrrhus, remarks:

> at the moment of the sacrament when we receive the members of the Spouse, we kiss and embrace him . . . and we imagine a kind of nuptial embrace; we consider that we unite ourselves to him by embracing and kissing him.[101]

The Eucharist is both the pattern and the fulfillment of sexual desire.

"Love (III)" exploits just such a conflation of the imagery of eating and of sexual intercourse. In offering himself to all at each celebration of the communion, Christ is like a desirable and desiring lover. In the act of eating, and in the sexual intercourse that act could represent, divinity and humanity are conjoined. "Love (III)" may begin with an impulse of "my soul" but its conclusion emphasizes the body—"my meat." As Donne insists in "The Extasie," "Loves mysteries in soules doe grow, / But yet the body is his booke."[102] Because the Christian God willingly assumed human flesh, all bodily phenomena are potential manifestations of grace. In an uncharacteristically sybaritic passage, Richard Hooker describes the incarnation as a "copulation [of flesh] with Deity," and imagines receiving the Eucharist as the moment when "in the wounds of our Redeemer we there dip our tongues, we are dyed red both within and without, our hunger is satisfied and our thirst for ever quenched."[103] Lancelot Andrewes, too, waxes sensual on the subject; he remarks that in the incarnation, "He, and we, become not only *one flesh* (as *man* and *wife* do, by *conjugal union*); but even one *bloud* too."[104] Like Andrewes and Hooker, Herbert finds in sexual union and sensual pleasure a compelling model for the intimacy between humanity and God signaled by the incarnation, and celebrated in the Eucharist. For Herbert the body is both the locus of ungodly desires and the site of divinity. "The Glimpse" describes a tantalizing God whose "short abode and stay / Feeds not, but addes to the desire of meat." In "Ungratefulnesse," Herbert declares that God donned human flesh in order to "allure us with delights," and describes "the *Trinitie*, and *Incarnation*" as "jewels to betroth / The work of thy creation / Unto thy self in everlasting pleasure." "The Invitation," as Strier remarks, "presents the Eucharist as the ideal fulfillment of the passions involved in sinning."[105] It welcomes all to "feast" on a "God, in whom all dainties are," and tells those "whose love / Is your dove" that "Here is love, which having breath / Ev'n in death, / After death can never die." The incarnation, and its eucharistic re-enactment, seems for Herbert to have been a true banquet of the senses, inextricably linked to somatic pleasure. By representing eucharistic tasting as sexual indulgence, "Love (III)" highlights the voluptuous qualities of the feast of love stressed in "The Glimpse," "Ungratefulnesse," and "The Invitation"; it also flaunts the divine willingness to take on a body that is exposed in "The Bag" and "Marie Magdalene." In both senses, it accents the carnality immanent in the incarnation.

In two of his Holy Sonnets Donne engages in a superficially similar sexualization of his relationship with God. But in Donne, the stunning blend of erotic and religious impulses is easily comprehended precisely because the eroticism is so explicit. In "Show me dear Christ thy spouse," the vast differences between earthly and heavenly promiscuity are underscored by the apparent contradiction of the final couplet, in which Christ's spouse, the Church, is "most trew, and pleasing to thee, then / When she'is embrac'd and open to most men." Similarly, in "Batter my heart, three-person'd God," the paradox of a rape which makes one chaste is readily understood as a form of divine rapture stated in erotic terms:

> Take mee to you, imprison mee, for I
> Except you'enthrall mee, never shall be free,
> Nor ever chast, except you ravish mee.[106]

Donne's overt sensuality is marked by the spiritual models of his own mother church—a Counter Reformation Catholicism whose sensuality would reach its most explicit English statements in the work of Richard Crashaw.[107] With Donne we are meant to see, as William Kerrigan has eloquently demonstrated, the "awful discrimination" of heavenly and earthly love.[108]

But in "Love (III)" the reader experiences deep discomfort because the eroticism is at once more delicate and more deeply engrained in the divine. Rather than apprehending the awful discrimination of heavenly and earthly love, Herbert's reader is forced to grasp their equally awe-inspiring similarity. Like the speaker, the reader is at a loss for a fit response to this figure of divine Love. This uneasiness embodies a diminished version of the apprehension the speaker of "Love (III)" feels at this unexpected intimacy between him and his God. Indeed, the temptation to "draw back" from this aspect of "Love (III)" is great. For the erotic and the religious, although never separated in the poem, work against each other even as they are expressed in precisely the same language. In order to make simple sense of the poem, one must either suppress the erotic or cultivate it at the expense of the sacred. If this figure is an enticing lover, it is proper for the speaker to draw back, to grow slack, to refuse the seduction. But if this figure is God, then to draw back, to grow slack, to refuse to enter, is bad, evidence of unregenerate pride.

Such complications have led E. Pearlman to argue that the poem is best understood as an example of "the radical confusion in Herbert's mind between things maternal and things divine."[109] In feeding another, especially with the substance of his own body, divine Love does perform a traditionally maternal task. But when the speaker of "Love (III)" addresses his God as both "my deare" and "Lord," Herbert is not simply confusing his mother with his God. Rather, he is celebrating the remarkable intimacy God allows his creatures. In *Of Domesticall Duties*, William Gouge admonishes wives to refrain from calling husbands by such names as "Sweet, Sweeting, Hert, Sweet-heart, Love, Joy, [or] Deare" because "such tokens of familiaritie are not withall tokens of subjection and reverence."[110] But in "Love (III)," Herbert addresses his God in the very terminology that Gouge finds too "familiar" to pass between a husband and wife. As in "The Search," where he asks, "Whither, O, whither art thou fled, / My Lord, my Love?" Herbert carefully juxtaposes a terminology of "subjection and reverence" with one of familiarity and endearment.

"Love (III)," then, marks the last of the unexpected condescensions to humanity with which Herbert's God continues to astonish him. In "Redemption," for example, the speaker seeks his Lord "in great resorts; / In cities, theatres, gardens parks, and courts" only to find him

amidst "a ragged noise and mirth / Of theeves and murderers."
Throughout *The Temple*, Herbert has been looking for Love in all the
wrong places. In "Love (III)" he discovers it in an unanticipated
form—the guise of a seductive lover—thereby transforming a com-
edy of errors into a comedy of eros. In this way "Love (III)" exposes the
process by which "sin," in Julia Kristeva's phrase, is "turned upside
down into love."[111] Paradoxically, the very humanness and famil-
iarity of this incarnated God makes him so peculiar.[112] The life and
death of Christ truly is, as "The Bag" suggests, "a strange storie." As
in "Marie Magdalene," Herbert's God astonishes by his ability to as-
similate the sin he cancels, and to welcome the sinner his law would
condemn.

In a sermon on Psalm 2.12 ("Kisse the Son, lest he be angry") Donne
praises a God who similarly "stoops even to the words of our foule and
unchaste love, that thereby he might raise us to the heavenly love of
himselfe." Yet such condescension, Donne argues, places intense in-
terpretive pressure on the mortal reader: "Take heed lest those phrases
of love and kisses which should raise thee to him, do not bury thee in
the memory and contemplation of sinfull love." Donne promises the
wary reader that "there is corne under the chaffe . . . There is a heav-
enly love, under these ordinary phrases."[113] For Donne, the reader's
task is to distinguish spiritual and carnal senses. Yet in "Love (III)" the
corn keeps adhering to the chaff; the carnal continues to infiltrate the
spiritual. Such distinctions, however, are rendered irrelevant by Her-
bert's open-armed deity. Divine acceptance of the speaker, albeit
"guilty of dust and sin," entails an embrace of sexuality, that which
makes him feel guilty. And the embrace of sexuality, finally, is also a
cordial reception of the sexually impotent, he who cannot perform as
he would like for divine love.[114] Where Donne's God adopts erotic ter-
minology to test the interpretive and moral capacities of his followers,
Herbert's God assumes sexuality to attest his total absorption of sinful
humanity.

Such absorption also manifests itself in the curious blending of
gender-specific traits implicit in Herbert's representations of di-
vinity. Although Pearlman argues that Herbert's God "is threatening
when envisioned as father, consoling when envisioned as mother,"
rarely are the masculine and feminine characteristics of Herbert's
deity this distinct.[115] In "Longing," for example, Herbert depicts the
"Lord of my soul, love of my mind" (line 20) as a nourishing mother—
"Mothers are kinde, because thou art, / And dost dispose / To them a
part: / Their infants, them; and they suck thee / More free" (lines
13–18)—and a great lord who feasts all comers—"Thy board is full,

yet humble guests / Finde nests" (lines 54–55)—as well as a king
who left his "throne" in order to "relieve" humanity. Herbert repre-
sents himself not only as a "humble guest" and God's "childe" but
also as a "beggar" (line 77) and "thy dust . . . thy pile of dust" (lines
37, 41). In the final stanza, furthermore, God is envisaged both as the
speaker's beloved and as Cupid, the wounding God of Love, at whose
feet the speaker prostrates himself:

> My love, my sweetnesse, heare!
> By these thy feet, at which my heart
> Lies all the yeare,
> Pluck out thy dart,
> And heal my troubled breast which cryes,
> Which dyes.

For Herbert, God is simultaneously an image of patriarchal power and
a figure of maternal nourishment, the object of an inferior's supplica-
tion and the audience of a suitor's erotic pleas, an injuring Cupid and
the injured savior.[116] God is at once threatening and consoling, pierc-
ing and impaled, hospitable and coercive, powerful and submissive.

Stephen Greenblatt has recently argued that Shakespearean com-
edy, despite its array of women disguised as men, fails to represent male
characters dressed as women "in part because a passage from male to
female was coded ideologically as a descent from superior to inferior
and hence as an unnatural act or a social disgrace."[117] But this is pre-
cisely the trajectory taken by Herbert's condescending deity, stooping
to a culturally gendered inferiority while condescending to serve an
inferior. "Because of woman's marginal position in the world," re-
marks Simone de Beauvoir, "men will turn to her when they strive
through culture to go beyond the boundaries of their universe and gain
access to something other than what they have known."[118] Sur-
prisingly, the endowment of a traditionally patriarchal divinity with
elements of a socially marginal femininity underwrites Herbert's
struggle for spiritual transcendence.

By fusing masculine and feminine attributes, then, divine Love
breaks down normally discrete social categories, attaining an an-
drogyny that is political as well as sexual.[119] In "To Mr. Tilman after
he had taken orders," Donne terms the priest a "blest Hermaphro-
dite" because he couples heaven and earth (line 54); for Herbert, how-
ever, the hermaphrodite is not the priest but God, whose conjugation
of heaven and earth is replicated in the assimilation of masculine and
feminine traits.[120] In a sermon on Proverbs 8.17 ("I love them that
love me, and they that seek me early shall find me"), Donne explores

the androgyny of Christ's love in ways that illumine the tacit androgyny of Herbert's figure of Love:

> To shew the constancy and durableness of this love, the lover is a he, that is Christ; to show the vehemency and earnestness of it, the lover is a shee, that is wisdom . . . all that is good then, either in the love of man or woman is in this love; for he is expressed in both sexes, man and woman; and all that can be ill in the love of either sex, is purged away.[121]

Although Herbert never explicitly represents God as androgynous, his divinity quietly assimilates erotic qualities culturally encoded as masculine and feminine. Unlike Donne's androgynous deity, however, Herbert's God does not so much purge the "ill" present "in the love of either sex" as absorb it into his/her all-encompassing being. The result is both more unsettling, and more comforting.

Despite the unabashed misogyny of some of the participants in the dialogue of *The Courtier*, Castiglione nevertheless argues that the proper representation of divinity requires the inclusion rather than exclusion of traditionally female characteristics:

> And for so much as one kinde [gender] alone betokeneth an imperfection, the Divines of olde time referre both the one and the other to God: Wherefore Orpheus saide that Jupiter was both male and female: and it is read in scripture that God fashioned male and female to his likenesse. And the Poets many times speaking of the Gods, meddle the kindes together.[122]

The presence of masculine and feminine traits in Herbert's deity, then, is a manifestation of divine perfection, not the product of poetic deficiency or psychological confusion. An exclusively masculine divinity would be in some sense an "imperfection." Among the *Outlandish Proverbs* collected by Herbert is the common Renaissance expression that "words are women, deedes are men."[123] Perhaps Herbert's apprehension about performing before God is expressed so often in images of male potency because of this cultural equation of masculinity and accomplishment. In the encounter with the word-made-flesh in "Love (III)," though, Herbert's overwhelmingly beneficent deity robs him of both feminine words and masculine deeds, telling him neither to serve nor to speak but to "sit and eat." The theological anxiety generated by the need to serve an omnipotent God, then, finds an erotic corollary in the scenario of an amorous and androgynous divinity welcoming an impotent and hesitant mortal. Love literally becomes "the

Master Mistris" of the speaker's passion, the object of his sexual and social desires, an image of erotic invitation and political domination.

The apparition of an enticing, hermaphroditic deity brings us back to the work of Leonardo da Vinci, the figure with whom we began this chapter. In Leonardo's striking painting of a sexually ambiguous John the Baptist, divine invitation similarly occurs in the guise of sexual solicitation. The gesture of the right hand provocatively summons the viewer even as it points to a heaven above. Identified as a religious figure only by a thin cross nearly rendered invisible against the saint's luminous flesh, Leonardo's androgynous *St. John* unsettles the viewer he welcomes. "I felt far from comfortable in the presence of this apparition looming tenebrously out of the murky darkness," remembers Bernard Berenson of his first encounter with the painting. "I could not conceive why this fleshy female should pretend to be the virile, sun-dried Baptist, half starved in the wilderness."[124] Surprised by sensuality in a devotional context, the viewer of Leonardo's *St. John*, like the reader of Herbert's "Love (III)," must reconcile normally adverse impulses. The enigmatic smile of this figure, lurid but saintly, joins masculine and feminine, heaven and earth, flesh and spirit, temptation and transcendence. Like Herbert's smiling deity in "Love (III)," Leonardo's *St. John* embodies the sexual mystery at the core of religious experience.[125]

Throughout *The Temple*, Herbert voices his deep longing for the favor and love of his God by means of a complex set of homologies among divine, social, and sexual courtship. These homologies were in large part the product of the particular political situation of the English Renaissance. Where Queen Elizabeth had appropriated a rhetoric of masculine sovereignty, King James frequently assimilated images of matriarchal nurture.[126] Under both monarchs, furthermore, amorous language provided a medium of political courtship; political favor, in turn, was often expressed in erotic terms. When Elizabeth was on the throne, this process made possible the publishing of political desire in a vocabulary of heterosexual longing licensed by neo-Petrarchan convention.[127] When James was on the throne, however, this process resulted in a far more ideologically conflicted situation, in which political desire was articulated by means of a vocabulary that continually veered towards a homoeroticism condemned by Christian tradition. The chain of favorites at the Jacobean court—Esmé Stuart, Robert Carr, and George Villiers—each owed his political success in large part to the fact of James's erotic attraction to him. In the relationship of James and Buckingham, two figures Herbert knew and often

Figure 6.   Leonardo da Vinci, *St. John the Baptist* (1513–16). Paris. Musée du Louvre.

addressed, political longing and homosexual desire were mutually supporting passions; as Roger Lockyer argues, "By giving himself [sexually] to James, Buckingham confirmed his [political] supremacy."[128] Indeed James even defended his fervent love of Buckingham by reference to Christian precedent, invoking the close bond between Jesus and John the Evangelist to which Herbert's epigram "To John" (*Lucus* 34) also appeals. "You may be sure that I love the Earl of Buckingham more than anyone else," James told the Council. "I wish to speak in my own behalf and not to have it thought to be a defect, for Jesus Christ did the same and therefore I cannot be blamed. Christ had his John, and I have my George."[129] In a patriarchal and misogynistic culture such as the Renaissance, where women are valued primarily as agents of reproduction or as units of exchange, male homosexuality is the inevitable if brutally repressed outlet of the highest social bonds.[130] As *"Aethiopissa,"* Herbert's Latin poem to Bacon in the persona of a black woman, makes clear, male courtship of the favor of masculine superiors could easily be pulled from a socially warranted homosocial desire towards remarkably forthright homoerotic expression. In its eroticized love for a God addressed both as "Lord" and "my dear," Herbert's "Love (III)," like Leonardo's *St. John*, allows the culturally suppressed homoeroticism of the male love for a traditionally masculine deity to surface.[131] A composite of masculine and feminine authority and the object of political and erotic desire, Herbert's androgynous divinity functions as the absolute audience of the Renaissance lyric.[132]

"The terms of the social order," remarks Kenneth Burke, "incongruously shape our idea of God, inviting [mortals] to conceive of communication with God after the analogy of their worldly embarrassments."[133] In "Love (III)" and throughout *The Temple*, Herbert explores the intersection of social order, worldly embarrassment, and religious experience. Moreover, Herbert's historical moment—the early seventeenth century—has been identified by Norbert Elias, Michel Foucault, Lawrence Stone, and Francis Barker as inaugurating the withdrawal of sexuality into architectural privacy and linguistic euphemism. "The seventeenth century," remarks Foucault, "was the beginning of an age of repression emblematic of what we call the bourgeois societies, an age which perhaps we still have not completely left behind."[134] In their engagement with and recoil from a discourse of sexuality, Herbert's lyrics rest precariously on the fault lines of this cultural movement. "Pleasure promising drives and pleasure denying taboos and prohibitions, socially generated feelings of shame and repugnance, come to battle within" the Renaissance individual, argues Elias.[135] The pulls and tensions of "Love (III)," so elegantly voiced by the courtesy that records the internalization of social prohibition, thrive on just this battlefield. In its simple yet resonant final line, the speaker is told by the highest authority imaginable to satisfy a hunger that a range of political and scriptural authorities have demanded he suppress. Pleasure is at last reconciled to virtue. The poems of *The Temple* are a remarkable document in the history of sexuality. To draw back from their anxious eroticism is finally to retreat from this history, a miscellany of texts and practices infiltrating and enabling Herbert's devotional performances.

Recent scholarship has begun to exhume the importance of gender-specific and erotic imagery for past concepts of God. Leo Steinberg, for example, has called attention to a remarkable number of Renaissance depictions of Christ which emphasize the savior's genital potency as a measure of his adoption of human weakness.[136] Caroline Walker Bynum, conversely, has discovered an astonishing range and flexibility of gender imagery in medieval devotional discourse.[137] In our attempts to engage with texts from the past we must remain willing to attend to elements that upset rather than reinforce our modern prejudices. When dealing with sexuality in particular, we must resist the temptation to idealize or intellectualize it, to make it into a metaphor for an activity for which our conceptual apparatuses are better suited. The love that Herbert anatomizes and practices throughout *The Temple* is not just *caritas* but also *cupiditas*; not just *agape* but also *eros*.[138] Its medium is the flesh his God assumed as well as the spirit to which all life tends. Rather than functioning as an impertinent distraction from devotion, sexuality is the warp of that carefully woven fabric through which Herbert attempts to comprehend and express the divine. "To reproach mystics with loving God by means of the faculty of sexual love," remarks Simone Weil, "is as though one were to reproach a painter with making pictures by means of colors composed of material substances. We haven't anything else with which to love."[139] We should not then be as surprised as we nevertheless are to discover the plethora of erotic references pervading Herbert's religious poetry. We should, rather, admire the spiritual stamina of a poet who continually resists the temptation to draw back from the unsettling aspects of his encounter with the divine, and prize the capacity of his poetry to aspire to spirituality by embracing rather than repressing a remarkable range of corporeal experience.

Afterword

For pleasing words are like to Magick art.
                                        —Edmund Spenser

In the conclusion to *The Origin of Table Manners*, Claude Lévi-Strauss calls attention to

> the total opposition between the reasons for good manners believed in by so-called primitive people and ourselves. We wear hats to protect *ourselves* from rain, cold and heat; we use forks to eat with, and wear gloves when we go out, so as not dirty *our* fingers; we drink through a straw in order to protect *ourselves* from the coldness of the beverage . . . Yet in other societies, today as in former times, hats, gloves, forks, [and] drinking tubes . . . are meant as barriers against an infection emanating from the body of the user. Whereas we think of good manners as a way of protecting the internal purity of the subject against the external impurity of beings and things, in savage [*sic*] societies, they are a means of protecting the purity of beings and things against the impurity of the subject.[1]

In Herbert's devastatingly courteous lyrics, and in the Renaissance discourse of courtesy in general, we can see both functions of manners at work, as the courtly fear of contaminating others blends into the bourgeois anxiety about the world's infections. "The origin of table manners, and more generally that of correct behavior, is to be found," contends Lévi-Strauss, "in deference towards the world—good manners consisting precisely in respecting its obligations."[2] Afraid of defiling the sacred presence he approaches and equally terrified of external contagion, Herbert records in his anxiously man-

271

nered lyrics the impure subject's nervous encounter with an unclean domain. He defers to the world he fears.

Sweeping as it is, Lévi-Strauss's account of the origin of table manners nevertheless neglects the process by which such deference to the world can also be a tactic for controlling it. As a child I was fascinated by the power that the use of "please" and "thank you" seemed to bestow upon an otherwise powerless being. These were, my parents told me, "magic words"; my parents did not lie. When I used them, these words of supplication and gratitude really did seem to invest my utterances to adults with a near magical power (although they rarely worked with other children, who had not yet been socialized to appreciate their significance). A sprinkling of "Sir" and "Ma'am" only enhanced their thaumaturgic force. Suddenly adults listened and responded favorably to my requests, conquered by my glib "please," and gratified by my facile "thank you." My own "civilizing process" involved the discovery, however unformulated, that the act of submitting to societal norms of politeness is an ultimately empowering procedure. The gap between the absolute ease of speaking these words and the genuine power they bestowed did not seem worth examining; it was only another function of their magic. One does not ask how the spell works, only that one possess the power to cast it.

But Herbert does ask how the spell of his own courteous performances works. Preoccupied by the power that gestures of humility can exercise, he is also painfully aware of the desire for ascension they can disguise. Much of *The Temple* is devoted to analyzing the supernatural levitation by means of humiliation described in "Charms and Knots": "Who looks on ground with humble eyes, / Findes himself there, and seeks to rise." By turning on God the manipulative tactics of social supplication, Herbert empties the words of their magic in order to find out how they work. Yet in spite of, or rather because of, their saturation in this sullied social discourse, Herbert's poems attain an authenticity remarkable to religious utterance, so easily marred by self-congratulatory piety or masochistic self-indulgence. "*Herbert*," remarks the seventeenth-century Puritan divine Richard Baxter, "speaks *to God* like one that *really believeth a God*, and whose business in the world is most *with God. Heart-work* and *Heaven work* make up his Books."[3] Herbert writes like one whose business is most with God precisely because he uses the language of social exchange in his spiritual encounters with God. His heart-work and heaven-work are expressed in the idiom of court-work. The terms of terrestrial transaction between an inferior and a superior supply the vocabulary Herbert uses to negotiate between this world and the next.

A virtual anthology of supplicatory tactics, *The Temple* demonstrates how manners are not just an act of deference to the world but also a mode of exerting control over it. At once epidermal and profound, manners mediate social anxiety and delineate social boundaries, embodying the best and worst tendencies of a culture. Although manners are one of the many instruments we use to manipulate others, they are also the manacles that keep us from each other's throats. Manners include the most valued modes of conduct a society can muster: hospitality to strangers, beneficence to the destitute, and gratitude to benefactors. Yet they also supply the medium for expressing social contempt, class demarcation, and cultural superiority. Manners advertise one's willing submission to a status quo; yet mastery of their nuances is an empowering act. Manners come into being at the moment when behavior becomes art, when social intercourse finds formal solution. But once transformed into formulae, such conduct can easily be dissociated from the interior reality that produced it.

As I negotiate the network of pressing obligations and affective bonds that constitute my own social existence, the magic words of my childhood retain much of their power. I remain, moreover, intrigued by the capacity of the most apparently arbitrary gestures and phrases to shape and influence human conduct. In Herbert's works, I have found a site for measuring the contestatory and submissive energies of courtesy in a vital and compelling form. Their intensely self-conscious use of the supple discourse of courtesy offers a lexicon for transcribing the rhetorical energies of human conduct. An act of deference to the world and to the Christian God who uttered it into being, *The Temple* is also an attempt to harness these two unruly forces by means of human speech. Blending the techniques of poetry, the tactics of courtesy, the motives of praise, and the aspirations of prayer, Herbert welcomes the worldly reader and the profane world into the temple of his devotion. It is the paramount gesture of his beguiling civility.

Notes

Introduction

1. *Works*, p. 231.
2. William Shullenberger, *"Ars Praedicandi* in George Herbert's Poetry," in *"Bright Shootes of Everlastingnesse": The Seventeenth-Century Religious Lyric*, eds. Claude J. Summers and Ted-Larry Pebworth (Columbia: University of Missouri Press, 1987), p. 99.
3. Michel Foucault, "The Subject and Power," *Critical Inquiry* 8 (1982): 789. *Power* is one of Herbert's favorite words, occurring in its various forms (including "powerfull" and "powers") 92 times in his works.
4. Peter Laslett cites an unpublished manuscript (Bodleian, Tanner 233) in which Filmer refers to "the divine Poet and my intimate friend Mr. Geo. Herbert" ("Sir Robert Filmer: The Man versus the Whig Myth," *William and Mary Quarterly*, ser. 3, no. 4, vol. 5 [1948]: 527). No evidence of a relationship between the two survives from Herbert's hand.
5. Raymond Williams, *The Country and the City* (London: Oxford University Press, 1973), p. 31.
6. I borrow the phrase from James C. Scott's study of Malaysian peasantry, *Weapons of the Weak: Everyday Forms of Peasant Resistance* (New Haven: Yale University Press, 1985).
7. Edmund Spenser, *The Faerie Queene* (6.1.1.), ed. Thomas P. Roche, Jr. (Harmondsworth: Penguin, 1978), p. 878.
8. Stefano Guazzo, *The Civile Conversation*, trs. George Pettie (Books 1–3, 1581) and Bartholomew Young (Book 4, 1586), 2 vols. (London: Constable, 1925), 1:156.
9. *1 Henry IV* (3.2.50–52).
10. I am thinking here of Chilton Powell, *English Domestic Relations 1487–1653* (New York: Columbia University Press, 1917); Thomas F. Crane, *Italian Social Customs in the Sixteenth Century* (New Haven: Yale University Press, 1920); Elbert N. S. Thompson, "Books of Courtesy," in *Literary Bypaths of the Renaissance* (New Haven: Yale University Press, 1924),

pp. 127–71; Ruth Kelso, *The Doctrine of the English Gentleman in the Sixteenth Century*, in *University of Illinois Studies in Language and Literature* 14 (1929): 1–288; John E. Mason, *Gentlefolk in the Making: Studies in the History of English Courtesy Literature and Related Topics from 1531 to 1774* (Philadelphia: University of Pennsylvania Press, 1935); Jean Robertson, *The Arte of Letter Writing* (London: Hodder and Stoughton, 1942); John L. Lievsay, *Stefano Guazzo and the English Renaissance 1574–1675* (Chapel Hill: University of North Carolina Press, 1961); Joseph A. Mazzeo, "Castiglione's *Courtier*: The Self as a Work of Art," in *Renaissance and Revolution: Backgrounds to Seventeenth-Century Literature* (New York: Random House, 1965), pp. 131–60; Diane Bornstein, *Mirrors of Courtesy* (Hamden: Archon, 1975); and Wayne A. Rebhorn, *Courtly Performances: Masking and Festivity in Castiglione's "Book of the Courtier"* (Detroit: Wayne State University Press, 1978).

11. Daniel Javitch, *Poetry and Courtliness in Renaissance England* (Princeton: Princeton University Press, 1978); see also his "Rival Arts of Conduct in Elizabethan England: Guazzo's *Civile Conversation* and Castiglione's *Courtier*," *Yearbook of Italian Studies* 1 (1971): 178–98, and "*Il Cortegiano* and the Constraints of Despotism" in *Castiglione: The Ideal and the Real in Renaissance Culture*, eds. Robert W. Hanning and David Rosand (New Haven: Yale University Press, 1983), pp. 17–28. In the latter work, Javitch emphasizes more fully than in *Poetry and Courtliness* the ways in which Castiglione's ideal courtier responds to the pressures of Renaissance despotism.

12. Frank Whigham, *Ambition and Privilege: The Social Tropes of Elizabethan Courtesy Theory* (Berkeley: University of California Press, 1984), p. xi.

13. Edward Herbert, *Life and Reign of Henry VIII*, ed. Alexander Murray (London, 1870), pp. 139–40.

14. Norbert Elias, *The Court Society*, tr. Edmund Jephcott (New York: Pantheon, 1983), p. 108.

15. Peter Laslett, *The World We Have Lost* (New York: Charles Scribner's Sons, 1965), p. 52.

16. In his autobiography, Edward Herbert shows his familiarity with two of the most popular courtesy books of the English Renaissance, Stefano Guazzo's *Civile Conversation* and Giovanni della Casa's *Galateo*, stating: "I could say much more . . . concerning That discreete Civillity which is to bee observed in Communication either with freinds [sic] or strangers but that this worke would growe too bigg, And that many precepts conducing thereunto may bee had in Guazzo della Civile Conversatione and Galetaeus de Moribus" (*The Life of Edward, First Lord Herbert of Cherbury*, ed. J. M. Shuttleworth [London: Oxford University Press, 1976], p. 36). In *Stefano Guazzo and the English Renaissance*, pp. 141–44, Lievsay argues that "some fifty-odd" of George Herbert's *Outlandish Proverbs* "are to be found in Guazzo's *Civil conversatione*," but cautions against regarding Guazzo as an immediate source.

17. Amy Charles, *A Life of George Herbert* (Ithaca: Cornell University Press, 1977), p. 78.

18. M. M. Mahood, *Poetry and Humanism* (1949; repr. New York: Norton, 1970), p. 41.

19. Cristina Malcolmson, "George Herbert's *Country Parson* and the Character of Social Identity," *Studies in Philology* 85 (1988): 251.

20. Izaak Walton, "Life of Mr. George Herbert" (1670), in *Lives*, ed. George Saintsbury (London: Oxford University Press, 1927), p. 314. The phrase is from Walton's highly creative reconstruction of Herbert's last words.

21. I discuss "The Dedication" in greater depth in "Submission and Assertion: The 'Double Motion' of Herbert's 'Dedication,'" *John Donne Journal* 2, no. 2 (1983): 39–49, and in " 'Respective Boldnesse': Herbert and the Art of Submission," in *"A Fine Tuning": Studies of the Religious Poetry of Herbert and Milton*, ed. Mary Maleski (Binghamton, N.Y.: Medieval and Renaissance Texts and Studies, 1989), pp. 77–94.

22. In "Sanctifying the Aristocracy: 'Devout Humanism' in François de Sales, John Donne, and George Herbert," *Journal of Religion* 69 (1989): 51, Richard Strier rightly observes that "prudence and calculation are at the heart of 'The Church-porch.'" Strier's observation is borne out by the fact that about one-half "The Church-porch" is reproduced (without acknowledgment) in an anonymous pamphlet entitled *The Way to be Rich: According to the Practice of the Great Audley* (London, 1662), under the heading "His Rules of Thriving"; see Raymond A. Anselment, "Seventeenth-Century Adaptations of 'The Church-porch,'" *George Herbert Journal* 5, nos. 1 and 2 (1981–82): 66–68. A fascinating account of the discontinuity between "The Church-porch" and "The Church"—"corresponding to a parallel discontinuity in the cultural representation of selfhood"—is proffered by Debora K. Shuger in *Habits of Thought in the English Renaissance* (Berkeley: University of California Press, 1990), pp. 93–105.

23. Ben Jonson, *Volpone* (3.1.23–24), in *Ben Jonson*, eds. C. H. Herford, Percy Simpson, and Evelyn Simpson, 11 vols. (Oxford: Clarendon Press, 1925–52), 5:66–67.

24. Desiderius Erasmus, *De Civilitate Morum Puerilium*, tr. Robert Whitington (London, 1532).

25. *The Babees Book*, in *Manners and Meals in Olden Time*, ed. Frederick J. Furnivall (London: E.E.T.S., 1868), p. 3.

26. Louis B. Wright, *Middle-Class Culture in Elizabethan England* (Chapel Hill: University of North Carolina Press, 1935), explores in detail both "Handbooks to Improvement" (pp. 121–69) and "Guides to Godliness" (pp. 228–96). Douglas Bush, *English Literature in the Earlier Seventeenth Century 1600–1660* (London: Oxford University Press, 1962), p. 310, estimates that "more than two-fifths of the books printed in England from 1480 to 1640 were religious, and for the years 1600–40 the percentage is still higher."

27. The impulse to order and organize that emerged in response to this

anxiety is examined by William J. Bouwsma, "Anxiety and the Formation of Early Modern Culture," in *After the Reformation: Essays in Honor of J. H. Hexter*, ed. Barbara C. Malament (Philadelphia: University of Pennsylvania Press, 1980), pp. 215–46.

28. Gertrude Noyes, *Bibliography of Courtesy and Conduct Books in Seventeenth-Century England* (New Haven: Tuttle, Morehouse and Taylor, 1937), p. 4. Noyes includes both Herbert's *Country Parson* and his translation of Luigi Cornaro's *Treatise of Temperance and Sobriety* in her bibliography.

29. Abraham Fleming, *The Diamond of Devotion* (London, 1608), "A Preface to the true Christian Reader," pp. 2–4.

30. Ibid.

31. Walton, *Lives*, pp. 251–339. As David Novarr demonstrates in *The Making of Walton's "Lives"* (Ithaca: Cornell University Press, 1958), pp. 301–61, Walton emphasizes Herbert's worldliness "in order to show that even so noble and brilliant and worldly a man can see fit to renounce the worldly life for the holy one" (p. 353).

32. T. S. Eliot, *George Herbert*, British Writers and Their Work, no. 4, (Lincoln: University of Nebraska Press, 1964), p. 61.

33. *Life of Edward Lord Herbert of Cherbury*, ed. Shuttleworth, pp. 8–9.

34. Louis Martz, *The Poetry of Meditation: A Study in English Religious Literature of the Seventeenth Century* (New Haven: Yale University Press, 1954; rev. 1962), pp. 249–87. See in addition Martz's introduction to his edition, *George Herbert and Henry Vaughan* (Oxford: Oxford University Press, 1986), pp. xv–xxvi. From an opposite theological perspective—that of Puritanism rather than Catholicism—Jeanne Clayton Hunter also finds the relationship of friendship to mediate Herbert's interactions with God; see her "George Herbert and Puritan Piety," *Journal of Religion* 68 (1988): 237–40.

35. Helen Vendler, *The Poetry of George Herbert* (Cambridge: Harvard University Press, 1975), pp. 141–42. Anthony Low similarly finds in Herbert's relationship to God a mixture of intimacy and distance whose models are markedly social and political: "Although Herbert consistently views his God as a great king, utterly incommensurate with his creatures, paradoxically he also writes as if God were his familiar friend, sitting somewhere near the poet's elbow" ("Metaphysical Poets and Devotional Poets," in *George Herbert and the Seventeenth-Century Religious Lyric*, ed. Mario Di Cesare [New York: Norton, 1978], p. 222). Harold Toliver has recently remarked that Herbert's God "makes himself sufficiently available to allow overlapping between divine petition and the more ordinary situations of address" (*Lyric Provinces in the English Renaissance* [Columbus: Ohio State University Press, 1985], p. 129).

36. Malcolm Mackenzie Ross, *Poetry and Dogma: The Transfiguration of Eucharistic Symbols in Seventeenth-Century English Poetry* (New Brunswick: Rutgers University Press, 1954), p. 141.

37. Ibid., pp. 142, 153. Ross's emphasis upon the abjuratory aspects of Herbert's poetry is endorsed by Richard Strier, "George Herbert and the

World," *Journal of Medieval and Renaissance Studies* 12 (1981): 211–36. Similarly, in "Herbert's 'Decay' and the Articulation of History," *Southern Review* 18 (1983): 3–21, the only vestige of history that Jonathan Goldberg finds in *The Temple* is "the story of salvation played out in the Bible" (p. 3).

38. Ross, *Poetry and Dogma*, p. 143.

39. Leah Sinanoglou Marcus, *Childhood and Cultural Despair: A Theme and Variations in Seventeenth-Century Literature* (Pittsburgh: University of Pittsburgh Press, 1978), p. 113.

40. Ibid., p. 114. In "George Herbert and the Anglican Plain Style," in *Too Rich to Clothe the Sunne*, eds. Summers and Pebworth, pp. 179–93, Marcus profitably relocates Herbert in the world of ecclesiastical controversy. In "George Herbert's God," *English Literary Renaissance* 13 (1983): 90, E. Pearlman similarly proposes that "the most remarkable feature of [Herbert's] literary work taken as a whole" is "its deliberate isolation not only from political, economic, and social reality, but from human fellowship as well."

41. Marion White Singleton, *God's Courtier: The Configuring a Different Grace in George Herbert's "Temple"* (Cambridge: Cambridge University Press, 1987). I examine Singleton's arguments in more detail in a review in *Journal of English and Germanic Philology* 88 (1989): 411–14. In *The Golden Age Restor'd: The Culture of the Stuart Court, 1603–1642* (New York: St. Martin's Press, 1981), p. 243, Graham Parry asserts a similar spiritual quixotism: "In contrast to the earthly Court that had been so unresponsive to his pleas, in the poems that form the record of his spiritual life Herbert was to envisage an ideal Court, whose lord was the King of Kings . . . In the service of the Lord there is always satisfaction and reward, and the Lord of the heavenly Court is always attentive."

42. Stanley Fish, *Self-Consuming Artifacts: The Experience of Seventeenth-Century Literature* (Berkeley: University of California Press, 1972), p. 182.

43. Ibid., p. 157.

44. Barbara Harman, *Costly Monuments: Representations of the Self in George Herbert's Poetry* (Cambridge: Harvard University Press, 1982), p. 27.

45. Chana Bloch, *Spelling the Word: George Herbert and the Bible* (Berkeley: University of California Press, 1985).

46. Richard Strier, *Love Known: Theology and Experience in George Herbert's Poetry* (Chicago: University of Chicago Press, 1983), p. 253.

47. Ibid., p. xxi.

48. Ilona Bell, "Herbert's Valdesian Vision," *English Literary Renaissance* 17 (1987): 304. Proponents of the former include Rosemond Tuve, *A Reading of George Herbert* (Chicago: University of Chicago Press, 1952); Martz, *The Poetry of Meditation*; Claude J. Summers and Ted-Larry Pebworth, "Herbert, Vaughan, and Public Concerns in Private Modes," *George Herbert Journal* 3, nos. 1–2 (1979–80): 1–21, and "The Politics of *The Temple*: 'The British Church' and 'The Familie,'" *George Herbert Journal* 8, no. 1 (1984): 1–15; Sidney Gottlieb, "Herbert's Case of 'Conscience': Public or Private Poem?"

SEL 25 (1985): 109–26, and "The Social and Political Backgrounds of George Herbert's Poetry," in *"The Muses Common-Weale": Poetry and Politics in the Seventeenth Century,* eds. Claude J. Summers and Ted-Larry Pebworth (Columbia: University of Missouri Press, 1988), pp. 107–118; and Stanley Stewart, *George Herbert* (Boston: G. K. Hall, 1986). Adherents of the latter position include Joseph Summers, *George Herbert: His Religion and His Art* (Cambridge: Harvard University Press, 1954); William Halewood, *The Poetry of Grace: Reformation Themes and Structures in English Seventeenth-Century Poetry* (New Haven: Yale University Press, 1970); Ilona Bell, "'Setting Foot into Divinity': George Herbert and the English Reformation," *Modern Language Quarterly* 38 (1977): 219–44, reprinted in *Essential Articles for the Study of George Herbert's Poetry* (Hamden: Archon, 1979), pp. 63–83; Barbara Kiefer Lewalski, *Protestant Poetics and the Seventeenth-Century Religious Lyric* (Princeton: Princeton University Press, 1979); and Richard Strier, "History, Criticism, and Herbert: A Polemical Note," *Papers on Language and Literature* 17 (1981): 347–52, and *Love Known.* Bell proceeds to use Herbert's brief notes on Nicholas Ferrar's translation of *The Hundred and Ten Considerations of Signior John Valdesso* to establish Herbert's "Protestant view of justification," and so to endorse Strier's and Lewalski's conclusions about Herbert's firm protestantism.

49. Strier, *Love Known,* p. xxi.

50. Kenneth Burke, *A Rhetoric of Motives* (1950; repr. Berkeley: University of California Press, 1969), pp. 178–79. I have profited immensely from Burke's explorations of the hierarchical principal in theology and society in this book and in *The Rhetoric of Religion: Studies in Logology* (Boston: Beacon Press, 1961).

51. Moshe Greenberg, *Biblical Prose Prayer as a Window to the Popular Religion of Ancient Israel* (Berkeley: University of California Press, 1983), pp. 19–38. See also Ernst R. Curtius, *European Literature and the Latin Middle Ages,* tr. Willard R. Trask (Princeton: Princeton University Press, 1953), pp. 83–85, on the interchangeability between classical Roman formulae of self-disparagement and early Christian expressions of humility.

52. G. B. Caird, *Language and Imagery of the Bible* (London: Duckworth, 1980), p. 176.

53. The phrase "poetics of culture" was used by Stephen Greenblatt in his pioneering work, *Renaissance Self-Fashioning: From More to Shakespeare* (Chicago: University of Chicago Press, 1980), pp. 4–5. "New historicism" was first employed by Greenblatt in his introduction to *The Forms of Power and the Power of Forms in the Renaissance, Genre* 15 (1982): 3–6. Useful essays analyzing and defining the new historicism include Louis Montrose, "Renaissance Literary Studies and the Subject of History," *ELR* 16 (1986): 5–12; Jean E. Howard, "The New Historicism in Renaissance Studies," *ELR* 16 (1986): 13–43; Jonathan Dollimore, "Introduction: Shakespeare, Cultural Materialism, and the New Historicism," in *Political Shakespeare: New Essays in Cultural Materialism,* eds. Dollimore and Alan Sinfield

(Ithaca: Cornell University Press, 1985), pp. 2–17; Stephen Greenblatt, "The Circulation of Social Energy," chap. 1 of his *Shakespearean Negotiations: The Circulation of Social Energy in Renaissance England* (Berkeley: University of California Press, 1988), pp. 1–20; and Alan Liu, "The Power of Formalism: The New Historicism," *ELH* 56 (1989): 721–71.

54. In "History as Usual?: Feminism and the 'New Historicism,'" *Cultural Critique* 9 (Spring 1988): 87–121, Judith Newton helpfully analyzes the implicit if often suppressed relationship between feminist and new historicist approaches.

55. Three recent collections of essays attempt to comprehend the current attention to literature and history while avoiding the polemics that have characterized much new historicist work: *Politics of Discourse: The Literature and History of Seventeenth-Century England*, eds. Kevin Sharpe and Steven N. Zwicker (Berkeley: University of California Press, 1987); *The Historical Renaissance: New Essays on Tudor and Stuart Literature and Culture*, eds. Heather Dubrow and Richard Strier (Chicago: University of Chicago Press, 1988); and *The Muses Common-Weale*, eds. Summers and Pebworth.

56. Burke, *A Rhetoric of Motives*, p. 268. Daniel Javitch, "The Impure Motives of Elizabethan Poetry," in *The Forms of Power and the Power of Forms in the Renaissance*, pp. 225–38, suggestively employs the concept of impure persuasion in relation to Elizabethan secular poetry. On pure persuasion in a theological context, see also Burke, *The Rhetoric of Religion*, pp. 34–35 n.

Chapter 1

1. Joseph Summers, *The Heirs of Donne and Jonson* (London: Oxford University Press, 1970), p. 16.

2. Kenneth Burke, "On Covery, Re- and Dis-," *Accent* 13 (1953): 222. Burke's essay is actually a review of Rosemond Tuve, *A Reading of George Herbert* (Chicago: University of Chicago Press, 1952).

3. See John Knott, *The Sword of the Spirit: Puritan Responses to the Bible* (Chicago: University of Chicago Press, 1980), for the religious associations of this phrase.

4. Ps. 37.34—"Wait on the Lord, and keepe his way, and he shall exalt thee to inherit the land"—along with Luke 12.36–37—"And ye your selves [are] like unto men that waite for their Lord . . . Blessed are those servants, whom the Lord when he commeth, shall find watching"—provide the biblical foundation for this ideal.

5. Frank Whigham, *Ambition and Privilege: The Social Tropes of Elizabethan Courtesy Theory* (Berkeley: University of California Press, 1984), p. 40.

6. Walter Cohen, "Political Criticism of Shakespeare," *Shakespeare Reproduced: The Text in History and Ideology*, eds. Jean E. Howard and Marion F. O'Connor (New York: Methuen, 1987), p. 35. Cohen views the emphasis on

containment as a crucial difference between American new historicists and British cultural materialists.

7.   *Paradise Lost* (7:613–16), in *John Milton: Complete Poems and Major Prose*, ed. Merritt Y. Hughes (New York: Macmillan, 1957); all subsequent references to Milton's poetry are to this edition.

8.   *The Sermons of John Donne*, eds. George R. Potter and Evelyn M. Simpson 10 vols. (Berkeley: University of California Press, 1953–62), 1:236.

9.   Arthur Marotti, *John Donne, Coterie Poet* (Madison: University of Wisconsin Press, 1986), p. 254, offers a provocative account of these continuities in Donne's career: "The language of courtly suitorship is drawn into the *Holy Sonnets* to define the Christian's relationship to a strong kingly God, which suggests that behind Donne's theological preoccupation with strength and weakness lay his experiences in the secular world."

10.   T. S. Eliot, *George Herbert*, British Writers and Their Work, no. 4 (Lincoln: University of Nebraska Press, 1964), p. 54.

11.   Joan Thirsk, "Younger Sons in the Seventeenth Century," *History* 54 (1969): 358–77, explores the precarious economic and social status of younger sons such as Herbert.

12.   Cristina Malcolmson, "George Herbert's *Country Parson* and the Character of Social Identity," *Studies in Philology* 85 (1988): 247.

13.   Amy M. Charles, *A Life of George Herbert* (Ithaca: Cornell University Press, 1977), pp. 48–49, 101, examines the circumstances of Herbert's annuity and compares it to the support received by some contemporaries. Many of Herbert's letters to Danvers ask him to advance money against the annuity (see *Works*, pp. 364–65, 367).

14.   *Works*, p. xxvii.

15.   John Hacket, *Scrinia Reserata*, 2 vols. (London, 1693), 1:175; quoted in Charles, *A Life*, p. 98, and in *Works*, p. xxvii. Charles is surely right, contra Hutchinson, that Hacket means to praise rather than "comment severely" on Herbert's choice of a subject. Hacket prefaces this entry by observing of James's speech to Parliament—"his Majesty Feasted them with a Speech, then which nothing could be apter for the Subject, or more Eloquent for the matter. All the helps of that Faculty were extreamly perfect in him, abounding in Wit by Nature, in Art by Education, in Wisdom by Experience"—and concludes by noting—"The Speech which was had at the opening of this Parliament; doth commend Mr. *Herbet* [sic] for his Censure." These statements allow us to glimpse how a contemporary could accept, unashamedly and approvingly, such effusive flattery.

16.   A. G. Hyde, *George Herbert and His Times* (New York: G. P. Putnam's Sons, 1907), pp. 65–66.

17.   Perez Zagorin, *The Court and the Country: The Beginning of the English Revolution* (New York: Atheneum, 1971), p. 42. On the system of Renaissance patronage, see also the essays collected in *Patronage in the Renaissance*, eds. Guy Fitch Lytle and Stephen Orgel (Princeton: Princeton University Press, 1981); Linda Levy Peck, *Northampton: Patronage and Poli-*

tics at the Court of James I (London: Allen and Unwin, 1982), and "'For a King not to be bountiful were a fault': Perspectives on Court Patronage in Early Stuart England," *Journal of British Studies* 25 (1986): 31–61; and Derek Hirst, *Authority and Conflict: England, 1603–1658* (Cambridge: Harvard University Press, 1986), pp. 30–33.

18. *The Complete Works in Verse and Prose of George Herbert*, ed. A. B. Grosart, 3 vols. (London: Fuller Worthies' Library, 1874), 3:448–51; *Works*, pp. 458–59. Unless otherwise noted, all translations of Herbert's Latin works are from this edition (hereafter cited as *Complete Works*).

19. Quoted in J. P. Kenyon, ed., *The Stuart Constitution* (Cambridge: Cambridge University Press, 1966), pp. 12–14. Kenyon claims that James's "absolutism was confined to the realm of theory," and that he "was careful always to operate within the framework of the Common Law" (p. 8). On James's particular interpretation of divine right, see also J. N. Figgis, *The Divine Right of Kings* (Cambridge: Cambridge University Press, 1914), and G. R. Elton, "The Divine Right of Kings," in *Studies in Tudor and Stuart Politics and Government*, 2 vols. (Cambridge: Cambridge University Press, 1974), 2:193–214.

20. *Works*, p. 444. Since Grosart did not know this oration (Hutchinson prints it for the first time), I use the translation of Kenneth Alan Hovey, who graciously shared with me his unpublished translations of various Latin works by Herbert.

21. *Works*, p. 370. Herbert also aligns preferment in the courts of earth and heaven in a letter to Buckingham congratulating him for his marquisate, and in an epistle to Sir Robert Naunton, a former University Orator, complimenting him on being elected to Parliament; see *Complete Works*, 3:434; *Works*, pp. 456–57, and *Complete Works*, 3:441; *Works*, p. 465.

22. Charles, *A Life*, p. 91.

23. Marotti, *John Donne*, p. 246.

24. *Complete Works*, 2:111–12; *Works*, p. 386.

25. Keith Thomas, "Age and Authority in Early Modern England," *Proceedings of the British Academy* 62 (1977): 207.

26. Whigham, *Ambition and Privilege*, pp. 24, 32. Courtly discourse, moreover, often resembled academic disputation under the rule of the self-styled English Solomon. Sir John Harington remembers of his first encounter with James that "he enquyrede much of lernynge, and showede me his owne in suche sorte, as made me remember my examiner at Cambridge aforetyme" (quoted in *James I by His Contemporaries*, ed. Robert Ashton [London: Hutchinson, 1969], p. 159).

27. *Works*, pp. 598, 600, citing a letter by Joseph Mede (Meade) to Martin Stutevile (B.M. Harl. MS. 389, fol. 298), and a letter from Thomas Baker, Cambridge Collections (B.M. Harl. MS. 7041, fol. 38v).

28. In *Works*, p. 598, Hutchinson is noncommittal on the question of whether the translation of *"Dum petit Infantem"* first printed with the Latin is by Herbert.

29. Cited in *The Herbert Allusion Book: Allusions to George Herbert in the Seventeenth Century,* ed. Robert H. Ray, *Studies in Philology: Texts and Studies* 83 (1986): 3, from the same manuscript that Hutchinson selectively quotes.

30. In *The Politics of Mirth: Jonson, Herrick, Milton, Marvell, and the Defense of Old Holiday Pastimes* (Chicago: University of Chicago Press, 1986), p. 9, Leah S. Marcus argues that the Stuart kings "allowed considerably more latitude" to the utterances of their subjects than we have been willing to grant, "and not merely by default or out of some sleepy incapacity to perceive what their supposed panegyrists were up to . . . considerable freedom was tolerated so long as it could be contained—or at least could *seem* to be contained—within a framework upholding authority." Whether sleepy incapacity or genuine toleration was at work in James's grateful reception of Herbert's quietly equivocal epigram, I do not know.

31. Those who see this oration on Charles's return as the watershed of Herbert's political and religious careers include Joseph Summers, *George Herbert: His Religion and Art* (Cambridge: Harvard University Press, 1954), pp. 40–42; Marchette Chute, *Two Gentle Men: The Lives of George Herbert and Robert Herrick* (New York: Dutton, 1959), pp. 83–84; and Charles, *A Life,* p. 100. Both Summers and Charles stress the strong personal reason that may have disposed Herbert to speak out against war—he had lost two brothers, Richard and William, in battle. Kenneth Alan Hovey explores Herbert's use of the terminology of war and peace in this oration in "Holy War and Civil Peace: George Herbert's Jacobean Politics," *Explorations in Renaissance Culture* 11 (1985): 112–19. Herbert's anti-war sentiments are also vented in *Lucus* 32, "Triumphus Mortis"; see Hovey, "'Inventa Bellica' / 'Triumphus Mortis': Herbert's Parody of Human Progress and Dialogue with Divine Grace," *Studies in Philology* 78 (1981): 275–304.

32. Samuel R. Gardiner, *History of England from the Accession of James I to the Outbreak of the Civil War: 1603–1642,* 10 vols. (London: Longmans, Green, 1883–84), 7:266. On the bitter public outcry against the quest for a Spanish marriage and the spontaneous rejoicing that overtook the country when Charles returned from Spain without a bride, see Roger Lockyer, *Buckingham: The Life and Political Career of George Villiers, First Duke of Buckingham, 1592–1628* (London: Longman, 1981), pp. 125–97; and R. Malcolm Smuts, *Court Culture and the Origins of a Royalist Tradition in Early Stuart England* (Philadelphia: University of Pennsylvania Press, 1987), pp. 32–36.

33. "Of Praise," in *Francis Bacon: A Selection of His Works,* ed. Sidney Warhaft (New York: Odyssey, 1965), p. 179. In the *Discoveries,* Ben Jonson also recommends that the courtier should counsel his prince "not with insolence, or precept; but as the *Prince* were already furnished with the parts hee should have, especially in affaires of *State*" (C. H. Herford, Percy Simpson, and Evelyn Simpson, eds., *Ben Jonson,* 11 vols. [Oxford: Clarendon Press, 1925–52], 8:566).

34. Gardiner, *History of England,* 7:267.

35. *Complete Works*, 3:399; *Works*, p. 445.
36. *Complete Works*, 3:406–7; *Works*, p. 447.
37. Herbert also uses this gruesome image in "Content" to qualify (near-ly out of existence) the distinctions upon which the earthly hierarchy de-pends: "after death the fumes that spring / From private bodies make as big a thunder, / As those which rise from a huge King" (lines 22–24).
38. *Complete Works*, 3:411–12; *Works*, pp. 452–53. Those who have suggested the oration was unwelcome at court simply because of its un-timely expression of antiwar sentiment have missed the threads of resent-ment and criticism woven into its fabric of praise.
39. *Complete Works*, 3:408; *Works*, p. 450.
40. *Works*, p. 277. This Parliament, described by an "old Scottish cour-tier" as one that "dois evrye daye grate upone the King's prerogative soe mutche" (quoted in Zagorin, *Court and the Country*, p. 64), was also marked by the dissolution of the Virginia Company, in which both Nicholas Ferrar and Sir John Danvers had been major figures. See Robert E. Ruigh, *The Parlia-ment of 1624: Politics and Foreign Policy* (Cambridge: Harvard University Press, 1971).

In "Herbert's Experience of Politics and Patronage in 1624," *George Herbert Journal* 10, nos. 1 and 2 (1986/87): 33–45, Diana Benet contends that Herbert's parliamentary experience precipitated his apparent disillusion-ment with state employment, and his subsequent turn to the church. But Herbert's country parson is far less a figure in retreat from the political cur-rents of his time than such a pattern assumes. He encourages the youth of his parish not only to "endeavour by all means" to participate in Parliament but also (albeit less avidly) to encounter the court: "sometimes he may go to Court, as the eminent place both of good and ill" (p. 277).
41. Charles, *A Life*, pp. 112–18; A. L. Maycock, *Nicholas Ferrar of Little Gidding* (London: S.P.C.K., 1938), p. 120. "The idea of the [diaconate] as pri-marily a preparation for the [priesthood] is comparatively modern," remarks Maycock, dating from "at least the latter part of the seventeenth century."
42. Herbert may have delivered the oration at Buckingham's installation as Chancellor of Cambridge in 1626, but the oration is not extant. See Charles, *A Life*, p. 121.
43. In 1626 Herbert contributed "*In obitum incomparabilis Francisci Vicecomitis Sancti Albani*" to an unofficial tribute to Sir Francis Bacon from members of Cambridge, *Memoriae Francisci, Baronis de Verulamio, Vice-Comitis Sancti Albani Sacrum* (London, 1626). Bacon had died earlier that year in disgrace. In 1627 Herbert published *Memoriae Matris Sacrum*, his Latin verse elegy to his mother, alongside the text of Donne's funeral sermon for her.
44. Barnabus Oley, *Herbert's Remains* (London, 1652), sigs. a11v-a12r. Hutchinson, *Works*, p. 556, points out that Oley was a student at Clare Hall, Cambridge, from 1617 and a Fellow from 1623–44, and therefore "must have known [Herbert] well by repute, if not personally."

45. Amy M. Charles, "Herbert and the Ferrars: Spirituall Edification," in *"Like Season'd Timber": New Essays on George Herbert*, eds. Edmund Miller and Robert DiYanni (New York: Peter Lang, 1987), p. 16.

46. *Aubrey's Brief Lives*, ed. Oliver Lawson Dick (Harmondsworth: Penguin, 1962), p. 218.

47. *Works*, p. 249. In *The Foul and the Fragrant: Odor and the French Social Imagination* (Cambridge: Harvard University Press, 1986), Alan Courbin explores the aristocratic stress upon odor as a register of social distinction. Although lacking attention to its social ramifications, Terry G. Sherwood, "Tasting and Telling Sweetness in George Herbert's Poetry," *English Literary Renaissance* 12 (1982): 319–40, examines the significance of sweetness in Herbert's poetry. The country parson, Herbert relates, wears "apparell" that is "plaine, but reverend, and clean, without spots, or dust, or smell; the purity of his mind breaking out, and dilating it selfe even to his body, cloaths, and habitation" (p. 228). A bizarre version of such odoriferous suffusion is offered in the *Autobiography* of George's brother Edward: "It is well knowne to those that wayt in my chamber That the shirts waste Coates and other Garments I weare next my body are sweete beyond what either easily can bee beleived or hath bin observed in any els" (*The Life of Edward, First Lord Herbert of Cherbury*, ed. J. M. Shuttleworth [London: Oxford University Press, 1976], pp. 101–2).

48. [Thomas Powell], *The Art of Thriving* (London, 1635), p. 37. The chapter on "Attaining a Benefice" runs from pp. 33–49.

49. Charles, *A Life*, p. 81.

50. In "Ritual Man: On the Outside of Herbert's Poetry," *Psychiatry* 48 (1985): 69, William Kerrigan offers a compelling if somewhat different model from my own for apprehending continuity between Herbert's secular and sacred careers: "whether at Cambridge or Bemerton, as Claudian or as Aaron, orating in Latin or sermonizing in English, Herbert presided over ritual occasions."

51. *Ben Jonson*, 8:640.

52. On the terrifying ambivalence of this stanza and this poem, see the brilliant reading by William Empson, *Seven Types of Ambiguity* (New York: New Directions, 1947), pp. 226–33.

53. Louis Adrian Montrose, "Gifts and Reasons: The Contexts of Peele's *Araygnement of Paris*," *ELH* 47 (1980): 433–61; and Patricia Fumerton, "Exchanging Gifts: The Elizabethan Currency of Children and Poetry," *ELH* 53 (1986): 241–78.

54. Marcel Mauss, *The Gift: Forms and Functions of Exchange in Archaic Societies*, tr. Ian Cunnison (New York: Norton, 1967), pp. 1–13.

55. *Complete Works*, 3:450; *Works*, p. 459.

56. Pierre Bourdieu, *Outline of a Theory of Practice*, tr. Richard Nice (Cambridge: Cambridge University Press, 1977), p. 5. Bourdieu's work builds on and critiques Mauss.

57.   Richard Strier, *Love Known: Theology and Experience in George Herbert's Poetry* (Chicago: University of Chicago Press, 1983), p. 50.

58.   Ilona Bell, " 'Setting Foot into Divinity': George Herbert and the English Reformation," *Modern Language Quarterly* 38 (1977): 219–44, repr. *Essential Articles for the Study of George Herbert's Poetry*, ed. John R. Roberts (Hamden: Archon, 1979), pp. 63–83.

59.   Bourdieu, *Outline of a Theory of Practice*, p. 195.

60.   Donne, *Sermons*, 2:138.

61.   Lorenzo Ducci, *Ars aulica; or, The Courtiers Arte*, tr. [Ed. Blount?] (London, 1607), pp. 226–27. This translation is dedicated to Herbert's two noble kinsmen, William Herbert, earl of Pembroke, and Philip Herbert, earl of Montgomery. In *Civility and Society in Western Europe, 1300–1600* (Bloomington: Indiana University Press, 1988), p. 34, Marvin Becker describes the *Ars aulica* as "perhaps the most psychologically troubling, as well as the most esthetically wrought[,] work of the genre." This bitterly incisive work is also discussed by Sydney Anglo, "The Courtier: The Renaissance and Changing Ideals," *The Courts of Europe: Politics, Patronage and Royalty 1400–1800*, ed. A. G. Dickens (New York: McGraw-Hill, 1977), pp. 51–53.

62.   Mauss, *The Gift*, pp. 72–73. William Nestrick cites Mauss in his stimulating study of prestation in Herbert's poetry, "George Herbert—The Giver and the Gift," *Ploughshares* 2, no. 4 (1975): 187–205. On the political superiority of giving to receiving, see also Aristotle, *Nichomachean Ethics*, tr. Martin Oswald (Indianapolis: Bobbs and Merrill, 1962), pp. 96–97.

63.   On the inexpressibility topos, see Ernst Robert Curtius, *European Literature and the Latin Middle Ages*, tr. Willard R. Trask (Princeton: Princeton University Press, 1953), pp. 159–62. On Herbert's employment of this topos, see the two letters to King James (*Complete Works*, 3:450, 452; *Works*, pp. 458–59, 460), and a letter to George Abbott, archbishop of Canterbury (*Complete Works*, 3:458; *Works*, pp. 466–67).

64.   Milton too attempted a poem on "The Passion," as a companion-piece to his precocious "Ode: On the Morning of Christ's Nativity." But Milton—a poet who would not allow blindness and political disfavor to interfere with the composition of one major and one "brief" epic as well as a tragedy—uncharacteristically found himself unable to complete the poem; instead, he published an unfinished version in the 1645 *Poems* with the note: "This subject the author finding to be above the years he had when he wrote it, and nothing satisfied with what was begun, left it unfinished." As in Herbert's "The Thanksgiving," the extraordinary quality of the passion seems to incapacitate mortal response to it.

65.   Bell, "Setting Foot into Divinity," p. 231; see also William Nestrick, " 'Mine' and 'Thine' in *The Temple*," in *"Too Rich to Clothe the Sunne": Essays on George Herbert*, eds. Claude J. Summers and Ted-Larry Pebworth (Pittsburgh: University of Pittsburgh Press, 1980), p. 118; and William H.

Pahlka, *Saint Augustine's Meter and George Herbert's Will* (Kent, Ohio: Kent State University Press, 1987), pp. 3–15.

66. G. W. Pigman III, "Versions of Imitation in the Renaissance," *RQ* 33 (1980): 1–32. On competitive and submissive imitation, see also Thomas Greene, *The Light in Troy: Imitation and Discovery in Renaissance Poetry* (New Haven: Yale University Press, 1982).

67. Erasmus, *Ciceronianus*, quoted in Pigman, p. 24.

68. Ducci, *Ars aulica*, p. 111.

69. Ibid., pp. 111–12.

70. *Ben Jonson*, 8:638.

71. Strier, *Love Known*, p. 50; Strier is citing Luther's *Commentary on St. Paul's Epistle to the Galatians: A Revised and Completed Translation of the "Middleton" Edition of the English Version of 1575*, ed. Philip S. Watson (London: J. Clarke, 1953), p. 270.

72. *D. Martin Luthers Werke Kritische Gesamtausgabe*, ed. J. C. F. Knaake, et al. (Weimar: Bohlau, 1883), 40:404; quoted in Anders Nygren, *Agape and Eros*, tr. Philip S. Watson (New York: Harper Torchbooks, 1969), p. 702, n. 1. Nygren is discussed in relation to Herbert by both Rosemond Tuve, "George Herbert and *Caritas*," *Journal of the Warburg and Courtauld Institute* 22 (1960): 303–31, repr. in *Essays by Rosemond Tuve*, ed. Thomas P. Roche, Jr. (Princeton: Princeton University Press, 1970), pp. 167–206, and Strier, *Love Known*, passim.

73. Erwin Panofsky, *The Life and Art of Albrecht Dürer* (Princeton: Princeton University Press, 1955), p. 43. Three drawings in which Dürer likewise imagines himself as Christ are examined by Robert Smith in "Dürer as Christ?" *Sixteenth-Century Journal* 6, no. 2 (1975): 26–36.

74. Baldassare Castiglione, *The Book of the Courtier*, tr. Thomas Hoby [1561] (London: Dent, 1928), p. 45.

75. George Puttenham, *The Arte of English Poesie*, eds. Gladys Doidge Willcock and Alice Walker (Cambridge: Cambridge University Press, 1936), pp. 293, 295–96. As Daniel Javitch argues in *Poetry and Courtliness* (Princeton: Princeton University Press, 1978), Puttenham conflates the art of poetry with the art of courtly conduct.

76. Denys de Refuges, *A Treatise of the Court; or, Instructions for Courtiers*, tr. John Reynolds, 2 vols. (London, 1622), 2:186.

77. *The Courtier*, tr. Hoby, p. 46. *Sprezzatura*, declares Whigham, "is equivalent to making a fetish of effortlessness" (*Ambition and Privilege*, p. 150).

78. De Refuges, *A Treatise of the Court*, 2:187.

79. *Love's Labor's Lost* (5.2.512–13)

80. Quoted in Marjorie Cox, "The Background to English Literature: 1603–1630," in *From Donne to Marvell*, ed. Boris Ford (Harmondsworth, England: Penguin, 1982), p. 25.

81. C. A. Patrides, ed., *The English Poems of George Herbert* (London: Dent, 1974), p. 57n.

82. *Ben Jonson,* 8:597.

83. Puttenham, *Arte of English Poesie,* pp. 227–28, 215.

84. Ira Clark, "'Lord, in Thee the Beauty Lies in the Discovery': 'Love Unknown' and Reading Herbert," *ELH* 39 (1972): 560–84, repr. in *Essential Articles,* ed. Roberts, pp. 473–93, and Barbara Harman, *Costly Monuments: Representations of the Self in George Herbert's Poetry* (Cambridge: Harvard University Press, 1982), pp. 170–96.

85. Whigham, *Ambition and Privilege,* p. 140.

86. In chap. 3, I explore the various manifestations throughout *The Temple* of divine violence against humanity—a violence which could also be seen to fulfill this threat of revenge.

87. Louis Martz, *The Poetry of Meditation* (New Haven: Yale University Press, 1962), p. 292; Harman, *Costly Monuments,* p. 61; Strier, *Love Known,* p. 53; Stanley Fish, *Self-Consuming Artifacts: The Experience of Seventeenth-Century Literature* (Berkeley: University of California Press, 1972), p. 183; and Michael McCanles, *Dialectical Criticism and Renaissance Literature* (Berkeley: University of California Press, 1975), p. 82.

88. *Complete Works,* 3:433; *Works,* p. 456.

89. *Complete Works,* 3:439; *Works,* p. 465. See also the letters to Robert Naunton (*Complete Works,* 3:441; *Works,* p. 465) and to James Leigh (*Complete Works,* 3:462; *Works,* p. 468).

90. Martin Luther, *Instructio,* in *Luther's Works: American Edition,* eds. Jaroslav Pelikan et al., 55 vols. (Philadelphia and St. Louis, 1955–), 1:264; quoted in Thomas Tentler, *Sin and Confession on the Eve of the Reformation* (Princeton: Princeton University Press, 1977), p. 358.

91. My sense of the power relationship immanent in confessional utterance was inspired by Michel Foucault's brief comments in *The History of Sexuality,* vol. 1, *An Introduction,* tr. Robert Hurley (New York: Random House, 1978), pp. 61–62.

92. John Bramhall, *Works* (Dublin, 1676), pp. 974–75. On the structures of confession, see Tentler, *Sin and Confession;* and John Bossy, "The Social History of Confession in the Age of the Reformation in the Age of the Reformation," *Transactions of the Royal Historical Society,* 5th ser., 25 (1975): 21–38. In describing his attitude to his own momentary (and largely unintentional) complicity with the Communist authorities in Czechoslovakia, Vaclav Havel incisively describes the bad faith that such confessional objectifications of past actions can involve: "This dividing of my self . . . into an alien, prior and incomprehensible 'I' that failed, and a living, present, genuine 'I,' genuinely mine, which does not understand and condemns the former 'I' . . . all that was simply an unacknowledged attempt to lie my way out of my responsibility for myself and shift it onto someone else, as it were" (quoted in Janet Malcolm, "The Trial of Alyosha," a review of Havel's *Letters to Olga, June 1979-September 1982* in *New York Review of Books* 37, no. 10 [June 14, 1990]: 37). Havel appropriately compares this insight into his own subjectivity to standing "directly in the study of the Lord God himself."

93. Jacques Lacan, *The Language of the Self: The Function of Language in Psychoanalysis*, tr. Anthony Wilden (Baltimore: Johns Hopkins University Press, 1968), p. 11.

94. Stephen Greenblatt, *Renaissance Self-Fashioning: From More to Shakespeare* (Chicago: University of Chicago Press, 1980), p. 245. My discussion of confession is indebted to his analysis of confessional utterance in *Othello*.

95. Walton, *Lives*, p. 315. His account is corroborated by John Ferrar, Nicholas's brother, who remembers that *The Temple* "was licensed at Cambridge (with some kind of Scruple by some, if I was not misinformed) only for those his Verses upon America &c" (quoted in Charles, *A Life*, p. 182).

96. See *The Bodleian Manuscript of George Herbert's Poems: A Facsimile of Tanner 307*, eds. Amy M. Charles and Mario A. Di Cesare (Delmar, N.Y.: Scholars' Facsimiles & Reprints, 1984), p. 10. Ironically, had Ferrar chosen to have Herbert's poems published in London rather than bridge, George's younger brother Henry "would have been the official responsible for allowing their entry in the Stationers' Register" (Charles, *A Life*, p. 181).

97. See the account of Laudianism at Cambridge by Hugh R. Trevor-Roper, "Laudianism and Political Power," in *Catholics, Anglicans and Puritans: Seventeenth Century Essays* (London: Secker & Warburg, 1987), pp. 76–90.

98. William Prynne, *Canterburies Doome* (London, 1646), p. 361 (my italics), quoted in Ray, ed., *The Herbert Allusion Book*, p. 22. In *The Puritan Origins of the American Self* (New Haven: Yale University Press, 1975), pp. 104–5, 145–46, Sacvan Bercovitch explores the use of these lines by early American authors in their attempts to place themselves in a pattern of redemptive history.

99. Michel Foucault, *The History of Sexuality*, vol. 1, pp. 88–89.

100. See, for example, Zagorin, *The Court and the Country*, passim; P. W. Thomas, "Two Cultures? Court and Country under Charles I," in *The Origins of the English Civil War*, ed. Conrad Russell (New York: Barnes and Noble, 1973), pp. 168–93. Recent work by revisionist historians, however, has complicated this picture by showing how frequently political factions spanned this traditional divide; see Derek Hirst, "Court, Country, and Politics before 1629," in *Faction and Parliament*, ed. Kevin Sharpe (Oxford: Oxford University Press, 1978), pp. 105–38; Peck, *Northampton*; Smuts, *Court Culture*; and Kevin Sharpe, *Criticism and Compliment: The Politics of Literature in the England of Charles I* (Cambridge: Cambridge University Press, 1987), pp. 11–22.

101. On Edward Herbert, see Sidney Lee, ed., *The Autobiography of Edward Lord Herbert of Cherbury* (New York: E. P. Dutton, 1906), pp. 145–59; on the other Herberts, see Michael Brennan, *Literary Patronage in the*

English Renaissance: The Pembroke Family (London: Routledge, 1988), pp. 198–206.

102. The legend is first recorded by Thomas Herbert in *Threnodia Carolina*, written in 1678, published in 1702; see Ray, ed., *The Herbert Allusion Book*, p. 128.

Chapter 2

1. See Annabel Patterson, *Censorship and Interpretation: The Conditions of Writing and Reading in Early Modern England* (Madison: University of Wisconsin Press, 1984). I explore the circumstances of the licensing of *The Temple* in chap. 1.

2. Marion White Singleton, *God's Courtier: Configuring a Different Grace in George Herbert's "Temple"* (Cambridge: Cambridge University Press, 1987), p. 105; Anthony Low, "Herbert's 'Jordan (I)' and the Court Masque," *Criticism* 14 (1972): 109–18.

3. Kenneth Burke, *The Rhetoric of Religion: Studies in Logology* (Berkeley: University of California Press, 1970), p. 56.

4. Quoted in Patrick Collinson, *Archbishop Grindal 1519–1583: The Struggle for a Reformed Church* (Berkeley: University of California Press, 1979), p. 242. On the Puritan attack on mortal kingship, see Michael Walzer, *The Revolution of the Saints: A Study in the Origins of Radical Politics* (Cambridge: Harvard University Press, 1965), pp. 148–98.

5. *Volpone* (3.5.36) suggests a slightly salacious context for the game in its reference to "your wanton gam'ster, at *primero*" (*Ben Jonson*, eds. C. H. Herford, Percy Simpson and Evelyn Simpson, 11 vols. [Oxford: Clarendon Press, 1925–52], 5:76). Thomas Middleton's play, *Your Five Gallants* (London, 1607), has a player named Primero who expresses aristocratic disgust at the prospect of a gentleman being whipped: "Whipping? you find not that in the statute to whip satin" (5.2).

6. Wilbur Sanders, " 'Childhood is Health': The Divine Poetry of George Herbert," *Melbourne Critical Review* 5 (1962): 6.

7. Edward Tayler, *Nature and Art in Renaissance Literature* (New York: Columbia University Press, 1964), p. 5.

8. George Puttenham, *The Arte of English Poesie*, eds. Gladys Doidge Willcock and Alice Walker (Cambridge: Cambridge University Press, 1936), p. 38. My sense of the politics of pastoral is deeply indebted to Louis Adrian Montrose, "Of Gentlemen and Shepherds: The Politics of Elizabethan Pastoral Form," *ELH* 50 (1983): 415–59.

9. Phoebe Sheavyn, *The Literary Profession in the Elizabethan Age* (Manchester: Manchester University Press, 1909), p. 58.

10. Patterson, *Censorship and Interpretation*, passim.

11. Quoted in G. P. V. Akrigg, *Jacobean Pageant: The Court of King James I* (New York: Atheneum, 1967), pp. 225–26.

Notes to Pages 62–68

12. Frank Whigham, *Ambition and Privilege: The Social Tropes of Elizabethan Courtesy Theory* (Berkeley: University of California Press, 1984), p. 61.

13. Norbert Elias, *The Civilizing Process*, vol. 1, *The History of Manners*, tr. Edmund Jephcott (New York: Urizen, 1978), p. 190.

14. *The Book of Common Prayer 1559: The Elizabethan Prayer Book*, ed. John E. Booty (Washington, D.C.: Folger Shakespeare Library, 1976), p. 73.

15. Keith Thomas, *Religion and the Decline of Magic* (New York: Charles Scribner's Sons, 1971), p. 152.

16. Stefano Guazzo, *The Civile Conversation*, tr. George Pettie (1581), ed. Edward Sullivan, 2 vols. (London: Tudor Translations, 1925), 1:198. The medieval background to such notions is explored by Ernst H. Kantorowicz, *The King's Two Bodies: A Study in Medieval Political Theology* (Princeton: Princeton University Press, 1957). A brilliant and nuanced account of the Renaissance "mystification of kingship" and its attendant "theology of absolutism" is available in chap. 4, "Holy Church and Sacred King," of Debora Kuller Shuger, *Habits of Thought in the Renaissance: Religion, Politics, and the Dominant Culture* (Berkeley: University of California Press, 1990), pp. 120–58.

17. Guazzo, *Civile Conversation*, 1:199–200.

18. Ibid., 1:166.

19. George Downame, *A Godly and Learned Treatise of Prayer* (Cambridge, 1640), p. 135.

20. Daniel Featley, *Ancilla Pietatis: Or, The Hand-maid to Private Devotion* (London, 1626), p. 11.

21. Quoted in *The Works of John Whitgift*, ed. John Ayre, 3 vols. (Cambridge: Parker Society, 1852), 2:488–89. In *Habits of Thought*, p. 160, Shuger comments on "the extraordinary tendency to analyze and legitimate religious ritual as an analogue of courtly ceremony," whereby "sacred symbolism appears as a variant of political gesture."

22. Ibid., 2:489.

23. Ibid.

24. Richard Hooker, *Of the Laws of Ecclesiastical Polity* (5.34.2), ed. Christopher Morris, 2 vols. (London: Dent, 1954), 2:137.

25. I quote from *The Book of Common Prayer*, ed. Booty, p. 52.

26. Hooker, *Laws* (5.34.3), 2:139. In the constitutionalist passages in Book 8, likewise, Hooker remains consistently reluctant to imbue kings with the traits of divinity; see, e.g., 8.2.12, and all of 8.4, in *The Works of Mr. Richard Hooker*, ed. John Keeble, 3 vols. (Oxford, 1888).

27. Hooker, *Laws* (1.2.1–6), 1:150–54.

28. Michael and Marianne Shapiro, *Figuration in Verbal Art* (Princeton: Princeton University Press, 1988), p. 27. They contrast metaphor to metonymy, "that trope in which a hierarchy of signata is either established or instantiated."

29. Rosalie L. Colie, *Paradoxia Epidemica: The Renaissance Tradition of*

Paradox (Princeton: Princeton University Press, 1966), p. 145. Colie, pp. 145–89, explores the use of negative theology in the works of Thomas Traherne and John Milton, and contrasts Herbert with them.

30. Ibid., p. 215.
31. John Donne, *Sermons*, eds. George Potter and Evelyn Simpson, 10 vols. (Berkeley: University of California Press, 1953–62), 9:227.
32. Richard Strier, " 'To all Angels and Saints': Herbert's Puritan Poem," *Modern Philology* 74 (1976): 135.
33. Louis Martz, *The Poetry of Meditation: A Study in English Religious Literature of the Seventeenth Century* (New Haven: Yale University Press, 1962), p. 98.
34. Perez Zagorin, *The Court and the Country: The Beginning of the English Revolution* (New York: Atheneum, 1971), p. 84.
35. Donne, *Sermons*, 9:321–22.
36. Whigham, *Ambition and Privilege*, p. 12. Whigham pointedly distinguishes between notions of patronage which "resemble the protestant theological universe: the near-divine patron seems equidistant from all suitors and is their sole point of reference" and the "fact" of this "many-layered matrix of mediation." On courtly mediation see also Whigham, "The Rhetoric of Elizabethan Suitors' Letters," *PMLA* 96 (1981): 868–69.
37. Strier, "To all Angels and Saints," pp. 143–44.
38. Helen Vendler, *The Poetry of George Herbert* (Cambridge: Harvard University Press, 1975), p. 43.
39. Autobiographical readings of the poem begin with Izaak Walton, "The Life of Mr. George Herbert," in *Lives of John Donne, Sir Henry Wotton, Richard Hooker, George Herbert, and Robert Sanderson* (1670), ed. George Saintsbury (London: Oxford University Press, 1928), pp. 275–76, and continue in more sophisticated form in L. C. Knights, "George Herbert," in *Explorations* (London: Chatto and Windus, 1946), pp. 141–44, and Amy M. Charles, *A Life of George Herbert* (Ithaca: Cornell University Press, 1977), pp. 84–87.
40. Ilona Bell, "Revision and Revelation in Herbert's 'Affliction (I),' " *John Donne Journal* 3, no. 1 (1984): 79–80.
41. Lorenzo Ducci, *Ars Aulica; or, The Courtiers Arte*, tr. [Ed. Blount?] (London, 1607), p. 232. Lawrence Stone, *The Crisis of the Aristocracy 1558–1641* (Oxford: Clarendon Press, 1965), pp. 476–77.
42. Denys de Refuges, *A Treatise of the Court; or, Instructions for Courtiers*, tr. John Reynolds, 2 vols. (London, 1622), 2:40.
43. Quoted in Wallace MacCaffrey, "Place and Patronage in Elizabethan Politics," in *Elizabethan Government and Society*, eds. S. T. Bindoff et al. (London: Athlone, 1961), p. 108. Walton, *Lives*, p. 276, contends the "friends" were Herbert's "most obliging and most powerful friends, *Lodowick* Duke of *Richmond*, and *James* Marquess of *Hamilton*," as well as King James; "with them," posits Walton, "all Mr. *Herbert's* Court-hopes" died. In order to place the disturbing poem as early as possible in Herbert's career, Charles argues unconvincingly that the friends were Herbert's two brothers, who died in

1616–17 (*A Life,* pp. 85–86). Neither Walton nor Charles mentions the deaths in 1626 of both Francis Bacon and Lancelot Andrewes, figures with whom Herbert was in frequent correspondence.

44. C. A. Patrides, ed., *The English Poems of George Herbert* (Totowa: Rowman and Littlefield, 1975), p. 180 n.

45. On "simper" in a courtly context, see OED (v².1.b), which cites *Philibert's Philosopher at Court,* tr. Thomas North (1575): "Counterfaite Courtiers which simper it in outwarde shewe, making pretie mouthes . . . " On "lay-hypocrisie," I cite the rich annotation of this difficult phrase by Louis Martz, ed., *George Herbert and Henry Vaughan* (Oxford: Oxford University Press, 1986), p. 436.

46. Angel Day, *The English Secretarie* (1599), ed. Robert O. Evans, 2 vols. in 1 (Gainesville: Scholars' Facsimiles and Reprints, 1967), 2:27–30.

47. Ibid., 2:18–19.

48. Antony de Guevara, *The Dial of Princes,* tr. Thomas North (London, 1582), p. 380; my italics.

49. James I to Parliament, Mar. 21, 1610, in J. P. Kenyon, ed., *The Stuart Constitution: Documents and Commentary* (Cambridge: Cambridge University Press, 1966), p. 14.

50. Barbara Harman, *Costly Monuments: Representations of the Self in George Herbert's Poetry* (Cambridge: Harvard University Press, 1982), pp. 89–105, cogently explores the complex narrative and temporal sequence of "Affliction (I)."

51. Richard Strier, *Love Known: Theology and Experience in George Herbert's Poetry* (Chicago: University of Chicago Press, 1983), p. 176.

52. Michael Dalton, *The Country Justice* (London, 1618), p. 64. Herbert recommends that the parson acquaint himself with this work in *The Country Parson,* p. 260.

53. Donne, *Sermons,* 5:339.

54. Saint Augustine, *Confessions,* tr. R. S. Pine-Coffin (Harmondsworth: Penguin, 1961), p. 50.

55. Bell, "Revision and Revelation," p. 89. An example of the intransitive use of "forgot" is *Othello* (2.3.188): "How comes it Michael that you are thus forgot?" asks Othello of a drunken Cassio.

56. My sense of the richness of these lines is indebted to the ingenious reading offered by William Empson in *Seven Types of Ambiguity* (New York: New Directions, 1947), pp. 183–84.

57. Martz, *Poetry of Meditation,* pp. 270–71.

58. Bell, "Revision and Revelation," p. 90.

59. Donne, *Sermons,* 5:284.

60. Vendler, *The Poetry of George Herbert,* p. 46. See also Bill Smithson, "Herbert's 'Affliction' Poems," *Studies in English Literature* 15 (1975): 130; Daniel Rubey, "The Poet and the Christian Community: Herbert's Affliction Poems and the Structure of *The Temple,*" *Studies in English Literature* 20 (1980): 105–23; Anne C. Fowler, " 'With Care and Courage': Herbert's 'Afflic-

tion' Poems," in *"Too Rich to Clothe the Sunne": Essays on George Herbert,*
eds. Claude J. Summers and Ted-Larry Pebworth (Pittsburgh: University of
Pittsburgh Press, 1980), pp. 129–45; and Daniel Doerksen, "'Growing and
Groning': Herbert's 'Affliction (I),'" *English Studies in Canada* 8, no. 1
(1982): 6–7.

61. Harman, *Costly Monuments,* p. 101.

62. Strier, *Love Known,* pp. 183, 73.

63. Quoted in James Turner, *The Politics of Landscape* (Cambridge:
Harvard University Press, 1979), p. 87.

64. Examples are given in R. H. Tawney, *The Agrarian Problem in the
Sixteenth Century,* intro. Lawrence Stone (New York: Harper and Row, 1967),
pp. 412–15. Tawney's book offers a fine account of the relationship between
landlords and tenants in the period.

65. Strier, *Love Known,* p. 55.

66. Indeed, James was so concerned about the number of gentry dwelling
in London that he issued frequent proclamations urging aristocrats to return
to their country estates; see Leah S. Marcus, *The Politics of Mirth: Jonson,
Herrick, Milton, Marvell, and the Defense of Old Holiday Pastimes*
(Chicago: University of Chicago Press, 1986), p. 66.

67. Chauncey Wood, "George and Henry Herbert on Redemption,"
Huntington Library Quarterly, 46 (1983): 306.

68. Strier, *Love Known,* p. 57.

69. *Complete Works,* 3:459; *Works,* p. 467.

70. Hooker, *Laws* (5.79.1), 2:443.

71. John Mulder, *The Temple of the Mind: Education and Literary Taste
in Seventeenth-Century England* (New York: Pegasus, 1969), p. 77.

72. See Barbara Lewalski, *Protestant Poetics and the Seventeenth-
Century Religious Lyric* (Princeton: Princeton University Press, 1979),
pp. 283–316; and Strier, *Love Known,* pp. 84–113.

73. Lawrence Stone, *The Family, Sex and Marriage in England 1500–
1800* (New York: Harper and Row, 1977), p. 97.

74. Strier, *Love Known,* p. 18, n. 32, claims that "the only interest in this
remarkably weak line is what it tells us of Herbert's personal fastidiousness."
Such fastidiousness is certainly at work, but as Elias demonstrates, the pros-
cription of spitting was part of the larger "civilizing process" of the period
(*The History of Manners,* pp. 153–56).

75. Strier, *Love Known,* p. 20.

76. Friendship as a central model for Herbert's relationship with God has
been explored from very different theological and critical presuppositions by
Louis Martz, *Poetry of Meditation,* pp. 249–87; Stanley Fish, *Self-Consuming
Artifacts: The Experience of Seventeenth-Century Literature* (Berkeley: Uni-
versity of California Press, 1972), p. 198; Edmund Miller, *"Drudgerie Divine":
The Rhetoric of God and Man in George Herbert* (Salzburg: Salzburg Studies in
English, 1979), pp. 58–83; and Jeanne Clayton Hunter, "George Herbert and
Friend," *Notes and Queries* 32 (1985): 161–62, and "George Herbert and Pu-

ritan Piety," *Journal of Religion* 68 (1988): 237–40. None of these critics, however, deals with a fully historical notion of friendship.

77.   Strier, *Love Known*, p. 183.

78.   Donne, *Sermons*, 1:223.

79.   Elizabeth Stambler, "The Unity of Herbert's *Temple*," *Cross Currents* 10 (1960): 259.

80.   Chana Bloch, *Spelling the Word: George Herbert and the Bible* (Berkeley: University of California Press, 1985), p. 37, n. 43, lists the relevant biblical verses.

81.   John Martin Heissler, ed., "Mr. Herbert's Temple and Church Militant Explained and Improved . . .   by George Ryley: A Critical Edition," 2 pts., diss., University of Illinois, 1960, p. 557.

82.   Singleton, *God's Courtier*, pp. 115–61, and Diana Benet, *Secretary of Praise: The Poetic Vocation of George Herbert* (Columbia: University of Missouri Press, 1984), pp. 101–99.

83.   Cf. Strier, *Love Known*, p. 173, on these lines: "The ontological framework which is the original and primary domain of the great chain idea has been entirely replaced by a functionalist framework."

84.   Christina Malcolmson, "George Herbert's *Country Parson* and the Character of Social Identity," *Studies in Philology* 85 (1988): 261.

85.   Hutchinson, *Works*, p. xxviii.

86.   Despite the fact that she takes the title of her book from this rich phrase, Diana Benet does little with its social implications (see her *Secretary of Praise*).

87.   Stein, *George Herbert's Lyrics*, p. 106. See also Parker H. Johnson, "The Economy of Praise in George Herbert's 'The Church,'" *George Herbert Journal* 5, nos. 1 and 2 (1981/82): 45–62.

88.   *Complete Works*, 3:452–53; *Works*, p. 460. See also the letter to James, 3:450, and a letter to Archbishop Abbot, 3:458.

89.   For the history and traditional use of this topos, see E. R. Curtius, *European Literature in the Latin Middle Ages*, tr. Willard R. Trask (Princeton: Princeton University Press, 1953), pp. 159–62.

90.   Bloch, *Spelling the Word*, p. 36.

91.   Leah S. Marcus, *Childhood and Cultural Despair: A Theme and Variations in Seventeenth-Century Literature* (Pittsburgh: University of Pittsburgh Press, 1978), p. 99.

92.   Strier proposes this in "Sanctifying the Aristocracy: 'Devout Humanism' in Francois de Sales, John Donne, and George Herbert," *Journal of Religion* 69 (1989): 57–58, citing the stanza as proof that "Herbert clearly transcended the disingenuousness with regard to wealth and worldly position that seems intrinsic to 'devout humanism.'"

93.   Donne, *Sermons*, 7:425.

94.   Strier, *Love Known*, p. 205. His discussion of "Faith" is on pp. 206–7.

95.   This image is also used in Herbert's oration on the return of Prince Charles from Spain (which I discuss in chap. 1).

96. Sidney Gottlieb, "The Social and Political Backgrounds of George Herbert's Poetry," *"The Muses Common-Weale": Poetry and Politics in the Seventeenth Century*, eds. Claude J. Summers and Ted-Larry Pebworth (Columbia: University of Missouri Press, 1988), p. 110.

97. *The Complete Works in Verse and Prose of George Herbert*, ed. A. B. Grosart, 3 vols. (London: Fuller Worthies' Library, 1874), 2:205; *Works*, p. 413.

98. Walton, *Lives*, p. 270.

99. Malcolmson, "George Herbert's *Country Parson*," p. 256.

100. Ivan Earle Taylor, "Cavalier Sophistication in the Poetry of George Herbert," *Anglican Theological Review* 39 (1957): 230.

101. L. C. Knights, "George Herbert" (1944), in *Explorations: Essays in Criticism Mainly on the Literature of the Seventeenth Century* (New York: George W. Stewart, 1947), p. 131. Knights also praises Herbert for his "invariable courtesy" (p. 131, n. 3).

102. Empson, *Seven Types of Ambiguity*, p. 120.

103. Joseph Summers, *George Herbert: His Religion and Art* (Cambridge: Harvard University Press, 1954), p. 151.

104. Christopher Hill, "Pottage for Freeborn Englishmen: Attitudes to Wage-Labour," in *Change and Continuity in Seventeenth-Century England* (Cambridge: Harvard University Press, 1975), p. 234.

105. The date is Hutchinson's (*Works*, p. 608), surmised from internal evidence.

106. *Complete Works*, 3:472; *Works*, pp. 471–73.

107. Strier, "Sanctifying the Aristocracy," pp. 57–58.

108. *The Latin Poetry of George Herbert*, tr. Mark McCloskey and Paul R. Murphy (Athens: Ohio University Press, 1965), p. 149; *Works*, p. 429.

109. *Latin Poetry*, pp. 141–43; *Works*, p. 427. Hutchinson identifies the political events to which the lines refer: "On 27 June 1627, within a few weeks of Lady Danvers's death, Buckingham sailed from Stokes Bay with about one hundred ships and 6,000 troops for the relief of La Rochelle," while "Count Tilly, commanding the army of the Catholic League, totally defeated Christian IV of Denmark at Lutter on 27 Aug. 1626" (*Works*, p. 595).

110. In "Proverbial Wisdom and Popular Errors," *Society and Culture in Early Modern France* (Stanford: Stanford University Press, 1965), pp. 227–57, Natalie Zemon Davis analyzes the Renaissance phenomenon of collecting common proverbs, although without reference to Herbert. Herbert's proverbs as a collection are discussed by James Thorpe, "Reflections and Self-Reflections: *Outlandish Proverbs* as a Context for George Herbert's Other Writings," *Illustrious Evidence: Approaches to English Literature of the Early Seventeenth Century*, ed. Earl Miner (Berkeley: University of California Press, 1975), pp. 23–37; and Michael Piret, "Herbert and Proverbs," *The Cambridge Quarterly* 17 (1988): 222–43.

111. *Works*, p. 352, no. 945. In the *Discoveries*, Ben Jonson shares a similar vision of social exploitation, with an added cannibalistic twist: "a fain'd famil-

iarity in great ones, is a note of certaine usurpation on the lesse . . . So the Fisher provides baits for the trowte, Roch, Dace, &c. that they may be food to him" (*Ben Jonson*, 8:597–98). I explore this passage in greater depth in " 'The Mysteries of Manners, Armes, and Arts': 'Inviting a Friend to Supper' and 'To Penshurst,' " in *The Muses Common-Weale*, eds. Summers and Pebworth, p. 72.

112. Richard Baxter, *The Crucifying of the world, By The Cross of Christ* (London, 1658), sig. (a3), quoted in *The Herbert Allusion Book: Allusions to George Herbert in the Seventeenth Century*, ed. Robert H. Ray, *Studies in Philology* 83, no. 4 (1986): 66.

113. Richard Baxter, *Of Redemption of Time* (1667), quoted in Ray, ed., *The Herbert Allusion Book*, pp. 78–79. Baxter proceeds to quote stanzas 14, 16, 17, and 18 of "The Church-porch."

114. Malcolmson, "George Herbert's *Country Parson*," p. 264.

115. *Works*, p. 236. Donne likewise remarks: "What a Coronation is our taking of Orders, by which God makes us a Royall Priesthood? And what an inthronization is the comming up into a Pulpit?" (*Sermons*, 7:134).

116. On secrets of state, see Jonathan Goldberg, *James I and the Politics of Literature* (Baltimore: Johns Hopkins University Press, 1983), pp. 55–112. Edward Herbert has a remarkably similar account of the pastoral power over the interior of subjects that the institution of confession bestows upon the Roman Catholic Church; Rome, he says, is "that place which first found meanes to establish soe greate an empire over the persons of men and afterwards over theire Consciences: The Articles of Confessing and Absolving sinners being a greater *Arcanum Imperii* for Governing the world then all the Acts invented by Statists formerly were" (*The Life of Edward, First Lord Herbert of Cherbury*, ed. J. M. Shuttleworth [London: Oxford University Press, 1976], p. 74).

117. In a remarkable passage from the *Conversations*, Ben Jonson, too, finds in the church a forum for speech liberated from the constraints of the social hierarchy; Jonson, remarks Drummond, "hath a minde to be a churchman, & so he might have favour to make one Sermon to the King, he careth not what yrafter sould befall him, for he would not flatter though he saw Death" (*Ben Jonson*, 1:141).

118. Malcolmson, "George Herbert's *Country Parson*," p. 253.

119. Hutchinson makes this point in his commentary (*Works*, p. 587).

120. Michael Brennan, *Literary Patronage in the English Renaissance: The Pembroke Family* (London: Routledge, 1988), p. 154.

121. T[homas] S[heppard?], Preface to Leonard Lessius, *Hygiasticon* (Cambridge, 1634), in which Herbert's translation first appeared, quoted from Ray, ed., *The Herbert Allusion Book*, p. 10.

122. *Works*, p. 538.

123. Featley, *Ancilla Pietatis*, pp. 99–100.

124. *Latin Poetry*, p. 93; *Works*, p. 413.

125. Stone, *Crisis*, p. 452.

126. Ibid., pp. 453–54.

127. Strier, *Love Known*, p. 210.

128. Martz, *Poetry of Meditation*, p. 314. For Martz, though, this regret is interpreted as a sign that "the poet loves his art: the devout humanist cannot bring himself to renounce it utterly," rather than as a manifestation of Herbert's resentment of this encroachment of royal power. The two readings, of course, are not exclusive.

129. Fish, *Self-Consuming Artifacts*, p. 222.

130. Strier, *Love Known*, p. 216.

131. Fish, *Self-Consuming Artifacts*, p. 223.

132. "Of Ambition," in *Francis Bacon: A Selection of His Works*, ed. Sidney Warhaft (New York: Odyssey, 1965), p. 143.

133. Summers, *George Herbert*, p. 90. Richard L. Sears of the Department of Astronomy at the University of Michigan informs me that "The Collar" was a favorite poem of Robert Oppenheimer; some of its attraction, I would like to think, derived from this complex intuition of order amidst apparent chaos. See Freeman Dyson, *Disturbing the Universe* (New York: Harper and Row, 1979), pp. 81–83.

134. Jeffrey Hart, "Herbert's 'The Collar' Re-Read," in *Essential Articles for the Study of George Herbert's Poetry*, ed. John R. Roberts (Hamden: Archon, 1979), p. 455.

135. Ibid.

136. *Spenser: Poetical Works*, eds. J. C. Smith and E. de Selincourt (London: Oxford University Press, 1912), p. 504, lines 895–905.

137. Martz, *Poetry of Meditation*, p. 303.

138. Hart, "Herbert's 'The Collar' Re-Read," p. 455.

139. In *The Doctrine and Discipline of Divorce*, Milton uses the phrase to denote powerless and meaningless bondage: "To couple hatred therfore though wedlock try all her golden links, and borrow to her aid all the iron manacles and fetters of Law, it does but seek to twist a rope of sand, which was a task, they say, that pos'd the divell" (in John Milton, *The Complete Prose Works*, eds. Don M. Wolfe et al., 8 vols. [New Haven: Yale University Press, 1953–82], 2:345).

140. Guazzo, *Civile Conversation*, 1:210.

141. See Marcus, *Childhood*, pp. 104–5, and passim.

142. *The Book of Common Prayer*, ed. Booty, p. 89.

143. In chap. 5, I show how deferential disputation of divine judgment becomes in "Love (III)" the occasion of political aggression.

144. Gordon J. Schochet, *Patriarchalism in Political Thought: The Authoritarian Family and Political Speculation and Attitudes Especially in Seventeenth-Century England* (New York: Basic Books, 1975). See, though, *Habits of Thought*, chap. 6, "Nursing Fathers: Patriarchy as a Cultural Ideal," pp. 218–49, in which Shuger cautions against assuming that "a father's relation to his child" necessarily involves "political relations of submission, domination, and the struggle to acquire power" (p. 219).

145. *Works*, pp. 363–71. His brother Edward, by contrast, addresses Sir

George More, the clerk of his wardship (and future father-in-law of John Donne), as "worthy Father," "loving Father," and "my much honoured father," and signs himself "your son," "the son that lives more than half in his loving father," and "your adopted son in name, but natural all other ways" (from Sidney Lee, ed., *The Autobiography of Edward, Lord Herbert of Cherbury* [New York: Dutton, 1906], pp. 188–90). Charles, *A Life*, pp. 30–31, discusses Edward's relationship to More.

Chapter 3

1. I received the letter on Oct. 5, 1988.
2. Elaine Scarry, *The Body in Pain: The Making and Unmaking of the World* (Oxford: Oxford University Press, 1985), pp. 27–59.
3. Cited in *Amnesty International: Report on Torture* (London: Duckworth, 2nd edition, 1975), p. 31.
4. Scarry, *Body in Pain*, p. 29.
5. Joseph H. Summers, *George Herbert: His Religion and Art* (Cambridge: Harvard University Press, 1954), pp. 128–29.
6. Robert Southwell, *An Humble Supplication to Her Majestie* (1591), ed. R. C. Bald (Cambridge: Cambridge University Press, 1953), p. 34.
7. Summers, *George Herbert*, p. 129.
8. Michel Foucault, *The History of Sexuality*, vol. 1, *An Introduction*, tr. Robert Hurley (New York: Random House, 1978), p. 86.
9. Richard Todd, *The Opacity of Signs: Acts of Interpretation in George Herbert's "The Temple"* (Columbia: University of Missouri Press, 1986), p. 65.
10. William Harrison, *The Description of England* (1587), ed. Georges Edelen (Ithaca: Cornell University Press, 1968), p. 187. Harrison is paraphrasing Sir Thomas Smith, *De republica Anglorum* (1583).
11. Sir Edward Coke, *The Third Part of the Institutes of the Laws of England* (London, 1797 ed.), p. 35, quoted in John H. Langbein, *Torture and the Law of Proof: Europe and England in the Ancien Regime* (Chicago: University of Chicago Press, 1976), p. 129. On the history and structure of torture, I have also consulted David Jardine, *A Reading on the Use of Torture in the Criminal Law of England Previously to the Commonwealth* (London, 1837); H. C. Lea, *Superstition and Force: Essays on the Wager of Law, the Wager of Battle, the Ordeal, Torture* (Philadelphia, 1878); Edward Peters, *Torture* (Oxford: Basil Blackwell, 1985); and James Heath, *Torture and English Law: An Administrative and Legal History from the Plantagenets to the Stuarts* (Westport, Conn.: Greenwood Press, 1982).
12. Cited in Langbein, *Torture and the Law of Proof*, p. 76.
13. Langbein, *Torture and the Law of Proof*, pp. 73–77.
14. Ibid., p. 82.
15. See L. A. Parry, *The History of Torture in England* (London: Sampson Low, Marston and & Co., 1934), pp. 36–62, 76–88. On the issue of torture and

power, see Michel Foucault, *Discipline and Punish: The Birth of the Prison*, tr. Alan Sheridan (New York: Vintage, 1979), pp. 3–69.

16. In *Torture and English Law*, pp. 201–239, Heath gives the texts of these letters.

17. Quoted in Malise Ruthven, *Torture: The Grand Conspiracy* (London: Weidenfeld and Nicolson, 1978), p. 54.

18. John N. Wall, *Transformations of the Word: Spenser, Herbert, Vaughan* (Athens: University of Georgia Press, 1988), p. 215.

19. 1 Cor. 3.16. The OED (sb²) records the earliest use of the anatomical meaning of "temple" from the fourteenth century.

20. Samuel Y. Edgerton, Jr., "*Maniera* and the *Mannaia*: Decorum and Decapitation in the Sixteenth Century," in *The Meaning of Mannerism*, eds. Franklin W. Robinson and Stephen G. Nichols, Jr. (Hanover: University Press of New England, 1972), p. 79.

21. Karen Cunningham, "Renaissance Execution and Marlovian Elocution: The Drama of Death," *PMLA* 105 (1990): 213.

22. Penry Williams, *The Tudor Regime* (Oxford: Clarendon Press, 1979), p. 398. Rare first-hand testimony of the experience of torture in the Renaissance is available in the Catholic autobiography of John Gerard, entitled in its modern translation *The Autobiography of a Hunted Priest*, tr. Philip Caraman (New York: Pellegrini and Cudahy, 1952), pp. 104–15.

23. William Harrison, *Description of England*, p. 189. One might want to speculate on the legal algebra by which errors of speech are punished by amputation of the organ of listening.

24. As Foucault argues in *Discipline and Punish*, the notion of prison as a house of correction rather than just a place of punishment is an eighteenth-century phenomenon. In *Imagining the Penitentiary: Fiction and the Architecture of Mind in Eighteenth-Century England* (Chicago: University of Chicago Press, 1987), John Bender correlates the construction of penitentiaries with novelistic fictions of personal identity.

25. Langbein, *Torture and the Law of Proof*, pp. 6–7.

26. Quoted in Georg Rusche and Otto Kirchheimer, *Punishment and Social Structure* (New York: Columbia University Press, 1939), p. 22.

27. Stanley Fish, *Self-Consuming Artifacts: The Experience of Seventeenth-Century Literature* (Berkeley: University of California Press, 1972), p. 160.

28. Richard Strier, *Love Known: Theology and Experience in George Herbert's Poetry* (Chicago: University of Chicago Press, 1983), p. 229.

29. Ibid., p. 231.

30. Southwell, *Humble Supplication*, p. 34.

31. Such imagery is explicated at length in Fredson Bowers, "Herbert's Sequential Imagery: 'The Temper,'" *Modern Philology* 59 (1962): 202–13.

32. Strier, *Love Known*, p. 233.

33. Foucault, *Discipline and Punish*, p. 11.

34. Strier, *Love Known*, pp. 31–32.

35. *Works*, p. 475.

36. In *An Humble Supplication*, Southwell suggests that Elizabethan torturers also direct their attentions to "the tendrest parts": "Some have bene tortured in such parts, as is almost a torture to Christian eares to heare it" (p. 34).

37. Harrison, *Description of England*, p. 187, observes that "the greatest and most grievous punishment used in England for such as offend against the state is drawing from the prison to the place of execution upon an hurdle or sled, where they are hanged till they be half dead and then taken down and quartered alive; after that, their members and bowels are cut from their bodies and thrown into a fire provided near-hand and within their own sight."

38. Francis Barker, *The Tremulous Private Body: Essays on Subjection* (London: Methuen, 1984), p. 22.

39. Harrison, *Description of England*, p. 187.

40. On display in the Tower of London is a device called "the collar," weighing ten pounds, and lined with studs, which locked around a prisoner's neck. I discuss "The Collar" in more detail in chap. 2.

41. Richard Strier, "Changing the Object: George Herbert and Excess," *George Herbert Journal* 2, no. 1 (1978): 26. See also Terry G. Sherwood, *Herbert's Prayerful Art* (Toronto: University of Toronto Press, 1989), p. 107: "Herbert is not like Paul or Donne after him in finding joy in suffering. The matter is more subtle, more complicated, and less easily comprehended. Herbert never ceases to weary of the grief that saves him."

42. Edmund Miller, *Drudgerie Divine: The Rhetoric of God and Man in George Herbert* (Salzburg: Salzburg Studies in English Literature, 1979), p. 56.

43. Scarry, *The Body in Pain*, p. 56.

44. John Donne, *Sermons*, eds. George Potter and Evelyn Simpson, 10 vols. (Berkeley: University of California Press, 1953–62), 1:233. In *Habits of Thought in the English Renaissance: Religion, Politics, and the Dominant Culture* (Berkeley: University of California Press, 1990), pp. 159–217, Debora Kuller Shuger offers an illuminating account of "the intersection of dependence, terror, and adoration" in Donne's relations with the divine.

45. Donne, *Sermons*, 1:234–35.

46. Ibid., 7:65–67.

47. Richard Hooker, *Of the Laws of Ecclesiastical Polity* (5.72.2), ed. Christopher Morris, 2 vols. (London: Dent, 1954), 2:374.

48. Southwell, *An Humble Supplication*, p. 33. The fact that God possesses the omniscience governments covet renders his recourse to torture all the more gratuitous.

49. Michel Foucault, "The Subject and Power," *Critical Inquiry* 8 (1982): 783.

50. Steven Mullaney, *The Place of the Stage: License, Play, and Power in Renaissance England* (Chicago: University of Chicago Press, 1988), pp. 105–7.

51. Foucault, *Discipline and Punish*, p. 201; see also Bender, *Imagining*

the Penitentiary. My sense of the appropriateness of Foucault to this passage was sharpened by hearing a yet unpublished paper by Stanley Fish, " 'Voide of Storie': Anti-Narrative in Seventeenth-Century Poetry," which offers a profound account of Foucauldian surveillance in *The Country Parson.*

52. Strier, *Love Known,* p. 134.

53. Ibid., p. 136.

54. Gen. 9.12–17. Scarry, *Body in Pain,* p. 361, n. 34, finds the same ambivalence in the Bible: "The word 'bow' (*keshet*) used as a noun elsewhere in the scriptures refers to the weapon: the curved or arched shape of the rainbow makes it a bow whose scale and splendor are appropriate to God; as a bow that is set aside, it becomes an image of the now benign (because unused) divine weapon."

55. Aldous Huxley, *Texts and Pretexts* (New York: Harper, 1933), p. 13, quoted from *George Herbert and the Seventeenth-Century Religious Poets,* ed. Mario A. Di Cesare (New York: Norton, 1978), p. 233.

56. Stephen Orgel makes the comparison in his discussion of *The Tempest* in *The Illusion of Power: Political Theater in the English Renaissance* (Berkeley: University of California Press, 1975), p. 49. In his *Autobiography,* pp. 58–59 and 96, Edward Herbert records his experience of two terrifying tempests while at sea, including one which sounds like the opening of *The Tempest:* "The master of our ship lost both the use of his compass and his reason" (*The Life of Edward, First Lord Herbert of Cherbury,* ed. J. M. Shuttleworth [London: Oxford University Press, 1976], p. 58).

57. *Lucus 19,* in *The Latin Poetry of George Herbert,* tr. Mark McCloskey and Paul R. Murphy (Athens: Ohio University Press, 1965), p. 95; *Works,* p. 414.

58. *Latin Poetry,* p. 145; *Works,* p. 428.

59. *Sir Thomas Wyatt: The Complete Poems,* ed. R. A. Rebholz (New Haven: Yale University Press, 1981), p. 81. The poem is a translation of Petrarch, *Rime,* no. 189.

60. *Works,* pp. 438–39. I quote from the translation first published in *Poems, by J. D.* (1650). In *The Divine Poems of John Donne* (Oxford: Clarendon Press, 2nd ed., 1978), pp. 138–47, Helen Gardner examines both poems in detail.

61. Hutchinson, *Works,* p. 502, cites Donne, "A Valediction: of weeping" (lines 26–27): "Since thou and I sigh one anothers breath, / Who e'r sighes most, is cruellest, and hasts the others death." See also Donne's "Song" ("Sweetest love, I do not goe"), lines 25–32.

62. Orgel, *Illusion of Power,* p. 57.

63. Ben Jonson, *Pan's Anniversary, or the Shepherds' Holiday* (lines 174–76), and *News from the New World Discovered in the Moon* (lines 285–87), in *Ben Jonson: Selected Masques,* ed. Stephen Orgel (New Haven: Yale University Press, 1970), pp. 197, 274.

64. M. C. Bradbrook, "Herbert's Ground," *Essays and Studies* 34 (1981): 68; *Neptune's Triumph for the Return of Albion* (line 365), in *Ben Jonson: Selected Masques,* p. 274.

65. Anthony Low, "Herbert's 'Jordan (I)' and the Court Masque," *Criticism* 14 (1972): 109–18.
66. *Latin Poetry*, tr. McCloskey and Murphy, p. 91; *Works*, p. 412.
67. Fish, *Self-Consuming Artifacts*, p. 184.
68. Chana Bloch, *Spelling the Word: George Herbert and the Bible* (Berkeley: University of California Press, 1985), p. 162.
69. Fish, *Self-Consuming Artifacts*, p. 187.
70. Donne, *Sermons*, 2:300.
71. Shuger, *Habits of Thought*, p. 198.
72. Bloch, *Spelling the Word*, p. 161.
73. Strier, *Love Known*, pp. 246–47.
74. Vendler, *Poetry of George Herbert*, p. 53.
75. In chap. 5, I analyze the sexual energy of these lines, and of the conclusion of "The Flower."
76. Vendler, *Poetry of George Herbert*, p. 51.
77. Ibid., p. 52.
78. Strier, *Love Known*, p. 252.
79. Ibid., pp. 250–51, highlights the discontinuity between past and present in the poem.
80. Ibid., p. 251.
81. Quoted from Ted-Larry Pebworth, "George Herbert's Poems to the Queen of Bohemia: A Rediscovered Text and a New Edition," *English Literary Renaissance* 9 (1979): 117, lines 15–16. Herbert's authorship of the poem is discussed by Pebworth, and by Kenneth Alan Hovey, "George Herbert's Authorship of 'To the Queene of Bohemia,'" *Renaissance Quarterly* 30 (1977): 43–50.

Chapter 4

1. Coburn Freer, *Music for a King: George Herbert's Style and the Metrical Psalms* (Baltimore: Johns Hopkins University Press, 1972), p. 206.
2. Rosemond Tuve, *A Reading of George Herbert* (Chicago: University of Chicago Press, 1952), p. 165.
3. Baldassare Castiglione, *The Book of the Courtier*, tr. Thomas Hoby [1561] (London: Dent, 1928), pp. 264, 261.
4. Ibid., p. 279.
5. John Donne, *Sermons*, ed. George Potter and Evelyn Simpson, 10 vols. (Berkeley: University of California Press, 1953–62), 3:152; see also 5:345.
6. Ilona Bell, " 'Setting Foot Into Divinity': George Herbert and the English Reformation," *Modern Language Quarterly* 38 (1977): 219–44, repr. in *Essential Articles for the Study of George Herbert's Poetry*, ed. John R. Roberts (Hamden: Archon, 1979), p. 70.
7. "He may wish that his own grief may never be exceeded among the humanity he pities . . . or he may mean *mine* as a quotation from the *others*, 'Only let there *be* a retribution, only let my torturers say never was grief like

theirs, in the day when my agony shall be exceeded'" (William Empson, *Seven Types of Ambiguity* [New York: New Directions, 3rd ed., 1947], pp. 228–29).

8. "Amaze" is given as "amuse" in the Bodleian manuscript (the poem is not in the Williams manuscript); "either Herbert on second thoughts or his editor substituted *Amaze*," proposes Hutchinson (*Works*, p. 523). Nevertheless, the meaning of the two words was far closer then than it is now.

9. Richard Strier, *Love Known: Theology and Experience in George Herbert's Poetry* (Chicago: University of Chicago Press, 1983), p. 186.

10. Ibid., p. 187.

11. Wilson F. Engel, III, "Christ in the Winepress: Backgrounds of a Sacred Image," *George Herbert Journal* 3, nos. 1 and 2 (1979/80): 47. Engel offers a thorough explication of the patristic tradition of commentary on the image.

12. William Harrison, *The Description of England* (1587), ed. Georges Edelen (Ithaca: Cornell University Press, 1968), p. 191; see also John H. Langbein, *Torture and the Law of Proof: Europe and England in the Ancien Regime* (Chicago: University of Chicago Press, 1976), pp. 74–77.

13. OED, *vice*, sb.², 3b, cites these lines from Herbert.

14. Elaine Scarry, *The Body in Pain: The Making and Unmaking of the World* (Oxford: Oxford University Press, 1985), p. 190.

15. The passage is from Exod. 20.25; see also Deut. 27.2, 5–6, and Josh. 8.31. On this quotation's relevance to "The Altar," see, e.g., Stanley Fish, *Self-Consuming Artifacts: The Experience of Seventeenth-Century Literature* (Berkeley: University of California Press, 1972), pp. 211–12; Strier, *Love Known*, p. 193; and Chana Bloch, *Spelling the Word: George Herbert and the Bible* (Berkeley: University of California Press, 1985), pp. 63–64.

16. Jeremiah Dyke, *A Sermon Dedicatory* (London, 1622), p. 3. The *DNB* describes Dyke as a Cambridge man (as was Herbert), "of moderate views, and one who, although he disliked ceremonies, submitted, so far as his conscience permitted, to their use, yet as being a thorough Puritan at heart."

17. Dyke, *Sermon Dedicatory*, p. 5

18. Ibid., p. 12.

19. Quoted in Robert Daly, *God's Altar: The World and the Flesh in Puritan Poetry* (Berkeley: University of California Press, 1978), p. 1.

20. Dyke, *Sermon Dedicatory*, p. 12

21. Strier, *Love Known*, p. 194. Fish, *Self-Consuming Artifacts*, p. 214, argues that Herbert reverses this commonplace: "if these lines have any value, it is because eternity, in the form of god's active presence, has (literally) graced them . . . He trusts not in his art, but in the appropriation of that art by God."

22. The antecedent tradition is explored in depth by J. B. Leishman, *Themes and Variations in Shakespeare's Sonnets* (London: Hutchinson University Library, 1963), pp. 25–91.

23. Richard Todd, *The Opacity of Signs: Acts of Interpretation in George Herbert's "The Temple"* (Columbia: University of Missouri Press, 1986), p. 183.

24. Robert B. Shaw, *The Call of God: The Theme of Vocation in the Poetry of Donne and Herbert* (Cambridge, Mass.: Cowley Publications, 1981), p. 104, was the first critic to call attention to this likeness.

25. Joel Fineman, *Shakespeare's Perjured Eye: The Invention of Poetic Subjectivity in the Sonnets* (Berkeley: University of California Press, 1986), p. 5.

26. George Puttenham, *The Arte of English Poesie*, eds. Gladys Doidge Willcock and Alice Walker (Cambridge: Cambridge University Press, 1936), p. 91.

27. Thomas Hobbes, *Answer to Davenant's Preface to "Gondibert"* (1650), in *Critical Essays of the Seventeenth Century*, ed. J. E. Spingarn, 3 vols. (Oxford: Clarendon Press, 1908), 2:57. Hobbes does not censure Herbert by name, but certainly has him in mind.

28. The point is made by Joseph Summers, *George Herbert: His Religion and Art* (Cambridge: Harvard University Press, 1954), p. 142; and Mary Ellen Rickey, *Utmost Art: Complexity in the Verse of George Herbert* (Lexington: University of Kentucky Press, 1966), pp. 10–15, who cites several relevant examples from the *Greek Anthology* (first English edition 1555) and from Francis Davison's *Poetical Rhapsody* (1602).

29. Puttenham, *Arte of English Poesie*, p. 97. Indeed, in "The pillar of Fame," the penultimate poem in the *Hesperides* (1648), Robert Herrick employs the form to establish his claim for the permanence of poetry "tho Kingdoms fal"; *The Complete Poetry of Robert Herrick*, ed. J. Max Patrick (New York: Norton, 1968), p. 443.

30. Donald R. Dickson, *The Fountain of Living Waters: The Typology of the Waters of Life in Herbert, Vaughan, and Traherne* (Columbia: University of Missouri Press, 1987), p. 89.

31. William V. Nestrick, "'Mine and Thine' in *The Temple*," in *"Too Riche to Clothe the Sunne": Essays on George Herbert*, eds. Claude J. Summers and Ted-Larry Pebworth (Pittsburgh: University of Pittsburgh Press, 1980), p. 116.

32. Fish, *Self-Consuming Artifacts*, p. 215. A similar construction is offered by Barbara Harman, *Costly Monuments: Representations of the Self in George Herbert's Poetry* (Cambridge: Harvard University Press, 1982), p. 218, n. 5; she sees the poem as "an illustration of what happens when agency and the *capacity to appear in one's own shape* have already been relinquished."

33. Strier, *Love Known*, pp. 192–93.

34. Fish, *Self-Consuming Artifacts*, p. 197.

35. J. W. Saunders explores the engrained aristocratic bias against publishing in the Renaissance in "The Stigma of Print: A Note on the Social Bases of Tudor Poetry," *Essays in Criticism* 1 (1951): 139–64, and *The Profession of English Letters* (London: Routledge and Kegan Paul, 1964), pp. 31–48. Herbert, of course, did not publish any of the poems in *The Temple* in his lifetime, and seems not to have circulated them in manuscript either.

36. Albert of Monte Cassino, *Flores rhetorici*, quoted in R. Howard Bloch, *Etymologies and Genealogies: A Literary Anthropology of the French Middle Ages* (Chicago: University of Chicago Press, 1983), p. 126. Bloch

views the focus upon the "disengagement of words from their conventional and proper meaning" as symptomatic of "the disruption that the reintroduction of money within the circuit of human affairs represented for the great lineages, the 'men of property,' of twelfth-century France"—a disruption similar to the tension in Herbert's poem between writing as if for popular or aristocratic audiences and composing for God.

37. Interestingly, in "George and Henry Herbert on Redemption," *Huntington Library Quarterly* 46 (1983): 308, n. 6, Chauncey Wood refers to a prose manuscript work by Henry Herbert, George's younger brother, entitled *Herbert's Golden Harpe or His Heavenlie Hymne*, in which "Biblical references . . . account for perhaps 70 to 80% of the wording in the text." Perhaps this is what it means to copy out the sweetness ready penned of love.

38. Daniel Featley, *Ancilla Pietatis: Or, The Hand-maid to Private Devotion* (London, 1626), p. 24.

39. Fish, *Self-Consuming Artifacts*, p. 199.

40. *Works*, no. 440, p. 336. My wife informs me that there is a tradition among American quilters which demands the inclusion of deliberate imperfection in order to avoid the pride of trying to make something perfect.

41. Summers, *George Herbert*, p. 84.

42. *Works*, pp. 224, 232. In "Submission and Assertion: The 'Double Motion' of Herbert's 'Dedication,'" *John Donne Journal* 2, no. 2 (1983): 39–49, I explore this vertiginous process in the first two-and-a-half lines of the "Dedication" prefacing the poems of *The Temple*: "Lord, my first fruits present themselves to thee; / Yet not mine neither: for from thee they came, / And must return."

43. Strier, *Love Known*, p. 180.

44. Ibid., p. 181.

45. Ibid. Strier, though, takes "he" as referring unequivocally to God.

46. Scarry, *Body in Pain*, p. 172.

47. C. A. Patrides, ed., *The English Poems of George Herbert* (London: Dent, 1974), p. 120 n.

48. Strier, *Love Known*, pp. 182–83.

49. Cited in David Harris Willson, *James VI and I* (London: Cape, 1956), p. 195.

50. Helen Vendler, *The Poetry of George Herbert* (Cambridge: Harvard University Press, 1975), p. 190.

51. Arnold Stein, *George Herbert's Lyrics* (Baltimore: Johns Hopkins University Press, 1968), pp. 1–44. See also Douglas L. Peterson, *The English Lyric from Wyatt to Donne: A History of the Plain and Eloquent Styles* (Princeton: Princeton University Press, 1967); Leah S. Marcus, "George Herbert and the Anglican Plain Style," in *Too Rich to Clothe the Sunne*, eds. Summers and Pebworth, pp. 179–93; and Frank Manley, "Toward a Definition of Plain Style in the Poetry of George Herbert," in *Poetic Traditions of the English Renaissance*, eds. Maynard Mack and George deForest Lord (New Haven: Yale University Press, 1982), pp. 203–17.

52. Claude J. Summers and Ted-Larry Pebworth, " 'Too Rich to Clothe the Sunne': Celebrating George Herbert," in *Too Rich to Clothe the Sunne,* eds. Summers and Pebworth, p. xi.

53. Todd, *The Opacity of Signs,* passim.

54. Donne, *Sermons,* 7:315.

55. Ibid., pp. 315–16. As evidence of the premium Donne placed on obscurity, Ben Jonson told Drummond "That Done said to him, he wrott that Epitaph on Prince Henry, *Look to me Faith,* to match Sir Ed: Herbert in obscurenesse" *(Ben Jonson,* eds. C. H. Herford, Percy Simpson, and Evelyn Simpson, 11 vols. [Oxford: Clarendon Press, 1925–52], 1:136).

56. Castiglione, *The Courtier,* p. 51.

57. Daniel Javitch, *Poetry and Courtliness in Renaissance England* (Princeton: Princeton University Press, 1978), p. 66.

58. Joseph Anthony Mazzeo, "St. Augustine's Rhetoric of Silence: Truth vs. Eloquence and Things vs. Signs," in *Renaissance and Seventeenth-Century Studies* (New York: Columbia University Press, 1964), p. 17.

59. Frank Whigham, *Ambition and Privilege: The Social Tropes of Elizabethan Courtesy Theory* (Berkeley: University of California Press, 1984), p. 102.

60. On the moral weight given to simplicity in the period, see Richard Foster Jones, "The Moral Sense of Simplicity," in *Studies in Honor of Fredrick W. Shipley, Washington University Studies,* n.s. 14 (1941): 265–88.

61. Izaak Walton, *Lives,* ed. George Saintsbury (London: Oxford University Press, 1927), p. 295.

62. Leah S. Marcus, "George Herbert and the Anglican Plain Style," in *Too Rich to Clothe the Sunne,* eds. Summers and Pebworth, pp. 179–93.

63. Neil Rhodes, "Nashe, Rhetoric and Satire," in *Jacobean Poetry and Prose: Rhetoric, Representation and the Popular Imagination,* ed. Clive Bloom (London: Macmillan, 1988), p. 30.

64. Stefano Guazzo, *The Civile Conversation,* tr. George Pettie (1581), ed. Edward Sullivan (London: Tudor Translations, 1925), 1:165–66.

65. Featley, *Ancilla Pietatis,* pp. 20–22.

66. Ibid., p. 108.

67. It is interesting in the context of Herbert's spiritualization of alchemical inquiry that Sir William Herbert, a relative whose daughter married George's brother Edward, was preoccupied by the project of attaining the philosopher's stone, and was the intimate friend of the period's most famous alchemist, John Dee; see *The Autobiography of Edward, Lord Herbert of Cherbury,* ed. Sidney Lee (New York: Dutton, 1906), p. 22 and n. 3.

68. A detailed discussion of these revisions and a parallel account of the theology they imply is available in Janis Lull, *The Poem in Time: Reading George Herbert's Revisions of "The Church"* (Newark: University of Delaware Press, 1990), pp. 94–100.

69. *The Geneva Bible: A Facsimile of the 1560 Edition,* ed. Lloyd E. Berry (Madison: University of Wisconsin Press, 1969), p. 314.

70. Claude Lévi-Strauss, *The Jealous Potter*, tr. Benedicte Chorier (Chicago: University of Chicago Press, 1988).

71. Richard Strier, " 'To all Angels and Saints': Herbert's Puritan Poem," *Modern Philology* 77 (1979): 140.

72. *Geneva Bible*, p. 138; Strier, "To all Angels and Saints," p. 140, where he also quotes the gloss from the Geneva Bible.

73. Strier, *Love Known*, p. 183.

74. John Donne, *Letters to Severall Persons of Honour* (1651), ed. M. Thomas Hester (New York: Scholars' Facsimiles and Reprints, 1977), pp. 111–12. In *A Godly and Learned Treatise of Prayer* (Cambridge, 1640), p. 215, George Downame likewise remarks, "The readiest way to obtein new blessings, is to give thanks for the old."

75. M. C. Bradbrook, "Herbert's Ground," *Essays and Studies* 34 (1981): 78.

76. Donne, *Sermons*, 5:347.

77. Featley, *Ancilla Pietatis*, p. 398.

78. Frank Whigham, "The Rhetoric of Elizabethan Suitors' Letters," *PMLA* 96 (1981): 872–74.

79. Puttenham, *Arte of English Poesie*, pp. 293–94. Whigham, "The Rhetoric of Elizabethan Suitors' Letters," p. 871, cites this passage from Puttenham as an explanation for "the absence of claims of merit" in the supplicatory letters he examines.

80. Lewis Hyde, *The Gift: Imagination and the Erotic Life of Property* (New York: Vintage, 1979), pp. 143, 149.

81. Angel Day, *The English Secretary (1599)*, ed. Robert O. Evans, 2 vols. in 1 (Gainesville: Scholars' Facsimiles and Reprints, 1967), 1:99. Whigham, "The Rhetoric of Elizabethan Suitors' Letters," p. 874, analyzes this letter in terms of the social rank of the interlocutors.

82. Strier, *Love Known*, p. 184.

83. Ibid., p. 95.

84. Ibid., p. 96.

85. In "The Match," Henry Vaughan explicitly answers this invitation: "Here I join hands, and thrust my stubborn heart / Into thy *deed*" (*Henry Vaughan: The Complete Poems*, ed. Alan Rudrum [New Haven: Yale University Press, 1981], p. 191). In *Henry Vaughan: The Unfolding Vision* (Princeton: Princeton University Press, 1982), Jonathan F. S. Post explores in depth the profound relationship between Vaughan and Herbert, and suggests that "The Match" "defines the necessary ingredients for a successful transfer of power" (p. 119).

86. Strier, *Love Known*, p. 109.

87. Ibid., p. 110.

88. Featley, *Ancilla Pietatis*, p. 108.

89. *The Latin Poetry of George Herbert*, tr. Mark McCloskey and Paul R. Murphy (Athens: Ohio University Press, 1965), p. 63; *Works*, p. 404.

90. Donne, *Sermons*, 5:270–72.

91. Ibid., 5:233.

92. Ibid., 5:364.

93. Marion White Singleton, *God's Courtier: Configuring a Different Grace in George Herbert's "Temple"* (Cambridge: Cambridge University Press, 1987), p. 192. Singleton does not explore what it might mean to try to lead God to virtue.

94. Day, *English Secretary*, 1:68.

95. Ibid., 1:47.

96. *Latin Poetry*, tr. McCloskey and Murphy, pp. 113–17; *Works*, pp. 419–20. In " 'Inventica Bellica' / 'Triumphus Mortis': Herbert's Parody of Human Progress and Dialogue with Divne Grace," *Studies in Philology* 78 (1981): 275–304, Kenneth Alan Hovey examines the circumstances of the poem's composition, and its relation to Herbert's antiwar sentiments in his oration on the return of a belligerent Prince Charles from Spain (*Complete Works*, ed. Grosart, 3:403–7; *Works*, pp. 448–49).

97. Strier, *Love Known*, p. 99.

98. William V. Nestrick, " 'Mine and Thine' in *The Temple*," in *Too Rich to Clothe the Sunne*, ed. Summers and Pebworth, p. 122.

99. Richard Hooker, *Of the Laws of Ecclesiastical Polity* (1.2.2,6), ed. Christopher Morris, 2 vols. (London: Dent, 1954), 1:150–54. Rather than implicating the speaker in the aggressive action Hooker proscribes, Strier, *Love Known*, p. 102, opposes Herbert to Hooker on the question of God's law.

100. Strier, *Love Known*, pp. 103–4.

101. Ibid., p. 104.

102. A. L. Clements, "Theme, Tone, and Tradition in George Herbert's Poetry," in *Essential Articles for the Study of George Herbert's Poetry*, ed. Roberts, pp. 33–51.

103. Stanley Fish, *The Living Temple: George Herbert and Catechizing* (Berkeley: University of California Press, 1978), p. 135, observes that the speaker of "Love (III)" is "killed with kindness."

Chapter 5

1. *The Collected Works of Samuel Taylor Coleridge: Marginalia*, ed. George Whalley, 12 vols., Bollingen Foundation (Princeton: Princeton University Press, 1984), no. 12, vol. 2, p. 1034.

2. I agree with Louis Martz, *The Poetry of Meditation* (New Haven: Yale University Press, 1962), p. 319, and Chana Bloch, *Spelling the Word: George Herbert and the Bible* (Berkeley: University of California Press, 1985), p. 100, that "Love (III)" represents *both* the soul's reception of the Eucharist and heaven's reception of the soul.

3. Jacques Revel, "The Uses of Civility," in *A History of Private Life*, vol. 3, *Passions of the Renaissance*, ed. Roger Chartier, tr. Arthur Goldhammer (Cambridge: Harvard University Press, 1989), pp. 183–84. Revel is making particular use of Norbert Elias, *The History of Manners*, vol. 1 of *The Civilizing Process*, tr. Edmund Jephcott (New York: Urizen, 1978), pp. 84–129.

4. Heinrich Bullinger, *Commonplaces of Christian Religion*, tr. John Stockwood (London, 1572), p. 200v.

5. *Certaine Sermons or Homilies Appointed to be Read in Churches In the Time of Queen Elizabeth I (1547–1571): A Facsimile Reproduction of the Edition of 1623*, eds. Mary Ellen Rickey and Thomas B. Stroup, 2 vols. in 1 (Gainesville: Scholars' Facsimiles and Reprints, 1968), 2:197, 205.

6. Stephen Booth, ed., *Shakespeare's Sonnets* (New Haven: Yale University Press, 1977), pp. 488–89, in the midst of a provocative note on the capacity of puns to structure a poem in which they do not appear.

7. Many readers have noted the elements of a courtesy-contest in the poem, but none has explored its relation to the contemporaneous practices of courtesy. Arnold Stein, *George Herbert's Lyrics* (Baltimore: Johns Hopkins University Press, 1968), pp. 192–94, calls attention to the poem's "movements and language of polite service," and describes it as "contest in courtesy and humility." Leah S. Marcus, *Childhood and Cultural Despair: A Theme and Variations in Seventeenth-Century Literature* (Pittsburgh: University of Pittsburgh Press, 1978), p. 117, terms the poem "a playful contest of wit and courtesy." Richard Strier, *Love Known: Theology and Experience in George Herbert's Poetry* (Chicago: University of Chicago Press, 1983), p. 74, terms the poem a "comedy of manners," and is attentive to the theological nuances of "the courtesy-contest situation."

8. Amy M. Charles, *A Life of George Herbert* (Ithaca: Cornell University Press, 1977), p. 119.

9. Ibid., p. 41. Over a period of thirteen weeks, Charles records 95 different visitors.

10. *The Life of Edward, First Lord Herbert of Cherbury*, ed. J. M. Shuttleworth (London: Oxford University Press, 1976), p. 7. As a testimony to the importance of hospitality to the family mythology, Edward also remembers that his grandfather "delighted also much in Hospitality, as having a very long Table twice covered every Meal with the best Meats that could be gotten" (p. 3).

11. Marcus, *Childhood and Cultural Despair*, p. 114.

12. Felicity Heal, "The Idea of Hospitality in Early Modern England," *Past and Present* 102 (1984): 67, 73, and passim.

13. Charles, *A Life*, p. 120.

14. Helen Vendler, *The Poetry of George Herbert* (Cambridge: Harvard University Press, 1975), pp. 275–76.

15. Frank Whigham, *Ambition and Privilege: The Social Tropes of Elizabethan Courtesy Theory* (Berkeley: University of California Press, 1984), pp. 102–12.

16. Stefano Guazzo, *The Civile Conversation*, tr. George Pettie (1581), ed. Edward Sullivan, 2 vols. (London: Tudor Translations, 1925), 1:166.

17. Baldassare Castiglione, *The Book of the Courtier*, tr. Thomas Hoby [1561] (London: Dent, 1928), p. 109.

18. Whigham, *Ambition and Privilege*, p. 109.

19. James Cleland, *The Institution of a Young Noble Man* (1607), ed. Max Molyneux, 2 vols. (Delmar, N.Y.: Scholars' Facsimiles and Reprints, 1948), 1:179.

20. Giovanni della Casa, *A Renaissance Courtesy-Book: Galateo of Manners and Behaviours*, tr. Robert Peterson (1576), ed. Joel E. Spingarn (London: Humanist's Library, 1914), p. 44.

21. Ibid., p. 45.

22. George Puttenham, *The Arte of English Poesie*, eds. Gladys Doidge Willcock and Alice Walker (Cambridge: Cambridge University Press, 1936), p. 277.

23. Ibid.

24. Ibid.

25. Strier, *Love Known*, p. 78.

26. I owe the reference to talking with one's mouth full to personal correspondence with M. Thomas Hester. In *Epigramme* 107, "To Captayne Hungry," Jonson similarly tells his guest to eat, not speak: "Doe what you come for, Captayne, with your newes; / That's, sit, and eate: doe not my eares abuse" (*Ben Jonson*, eds. C. H. Herford, Percy Simpson, and Evelyn Simpson, 11 vols. [Oxford: Clarendon Press, 1925–52] 8:68, lines 1–2).

27. Stein, *George Herbert's Lyrics*, p. 194.

28. "An Interview with Donald Sheehan," in *Recitative: Prose by James Merrill*, ed. J. D. McClatchy (San Francisco: North Point Press, 1986), p. 33.

29. Anonymous, *The Mirror of Complements* (London, 1635), pp. 27–29.

30. See my "'Mysteries of Manners, Armes, and Arts': 'Inviting a Friend to Supper' and 'To Penshurst,'" in *"The Muses Common-Weale": Poetry and Politics in the Seventeenth Century*, eds. Claude J. Summers and Ted-Larry Pebworth (Columbia: University of Missouri Press, 1988), pp. 62–79.

31. Herbert does not of course believe that he can actually put God in his debt, but political indebtedness would be the social product of the deferential maneuvering to which his dialogue with God appeals. For a fascinating account of one who did believe in the possibility of obligating God, see Richard A. Grusin, "'Put God in Your Debt': Emerson's Economy of Expenditure," *PMLA* 103 (1988): 35–44.

32. Norbert Elias, *The Court Society*, tr. Edmund Jephcott (New York: Pantheon, 1983), p. 94.

33. Frank Whigham, "The Rhetoric of Elizabethan Suitors' Letters," *PMLA* 96 (1981): 867.

34. See, e.g., Sir William Segar, *The Booke of Honor and Armes* (London, 1590), and *Honor, Military and Civil* (London, 1602); Vincent Saviolo, *His Practice of the Rapier and Dagger* (London, 1595); George Silver, *Paradoxes of Defense* (London, 1599); Thomas Milles, *The Catalogue of Honor* (London, 1610); and John Selden, *Titles of Honour* (London, 1614), for which Ben Jonson wrote "An Epistle to Master John Selden." Segar is discussed in Diane Bornstein, *Mirrors of Courtesy* (New York: Archon, 1975), pp. 120–27.

In *As You Like It* (5.4.44–103), Touchstone offers a devastating parody of the ways in which these works, which he calls "books for good manners" (line 91), circumscribe social violence.

35. Norbert Elias, *Power and Civility*, vol. 2 of *The Civilizing Process*, tr. Edmund Jephcott (New York: Pantheon, 1982), p. 259.

36. I borrow the phrase from Erving Goffman, *Encounters: Two Studies in the Sociology of Interaction* (Indianapolis: Bobbs-Merrill, 1961), p. 78. Goffman uses the term in relation to the twentieth-century's arena of polite behavior—the dinner party. On the "rhetoric of social combat," see Whigham, *Ambition and Privilege*, pp. 137–50.

37. Lawrence Stone, *The Family, Sex and Marriage in England 1500–1800* (New York: Harper & Row, 1977), p. 93.

38. Lawrence Stone, *The Crisis of the Aristocracy 1558–1641* (Oxford: Clarendon Press, 1965), pp. 223–24.

39. *The Letters of John Chamberlain*, ed. Norman Egbert McClure, 2 vols. (Philadelphia: American Philosophical Society, 1939), 2:344. I owe this reference to Michael MacDonald of the Department of History, University of Michigan.

40. William Camden, *Annales Rerum Anglicarum et Hibernicarum regnante Elizabetha*, tr. R. Norton (London, 1625), quoted in R. C. Bald, *Donne and the Drurys* (Cambridge: Cambridge University Press, 1959), p. 15.

41. *The Life of Edward, Lord Herbert*, ed. Shuttleworth, p. 28.

42. Henry Peacham, *The Garden of Eloquence* (1593), ed. William G. Crane (Gainesville: Scholars' Facsimiles and Reprints, 1954), pp. AB3ᵛ-AB4.

43. Guazzo, *Civile Conversation*, 1:166.

44. Denys de Refuges, *A Treatise of the Court*, tr. John Reynolds, 2 vols. in 1 (London, 1622), 1:80.

45. Aristotle, *The Nichomachean Ethics*, tr. Martin Oswald (Indianapolis: Bobbs-Merrill, 1962), 1124b, pp. 96–97. Aristotle's comment is borne out by the anthropological work of Marcel Mauss, *The Gift: Forms and Functions of Exchange in Archaic Societies*, tr. Ian Cunnison (New York: Norton, 1967), p. 72.

46. Erving Goffman, "The Nature of Deference and Demeanor," *Interaction Ritual: Essays on Face-to-Face Behavior* (Garden City: Anchor, 1967), p. 62.

47. Guazzo, *Civile Conversation*, 1:167.

48. Henry Peacham, *The Truth of Our Times* (1638), in *The Complete Gentleman, The Truth of Our Times, and The Art of Living in London*, ed. Virgil B. Heltzel (Ithaca: Cornell University Press, 1962), p. 203.

49. Ibid., p. 196; "To Penshurst," lines 65–66, in *Ben Jonson*, 8:95.

50. Stone, *Crisis*, p. 42.

51. In " 'Anger's My Meat': Feeding, Dependency, and Aggression in *Coriolanus*," in *Representing Shakespeare*, eds. Murray M. Schwartz and Coppelia Kahn (Baltimore: Johns Hopkins University Press, 1980), pp. 129–49, Janet Adelman highlights the nightmarish aspects that the social curren-

cy of food could assume, tracing in *Coriolanus* both a fear of the dependence produced by eating and terror at the prospect of being consumed.

52. Anne Williams, "Gracious Accommodations: Herbert's 'Love (III),'" *Modern Philology* 82 (1984): 18, n. 17. See also the etymology of "authority" as *"augeo, 'increase, nourish, cause to grow'"* explored by Stephen Orgel in "Prospero's Wife," *Representations* 8 (1984): 9.

53. Anonymous, *Cyvile and Uncyvile Life* (London, 1579), cited in Felicity Heal, "The Idea of Hospitality in Early Modern England," p. 74.

54. Antony de Guevara, *The Diall of Princes,* tr. Thomas North (London, 1619), p. 619.

55. A fascinating study of such motifs is Maggie Kilgour, *From Communion to Cannibalism: An Anatomy of Metaphors of Incorporation* (Princeton: Princeton University Press, 1990).

56. Guazzo, *Civile Conversation,* 1:192.

57. Whigham, *Ambition and Privilege,* p. 66.

58. *Ben Jonson,* 8:597–98. On Jonson's enigmatic relationship to the authorities his poems address, see Stanley Fish's provocative essay, "Authors-Readers: Jonson's Community of the Same," *Representations* 7 (1984): 26–58.

59. Pierre Bourdieu, *Outline of a Theory of Practice,* tr. Richard Nice (Cambridge: Cambridge University Press, 1977), p. 191.

60. *Ben Jonson,* 4:368.

61. Ben Jonson, *Bartholomew Fair* (2.1.27–29). Despite these unmistakable lower class mercantile associations, the phrase seems already to have acquired the potential that Herbert exploits for the expression of a genuinely tender solicitude; in Shakespeare's *King John,* Arthur hopes to mollify Hubert (who is about to torture Arthur) by reminding him of when he had "with my hand at midnight held your head; / And like the watchful minutes to the hour, / Still and anon cheer'd up the heavy time, / Saying '*What lack you?*' and '*Where lies your grief?*' / Or '*What good love may I perform for you?*'" (4.1.45–49; my italics).

62. Claudius Hollyband, *The French Schoole-maister* (1573), in *The Elizabethan Home Discovered in Two Dialogues by Claudius Hollyband and Peter Erondell,* ed. Muriel St. Clare Byrne (London: Methuen, 1949), p. 21.

63. Bloch, *Spelling the Word,* pp. 99–112; Vendler, *Poetry of George Herbert,* pp. 54–55, 58–60, 232, 274–76; Michael McCanles, *Dialectical Criticism and Renaissance Literature* (Berkeley: University of California Press, 1975), pp. 75–76; Marcus, *Childhood and Cultural Despair,* pp. 116–17.

64. Stanley Fish, *The Living Temple: George Herbert and Catechizing* (Berkeley: University of California Press, 1978), pp. 131–36; Stein, *George Herbert's Lyrics,* pp. 190–95.

65. Strier, *Love Known,* p. 77, n. 37.

66. Ibid., p. 82. Strier's assertion that "God is a host Who will not take no for an answer" (ibid., p. 83) is very close to Fish's characterization of the invitation as "an offer you can't refuse" (*Living Temple,* p. 134).

67. Fish, *Living Temple,* p. 134.

68. Miguel de Cervantes, *Don Quixote* (P. 1, Bk. 2, chap. 3), tr. Peter Motteux, rev. Ozell (New York: Modern Library, 1930), p. 62.

69. Ibid., pp. 62–63.

70. Ibid., p. 63.

71. Castiglione, *The Courtier*, p. 109. Frederigo refers here to the parable of the great supper, Luke 14.7–10. Bloch, *Spelling the Word*, pp. 99–112, identifies the many biblical precedents for "Love (III)," including this parable.

72. Guazzo, *Civile Conversation*, 1:192; my italics.

73. Joseph H. Summers, "Sir Calidore and the Country Parson," in *Like Season'd Timber: New Essays on George Herbert*, eds. Edmund Miller and Robert DiYanni (New York: Peter Lang, 1987), p. 216.

74. Barnabus Oley, "A Prefatory View of the Life and Vertues of the Authour, and Excellencies of This Book," in *Herbert's Remains. Or, Sundry Pieces of that sweet Singer of the Temple, Mr. George Herbert* (London, 1652), sigs. a11v–a12r. Hutchinson, *Works*, p. 556, suggests that Oley "must have known [Herbert] well by repute, if not personally."

75. John Donne, *Sermons*, eds. George Potter and Evelyn Simpson, 10 vols. (Berkeley: University of California Press, 1953–62), 1:271.

76. Samuel Taylor Coleridge, *Collected Letters*, ed. Earl Leslie Griggs (Oxford: Clarendon Press, 1956–), 6:573.

77. See George Ryley, "Mr. Herbert's Temple and Church Militant Explained and Improved," ed. John Martin Heissler (diss., University of Illinois, 1960), pp. 647–48, and Strier, *Love Known*, pp. 80–83.

78. Strier, *Love Known*, pp. 73–74.

79. Luke 17.7–10. The headnote to this passage in the AV declares: "How we are bound to God and not he to us."

80. Edwin Sandys, *Sermons*, ed. John Ayre (Cambridge, 1841), p. 297. Sandys is paraphrasing Augustine on the Psalms.

81. Marion White Singleton, *God's Courtier: Configuring a Different Grace in George Herbert's "Temple"* (Cambridge: Cambridge University Press, 1987), p. 194.

82. Samuel Torshell, *The Saints Humiliation* (London, 1633), p. 115.

83. John Wing, *Jacobs Staffe* (Flushing, 1621), pp. 126–30.

84. Donne, *Sermons*, 9:272.

85. *The Book of Common Prayer 1559: The Elizabethan Prayer Book*, ed. John E. Booty (Washington, D. C.: Folger Shakespeare Library, 1976), pp. 254–56. Bloch, *Spelling the Word*, pp. 102–4, also discusses the relevance of the Prayer Book exhortations to "Love (III)."

86. *Book of Common Prayer*, pp. 256–57.

87. Fish, *Living Temple*, pp. 111–32.

88. *Book of Common Prayer*, p. 258. This sense of danger seems to have been bound up for Herbert in the approach to the sacred. Herbert's country parson "often tels [his congregation], that Sermons are dangerous things, that none goes out of Church as he came in, but either better, or worse" (p. 233).

Similarly, "The Church-porch" admonishes the church-goer to "look to thy actions well: / For churches are either our heav'n or hell" (lines 425–26).

89. Guazzo, *Civile Conversation*, 1:210.

90. *The Lytylle Childrenes Lytil Boke*, lines 3–6; see also *The Young Children's Book*, lines 5–8, both in *Manners and Meals in Olden Time*, ed. Frederick J. Furnivall (London: E.E.T.S., 1868), pp. 16–17. I have somewhat updated the orthography.

91. In *Painting and Experience in Fifteenth-Century Italy* (Oxford: Oxford University Press, 1972), pp. 32–56, Michael Baxandall explores how "fifteenth-century people differentiated more sharply than us between successive stages of the Annunciation," and uses the work of Fra Roberto da Lecce to identify five stages of Mary's response: *Conturbatio* (disquiet), *Cogitatio* (reflection), *Interrogatio* (inquiry), *Humiliatio* (submission), and *Meritatio* (merit). The two Annunciations that I consider explore the first stage of *Conturbatio*; *Meritatio* would of course be theologically irrelevant to "Love (III)," whose point is the undeservedness of divine grace.

92. *Works*, p. 259. Donald J. McGinn, ed., *The Admonition Controversy* (New Brunswick: Rutgers University Press, 1949), pp. 209–13, collects the major texts by Whitgift and Cartwright on the issue of the proper posture for reception of the Eucharist.

93. Strier, *Love Known*, p. 78, n. 41.

94. James I, *A Meditation Upon the Lords Prayer* (London, 1619), p. 22.

95. Daniel Featley, *Ancilla Pietatis: Or, The Hand-maid to Private Devotion* (London 1626), p. 14.

96. Ibid., p. 17.

97. John Milton, *Of Reformation touching Church-Discipline* (1641), in *The Complete Prose Works of John Milton*, eds. Don M. Wolfe et al., 8 vols. (New Haven: Yale University Press, 1953–82), 1: 523.

98. Ibid., p. 524. Milton here refers to John 13.5–11.

99. On rituals of status reversal, see Victor Turner, *The Ritual Process: Structure and Anti-Structure* (Ithaca: Cornell University Press, 1969).

100. Bloch, *Spelling the Word*, p. 109.

101. Julia Kristeva, *Tales of Love*, tr. Leon S. Roudiez (New York: Columbia University Press, 1987), p. 9.

102. Stein, *George Herbert's Lyrics*, p. 195, suggests that the poem is "not finished, not even transformed, but in effect consumed." Fish, *Living Temple*, p. 136, argues even more forcefully that the closure communicated by "Love (III)" is "a closure which, rather than being earned, is imposed." Strier, *Love Known*, p. 82, n. 50, allows that "one can grant Fish's point and still not see it as making the poem bitter or unsatisfying."

103. I am thinking here particularly of Arthur F. Marotti's politically attentive but occasionally tendentious work on the Renaissance lyric in " 'Love Is Not Love': Elizabethan Sonnet Sequences and the Social Order," *ELH* 49 (1982): 396–428, and in *John Donne, Coterie Poet* (Madison: University of Wisconsin Press, 1986). Love, I would argue, sometimes is love.

104. I borrow the phrase from Richard Todd, *The Opacity of Signs: Acts of Interpretation in George Herbert's "Temple"* (Columbia: University of Missouri Press, 1986), p. 190.

Chapter 6

1. Leonardo da Vinci, *Treatise on Painting*, tr. A. Philip McMahon, 2 vols. (Princeton: Princeton University Press, 1956), 1:22. The Italian text is quoted from *The Literary Works of Leonardo da Vinci*, ed. Jean Paul Richter, 2 vols. (London: Phaidon, 1970), 1:64.

2. Russell Fraser, "George Herbert's Poetry," *Sewanee Review* 95 (1987): 581. Fraser's essay explores in fascinating ways the "occulted sexual energy" (p. 575) of Herbert's poetry, and offers a fine reading of "Vertue." In "Reading (Herbert's 'Vertue') Otherwise," *Mississippi Review* 33 (1983): 61, Jonathan Goldberg also sees "Vertue" as "a sexual scene, sweet, perfumed, filled with roses and spring." Robert Rogers, *Metaphor: A Psychoanalytic View* (Berkeley: University of California Press, 1978), pp. 55–57, likewise attends to the poem's erotic overtones.

Yvor Winters's pronouncements on the irrelevance of sexual to religious experience in *Forms of Discovery* (Chicago: Swallow Press, 1967), p. 92, articulately voice the cultural assumptions Fraser describes: "the poet who insists on dealing with [religious] experience and who becomes involved emotionally in the sexual analogy runs the risk of corrupting his devotional poetry with sexual imagery. It is not that sexual experience is 'immoral'; but it is irrelevant to the religious experience, and in so far as it is introduced into the religious experience, can result in nothing but confusion." Winters has the excesses of Richard Crashaw in mind, but argues that such excesses are the inevitable product of mixing religion and sex rather than symptoms of Crashaw's particular poetic. A sympathetic and intelligent reading of Crashaw is available in R. V. Young, *Richard Crashaw and the Spanish Golden Age* (New Haven: Yale University Press, 1982).

3. Even Helen Vendler, one of the readers most attentive to the erotic intimations of Herbert's poems, begs the question of Herbert's carnal knowledge in her account of these lines: "Herbert may say in 'The Forerunners' that his words, before his employ, knew only stews and brothels, but it would seem that he knew just enough to have a perfect horror of such places and of their inhabitants" (*The Poetry of George Herbert* [Cambridge: Harvard University Press, 1975], p. 162).

4. Charles Davis, *Body as Spirit: The Nature of Religious Feeling* (New York: Seabury, 1976), pp. 130–31. Two recent works explore the genesis of this inconsistency in early Christian attitudes: Elaine Pagels, *Adam, Eve, and the Serpent* (New York: Random House, 1988), and Peter Brown, *The Body and Society: Men, Women and Sexual Renunciation in Early Christianity* (New York: Columbia University Press, 1988).

5. Norbert Elias, *The Civilizing Process*, vol. 1, *The History of Manners*, tr. Edmund Jephcott (New York: Pantheon Books, 1978) pp. 134–43.

6. Ibid., pp. 187–88.

7. Peter Stallybrass and Allon White, *The Politics and Poetics of Transgression* (Ithaca: Cornell University Press, 1986), p. 90.

8. Frank Whigham, *Ambition and Privilege: The Social Tropes of Elizabethan Courtesy Theory* (Berkeley: University of California Press, 1984), attentively foregrounds the materialist motives that infuse Renaissance courtesy literature, but at the expense of attention to its use as a discourse of affection and self-construction.

9. Michel Foucault, *The History of Sexuality*, vol. 2, *The Use of Pleasure*, and vol. 3, *The Care of the Self*, tr. Robert Hurley (New York: Random House, 1985, 1986).

10. Foucault, *The Use of Pleasure*, pp. 10–11.

11. Foucault, *The Care of the Self*, p. 51.

12. Frank Whigham, "The Rhetoric of Elizabethan Suitors' Letters," *PMLA* 96 (1981): 878. Whigham does not, however, suggest what these lessons might be.

13. As Ann Rosalind Jones and Peter Stallybrass note, "under 'courtship' the *OED* gives headings both for 'behaviour or action befitting a courtier' (first example, 1588) and for 'the action or process of paying court to a woman' (first example, 1596)" ("The Politics of *Astrophil and Stella*," *SEL* 24 [1984]: 53–68).

14. Kenneth Burke, *A Rhetoric of Motives* (1950; repr. Berkeley: University of California Press, 1969), p. 217.

15. Hutchinson, ed., *Works*, pp. 551, 597–98, recounts the arguments for Herbert's authorship. The claims are solid, based on manuscript (B.M. Add. MS. 22602) as well as textual (James Duport, *Ecclesiastes Solomonis* [1662]) authority. The only real argument against identifying it with Herbert is the circular claim (which I would dispute) that the poem is atypical of him. The translation I cite is from A. B. Grosart, ed., *The Complete Works in Verse and Prose of George Herbert*, 3 vols. (London: Fuller Worthies' Library, 1874), 2:165. The poem has received little critical attention, but was apparently very popular in the seventeenth century; see Gerard Previn Meyer, "The Blackamoor and Her Love," *Philological Quarterly* 17 (1938): 371–76, and Elliot H. Tokson, "The Image of the Negro in Four Seventeenth-Century Love Poems," *Modern Language Quarterly* 30 (1969): 508–22.

16. Exemplary of the cultural antipathy towards blackness is the moment in *Much Ado About Nothing* (5.4.38) where Claudio emphasizes his willingness to marry an unknown woman by promising that "I'll hold my mind were she an Ethiope."

17. At the end of his life Bacon dedicated his *Translation of Certaine Psalmes into English Verse* (1625) to "his very good frend, Mr. George Herbert," because "in respect of Divinitie, and Poesie, met (whereof the one is the Matter, the other the Stile of this little Writing) I could not make better choice" (quoted in *Works*, p. xl). The relationship between Bacon and Herbert

has been analyzed (although with little attention to these two poems) by William A. Sessions, "Bacon and Herbert and an Image of Chalk," in *"Too Rich to Clothe the Summe": Essays on George Herbert*, eds. Claude J. Summers and Ted-Larry Pebworth (Pittsburgh: University of Pittsburgh Press, 1980), pp. 165–78; and Charles Whitney, "Bacon and Herbert as Moderns," in *Like Season'd Timber: New Essays on George Herbert*, eds. Edmund Miller and Robert DiYanni (New York: Peter Lang, 1987), 231–39.

18. Hutchinson, *Works*, p. 551, cites the opinion of J. Fry, *Bibliographical Memoranda* (Bristol, 1816), that the diamond was actually a copy of Bacon's *Essays*, but as Hutchinson points out, "no edition [of the *Essays*] appeared between 1614 and 1624," when Bacon was Lord Chancellor. Sessions, "Bacon and Herbert," p. 169, suggests the diamond was "most likely" Bacon's *Magna Instauratio* (1620). No one seems to consider the possibility that the diamond was actually a diamond.

19. See *The Poems English and Latin of Edward Lord Herbert of Cherbury*, ed. G. C. Moore Smith (Oxford: Clarendon Press, 1923), "Sonnet of Black Beauty," "Another Sonnet of Black it self," "The Brown Beauty," and "To one Blacke, and not very Hansome, who expected commendation," pp. 38–39, 60, 97–98.

20. *Francis Bacon: A Selection of His Works*, ed. Sidney Warhaft (New York: Odyssey, 1965), p. 443. This passage was brought to my attention by a fine article by Karen Newman on sexual and racial anxiety in *Othello*, "'And wash the Ethiop white': Femininity and the Monstrous in *Othello*," in *Shakespeare Reproduced: The Text in History and Ideology*, eds. Jean E. Howard and Marlon F. O'Connor (New York: Methuen, 1987), pp. 141–62.

21. It may be relevant that, as John Aubrey records, Bacon was a pederast, whose "Ganimeds and Favourites tooke Bribes" (*Aubrey's Brief Lives*, ed. Hugh Lawson Dick [Harmondsworth: Penguin, 1962], p. 120).

22. Stephen Greenblatt, *Shakespearean Negotiations: The Circulation of Social Energy in Renaissance England* (Berkeley: University of California Press, 1988), pp. 78–79. My understanding of the physiology of Renaissance sexuality is indebted to Greenblatt's provocative discussion of Shakespeare's transvestite theater, "Fiction and Friction," pp. 66–93, and to Thomas Laqueur, *Making Sex: Body and Gender from the Greeks to Freud* (Cambridge: Harvard University Press, 1990).

23. William Harvey, *Disputations Touching the Generation of Animals*, tr. Gweneth Whitteridge (Oxford: Blackwell Scientific Publications, 1981), p. 151 (my italics); quoted in Greenblatt, *Shakespearean Negotiations*, pp. 183–84, n. 39.

24. On the sexual meaning of "to serve," see Stephen Booth, ed., *Shakespeare's Sonnets* (New Haven: Yale University Press, 1977), p. 487, note on Sonnet 141, line 10. Under "turn," sb. 30b., the *OED* identifies the meaning of the phrase "to serve one's turn" as "to suffice for or satisfy a need." To serve Venus' turn is thus to satisfy venereal needs.

25. See Booth, *Sonnets*, pp. 441–42, note on Sonnet 129, line 1; and

Herbert Alexander Ellis, *Shakespeare's Lusty Punning in "Love's Labour's Lost"* (Mouton: The Hague, 1973), pp. 95–97. Ellis cites the following words of Mercutio in *Romeo and Juliet* (2.1.23–6): " 'Twould anger him / To raise a *spirit* in his mistress' circle / Of some strange nature, letting it there stand / Till she had laid it and conjur'd it down."

26. See Heather A. R. Asals, *Equivocal Predication: George Herbert's Way to God* (Toronto: University of Toronto Press, 1981), p. 96.

27. Vendler, *The Poetry of George Herbert*, p. 161.

28. Ibid., p. 162.

29. Richard Strier, "Changing the Object: Herbert and Excess," *George Herbert Journal* 2 (1978): 24.

30. Vendler, *The Poetry of George Herbert*, p. 163.

31. Booth, *Sonnets*, p. 177, and Ellis, *Shakespeare's Lusty Punning*, pp. 103–10.

32. Richard Strier, *Love Known: Theology and Experience in George Herbert's Poetry* (Chicago: University of Chicago Press, 1983), p. 39, n. 30. Strier, though, emphasizes the erotic as it embodies an intellectualized attack on reason, where I stress the importance in its own right of Herbert's somatic imagery to the poems' wish to negotiate between earthly and heavenly love.

33. *Sir Philip Sidney's Defense of Poesy*, ed. Lewis Soens (Lincoln: University of Nebraska Press, 1970), p. 51. In *Transformations of the Word: Spenser, Herbert, Vaughan* (Athens: University of Georgia Press, 1988), pp. 224–37, John N. Wall explores in detail the influence of Sidney's *Astrophil and Stella* on Herbert's *Temple*, and asserts that "love for Herbert does not exclude the erotic dimension" (p. 225).

34. In "I am a little world made cunningly," Donne likewise juxtaposes "the fire / Of lust" to the "fiery zeale" of God, "which doth in eating heale" (*The Divine Poems of John Donne*, ed. Helen Gardner, 2nd ed. [Oxford: Clarendon Press, 1978], p. 13).

35. On "strain" as a verb meaning "to embrace closely," see Eric Partridge, *Shakespeare's Bawdy* (New York: Dutton, 1960), p. 196.

36. This meaning, employed frequently and with great relish by Chaucer's Wife of Bath, is still available in Shakespeare's Sonnet 20, in which the young man is "not acquainted" (line 3) because nature has "pricked [him] out for women's pleasure" (line 13). In addition, the "quaint Honour" that the speaker of Marvell's "To his Coy Mistress" (line 29) prophesies will "turn to dust" is both his mistress's pudendum and a mocking reference to the societal value conferred by her control over it (*The Poems and Letters of Andrew Marvell*, ed. H. M. Margoliouth 2 vols. [Oxford: Clarendon Press, 1971], 1:28).

37. Strier, *Love Known*, p. 89.

38. Janis Lull, "George Herbert's Revisions in 'The Church' and the Carnality of 'Love' (III)," *George Herbert Journal* 9, no. 1 (1985): 5.

39. Jonathan Goldberg, *Voice Terminal Echo: Postmodernism and English Renaissance Texts* (New York: Methuen, 1986), p. 110. Goldberg specu-

lates, not always persuasively, on a range of auto-erotic possibilities in poems such as "Artillerie," "Home," and "The Bag."

40. On the sexual confusion and unnatural generation represented by the cockatrice, see Thomas Rogers Forbes, *The Midwife and the Witch* (New Haven: Yale University Press, 1966), pp. 1–17. The relevance of alchemical concepts of the uroboric cockatrice is explored in Laurence Breiner, "Herbert's Cockatrice," *Modern Philology* 77 (1979): 10–17.

41. On "cockatrice" as "prostitute," see James T. Henke, *Courtesans and Cuckolds: A Glossary of Renaissance Dramatic Bawdy (Exclusive of Shakespeare)* (New York: Garland, 1979), p. 43; and Ben Jonson, "On Lieutenant Shift" (lines 21–24), *Epigrammes* 12, in *Ben Jonson*, eds. C. H. Herford, Percy Simpson, and Evelyn Simpson, 11 vols. (Oxford: Oxford University Press, 1925–52), 8:31. John Garrett, "Sin and Shame in George Herbert's Poetry," *Rivesta Canaria de Estudios Ingleses* 8 (1984): 141–43, attempts to read the poem in strictly Freudian terms.

42. The phrase is from Shakespeare's *Sonnet* 62, line 1. Dissuasion from masturbation as a theme in the *Sonnets* is examined by Booth, *Sonnets*, pp. 140, 142–43, and Joseph Pequigney, *Such Is My Love: A Study of Shakespeare's Sonnets* (Chicago: University of Chicago Press, 1985), pp. 15–18.

43. Michel Foucault, *The Care of the Self*, p. 140.

44. Strier, *Love Known*, p. 39. Strier, however, does not attend to the poem's onanistic orientation, focusing exclusively on the intellectual activity the poem describes.

45. The phrase is from *Sonnet* 6, line 13. On the pen/penis pun, see Partridge, *Shakespeare's Bawdy*, p. 163; Booth, *Sonnets*, p. 270, note on Sonnet 78, lines 3, 7, 11; and Hilda M. Hulme, *Explorations in Shakespeare's Language* (New York: Barnes and Noble, 1963) pp. 135–36. All three point to Gratiano's jealous threat in *Merchant of Venice* (5.1.237) to "mar the . . . pen" of the "young clerk" that Nerissa teasingly promises to sleep with. In "Gascoigne's 'Poemata Castrata': The Wages of Courtly Success" (*Criticism* 27 [1985]: 34), Richard C. McCoy calls attention to George Gascoigne's deployment of this pun in *The Adventures of Master F. J* (1573). The anonymous author of *The Whore's Rhetorick* (London, 1683), a bizarre offshoot of courtesy literature, dedicates his work "To the Most Famous University of London Courtezans," and tells them how in this work, his first, "you have at this instant got the Maiden-head of my officious scribbling instrument, as you have some years since, the Virginity of another Quill. The ink of this is black and smutty, but that of the other was of a more innocent and pleasing colour" (p. 12).

46. Strier, *Love Known*, p. 252; Vendler, *Poetry of George Herbert*, p. 51; in addition, see Fraser, "George Herbert's Poetry," p. 576. Strier, p. 252, n. 63, also calls attention to Herbert's "use of 'store' in an at least implicitly sexual context" in "The Pearl," line 26: "the projects of unbridled store." In *The Choise of Valentines*, a bawdy poem by Thomas Nashe (the poem was commonly known as *Nashe His Dildo*), "store" suggests seminal fluid; the sex-

ually exhausted speaker complains of his voracious mistress that "all my store seemes to hir, penurie" (*The Works of Thomas Nashe*, ed. R. B. McKerrow, 5 vols. [London, 1904–10], 3:415, line 300).

47. Augustine, *The City of God* (14.16–18), tr. John Healey (1610), 2 vols. (London: Dent, 1945), 2:47–49; see Gerard O'Daly, *Augustine's Philosophy of Mind* (London: Duckworth, 1987), p. 53. Lull, "Herbert's Revisions," p. 3, suggests that "the substitution in [the Williams manuscript] of 'And prick mine eyes' for 'Troubling mine eyes' was inspired by the phallic connotations of 'Babel'—the quick growing tower of self-delusion in the poem's final lines."

48. Strier, *Love Known*, p. 48, n. 45.

49. In "Herbert and the Unveiling of Diana: Stanza Three of 'Vanitie (I),'" *George Herbert Journal* 1, no. 2 (1978): 35, Stanton J. Linden suggests that Herbert intends the reader "to perceive the arrogance and presumptuousness of his 'subtil' empiricist's penetration into a private sanctuary that is the domain of the chaste, modest, and divine Diana, the exploited 'creature,' nature, of stanza three." Evelyn Fox Keller has explored how Bacon's model of scientific inquiry involves the exercise of masculine domination over a nature conceived as female (*Reflections on Gender and Science* [New Haven: Yale University Press, 1985], pp. 33–42).

50. Strier, *Love Known*, p. 48, n. 45.

51. *The Sermons of John Donne*, eds. Evelyn Simpson and George R. Potter 10 vols. (Berkeley: University of California Press, 1954–62), 6:190–91.

52. Ibid., 6:192.

53. Ibid., 6:200.

54. Deut. 30.6–9; see also Gen. 17.6–14.

55. Vendler is cautiously attracted by a "psychoanalytic interpretation" which "might see this poem as a masochistic acquiescence in castration: to accept castration is to be reconciled with the father by no longer possessing a rival masculine member" (*Poetry of George Herbert*, p. 295, n. 12). But one need only consider the aggression that Donne and Herbert associate with male sexuality to comprehend the theological and emotional power of this castration. Legend suggests that Origen, on reading Matt. 19.12—"and there be Eunuches, which have made themselves Eunuches for the kingdome of heavens sake"—castrated himself. Also relevant is Paul's admonition in Gal. 5.12—"I would they were even cut off which trouble you." In "*Justus quidem tu es, Domine,*" line 13, Gerard Manley Hopkins describes himself as "time's eunuch" (*A Hopkins Reader*, ed. John Pick [London: Oxford University Press, 1953], p. 30).

56. Stanley Stewart, *The Enclosed Garden: The Tradition and the Image in Seventeenth-Century Poetry* (Madison: University of Wisconsin Press, 1966), p. 53.

57. In *Childhood and Cultural Despair: A Theme and Variations in Seventeenth-Century Literature* (Pittsburgh: University of Pittsburgh Press, 1978), pp. 94–120, Leah S. Marcus incisively examines the manner in which

"becoming the child of God" was the major goal of Herbert's devotional life, but she does not explore the ways in which childhood was bound up for Herbert in notions of asexual purity.

58.   E. Pearlman, "George Herbert's God," *English Literary Renaissance* 13 (1983): 107. See also Janel Mueller, "Women Among the Metaphysicals: A Case, Mostly, of Being Donne For," *Modern Philology* 87 (1989): 154, who argues that "in the child this negation of sexuality takes the explicit positive form of carnal innocence."

59.   Elaine Scarry, *The Body in Pain: The Making and Unmaking of the World* (Oxford: Oxford University Press, 1985), p. 210.

60.   Robert Graves, *Poetic Unreason and Other Studies* (London: Cecil Palmer, 1925), p. 62. Graves views "The Bag" as a poem of "the Jekyll and Hyde variety . . . where the manifest content and the latent content represent opposite sides of a conflict" (p. 57).

61.   Mueller, "Women Among the Metaphysicals," p. 153, likewise asserts that Herbert's Christ "assimilates nurturant female functions symbolically in his spear-pierced side that runs blood and water." Mueller, though, argues that this feminization is the product of Herbert's rejection of sexuality, not the result of his nervous engagement with it.

62.   I quote from the translation of Mark McCloskey and Paul R. Murphy, *The Latin Poetry of George Herbert: A Bilingual Edition* (Athens: Ohio University Press, 1965), p. 65; *Works*, p. 404. The *Soliloquies* attributed to Bonaventura likewise stress the relationship between divine vulnerability and penetrability; Christ's wound, observes the author, is "opened to suffer thee to enter therein" (Bonaventura, *Soliloquies* [London, 1655], p. 88; sig. E7ᵛ, quoted in Richard Todd, *The Opacity of Signs: Acts of Interpretation in George Herbert's "The Temple,"* [Columbia: University of Missouri Press, 1986], p. 25, n. 10).

63.   *Latin Poetry*, p. 107; *Works*, p. 417.

64.   *Latin Poetry*, p. 119; *Works*, p. 421. A rejected stanza of "Whitsunday" likewise envisions an overtly maternal God: "Show yᵗ thy brests can not be dry, / But yᵗ from them ioyes purle for ever/ Melt into blessings all the sky, / So wee may cease to suck: to praise thee, never" (*Works*, p. 59). See also the conclusion of the poem entitled "Perseverance" that Herbert did not include in *The Temple*: "Onely my soule hangs on thy promises / With face and hands clinging unto thy brest, / clinging and crying . . .   " (*Works*, p. 205). It is, I think, significant that such explicitly maternal imagery exists only in Latin or Greek or in vernacular material Herbert rejected from *The Temple*. As Fred J. Nichols contends, the Latin poetry of the Renaissance is often more "intimate and personal" than works in the "mother tongue" (*An Anthology of Neo-Latin Poetry*, ed. Nichols [New Haven: Yale University Press, 1979], pp. 1–3). The Latin and Greek lyrics and the rejected English poems offer explicit versions of motifs that are much quieter in the revised English poems.

65.   Pearlman, "George Herbert's God," p. 108. Isaiah 49.23 offers some

license for such imagery, where God promises his people: "And kings shall be thy nursing fathers, and their queenes thy nursing mothers."

66. Caroline Walker Bynum, *Jesus as Mother: Studies in the Spirituality of the High Middle Ages* (Berkeley: University of California Press, 1982), p. 133; see also Bynum, *Holy Feast and Holy Fast: The Religious Significance of Food to Medieval Women* (Berkeley: University of California Press, 1987), pp. 270–71; and Marsha L. Dutton, "Christ Our Mother: Aelred's Iconography for Contemplative Union," in *Goad and Nail: Studies in Medieval Cistercian History*, ed. E. Rozanne Elder (Kalamazoo, Mich.: Cistercian Publications, 1985), pp. 21–45.

67. On the tradition of such sentiments, see R. Howard Bloch, "Medieval Misogyny," *Representations* 20 (1987): 1–24.

68. "Mr. Herbert's Temple and Church Militant Explained and Improved by a Discourse Upon Each Poem Critical and Practical by George Ryley: A Critical Edition," ed. John Martin Heissler (Diss., University of Illinois, 1960), p. 357.

69. An earlier version of this poem concedes that such advice may "seeme Monkish," but goes on to recommend: "Let not each fansy make thee to detest / A Virgin-bed, wch hath a speciall Crowne / If it concurr wth vertue" (*W*, lines 19–21).

70. Richard Strier, "Sanctifying the Aristocracy: 'Devout Humanism' in Francois de Sales, John Donne, and George Herbert," *Journal of Religion* 69 (1989): 46, n. 41. Ryley, "Mr. Herbert's Temple Explained," 1:9–10, glosses these difficult lines by reference to "a Story, some tell, of a young man, upon some Specious promises from Satan, tempted by him, to kill his Mother, wch he, wth horror att ye Barbarity of ye thing, refused: afterward he tempted him to kill his Sister; wch, wth the like resentmt, he also rejected: a 3d time, he offered to give him ye thing he desired, if he wd be drunken; wch he lookt upon as so agreeable, Venial Crime, yt he Embrac't it: &, wn drunk, he came ranting home, &, in his fury, he Slew his Mother, yn wth child of a daughter."

71. Elias, *The History of Manners*, p. 190.

72. *Works*, p. 238. A fascinating counterpart to Herbert's coldly pragmatic attitude to the role of the country parson's wife is a mid-nineteenth-century work entitled *The Country Parson's Wife. Being Intended as a Continuation of and Companion for Herbert's Country Parson* (London: J. Hatchard and Son, 1842). The author L[ouisa] L[ane] carves out an arena for female religious activity—largely in the domestic realm—without threatening or critiquing the masculine hegemony that Herbert's remarks endorse.

73. *Complete Works*, 3:475–76; *Works*, p. 470.

74. On the background of this topos, see Joseph C. Plumpe, *Mater Ecclesia: An Enquiry into the Concept of Church as Mother in Early Christianity* (Washington, D.C.: Catholic University of America Press, 1943).

75. In "To His Coy Mistress," Marvell uses worms in just this way, admonishing his audience that after death "worms shall try / That long preserv'd Virginity" (*Poems*, ed. Margoliouth, 1:28).

76. The literary and biblical contexts of this poem are explored in rich detail by Claude J. Summers, "The Bride of the Apocalypse and the Quest for True Religion: Donne, Herbert, and Spenser," in *"Bright Shootes of Everlastingnesse": The Seventeenth-Century Religious Lyric*, eds. Claude J. Summers and Ted-Larry Pebworth (Columbia: University of Missouri Press, 1987), pp. 72–95. In *Equivocal Predication*, pp. 94–110, Asals speculates provocatively on the connections among Mother Church, Magdalene Herbert, and Mary Magdalene, in Herbert's mind.

77. Claude J. Summers and Ted-Larry Pebworth, "The Politics of *The Temple*: 'The British Church' and 'The Familie,'" *George Herbert Journal* 8, no. 1 (1984): 3.

78. John Milton, *Animadversions* (1641), ed. Don M. Wolfe, in *Complete Prose Works*, 8 vols. (New Haven: Yale University Press, 1953), 1:728.

79. Elizabeth Stambler, "The Unity of Herbert's *Temple*," in *Essential Articles for the Study of George Herbert's Poetry*, ed. John R. Roberts (Hamden: Archon, 1979), p. 329. See also Louis L. Martz, *The Poetry of Meditation: A Study in English Religious Literature of the Seventeenth Century* (New Haven: Yale University Press, 1962), pp. 259–73.

80. Stanley Stewart, *The Enclosed Garden*, offers a learned account of the reception of the Song of Solomon in the seventeenth century. See also George L. Scheper, "Reformation Attitudes toward Allegory and the Song of Songs," *PMLA* 89 (1974): 551–62. Chana Bloch, *Spelling the Word: George Herbert and the Bible* (Berkeley: University of California Press, 1985), exhaustively explores the variety of biblical sources that infiltrate "Love (III)."

81. See, e.g., Arnold Stein, *George Herbert's Lyrics* (Baltimore: Johns Hopkins University Press, 1968), pp. 190–95; Stanley Fish, *The Living Temple: George Herbert and Catechizing* (Berkeley: University of California Press, 1979), pp. 131–4; Strier, *Love Known*, pp. 73–83; Vendler, *Poetry of Herbert*, pp. 58–60, 274–6; Marcus, *Childhood and Cultural Despair*, pp. 116–7; and Anne Williams, "Gracious Accommodations: Herbert's 'Love (III),'" *Modern Philology* 82 (1984): 13–22.

82. Joseph H. Summers, *George Herbert: His Religion and Art* (Cambridge: Harvard University Press, 1954), p. 89. Summers, however, does not expand on these relationships.

83. Bloch, *Spelling the Word*, p. 339. Reuben Brower similarly describes the encounter between guest and host as one of "almost feminine intimacy" (*The Fields of Light: An Experiment in Critical Reading* [London: Oxford University Press, 1951], pp. 28–31). See also Robert Bagg, "The Electromagnet and the Shred of Platinum," *Arion* 8 (1969): 428–29.

84. Lull, "Herbert's Revisions," pp. 11, 14, 13.

85. The opening line of "Womans Honour," a poem by the notorious John Wilmot, earl of Rochester—"Love bade me hope, and I obeyed"—parodies the erotic connotations of this image. This allusion to Herbert not only reminds the reader of Rochester's poem "that Rochester's speaker desires a sexual version of the submission in which Herbert's meditation

ends" (Jeremy Treglown, "Satirical Inversion of Some English Sources in Rochester's Poetry," *Review of English Studies* 24 [1973]: 43), but it also awakens the dormant eroticism of "Love (III)"'s situation and opening line. Interestingly, though, the rest of Rochester's poem swerves from the erotic parody that the remainder of "Love (III)" invites; perhaps Rochester felt it was not enough of a challenge.

86.   In *Protestant Poetics and the Seventeenth-Century Religious Lyric* (Princeton: Princeton University Press, 1979), p. 293, Barbara Lewalski remarks that Herbert "makes little direct use" of the bridegroom-bride metaphor for his relationship with God, "and when he does, avoids its erotic connotation." I would argue that "Love (III)" is a notable exception to both statements.

87.   In "Sacred 'Parody' of Love Poetry, and Herbert," *Essays by Rosemond Tuve*, ed. Thomas P. Roche, Jr. (Princeton: Princeton University Press, 1970), pp. 207–51, Rosemond Tuve explores the kinds of sacred parody available to and practiced by Herbert. See also Martz, *Poetry of Meditation*, pp. 184–93.

88.   Malcolm Evans, " 'In Love with Curious Words': Signification and Sexuality in English Petrarchism," in *Jacobean Poetry and Prose: Rhetoric, Representation and the Popular Imagination*, ed. Clive Bloom (London: Macmillan Press, 1988), p. 131.

89.   The sexual implication of "slack" is noted, but not explored, by John R. Mulder, "George Herbert's *Temple*: Design and Methodology," *Seventeenth-Century News* 31, no. 2 (1973): 43; Greg Crossan, "Herbert's 'Love (III),' " *Explicator* 37, no. 1 (1978): 40–41; Todd, *The Opacity of Signs*, pp. 189–90; Garrett, "Sin and Shame," pp. 144–46; and William A. Sessions, "Abandonment and the Religious Lyric," in *Bright Shootes of Everlastingnesse*, eds. Summers and Pebworth, pp. 13–14.

90.   Shakespeare's Sonnet 20, e.g., bemoans the fact that nature, by "prick[ing]" the young man "out for women's pleasure," has "add[ed] one *thing* to my purpose nothing" (lines 12–13; my italics). Booth, *Sonnets*, p. 472, cites the following verse of the song "Fain wold I haue a pretie thing to give unto my Ladie" from *A Handful of Pleasant Delights* [1584], ed. Hyder E. Rollins (Cambridge: Harvard University Press, 1924), p. 58, which suggests a potential erotic model for the dialogue of "Love (III)": "The Mercers pull me going by, / the Silkie wiues say, *what lack ye*? / *The thing you haue not*, then say I" (my italics). See also the range of quotations collected by Partridge, *Shakespeare's Bawdy*, p. 203, and Henke, *Courtesans and Cuckolds*, p. 270.

91.   William Kerrigan, "The Fearful Accommodations of John Donne," *English Literary Renaissance*, 4 (1974): 357. Perhaps also relevant is Booth's claim that "diminished eyesight was particularly associated with the diminishment of 'spirits' " (p. 442).

92.   The point is made by Crossan, "Herbert's 'Love (III),' " p. 41, citing OED, "eye," 5a.

93.   Robert Burton, *The Anatomy of Melancholy*, Pt. 3, Sec. 2, Memb. 2,

Subs. 2; quoted in Donald Beecher, "The Lover's Body: The Somatogenesis of Love in Renaissance Medical Treatises," *Renaissance and Reformation* 24 (1988): 9.

94. OED, I.7. See, for example, Isaiah 47.3—"Thy nakednes shalbe uncovered, yea thy shame shalbe seene"—and Revelation 16.15—"Blessed is he that . . . keepeth his garments, least hee walke naked, and they see his shame."

95. William Kerrigan, "Ritual Man: On the Outside of Herbert's Poetry," *Psychiatry* 48 (1985): 69–70.

96. Terry G. Sherwood, *Herbert's Prayerful Art* (Toronto: University of Toronto Press, 1989), pp. 75–76.

97. I borrow the phrase from Mikhail Bakhtin, *Rabelais and His World*, tr. Helene Iswolsky (Cambridge: M.I.T. Press, 1968), pp. 368–436. Elias, *History of Manners*, pp. 82–83, 130–35, traces the changing attitude to farting, from a purgative and healthful activity to an indecorous and offensive function in the Renaissance.

98. Partridge, *Shakespeare's Bawdy*, pp. 105, 195. Henke, *Courtesans and Cuckolds*, p. 78, suggests that the use of "eat" to indicate "cunnilingus or fellatio" is an American coinage. An anonymous work entitled *The Crafty Whore: Or, the Mistery and iniquity of Bawdy Houses Laid Open* (London, 1628), makes frequent use of metaphors of erotic consumption, resulting in phrases such as "venereall banquet" and references to dining "both at Ceres and Venus table" (pp. 7, 53). In *Herbert's Prayerful Art*, by contrast, Sherwood wishes to separate eating from any erotic overtones: "Not heterosexual embrace, but assimilation through eating and speaking . . . expresses the love union in heaven" (p. 50).

99. *The Complete Poetry of Robert Herrick*, ed. J. Max Patrick (New York: Norton, 1968), p. 248. "Meat," argues Stephen Booth, "was and is a slang term for 'whore's flesh'" (Booth, *Sonnets*, p. 396, note on Sonnet 118, line 7).

100. *Meditations sur l'Evangile: Sermons de Notre-Seigneur, XXIV journée*, in *Oeuvres Complets de Bossuet*, 6 vols. (Paris, 1862), 6:369. I owe this reference, and the latter paragraph of the translation, to Nicholas J. Perella, *The Kiss Sacred and Profane: An Interpretive History of Kiss Symbolism and Related Religio-Erotic Themes* (Berkeley: University of California Press, 1969), p. 3. In *Holy Feast and Holy Fast*, Bynum suggestively explores the devotional importance of eating in the Middle Ages.

101. Theodoret, *Patrologiae cursus completus*, Series Graeca, 81:53; quoted in Perella, *The Kiss*, p. 46.

102. *The Complete English Poems of John Donne*, ed. C. A. Patrides (London: Dent, 1985), p. 102, lines 71–72.

103. Richard Hooker, *Of the Laws of Ecclesiastical Polity* (5.65.5, and 5.67. 12), ed. Christopher Morris, 2 vols. (London: Dent, 1907), 2:215, and 2:331.

104. Lancelot Andrewes, "Sermon 1 of the Nativitie: Christmas 1605,"

in *Sermons*, ed. G. M. Story (London: Oxford University Press, 1967), p. 11.

105.   Strier, "Changing the Object," p. 28. Strier, though, views "The Invitation" as unique in *The Temple* in its translation of sensuality into spirituality, where I find it symptomatic.

106.   *Divine Poems of Donne*, ed. Gardner, pp. 11, 15.

107.   See Young, *Crashaw and the Spanish Golden Age*, pp. 20–50, for a fine account of the continental sources of such spirituality. The lingering elements of Catholicism in Donne are explored by Dennis Flynn, "Donne's Catholicism: I," *Recusant History* 12 (1975): 1–17, and "Donne's Catholicism: II," *Recusant History* 13 (1976): 178–95; John Carey, *John Donne: Life, Mind and Art* (New York: Oxford University Press, 1981), pp. 15–59; and Richard Strier, "John Donne Awry and Squint: The 'Holy Sonnets,' 1608–1610," *Modern Philology* 86 (1989): 357–85.

108.   Kerrigan, "Fearful Accommodations," pp. 337–63.

109.   E. Pearlman, "George Herbert's God," p. 111.

110.   William Gouge, *Of Domesticall Duties* (London, 1622), pp. 283–84.

111.   Julia Kristeva, *Powers of Horror: An Essay on Abjection*, tr. Leon S. Roudiez (New York: Columbia University Press, 1982), pp. 122–23. I have learned much from this suggestive book and from Kristeva's *Tales of Love*, tr. Leon S. Roudiez (New York: Columbia University Press, 1987).

112.   Strier, *Love Known*, pp. 57–58, explores how Herbert's God violates decorum to demonstrate the strangeness of the means of divine grace.

113.   Donne, *Sermons*, 3:313 (quoted in part in Kerrigan, "Fearful Accommodations," p. 350). On the Protestant anxiety about the eroticism of the Song of Solomon, see Scheper, "Reformation Attitudes toward Allegory and the Song of Songs," pp. 557–59.

114.   As Pierre Darmon has demonstrated, the impotent were social outcasts in early modern Europe (*Trial by Impotence: Virility and Marriage in Pre-Revolutionary France*, tr. Paul Keegan [London: Chatto & Windus, 1985]). The embrace of the impotent, then, is a prototypically Christian acceptance of the socially marginal.

115.   Pearlman, "George Herbert's God," p. 103, n. 14. Vendler similarly suggests that "Herbert's tendency is certainly to see God, in any benevolent aspect, as more female than male" (*Poetry of George Herbert*, p. 292, n. 14).

116.   Strier, "Changing the Object," pp. 25–27, makes the important distinction between the ecstatic wounds of Crashaw's St. Theresa poems and Herbert's asexual treatment of the dart of Love in these lines; he argues that Herbert, unlike St. Theresa, desires "not a prolongation of his pain but a surcease from it." I explore Herbert's attitude to physical pain in chap. 4.

117.   Greenblatt, *Shakespearean Negotiations*, p. 92.

118.   Simone de Beauvoir, *The Second Sex*, tr. H. M. Parshley (New York: Bantam, 1961), p. 122.

119.   In "Androgyny, Mimesis, and the Marriage of the Boy Heroine on the English Renaissance Stage," *PMLA* 102 (1987): 29, Phyllis Rackin finds in

the Renaissance androgyne both "an image of transcendence" and "an image of monstrous deformity."

120. In "Adam, Christ, and Mr. Tilman: God's Blest Hermaphrodites," *American Benedictine Review* 40 (1989): 250–60, Frances M. Malpezzi surveys traditional analogues to Donne's striking image in "To Mr. Tilman."

121. Donne, *Sermons*, 1:239. Virginia Ramey Mollenkott explores Donne's use of androgynous imagery in "John Donne and the Limitations of Androgyny," *JEGP* 80 (1981): 22–38.

122. Baldassare Castiglione, *The Book of the Courtier*, tr. Thomas Hoby [1561], (London: Dent, 1928), p. 199. The scriptural precedent is examined in detail in James Grantham Turner, *One Flesh: Paradisal Marriage and Sexual Relations in the Age of Milton* (Oxford: Clarendon Press, 1987), chap. 1, and Mary Nyquist, "The Genesis of Gendered Subjectivity in the Divorce Tracts and in *Paradise Lost*," in *Re-membering Milton: Essays on the Texts and Traditions*, eds. Mary Nyquist and Margaret W. Ferguson (London: Methuen, 1987), pp. 99–127.

123. *Works*, no. 843, p. 349. In *Literary Fat Ladies: Rhetoric, Gender, Property* (London: Methuen, 1987), pp. 23–24, Patricia Parker analyzes this traditional opposition between womanly words and manly deeds in *Hamlet*.

124. Bernard Berenson, "An Attempt at Revaluation" (1916) in *Leonardo da Vinci: Aspects of the Renaissance Genius*, ed. Morris Philipson (New York: George Braziller, 1966), pp. 115, 120. Perhaps because of its unsettling blend of carnality and spirituality, of masculine and feminine, this painting is one of the least admired of Leonardo's works. Even Kenneth Clark, who offers probably the fullest appreciation of the painting, concludes that "it remains an unsatisfactory work" (*Leonardo da Vinci: An Account of His Development as an Artist* [Cambridge: Cambridge University Press, 1952], pp. 171–75). The painting, however, was certainly dear to the artist, being one of the few works to make the voyage with him from Italy to France. It was also, according to Clark, his "most influential," and most often copied, work (p. 174).

125. Fascinatingly, a painting of Bacchus (now in the Louvre) ascribed to Leonardo's studio began as a representation of John the Baptist. The seventeenth-century addition of a crown of vine leaves and a leopard's skin, and the conversion of the cross into a thyrsis, complete the metamorphosis from sacred to profane object desired by Leonardo's patron in the anecdote from the *Paragone* with which we began this chapter.

126. On Elizabeth's use of masculine terminology, see Leah S. Marcus, "Shakespeare's Comic Heroines, Elizabeth I, and the Political Uses of Androgyny," in *Women in the Middle Ages and the Renaissance: Literary and Historical Perspectives*, ed. Mary Beth Rose (Syracuse: Syracuse University Press, 1986), pp. 135–53. On the Jacobean imagination of the king as a nourishing father, combining male and female modes of authority, see especially Jonathan Goldberg, "Fatherly Authority: The Politics of Stuart Family Images," in *Rewriting the Renaissance: The Discourses of Sexual Difference in*

Early Modern Europe, eds. Margaret W. Ferguson, Maureen Quilligan, and Nancy J. Vickers (Chicago: University of Chicago Press, 1986), pp. 3–32; and Stephen Orgel, "Prospero's Wife," *Representations*, 8 (1984): 1–13.

127.   See, e.g., Louis Adrian Montrose, "Celebration and Insinuation: Sir Philip Sidney and the Motives of Elizabethan Courtship," *Renaissance Drama* ns. 8 (1977): 3–35, and Arthur Marotti, " 'Love is not Love': Elizabethan Sonnet Sequences and the Social Order," *ELH* 49 (1982): 396–428.

128.   Roger Lockyer, *Buckingham: The Life and Political Career of George Villiers, First Duke of Buckingham 1592–1628* (London: Longman, 1981), p. 22; on the relationship of Buckingham and James, see also Lockyer, pp. 25–52; Jonathan Goldberg, *James I and the Politics of Literature: Jonson, Shakespeare, Donne, and Their Contemporaries* (Baltimore: Johns Hopkins University Press, 1983), pp. 137–46; and Caroline Bingham, *James I of England* (London: Weidenfeld and Nicolson, 1981), pp. 83–84, 159–61.

129.   Quoted in David Harris Willson, *King James VI and I* (New York: Oxford University Press, 1967), p. 384. Christopher Marlowe was accused of asserting "That St John the Evangelist was bedfellow to Christ and leaned alwaies in his bosome, that he used him as the sinners of Sodoma" (quoted in Paul H. Kocher, *Christopher Marlowe: A Study of His Thought, Learning and Character* [Chapel Hill: University of North Carolina Press, 1946], p. 35). In "The Church-porch," the relationship between Christ and John epitomizes a love and friendship unavailable to Herbert's materialistic age: "But love is lost, the way of friendship's gone, / Though *David* had his *Jonathan*, Christ his *John*" (lines 275–76). The little known heresy of a homosexual relationship between Christ and John—probably based on John's frequent self-description as the best-loved of the apostles—is explored by Claude J. Summers in an unpublished paper, "The (Homo)sexual Temptation of *Paradise Regained*"; see also John Boswell, *Christianity, Social Tolerance, and Homosexuality: Gay People in Western Europe from the Beginning of the Christian Era to the Fourteenth Century* (Chicago: University of Chicago Press, 1980), pp. 225–26, and James M. Saslow, *Ganymede in the Renaissance: Homosexuality in Art and Society* (New Haven: Yale University Press, 1986), pp. 6, 42.

130.   In *Christianity, Social Tolerance, and Homosexuality*, Boswell describes the increasing intolerance with which homosexuality was greeted from the beginning of Christianity through the late Middle Ages. Alan Bray, *Homosexuality in Renaissance England* (London: Gay Men's Press, 1982), continues the pattern through eighteenth-century England. Also helpful is David F. Greenberg, *The Construction of Homosexuality* (Chicago: University of Chicago Press, 1988).

131.   In *John Donne, Coterie Poet* (Madison: University of Wisconsin Press, 1986), pp. 259–60, Arthur F. Marotti finds a similar process in Donne's "Batter my heart": "The sexualization of the speaker's relationship to God at

the end of the sonnet is shocking partly because it has the shape of a passive homosexual fantasy . . . Being loved in the spiritual homoerotic context of 'Batter my heart' corresponded to being favored in the political order." Summers, "The (Homo)sexual Temptation," mentions that the British newspaper *Gay News* was prosecuted in 1977 for blasphemy "for publishing a poem that uses homosexual imagery to *praise* Christ."

132. Compare Sherwood, *Herbert's Prayerful Art*, p. 49: "A mark of the love between God and man is that heterosexual love, embodied in the available conventions of secular love poetry, can suggest man's union with God only in a qualified way."

133. Burke, *A Rhetoric of Motives*, p. 234. In a review-essay of Rosemond Tuve's *Reading of George Herbert* (Chicago: University of Chicago Press, 1952), Burke glances at the possibility of androgyny in Herbert's God via Herbert's relationship to his mother ("On Covery, Re- and Dis-," *Accent* 13 [1953]: 225–26).

134. Elias, *The History of Manners*, and *Power and Civility*; Michel Foucault, *The History of Sexuality*, vol. 1, *An Introduction*, tr. Robert Hurley (New York: Random House, 1978), p. 17; see also especially pp. 3–13, 53–74, 115–31; Lawrence Stone, *The Family, Sex and Marriage in England 1500–1800* (New York: Harper and Row, 1977), especially pp. 519–27; and Francis Barker, *The Tremulous Private Body: Essays on Subjection* (London: Methuen, 1984), pp. 3–69.

135. Elias, *History of Manners*, p. 190.

136. Leo Steinberg, *The Sexuality of Christ in Renaissance Art and in Modern Oblivion* (New York: Pantheon, 1983). See also Bynum's fine response to Steinberg, "The Body of Christ in the Later Middle Ages: A Reply to Leo Steinberg," *Renaissance Quarterly* 39 (1986): 399–439.

137. Bynum, *Jesus as Mother* (1982), and *Holy Feast and Holy Fast* (1987). See also the feminist recovery of female images of the biblical God in Phyllis Trible, *God and the Rhetoric of Sexuality* (Philadelphia: Fortress Press, 1978), and Virginia Ramey Mollenkott, *The Divine Feminine: The Biblical Imagery of God as Female* (New York: Crossroad, 1984).

138. Tuve's otherwise impressive essay, "George Herbert and *Caritas*," offers the consummate statement of a de-sexualized love in Herbert: "when the love exchanged is between God and man, . . . the identical words and similar phrases of profane poetry cease to bear a comparable significance" (*Essays*, p. 181). The terms *agape* and *eros* are of course from Anders Nygren's monumental *Agape and Eros*, tr. Philip S. Watson (New York: Harper, 1969).

139. *The Notebooks of Simone Weil*, tr. Arthur Wills, 2 vols. (London, 1956), 2:472; quoted in Bynum, "A Reply to Leo Steinberg," p. 410, n. 26. Weil was a great admirer of Herbert, and particularly of "Love (III)." In "Simone Weil et George Herbert," *Etudes* 340 (1974): 250, Jean Mambrino cites Weil's judgment on "Love (III)" as "le plus beau poème du monde."

Afterword

1. Claude Lévi-Strauss, *The Origin of Table Manners*, tr. John and Doreen Weightman (New York: Harper and Row, 1978), pp. 503–4.

2. Ibid., p. 507.

3. Richard Baxter, *Poetical Fragments: Heart Imployment with God and It Self* (London, 1681), "The Epistle To The Reader," sigs. A7-A7v; quoted in Robert H. Ray, *The Herbert Allusion Book: Allusions to George Herbert in the Seventeenth Century, Studies in Philology* 83 (1986): 131–32. In *Love Known: Theology and Experience in George Herbert's Poetry* (Chicago: University of Chicago Press, 1983), p. 174, Richard Strier cites the final sentence of this quotation in order to emphasize the importance of emotion in *The Temple*.

Index of Herbert's Works

Latin Works

General Index

General Index

339

Scheper, George L., 325 n. 80, 328 n. 113
Schochet, Gordon, 110, 299 n. 144
Schoenfeldt, Michael C., 277 n. 21, 298
n. 111, 307 n. 42, 312 n. 30
Science, as rape, 246
Scott, James C., 275 n. 6
Scupoli, Lorenzo, 195
Sedgwick, Eve Kosofsky, 235–36
Segar, Sir William, 312 n. 34
Selden, John, 312 n. 34
Self-control, and power, 98–99
Service, 84–91, 178–84; sexual mean-
ings of, 237, 258, 319 n. 24
Sessions, William A., 318 n. 17, 319
n. 18, 326 n. 89
Sexual desire, 13–14, 16, 102–3, 251–52;
phallocentric discourse of, 236–37;
physiology of, 236; and religious feel-
ing, 230–31, 237–39, 240–41, 243–44,
260–63, 317 n. 2; and religious prefer-
ence, 254–55; and self-discipline, 232–
33
Shakespeare, William, 3, 31, 46, 74, 124,
130, 136, 139, 143, 195, 228, 235, 260,
275 n. 9, 294 n. 55, 313 n. 34, 314 n. 61,
318 n. 16, 319 n. 25, 320 n. 36, 321
n. 45, 326 n. 90
Shapiro, Michael and Marianne, 67, 292
n. 28
Sharpe, Kevin, 281 n. 55, 290 n. 100
Shaw, Robert B., 306 n. 24
Sheavyn, Phoebe, 61, 291 n. 9
Sherwood, Terry, 259, 286 n. 47, 302 n.
41, 327 n. 96, 327 n. 98, 330–31 n. 132
Shuger, Debora, 147–48, 277 n. 22, 292
n. 16, 292 n. 21, 299 n. 144, 302 n. 44
Shullenberger, William, 1, 275 n. 2
Sidney, Sir Philip, 239, 320 n. 33
Silver, George, 312 n. 34
Singleton, Marion White, 10, 60, 84–85,
191, 219, 279 n. 41, 291 n. 2, 310 n. 93,
315 n. 81
Smith, Robert, 288 n. 73
Smithson, Bill, 294 n. 60
Smuts, R. Malcolm, 284 n. 32, 290 n. 100
Southwell, Robert, 119, 127, 136, 300
n. 6, 302 n. 36
Spenser, Edmund, 3, 102, 105, 256, 271,
275 n. 7, 299 n. 136
Sprezzatura, 46, 164, 288 n. 77

Stallybrass, Peter, 232, 317 n. 7, 318 n. 13
Stambler, Elizabeth, 83, 256, 296 n. 79,
325 n. 79
Stein, Arnold, 87, 175, 213, 307 n. 51,
311 n. 7, 316 n. 102, 325 n. 81
Steinberg, Leo, 270, 331 n. 136
Stewart, Esmé, first duke of Lennox, 267
Stewart, Stanley, 248, 280 n. 48, 322
n. 56, 325 n. 80
Stone, Lawrence, 72, 83, 101, 207, 211,
269, 295 n. 73, 313 n. 37, 313 n. 38, 331
n. 134
Storms: and power, 139–44, 158–60; and
suffering, 139–40, 148–52
Strier, Richard, 11–12, 40, 43, 49, 68–
69, 76, 78, 80–81, 83, 92, 95, 102,
104, 126–27, 128, 131, 137, 149,
151, 152, 158–59, 167, 172–73, 182,
184, 186, 188, 189, 192–93, 195, 205,
213, 218, 225, 238, 239, 241, 243,
246, 252, 262, 277 n. 22, 278–79
n. 37, 279 n. 46, 280 n. 48, 281 n. 55,
287 n. 57, 288 n. 72, 293 n. 32, 294 n.
51, 295 n. 74, 296 n. 92, 301 n. 28,
302 n. 41, 305 n. 9, 309 n. 71, 310
n. 99, 311 n. 7, 314 n. 66, 316 n. 102,
320 n. 29, 320 n. 32, 321 n. 44, 321 n.
46, 324 n. 70, 325 n. 81, 327 n. 105,
328 n. 107, 328 n. 112, 328 n. 116, 332
n. 3
Submission, and rebellion, 24
Summeras, Claude J., 255, 279 n. 48, 281
n. 55, 324 n. 76, 325 n. 77, 330 n. 129,
330 n. 131
Summers, Joseph, 22, 94, 105, 118–19,
171, 217, 256, 280 n. 48, 281 n. 1, 284
n. 31, 297 n. 103, 300 n. 5, 306 n. 28,
315 n. 73, 325 n. 82
Surveillance: and comfort, 137–38; and
power, 135–37

Table manners, 199–200
Tawney, R. H., 295 n. 64
Tayler, Edward, 61, 291 n. 7
Taylor, Ivan Earle, 94, 297 n. 100
The Temple: licensing, 54, 290 n. 95, 290
n. 96; title, 123
Tentler, Thomas, 289 n. 90, 289 n. 92
Terror, intertwined with divine love,
110–11, 113, 131–35